THE PSYCHOLOGY
OF
EMOTION

The Psychology
of
Emotion

K. T. Strongman

Psychology Department, University of Exeter

JOHN WILEY & SONS

LONDON · NEW YORK · SYDNEY · TORONTO

Library of Congress Catalog Card No. 72-2643

ISBN 0 471 83409 2

Printed in Great Britain
By Unwin Brothers Limited
The Gresham Press, Old Woking, Surrey.
A member of the Staples Printing Group.

For Lara and Luke

Preface

In spending some years teaching an advanced undergraduate course on the psychology of emotion, I increasingly felt the need for a book which gathered together some of the very different approaches which have been made to the subject. Our knowledge of emotion has been gained in diverse ways; it is discussed in most areas of psychology and, indeed, permeates the whole subject. This inevitably means that its study within a single course is difficult--the relevant sources and their evaluations are spread very widely throughout the psychological literature. The present book is an attempt to simplify matters by drawing together and comparing representative examples of the better thought and research on emotion. In that it presupposes some knowledge of psychology, the book is not directed at the beginning student. It is meant for the second or third year undergraduate who wishes to gain a more specialized knowledge of the subject.

Although the basic aims of the book are to provide a broad coverage of emotion and to suggest guidelines for its study and research, it is not completely unbiased. It quite self-evidently reflects two fundamental viewpoints. First, emphasis is laid on research which is reasonably sound methodologically, and on theory which is reasonably well anchored to such research. Second, there is more than a faint leaning towards the behavioural (although not necessarily behaviouristic) approaches to the subject. In spite of this, it should be simple enough for the reader who is antipathetic to these types of analysis to skim over them or miss them out altogether. In any case, he should certainly forgo the last few pages of the book. However, I make no apologies for such biases, since I believe them to lead to research strategies which are important to the overall study of psychology.

Finally, I would like to express my gratitude to all those who have tolerated my vagaries during the writing of this book. In particular, I thank my friends and colleagues Philip Wookey and Robert Remington for their help, advice and encouragement, and my wife, Thelma, without whose support I should never have finished.

Acknowledgments

The author wishes to acknowledge the cooperation of the following for granting permission to reproduce diagrams from their publications:

Academic Press, Inc.
Figures 4 and 5 (M. Arnold, Ed., *Feelings and Emotions*, Academic Press, New York, 1970, pp. 10–11).

American Psychological Association
Figure 10 (V. H. Denenberg, *Psychol. Rev.*, 1964, **71**, 235–351). Copyright 1964 by the American Psychological Association and reproduced by permission.

McGraw-Hill Inc. and Appleton-Century-Crofts
Figure 7 (from *Physiological Psychology*, 3rd edn. by G. T. Morgan © 1965 McGraw-Hill Inc., adapted from *Bodily Changes in Pain, Hunger, Fear and Rage* by W. B. Cannon, published by Appleton-Century-Crofts).

New York Academy of Sciences
Figure 3 (D. Bindra, 'A unified interpretation of emotion and motivation', *Ann. New York Acad. Sci.*, 1969, **159**, p. 1073).

Contents

Preface vii

1. Introduction 1

2. Twenty theories of emotion 13

3. The physiology of emotion 36

4. Cognition and emotion 66

5. Emotional behaviour 92

6. Emotional development 126

7. Emotional expression and recognition 148

8. Pathological emotion—anxiety 170

9. Overview 191

References 196

Index 223

1

Introduction

As it is commonly conceived, emotion is bound up with feeling. Were you to produce an off-the-cuff definition of the term, it would probably make some reference to subjective feelings. Go one stage further and consult a dictionary, and yet again the word feeling would be prominent. For example, the *Shorter Oxford English Dictionary* defines emotion (in psychology) as a 'mental feeling or affection, distinct from cognitions or volitions'. Clearly, one thing we mean if we use the word emotion is personal, subjective feeling. We describe this feeling as pleasant or unpleasant, mild or intense, transient or long lasting, and as interfering with or enhancing our behaviour.

In his *Dictionary of Psychology*, Drever (1952) is a little less subjective in his definition. He describes emotion as a complex state of the organism involving widespread bodily changes. Mentally, this is accompanied by strong feelings and impulses to behave in particular ways. He has added two more ingredients to the mixture—bodily states and behaviour. To return to your off-the-cuff definition, it may well have included some reference to physiological changes, such as an increased pulse rate, or sweating, a feeling of palpitations or trembling. Or it may have referred to some behaviour such as fighting or running, or to some strained facial expression. Emotion then also involves physiological and behavioural change; again, such change may vary along several dimensions—it may, for example, be great or small, acute or chronic, we may enjoy it or we may not.

To take the exercise one stage further, were you to define a specific emotion, such as anger or fear, you might well begin your definition with some phrase like: 'It is when ...' or 'Yesterday, I was ...'. In other words, you would escape the definition by giving an example, and that example would describe some environmental situation that you had experienced.

Emotion is feeling, it is a bodily state involving various physical structures, it is gross or fine-grained behaviour, and it occurs in particular situations. When we use the term we mean any or all of these possibilities, each of which may show a wide range of variation. This points to the major difficulty which besets the academic study of the subject. Different theorists have taken different starting points. Any theory of emotion or any empirical research on emotion deals only with some part of the broad meaning that the term has acquired. Some theorists stress psychological factors, some behavioural, some subjective. Some deal only with extremes, some say emotion colours all behaviour. There is no consensus of opinion; at present emotion defies definition. It is impossible to make conclusive statements about the whole subject merely from ideas or research in only one of its aspects. And these aspects are often too disparate to attempt more than the slightest synthesis. At best we can perhaps suggest that some of the areas of study which make up emotion can be usefully and cogently reduced to others. For the moment, I will not add to the confusion by producing my own definition of emotion. Most of this book will be concerned with describing emotion rather than defining it. The aim is to give the reader more connotations to the word than he has at present.

FOUNDATIONS OF THE STUDY OF EMOTION

Leeper (1965) puts forward an interesting hypothesis to account for the rationalist, commonsense doctrine of the emotions which was generated by the early philosophers. Briefly, this doctrine contrasted reason and emotion by proposing that man is basically knowing and rational, but to achieve this must minimize his baser, emotional elements. Reason was equated with choice and emotion was regarded as an inbuilt response to significant environmental stimuli—we hear the roar of the lion, feel afraid and run, rather than coolly and rationally shooting it between the eyes.

Leeper argues that there are parallel trends in everyday thought about emotion and in its pre-scientific study. He suggests that these trends come from the emphasis which is usually laid on palpable factors in any new field of study. He describes palpable factors as tangible, highly invariable, and showing close relationships between cause and effect. He believes that stress on such factors led pre-scientific thought to focus on conscious, intense emotions, particularly those capable of strongest expression. Also, emotion (as a process underlying behaviour) was viewed as having its effects mainly by increasing the intensity and duration of primitive behaviours such as fighting, and as producing socially irresponsible actions.

Leeper suggests further that much of present-day scientific thought is still caught in this basic philosophy. For example, despite Freud, there is not much credence given to possible unconscious emotions. Emotions are still often thought of only as strong experiences, and it is mainly the negative ones which receive attention. Emotions continue to be regarded as fundamentally opposed to realistic, adaptive functioning.

Although the rationalist philosophy of the emotions began with Plato and Aristotle, it received its fullest expression by Descartes in the seventeenth century. Descartes' was the extreme dualistic philosophy, separating mind and body. In animals, he thought that there is simply an environmental input and a bodily output. In man, reason (or choice) intervenes. Emotions (or passions) were vital to his viewpoint since he thought of them as changing the flow of animal spirits, the basic determinants of action. Descartes suggested that there are six primitive emotions: admiration, love, hate, desire, joy and sadness. These combine to produce the introspective feelings which we regard as emotion. However, he also drew attention to the place of physiology and bodily functions in emotion. He regarded overt emotional behaviour as the result of instinctive attempts at achieving suitable responses to given environmental conditions.

Descartes believed emotions to have four main functions. They cause: (1) the appropriate flow of animal spirits in the body; (2) the body to be held ready for the various environmental goal objects which come its way; (3) the soul to desire these objects, which nature has already told us are of use; and (4) a persistence of the desire for these objects.

Descartes regarded the actual course taken by the emotions as beginning with an object in the environment which, via the sense organs and nerves, creates an impression on the pineal gland. This causes the soul to apprehend the stimulus and also causes the animal spirits in the brain and nerves to become active. These spirits act on the pineal gland to convert the feeling which is already there into a passion (emotion). Thus Descartes distinguishes between passions (in the soul), bodily commotion (in the viscera) and action (overt movement). However, although his view of emotion is considerably more sophisticated than previous ideas, and although he lays much emphasis on emotion as basic to behaviour, the problem of the relation between emotion and reason (and also between mental and bodily factors in emotion) is still very apparent. His theory of emotion can be summarized as suggesting that emotion intervenes between stimulus and response, causing the response to be less rational than it otherwise would have been.

After Descartes, the next significant discussion of emotion is to be found in Darwin's *Expression of the Emotions in Man and Animals* (1872). He stressed overt action as the biologically significant aspect of emotion and emphasized the importance of causative environmental stimulation. Also, of course, his theory of evolution pointed to the continuity between man and animals with respect to emotion, as well as in every other way. Shortly following this, James (1884) brought together the ideas of Descartes and Darwin and with a neat reversal of the commonsense view produced what was effectively the first psychological theory of emotion. James' theory will be discussed at length later, but, in summary, he suggested that the perception of emotional stimuli leads both to visceral reactions and to overt muscular reactions. The feeling of these reactions (i.e. cortical feedback from them) *is* the emotional experience. We hear the lion roar, run and then feel afraid. James' theory was important in that it pointed to a relationship between emotional stimuli, emotional behaviour and emotional experience. In fact, it is James who provided the obvious and necessary stimulus to academic thought about emotion. He removed the emphasis from considerations of how emotion might function.

MODERN APPROACHES TO EMOTION

Since James, the experimental and theoretical work on emotion has diversified considerably. Bindra (1970) provides a concise breakdown of the various experimental approaches. These have been clearly related to emotion as feeling, emotion as response, and the stimuli which produce emotion. (1) Emotional experience (or recognition); this refers to emotion as subjectively reported by man and as inferred by him about other men and about animals. (2) Emotional arousal; referring to changes in internal bodily processes, i.e. visceral, somatic and neural function, as produced by environmental stimuli. (3) Emotional action; referring to overt response patterns, obvious behaviour. (4) Emotional stimuli; here the stress has been on the stimulus features of the physical or social environment that produces (1), (2) and (3). This last line of attack carries an immediately obvious problem, its implicit circularity; it is difficult to define emotional stimuli independently of emotional responses. However, it has led to two research strategies. First, one aimed at finding what stimuli will produce a given range of emotional responses. And second, the selection of a particular stimulus pattern and a determination of what responses this will elicit under various organismic conditions, such as hormonal change.

Theoretically, the aim over the last 80 years or so has been to define emotion and to find a place for it in behaviour theory. Bindra again provides a cogent analysis of the three major theoretical approaches which have developed. The most common of these specifies emotion as a *unique* process. However, ideas on the workings of this process have taken many forms. As we have seen, James (1884), for example, viewed it as a 'feeling' of bodily changes stemming from a perception of an 'exciting' fact. Wenger (1950) regarded it as visceral reaction, Cannon (1927) as neural thalamic impulses which are generated by the release of cortical inhibition. Or Arnold (1950) regarded it as an appraisal in the brain of sensory stimuli, resulting in an 'emotional attitude' which produces the 'emotional experience', and Lindsley (1951) as behavioural activation due to arousal of the brain-stem reticular formation. There are many such theories, some of which will be discussed in detail later. However, none has gained general acceptance. This is probably because the idea of emotion as a single process cannot cater for all the data which have been gathered from empirical studies. And the studies themselves have been concentrated on very different aspects of emotion.

Emotion has sometimes been analysed as an intervening variable, anchored to observable stimuli and responses. McDougall's (1928) instinct theory, for example, posits an 'emotional impulse' which links stimuli and responses. Or Brown and Farber (1951) describe emotion within a Hullian framework. The third approach has the advantage of immediately fitting emotion into general behaviour theory. It explains all emotional phenomena without any theoretical recourse to emotion; a single set of processes are hypothesized to account for emotion, for motivation and for perception. Bindra (1969) and Leeper (1965) provide examples of such theories. If the theories which adopt this broad strategy can be judged as 'good' theories (see below) they are perhaps to be preferred, since they make considerable gains in parsimony. However, this remains to be seen.

The more recent theories of emotion can also be analysed in terms of their main emphasis. Such a breakdown points to at least five major approaches: (1) Emotions as conscious experiences, differentiated subjectively (for example the psychoanalytically oriented theories). (2) Emotions as psychological states, emphasizing either the automatic nervous system and/or the limbic system (for example Lindsley; Arnold). (3) Emotions as representing inadequate adaptation (for example Plutchik). (4) Emotions as motivational (for example Leeper). (5) Emotions as one aspect of behaviour (for example Millenson).

Finally, an even broader analysis, and one which will be used in this book, is simply into those theories which are primarily cognitive, those which are primarily physiological and those which are primarily behavioural.

It should be clear from what has been said so far that rather than simplifying the layman's view of emotion, modern academic psychology complicates it even further. Theory and research have stemmed from and developed the many intuitive meanings which emotion already has. More complexity is added to this increasingly complex picture by each line of enquiry appearing in several contexts. Most aspects of psychology are relevant to emotion. As will be explained below, it is hoped that the structure of this book will aid understanding of these various areas and approaches. However, before this, mention must be made of some more general issues. First, there is a brief description of what characterizes a good theory; in considering emotion it is necessary to evaluate many theories. There will follow a discussion of some problems which should be borne in mind in any appreciation of emotion. Some of these are germane to particular approaches such as the physiological or behavioural. Others occur with regularity across the whole sphere of emotion and indeed throughout much of psychology.

THEORY

To some extent any theory must be formal. It should employ terms with rules that tie them together. In turn, these rules should be defined or related to empirical events. The theory should account for and reduce these empirical events in a simplified manner and to a more simplified form. Many theories of emotion can be judged as reasonably successful in this respect (for example Plutchik; Millenson), although they are often lacking in a formal structure (for example Schachter). Perhaps the most important aspect of any theory is the degree to which it is anchored to an empirical base. Only thus can it be tested. A theory which is untestable is surely of less value than one which has been tested and proved wrong. So, any theoretical constructs should be linked semantically to empirical constructs. The empirical constructs themselves are mainly the descriptions of behaviour and of the situations in which it occurs. It is here that many theories of emotion are lacking (for example Arnold; Izard and Tomkins). They are too speculative and couched in terms which are often too nebulous to lead to clear prediction. One problem is that, as has already been pointed out, descriptions of emotion and of emotion-producing stimuli are very often made in quite disparate ways. Theories then become correspondingly difficult to compare.

(Compare, later, Arnold's cognitive/physiological theory with Millenson's behavioural model or Duffy's activation theory, for example.)

Whatever is referred to by the constructs of a theory, these must be a combination of economy and complexity. A theory should describe empirical relationships which already obtain and yet also explain both them and other possible relationships. It must be adequate in its formal structure and yet well grounded empirically. Essentially, it represents a compromise, but a compromise from which predictions can be made. Ultimately, the strength of a theory lies in its predictive power. Some theories of emotion are so broad as to predict almost anything (for example Izard and Tomkins; Leeper). Others hardly move any distance from the empirical observations on which they are based, and hence predict little (for example Davitz). As will become obvious, there is room for a good theory of emotion which takes into account all of its various overtones.

SOME BASIC PROBLEMS

At present, there are no right or wrong answers to the problems discussed below. Although they are pressing and important to the study of emotion, they have tended to be dealt with in idiosyncratic and arbitrary ways. Each investigator produces equally good solutions and an equally cogent supportive argument. For this reason they are problems about which the reader should for the most part draw his own conclusions.

Terminology

Within the literature on emotion many terms are employed quite freely. Their usage is inconsistent and they are seldom adequately defined. Not least of these is 'emotion' itself. Other words which have high association value but which nevertheless denote little are 'feeling', 'affect' and 'emotionality'. A similar lack of precision surrounds terms which refer to specific emotions, jealousy, fear, love, anger, for example (and particularly anxiety). To concentrate on 'emotion', it has sometimes been defined, for example, as a state of the organism which affects behaviour, and sometimes more directly as a response. When defined as a state, it is sometimes regarded as mentalistic and sometimes as physiological. When defined as a response, it is sometimes seen as physiological and sometimes as behavioural. The particular everyday connotation of emotion which has provided the starting point for any one theorist or researcher has led to an individualistic and biased definition. Occasional inconsistencies are even evident *within* as well as between those who study emotion.

At this point, I do not wish to add to extant definitions. When words such as feeling and affect are found in this book, it will be made clear whose usage is being followed. Otherwise they will be avoided. For the most part, the term emotion will itself be used broadly. In this way it is hoped that the reader will build up a general concept of emotion; and one which in fact reflects its everyday usage. It clearly does embody many different aspects at many levels of function. It is a large part of a complex subject.

Levels of discourse

The problem of the various levels of discourse to be found in the psychology of emotion has already been described. It devolves from the continuing division of emotion into experience, behaviour, physiological substrates and eliciting stimuli. Those who study emotion have their own preference for the terms in which they can most comfortably converse and presumably in which they regard emotion as most appropriately expressed. They may be restricted to one of the above types of discourse or they may be happy to handle them in combination. Whichever way, it is frequently difficult to compare the work and ideas of various researchers.

Subsuming the type of problem to be discussed here under the rubric of levels of discourse is perhaps mistaken since it implies that some 'levels' are higher (more worthy) than others. This in itself must be an arbitrary matter, since each level brings its own problems. Whether one believes the advantages to outweigh the disadvantages is ultimately a matter of personal predilection (or to make clear my own bias, depends on one's past history of reinforcement).

The problems of regarding emotion primarily as a matter of personal experience are the most self-evident; they concern the validity and reliability of data. It is many years since the introspectionist approach to psychology was thrown into disrepute. It would perhaps be a retrograde step to make it respectable once more. This is not to suggest that the subjective report of 'how a person is feeling' or of what emotion he is experiencing may not provide useful information, but rather that as a datum it cannot stand alone. We cannot place reliance on verbal report from one time to the next. It may be mistaken or aimed at pleasing. We cannot know whether one man's 'anger' is the same as his brother's. Results from any studies of emotion which stress subjective experience should be regarded as no more than indicative, as productive of hypotheses which can be more rigorously tested.

Problems which are an integral part of any discussion of emotional stimuli can also be quickly dealt with. How can we know that a stimulus is 'emotional' without finding that it leads to 'emotional behaviour'? It is difficult to define the stimulus independently of the response. For example, commonsense or intuition (i.e. everyday observation) tells us that if we jostle someone in the street he is likely to become angry, that is, he may shout at us or perhaps hit out. More systematic observations may confirm us in this belief. We would happily maintain our hypothesis until we met the man who ignored our jostling or who ran from it. Is jostling no longer an anger-producing stimulus? Did our man 'feel' anger but not show it in the usual way (statistically speaking)? Does jostling also act as a fear stimulus? It is difficult to break the circle between stimulus and response. Of course, if a definition of emotional stimuli can be made independently of the responses which they produce then these problems fade away.

But this has not usually been done. It is similar to the problem which, for example, has faced learning theorists in their considerations of punishment (see for example Azrin and Holz 1966).

Research and theory into the physiology of emotion has produced a vast literature, but has been beset by the insoluble problem of reductionism. As will be seen in Chapter 3, the physiological approach to emotion has been focused largely on the possible emotional functions of the autonomic nervous system (ANS) and the central nervous system (CNS)—mainly the limbic system. Subjectively, the reason for this emphasis is easy to see. For example, we can 'feel' our pulse rate increase and our face become red when we are experiencing what we have been taught to call anger. However, if this approach is taken too far, then psychology (as the study of behaviour) becomes reduced to physiology. It is conceivable that this is all to the good, though there are many psychologists who would not agree. Clearly, psychology can gain much from physiology, and physiological fact may well lead to useful behavioural predictions. Basically, there are two important questions which require an affirmative answer before we can argue that a reductionist approach is justified: (1) *Can* we reduce whatever we are studying to another level? (2) Is it useful to make this reduction? In studying the physiology of emotion these questions have usually received scant attention. The physiology has often been far removed from behaviour, and the physiological speculations have been frequently far removed from physiological fact. And, of course, there are the inevitable problems which vitiate most attempts to compare results from psychological and physiological studies of emotion— essentially different languages are being used and different experimental techniques followed. Emotion can be *studied* physiologically, but as this is but one of its many aspects it is unlikely that there could be any justification for reducing it entirely to this level.

Finally, there is a large body of work on emotion in which the main emphasis or level of discourse is on overt behaviour. Such work can have the advantages of increased objectivity. It is methodologically 'purer' to deal with observable behaviour than with more hypothetical experiences or feelings. However, this level of discourse is often criticized for oversimplifying complex problems. Internal feelings which we 'know' subjectively to exist are disregarded and little notice paid to physiological changes. The behavioural approach is good from the viewpoint of sound investigation, but may seem to give less than the whole picture. On the other hand, it may be that ultimately we shall be able to make any necessary predictions about emotion solely in terms of emotional behaviour. Whether there is any underlying feeling state which is in some way determining the overt behaviour may be immaterial if we can specify the external determinants of the state. We can then jump from environmental stimuli to overt behaviour. Such would be the standpoint of the more confirmed behaviourist.

Animals or humans—artificiality

Studies of emotion have been carried out on a large variety of species—from mice to man—and the primary emphasis has by no means been on human investigations. The reasons for (what at first sight might seem to be) the surprisingly large number of animal studies in this field are quite straightforward. In fact, they are just slightly more obvious than those that apply in many other areas of psychology. The first is rooted in the problem of artificiality. Are human 'laboratory' emotions, emotions at all? It is notoriously difficult to evoke human emotion in a laboratory setting, even with powerful, intense stimuli. The subjects' responses are tempered by the situation. In passing, it is worth noting that this idea brings out the 'language problem'. For example, we can say that the laboratory nature of a study will change the stimuli used from what they would otherwise have been in real life. They become fresh stimuli evoking new responses. Or we can say that the subject 'knows' that it is only an experiment and cuts down the tenor of his reactions accordingly. Either way, however, the result is artificiality.

The most obvious way around this problem is to use stimuli which are intense or powerful enough to produce responses which approximate to our everyday observations of emotion (although there is some circularity in this argument). Alternatively, the subjects may be so completely deceived that they are unaware that they are taking part in an experiment. The ethical objections to each of these solutions are immediately apparent. The other possibility is to use infrahuman subjects. Here, any objection that artificiality will lead to distorted results is weakened, particularly if laboratory-raised animals have been used; their 'natural' home is the laboratory. With such subjects a much closer control can be legitimately exercised over their emotional behaviour, making it that much more likely that its determinants will be found.

However, many psychologists would question the validity of using animal subjects at all in the study of emotion. Are 'animal' emotions emotion? They might argue that animals do not have emotions, or if they do then they may be so different from human emotion as to make comparison fruitless. Such an attitude would be most likely to be held by those who view emotion primarily at an experiential level. How can we meaningfully speak of the subjective experiences and feelings of animals? Conversely, it can be argued that if the determinants of emotion can be elucidated by well-defined and methodologically sound animal studies then they will lead to hypotheses which will be more easy to test at the human level. So the argument twists on, and it is for the individual to reach his own conclusions. However, it should be noted that if the decision is to be against the validity of animal studies of emotion then a vast amount of well-conceived and well-conducted research is rendered somewhat pointless. That much of the present book depends upon evidence from investigations of emotion using animal subjects shows the direction of my own views.

The relationship of emotion to other fields of study

The difficulty in defining emotion and the problem of its general breadth as a concept have led it to overlap considerably with some of the other equally wide concepts with which psychology abounds. Three in particular will be met frequently in this book: drive, motivation and arousal. Each of these will be briefly discussed below, but for the reader who is interested in them in more depth, a good starting point is provided by Bolles (1967) for drive and motivation and Bindra (1959) for arousal.

In some form or another the concept of motivation has existed for as long as man has been attempting to account for his own behaviour. It makes no reference to experience or to any behavioural fact, but is used as a *hypothetical* cause of behaviour. It is conceived of as a force which lies behind behaviour and which therefore aids in our understanding of it. Although not an essential construct in explanations of behaviour, motivation has tended to appear in most accounts of behaviour and has frequently led to highly productive investigations.

An attempt to give a firm theoretical and empirical basis to motivation is embodied in the idea of drive, taking over as it did from instinct. Like instincts, drives were first seen as basic to motivation, as a way of objectifying the subjective, and as of biological importance. These three qualities were itemized as a result of the idea that drive has a solid physiological foundation (in bodily need). If this were in fact the case then the concept of motivation would become less hypothetical than it is. From these hopeful if vague formulations four main lines of research developed. (1) Hunger and thirst were studied as central dynamic states, not just as stimuli. (2) It was demonstrated that animals become more active with increases in biological need, i.e. drives have general energizing effects. (3) Evidence accrued to support the idea of specific hungers. (4) Drive strength was measured. Although each of these avenues of research provided interesting information in its own right, it did not lead to any generally acceptable definition of drive. Instead there were many definitions, each of which could be objected to in some way. Some were too loose and others too tight; sometimes drive was regarded as a stimulus, sometimes as a central state.

At this point in the development of the drive concept, two further problems came to light. (1) How many drives are there? There may be just one which has a general effect, or there may be many. Should we invoke a new drive to account for every new sort of behaviour which is observed? (2) Do drives add to the direction of behaviour, or to its energy, or to both?

In the midst of this confusion, Hull (1943) gave drive a much firmer theoretical basis. Briefly, he related it to physiological need and viewed it as similar to, but independent of, habit. He regarded it as energizing behaviour, and when it was reduced as reinforcing behaviour. He saw it as nonspecific and nondirectional. Recent evidence concerning these and other defining characteristics of drive point to it as a not very robust concept. However, Hull's formulations were the most far-reaching, and so when the term is used in the present text it will be in the Hullian sense.

The other concept which inevitably keeps popping up within this book is that of arousal (or activation). Some psychologists (for example Duffy 1941) altogether replace 'emotion' with 'arousal'. This is yet another hypothetical construct, and one which is closely related to drive. Various theorists (for example Duffy 1951;

Bindra 1959; Lindsley 1951) believe the basis of drive to be the hypothetical physiological state of arousal. The fundamental suggestion is that the diffuse projection system in the reticular formation of the brain enhances the reception of specific stimuli and thus serves to influence any learning that is occurring at the time. Although, like drive, arousal is a heavily used concept, hard evidence to support it is not abundant. This state of affairs is worsened by the theoretical structure on which the concept of arousal is built. This depends on the notion that for a behavioural task of a given complexity there is an optimum level of arousal for optimal performance. Thus is derived the notorious inverted U-shaped function relating arousal to performance. The main problem integral to this idea is that of the whereabouts on the arousal curve of a particular behavioural performance. Is it approaching the optimal level or retreating from it? Overall, we are ignorant of any individual response patterning in arousal and there is little evidence for any individual differences.

Although there is little empirical support for the validity of a unitary concept of arousal, it is frequently used in accounts of emotion. It is often accepted that emotional behaviour occurs with high levels of arousal and that different emotions enjoy different positions on the arousal continuum. If physiological arousal involves pushing the sympathetic nervous system into action, then this is a reasonable idea, but it does not account for all emotional behaviour. A necessary condition for emotion to occur must be an aroused organism, but arousal need not imply emotion. A similar set of physiological changes may be seen in hard physical exercise. The general view adopted here is that arousal as a unitary concept is not very useful, particularly to our understanding of emotion. It is difficult to define and awkward to measure. As will be seen, people differ in their physiological response patterns and different situations may have similar or different physiological effects.

THE STRUCTURE OF THE BOOK

The various problems described above have led to the particular form taken by the present book. Essentially it is a compromise, but one which it is hoped will put the psychology of emotion into some sort of perspective. As so much of the area is characterized by theories or models, Chapter 2 presents twenty of these in summary form. Since many of these appear in greater detail in their specific contexts later in the book, no attempt is made to criticize them at this point. They are collected together to give some idea of the development of theoretical viewpoints of emotion and to allow the reader a comparative basis for evaluating them.

Following Chapter 2 are three chapters which each emphasize a different approach to the study of emotion: physiological, cognitive and behavioural. After these are three further chapters which deal with the study of emotion as it cuts across psychology. These are emotional development, the social psychological approach to the expression and recognition of emotion, and pathological or morbid emotion (particularly anxiety). Throughout the six basic chapters an attempt is made to present the major empirical facts and wherever possible to fit these into the existing theories. Also, where appropriate, critical comment is made. Finally, Chapter 9 offers a brief overview and a definition of emotion.

Although the coverage of the major topics within this book is fairly complete, or at least representative of the main work which has been done, not every aspect of the study of emotion is dealt with. For example, only very brief mention is made of the existential and psychoanalytic approaches to emotion, or of the ethological work on human sex and aggression. The prime reason for such omissions is that in my opinion these approaches have very little to offer. Essentially, they come from the soft underbelly of psychology and more space would therefore have to be spent in criticizing them than in presenting them. Much of the research and theory in the psychology of emotion which has come from the supposedly more rigorous branches of the subject can be all too easily criticized without considering the vaguer approaches. Of course, this argument may simply be a rationalization of my own prejudices, or just a straightforward (?) emotional reaction.

2

Twenty Theories of Emotion

There are many theories of emotion. They stem from various fundamental assumptions, they stress different problems, and they can be distinguished both in the degree of their formality and in the degree to which they are anchored to empirical fact. The present chapter contains straightforward summaries of some of these theories. No evidence will be presented either for or against them and they will be neither evaluated nor criticized. The aim is to provide some idea of the breadth of thought which has been put into theorizing about emotion. Also, it is intended that this chapter may be used as a quick comparative reference system to representative aspects of the many approaches which have been made to the subject. To describe all theories of emotion would necessitate a book in itself, so the number has been restricted to twenty. These have been chosen either because they are centrally important to modern thought in emotion and/or because they illustrate the breadth of the subject. Many of the theories which are described here will be analysed in greater detail later in the book. There, when appropriate, they will also receive criticism. Others, judged to be of less importance, will only be encountered in this chapter and the interested reader should study the references given for a fuller exposition of these.

Any sample of theories of emotion could be organized in a number of ways—according to the type of approach or emphasis which they take, their chronological order of appearance, the extent of their influence, and so on. Whichever way is followed leads to some confusion. The plan used here was devised to minimize such confusion. The earlier theories are arranged in chronological order, and the more recent are gathered into a broad classification according to the type of approach on which they depend, physiological, cognitive, behavioural, etc. As will be seen, the divisions are not distinct; there is overlap for two reasons. First, the confusion inherent in some theories makes them difficult to categorize, and second, in others equal emphasis is placed on more than one aspect of the subject. Where this is the case and where there are obvious grounds for comparison, it will be indicated. Finally, when reading the summaries which follow it is worth keeping in mind the problems mentioned in Chapter 1. It is here that they will first become evident.

W. James (the James–Lange theory)

The James–Lange theory of emotion is probably the most famous of all in that it generated a lasting controversy amongst psychologists. Also, it has acted as a stimulus for many more recent theories and a great deal of research (see Chapters 3 and 4). The theory is usually attributed to James and to Lange since it was put forward separately by each (James 1884; Lange 1885), although James was its main and clearest exponent.

James began by limiting his field of consideration to those emotions which have 'a distinct bodily expression'. He was attempting to distinguish between mental processes which have no obvious physiological concomitants and those in which straightforward, easily observable changes occur. He suggested that the everyday way of regarding these grosser emotions is: (1) we mentally perceive some fact, (2) this produces some mental affect (called the emotion) and (3) this in turn produces the bodily expression. His view was the converse of this:

'... the bodily changes follow directly the PERCEPTION of the existing fact, and that our feeling of the same changes as they occur IS the emotion'.

(1884, p. 189; italics and capitals his.)

So, for example, rather than face some public performance to which we are unused at this point we become anxious and then have 'butterflies in the stomach', tremble and stutter; in James' terms we face our public performance, have 'butterflies', tremble and stutter and as a result feel anxious. He was therefore (as have so many emotion theorists in lesser ways) making a volte face on what had gone before, the nub of his theory resting on the notion that the visceral discharges associated with some environmental situation actually lead to the emotion as we know it.

The argument which James used to support this theory can be reduced to a few main points; it was based largely on introspection. He asserted that any sensation has extremely complex physiological manifestations and that these are all felt, some obviously, some more obscurely. He suggested that we imagine some strong emotion and then try to push from our consciousness all of the feelings of the bodily symptoms associated with it. He maintained that if we do this successfully there will be nothing left; we shall have completely exorcized the emotion. Finally, he cited many examples of how everyday situations lead directly to these complex, strong (bodily) feelings (seeing a friend peering over the edge of a cliff, for example) and argued support of his case from the idea of how easy we find it to classify both abnormal and normal behaviour according to bodily symptoms.

The James–Lange theory can best be summarized as in Figure 1. This simply represents in diagrammatic form the way in which emotions are experienced as James saw it. (It is worthwhile to compare this figure with Figure 2, which represents the Cannon–Bard theory in a similar way.)

W. B. Cannon (the Cannon–Bard theory)

Cannon's ideas were the first of any note to appear after those of James, and his approach usually took the form of criticism of James (see Chapters 3 and 4)

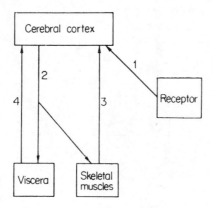

Figure 1. Diagrammatic representation of the James–Lange theory. Arrows show direction of function.

and then a statement of an alternative theory (1915; 1927; 1931; 1932). At different times, Cannon's theory has been referred to as a thalamic theory, the first of the emergency theories or as a neurophysiological theory. This last gives the clue as to why it is often described as the Cannon–Bard theory, since much of the experimental work on which it was based was carried out separately by Bard (for example 1928; 1934; 1950).

Cannon's attack on James will be left for Chapter 4. For now it is enough to say that he based his own theory on evidence (for example Bard 1928; Cannon and Britton 1927; Head 1921) which could be best interpreted as suggesting that the neurophysiological site of emotional expression is subcortical, or, more particularly, thalamic. He argued that in any emotion there is a similar chain of events. An environmental situation stimulates receptors which relay impulses to the cortex. The cortex, in turn, stimulates thalamic processes which act in particular patterns corresponding to particular emotional expressions. Cannon believed that nothing more specific is required than that the neurons in the thalamus be 'released'. He maintained that the nervous discharge from the thalamus has two functions, first to excite muscles and viscera and second to relay information back to the cortex. Thus in Cannon's words:

'... the peculiar quality of the emotion is added to simple sensation when the thalamic processes are aroused'.

(1927, p. 119; italics his.)

This implies that when the thalamus discharges, we experience the emotion at almost the same time that bodily changes occur.

Cannon's theory of emotion is diagrammatically summarized in Figure 2. Basically, Cannon brought into regard the importance of the thalamus and in so doing produced some cogent arguments against James, although these have since been seriously questioned. However, as will be seen later, the neurophysiological picture is far more complicated than Cannon painted it. At least

Figure 2. Diagrammatic representation of the Cannon–Bard
theory. Arrows show direction of function.

he drew attention to the neurophysiology of emotion and hence acted as the
progenitor of much research and theory.

W. McDougall

McDougall (1910; 1923; 1928) attempted to distinguish between emotions and
feelings, an endeavour made somewhat similarly by a few of the more Gestalt-
based European psychologists (for example Klages 1950; Krueger 1928). His
theory also depended on some basic biological considerations (compare with
Plutchik's theory). McDougall believed that the capacity to approach beneficial
goals is fundamental to psychology and that all behaviour stems from seeking
food and escaping or avoiding noxious stimuli. He argued that what we call
emotions and feelings occur as adjuncts to these basic processes; they come
from the way in which we perceive our environment and our various bodily
changes.

McDougall proposed that two feelings—pleasure and pain—modify all of our
goal-directed behaviour. However, he also regarded man as more complex than
this; man is cognitive and has expectations, he fuses together many experiences
and has odd concentrations of feelings. McDougall suggested that it is these more
cognitive aspects that set man apart from other organisms and direct that he no
longer alternates between pleasure and pain but continually ranges over a complexity of feelings. McDougall believed that through everyday usage these complex
feelings have become known as the various emotions. He then argued that in fact
these are not 'real' emotions and that science would profit if the term were not
used in their description (see Duffy for a similar argument).

McDougall's schema for emotion proper began with a statement that throughout the evolution of man goals became more specific and goal-directed behaviour became more specialized. The result was more precise and particularized bodily adjustment. The experience of each of these well-differentiated strivings gave the clear quality of a 'primary emotion'. If two or more of these main bodily reactions conflict, from the experiential point of view this results in '... the secondary or blended emotions' (1928), such complexities as shame or reproach.

McDougall also compared complex feelings (not really emotions) with emotions proper (whether primary or secondary). He suggested three main points of comparison. (1) Complex feelings are conditioned by success or failure in our strivings and therefore colour any subsequent impulse that may be similar. 'True' emotions are quite independent of this. They are simply what makes each impulse distinctive and so do not affect any later strivings. (2) McDougall believed that complex feelings were restricted to man since they depend for their appearance on the development of cognition. Real emotions must, however, have appeared much earlier on the evolutionary scale. (3) Finally, named complex feelings such as hope and anxiety are not entities. They just reflect ill-defined ranges of experience and feelings in which there is no blending. Conversely, McDougall viewed each primary emotion as long lasting; it is '... an enduring feature of the mental structure of the organism' (1928). Each emotion is only associated with desire and therefore, unlike complex feelings, conflicting desires may produce blends of emotion. Allowing that this was a very subjective analysis, it is possible to appreciate what McDougall was suggesting by comparing, in an everyday sense, the behaviours that tend to accompany 'complex feelings' of anxiety and hope with those that occur with 'true' emotions of, say, fear and curiosity.

J. W. Papez

After Cannon, Papez's (1937) theory of emotion was the next to have a neurophysiological basis. His starting point came from the idea that in lower vertebrates there are anatomical and physiological connections on the one hand between the cerebral hemisphere and the hypothalmus, and on the other between the cerebral hemisphere and the dorsal thalamus. These relationships become further elaborated in the mammalian brain. Papez believed emotion to be mediated by such cortico-hypothalamic interconnections.

Papez stated simply that emotion implies behaviour (expression) and feeling (experience or subjective feeling) and quoted Bard's (1929) results as showing that emotional expression depends on the hypothalamus. But he viewed the cortex as being necessary for the mediation of subjective emotional experience. And further, he suggested that emotional expression and emotional experience are phenomena which can be dissociated from one another in man. Papez also provided a general anatomical picture of the possible structures involved in a corticothalamic mechanism of emotion. Since by now this is a somewhat dated view it is not worth describing in detail. However, Papez believed that his hypothesized circuit could account for emotion as arising either from psychic (cortical) activity or hypothalamic activity.

Finally, Papez suggests three routes that might be taken by afferent connections from the receptors after they have arrived at the thalamus. He termed these the 'stream of movement', 'stream of thought' and 'stream of feeling', these names presumably reflecting their possible function.

Clearly, Papez's theory depended heavily on neurophysiologizing. However, it was couched in terms such that it could account for the apparently different origins of emotion, for emotion felt and emotion expressed, and for the emotional colouring which seems to be present in many other nonemotional experiences.

J. B. Watson

Watson (1929; 1930) provided the first of the clearly behaviourist theories of emotion. However, he stressed the physiological aspects of emotion as well as the behavioural. Thus:

'An emotion is an hereditary "pattern-reaction" involving profound changes of the bodily mechanism as a whole, but particularly of the visceral and glandular systems'.

(1929, p. 225; italics his.)

Given this definition, Watson went on to distinguish between emotional and instinctive reactions. He did this by asserting that an emotional stimulus shocks an organism into a state of chaos, at least for a brief period of time. So, to Watson, emotions were disorganizing.

On the basis of observational work with children, Watson postulated that there are three types of fundamental emotional reaction—fear, rage and love. However, he maintained that such words often cause confusion and that it might therefore be better to term them X, Y and Z. He suggested that the X (fear) dimension is caused by: (1) sudden removal of support from an infant, (2) loud sounds, and (3) mild but sudden stimuli when an infant is just falling asleep or awakening. Typical responses are breath-catching, hand-clutching, eye-closing, lip-puckering and crying. He viewed the Y (rage) dimension as caused by 'hampering an infant's movements'. Responses to this include crying, screaming, body-stiffening, limb-slashing and breath-holding. Finally, he saw the Z (love) dimension as caused by any gentle manipulation, particularly of the erogenous zones of the body, responses to which include smiling, gurgling and cooing. Watson believed each of these patterns of reaction to be built in and evident from birth.

Watson's main contributions to the study of emotion were to offer this three-dimensional theory and to place emphasis on behaviour rather than on internal states and feelings. This, and his classic study with Rayner (Watson and Rayner 1920) on Little Albert, proved to be the foundation on which later behavioural conceptions of emotion have been built (see Chapter 5). In the way in which Watson was the general father of behaviourism, so he was the particular father of the behaviourist approaches to emotion.

D. B. Lindsley

Lindsley's theory of emotion first appeared in 1950 and 1951. More recently (1957; 1970) he has extended it to broader aspects of behaviour. Essentially, it is similar to Duffy's theory in that it is based on the concept of arousal. However, it is expressed in neurophysiological rather than behavioural terms.

Lindsley's (1951) theory depended on his belief in five empirical findings. These are summarized below, although it should be borne in mind that some doubt has been cast on them by more recent thought and empirical work. (1) In emotion, the electroencephalogram (EEG) is characterized by desynchronization, i.e. alpha-blocking or activation. (2) EEG activation can be produced by stimulation of the brain-stem reticular formation, or of the sense modalities. (3) Synchrony is restored and EEG activation is abolished by destruction of the basal diencephalon. (4) The behaviour which occurs, at least in cats, if lesions appropriate to (3) above are produced is described by Lindsley as being opposite to that which is usually seen in emotional arousal. It is apathy, somnolence, etc. (5) Overlapping the cortically arousing EEG mechanism is that of the basal diencephalon, which is the substrate for the objective part of emotional expression.

Although Lindsley (1957; 1970) has added some empirical support to these basic points and has also revised some of the details of his theory, the fundamental idea remains the same: arousal/motivation mechanisms underlie emotion. He suggests that the mechanisms of arousal are the brain-stem reticular formation interacting with the diencephalic and limbic systems via the ascending reticular activating system. He also maintains that the diencephalic and limbic systems control emotional expression and emotional and motivational behaviour. He regards emotion as being expressed in three ways: (1) through cortical channels, for example thought, worry, anxiety (cortical arousal); (2) through visceral channels, for example sweating, crying, in fact ANS function (cortical, diencephalic and brain-stem arousal); (3) through somatomotor channels, for example facial expression, muscle tension (somatomotor arousal).

Lindsley is a wide-ranging neural arousal theorist. Although his research and theory are important to emotion, he also takes in such phenomena as sleep wakefulness, alerting, attention, selective attention, vigilance, and, of course, motivation. Such is the postulated ubiquity of function of the descending and ascending reticular systems, and of those other CNS structures with which they interact.

D. Bindra

Bindra (1968; 1969) puts forward an up-to-date neurophysiological theory of emotion, or more strictly, of emotion and motivation. He suggests that both emotional and motivational phenomena can best be accounted for in terms of one construct, that of the central motive state (CMS).

Bindra begins by denying that any useful distinction can be made between emotion and motivation and speaks instead of 'species-typical', biologically useful actions. He suggests that such actions are an interaction between environmental

20

stimuli (which he terms incentives) and physiological change. (Evidence in support of this contention is reviewed, for example, in Glickman and Schiff 1967.) Bindra believes this interaction to take place in the brain and to involve joint environmental and physiological action on a common group of neurons. He maintains that this produces a CMS; this is not in itself a drive but is simply a functional change in neurons which needs *both* an environmental stimulus and a physiological change before it will occur. Thus, for example, physiological hunger and the sight, smell and taste of food are not by themselves enough to produce a CMS; they must occur together.

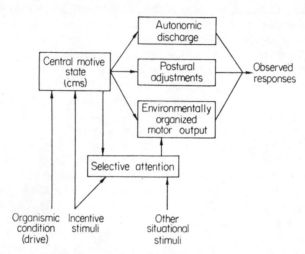

Figure 3. Bindra's central motive state mechanism (taken from Bindra 1969). The figure shows two ways in which the hypothetical CMS can bring about species-typical action. (1) Via organismic conditions and incentive stimuli from the environment, i.e. selective attention. (2) Via effects on sensory and motor mechanisms, i.e. motor facilitation or response bias.

The hypothetical notion of how a CMS produces a species-typical action is shown in Figure 3. A CMS is thought to increase the probability of a response to certain environmental stimuli by altering the effectiveness of the sensory input —shown as 'selective attention' in the figure. Or a CMS may increase the likelihood of a particular action by altering neural discharge to appropriate autonomic and somatic motor sites—'motor facilitation' or 'response bias'. Bindra argues that this scheme is equally apposite to considerations of both emotion and motivation. This leads him to the view that many words traditionally used in discussions of emotion and motivation can be replaced by common terms. For example, CMS instead of emotion or emotional state and motive or motivational state; physiological condition instead of emotional predisposition and drive.

Two further aspects of Bindra's CMS ideas are worth summarizing. (1) He believes that CMSs can be classically conditioned. Their nature depends on the actual physical state and environmental stimuli involved in this conditioning stimulus and the unconditioned stimulus (incentive). (2) Bindra asserts that the CMS can be used to resolve many of the long-enduring problems in the study of emotion. For example, the occurrence of emotion has often been thought to depend on external stimuli, whereas that of motivation has been seen to depend on internal stimuli. CMS analysis puts these together and implies that the traditional distinction has been drawn because of a difference in the value of the determining conditions—a very wide environmental stimulus can create an emotional CMS, whereas physiological states for motivational CMSs are very specific. To take another example, emotional behaviour has often been thought of as disorganized (but see Leeper) and motivational behaviour as organized. Bindra argues that both types of behaviour can be organized or disorganized depending on when they are observed during individual development. Thus a lack of experience with a particular environmental stimulus will lead to disorganized responding. However, he also suggests that motivational patterns start early on in development and occur frequently, whereas emotional patterns occur less frequently and involve more unusual situations. In this sense, he views motivation as organized and emotion as disorganized, but there seems to be little justification for this in terms of the CMS.

R. Plutchik

Although comparatively recent, Plutchik's theory of emotion has evolved over a number of years (see, for example, 1962; 1965; 1966; 1970). In his later formulation (1970) he begins as others have done by outlining what any theory of emotion should do and how some of the previous theories have not lived up to this. He suggests that his own theory, essentially biological in nature, does not have these shortcomings.

Plutchik regards emotion as multidimensional, the dimensions being those of intensity, similarity and polarity. Any emotion can vary in its intensity (for example between pensiveness and grief); any emotion varies as to its degree of similarity to any other emotion (for example joy and anticipation are more similar than loathing and surprise); and all emotions are polar (for example disgust is the opposite of acceptance.)

Plutchik represents these three dimensions in the form of a model shown in Figure 4. Vertically, on the inverted cone in this figure intensity is represented, whereas each section portrays a primary emotion. Figure 5 shows a cross-section through the cone, with the area in the centre denoting the conflict which Plutchik believes to be involved in mixed motives.

In developing his ideas, Plutchik discusses the problem of the language used in any analysis of emotion. He maintains that we normally use everyday, subjective language of the sort employed in the figures to describe emotion. However, he suggests that there are two other possible sorts of language—a purely descriptive one based on behavioural observation and a functional one based on

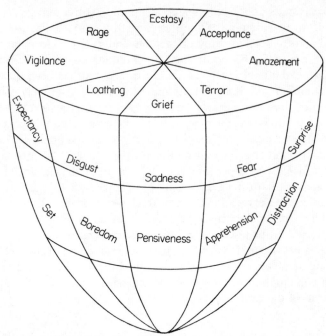

Figure 4. Plutchik's three-dimensional model of emotion (taken from Arnold 1970).

the adaptive function of what the organism does. Hence, in Plutchik's terms, we may be experiencing joy or ecstasy, whilst behaviourally we are mating or possessing and functionally we are reproducing. He argues that the functional/adaptive language is the best to use when discussing emotion since he views it as varying along the same three dimensions (i.e. intensity, similarity and polarity) as a number of basic adaptive functions. Adaptively speaking, an organism can protect, destroy, reproduce, deprive, incorporate, reject, explore or orient, four pairs of what Plutchik regards as opposites which can vary in intensity and in similarity to one another. Clearly, a behavioural language could also be generally applicable, and a subjective one could only be used with humans (and with caution). However, Plutchik prefers his adaptive language, simply viewing emotion as a bodily reaction of one of the types mentioned above.

This is a very broad, biological definition of emotion and as such is perhaps of limited use. But Plutchik suggests that it has a number of important implications: (1) emotion involves a prototypical adaptation; (2) emotion involves cognition; (3) emotion involves evolution; and (4) from a different viewpoint, emotion should be studied by specially devised methods—some of which Plutchik suggests.

M. B. Arnold

Arnold's theory of emotion has been developing for nearly three decades (see,

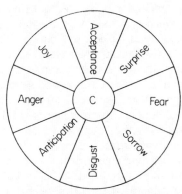

Figure 5. A cross-section through Plutchik's emotional solid (taken from Arnold 1970).

for example, 1945; 1960; 1968; 1970a; 1970b) and has appeared as a mixture of phenomenology (cognition) and physiology. It depends on the assumption that we can gain most knowledge about brain function in emotion (which to Arnold is of fundamental importance) by a cognitive analysis. This will enable us to identify the physiological mediation of the process running from perception to emotion and action.

Arnold's cognitive analysis of emotion depends very much on the construct of appraisal. She suggests that we immediately, automatically and *almost* involuntarily evaluate, with respect to ourselves, anything that we encounter. As long as no other appraisals interfere, this leads us to approach anything appraised as 'good', to avoid what is 'bad' and to ignore what is 'indifferent'. When we have a 'good' object we may well reappraise it and on the basis of this perhaps alter our behaviour. So Arnold regards appraisal as complementing perception and producing a tendency to *do* something. When this tendency is strong it is called emotion, although to Arnold all appraisals at least have the status of affective experiences.

Arnold suggests that in most new experiences memory is at the basis of our appraisals (the exceptions are 'simple' experiences such as taste or pleasure/pain). Anything new is evaluated in terms of our past experiences. She argues that the new object also evokes a memory of the *affect* associated with the previous experience. These affective memories are relivings of our past appraisals. Arnold regards them as continually distorting our judgment and therefore to be guarded against.

The final link in the appraisal chain comes from our imagination. Before we act, Arnold believes that the situation plus any relevant affective memories lead us to guess at the future. We imagine whether what will happen will be good or bad for us. Our appraisal then becomes dependent on memory plus expectation. From this we devise a plan of action which involves various possibilities for coping with the situation; we choose which is the best. It is worth pointing out again that Arnold suggests that this whole complex process of appraisal *may* well occur almost instantaneously.

For the most part, the remainder of Arnold's theory is concerned with hypothetical neural pathways which may mediate the hypothetical appraisal processes. These will be discussed in Chapter 3 (see also Chapter 4 for discussion of Arnold's theory). However, she also distinguishes between feeling and emotion. Emotional action patterns arise from positive or negative appraisals of perceived or imagined objects, whereas feeling action patterns are viewed as resulting from appraisals of something which may be either beneficial or harmful for our functioning. Although drawing this distinction, Arnold regards the hypothetical sequence of events involved in feeling as being much the same as that for emotion. For example, if I am sitting in a comfortable chair enjoying an amicable discussion, I may well be driven away if a pneumatic drill starts up in the roadway outside. Here is involved perception of the situation, appraisal, feeling, and finally a desire for action; just the same as if I had perceived a situation which had led me to be afraid and run away (emotion).

Arnold also discusses deliberate actions, which involve neither feeling nor emotion. Thus, I may sit writing this summary of Arnold's ideas on emotion without any desire to do so. Any pleasure comes when it is finished, not from the fairly mechanical progression of physically writing one word after another. Each successive word has no special attraction for me. If I were to express any emotion at all in the situation it would occur because I had had a period of difficulty in expressing myself, or alternatively had just completed a fluid two thousand words.

Arnold regards such deliberate action as: (1) making up the bulk of our everyday behaviour; (2) involving what we could call rational judgment; and (3) that which distinguishes us from the animals. So we judge situations both in terms of short-term (emotional) possibilities and long-term, more abstract, goals. And we often relinquish the former, which seem more immediately attractive, for the latter, which are better for us in the long run. Animals do not have this capacity; they can only make immediate, emotional appraisals. With her distinction between emotional action patterns and deliberate action patterns, Arnold believes that in reality she is separating emotion and will. In fact, she is nicely maintaining the traditional rationalist doctrine.

K. H. Pribram

Pribram's ideas concerning emotion overlap with many other theories. He begins from a neurophysiological viewpoint, takes into consideration ideas of appraisal (see Arnold) and motivation (see Leeper) and develops a cognitive/information theory position (see Siminov). Originally, Pribram (1970; Miller *et al.* 1960) regarded emotion as Plans, these being '... neural programs which are engaged when the organism is disequilibriated'. Pribram states that, normally, motivationally based Plans change because they are carried out, but if their execution is blocked then emotion results. Whether this emotion closes or opens the organism to more input (and Pribram allows both capacities) the Plan involved is stopped. When a Plan is held up in this way for a long period then 'regression' tends to occur. Pribram (Miller *et al.* 1960) goes on to argue that emotional expression is more primitive and basic than rational behaviour, although emotions need not be expressed at all. Thus, there are emotional Plans as well as motivational Plans, both of which are altered by experience. Pribram (1970) maintains that this idea of emotions as Plans brought with it too many problems. As an alternative, he speculates about feelings rather than emotions.

Pribram distinguishes between the 'objective' world of sense data and the subjective world of feelings, and proposes that where we have no evidence which will allow us to construct the objective world then we must rely on the subjective. In other words, if we have no good evidence that we are faced with something which we can see, hear, smell, taste or touch, then we must be feeling it inside. These feelings Pribram describes in his usual capitalized way as 'Feelings as Monitors'. He develops good, empirically based neurophysiological arguments to support such subjective feelings and affirms that this viewpoint is more fruitful than his previous idea of Plans.

We do not plan to be happy or sad or angry; rather, Pribram suggests, we simply *feel* happy or sad or angry. We construct Plans and implement them. They may be very easily executed, or they may fail, miserably or otherwise. We evaluate or appraise their success, and this process of appraisal is monitored, i.e. it is felt. Thus Feelings as Monitors are regarded as Images not Plans. Plans are merely constructed within the matrix that Images provide. A final contribution (and slight confusion) to the language of emotion suggested by Pribram is that 'go' Plans equal motivations and 'no-go' Plans equal emotions.

In summary, Pribram's most recent suggestion is that the study of emotion will benefit most by distinguishing between feelings and emotions, and then concentrating on the former. Feelings are Monitors are Images are appraisals of the degree of success attached to the execution of Plans. The Plans themselves may allow the organism to go ahead, in which case they are motivational, or they may be blocked, in which case the organism is thwarted and we have emotion. Although expressed in a somewhat idiosyncratic language, Pribram's theory of emotion is quite similar to Arnold's: basically, it is cognitive/phenomenological in nature and yet it draws on neurophysiological evidence for empirical support.

S. Schachter

This brief section on Schachter is included since no collection of summaries of the influential theories of emotion would be representative without his name. However, much of Schachter's contribution is through a cunningly devised series of experimental situations and the interpretation of the results which they have produced (see Chapter 4).

For an overview of Schachter's ideas the best sources are Schachter (1959; 1964). He develops what he terms a cognitive/physiological view of emotion. In fact, however, he suggests that emotional states are mainly determined by cognitive factors, a suggestion made by others before him (for example Ruckmick

1936), but not developed so far. He argues that emotional states are characterized by a general arousal of the sympathetic nervous system (SNS) and that from state to state this may differ slightly in its pattern. He maintains that we interpret and classify these states by clues from the situation which brought them about and also from our typical mode of perception. Physiological arousal occurs and is given its precise direction by our cognitions of what brought it about.

This formulation led Schachter to make three propositions. (1) If an individual is physiologically aroused but cannot explain why, what caused the arousal, then he will give his state a name and react to it in whatever cognitive way is open to him. Thus any *one* state could be labelled in many ways depending on the individual and his situation. (2) If an individual is physiologically aroused and has an entirely reasonable explanation of this available, it is improbable that he will entertain any alternative cognitive accounts. (3) The third proposition involves approaching the theory from the opposite direction. If from time to time an individual experiences the same cognition, he will only describe his feelings as emotions if he is also in some state of physiological arousal. Similarly, there will be no general emotional behaviour without this arousal. Hence, Schachter's basic idea is that emotions are controlled through a very close interrelationship and interaction between physiological arousal and cognitive appraisal.

P. V. Siminov

Although Siminov's (1970) theory of emotion is brief and simple, it is described here since it reflects a somewhat different approach to that of the remainder; it is presented directly in terms of information theory. Siminov begins with a definition of what he calls negative emotion:

$$E = - N(I_n - I_a)$$

where emotion equals need times the difference between the necessary information and the available information. In this context, information is the possibility of reaching a goal due to a particular communication. Thus, if an organism cannot organize itself appropriately through lack of information then the nervous mechanism leading to negative emotions starts to act. Siminov suggests that this has three main implications. (1) 'Dominant' reactions occur—i.e. previously neutral stimuli begin to be reacted to, and ineffectual (as regards any usual goals) activity is maintained. (2) This ineffectual activity leads to physiological changes typical of emotion. (3) The emotions themselves have a strong physiological activating influence. Consequently, if this mechanism becomes active, then some habitual response must have been disrupted.

Siminov views positive emotions in a similar way. When an organism's needs are satisfied it is emotionally quiescent, but if there is a surplus of information over and above that which is necessary for this satisfaction then positive emotion is the result. In the terms of the formula, $I_a > I_n$. Such positive emotions endure in the same way as do negative emotions and may facilitate behaviour.

Finally, Siminov suggests that emotions may be classified by taking into account: (1) the strength of the need; (2) the extent of the information deficiency or redundancy; and (3) the specificity of the action which is aimed at satisfying the need. He believes that it is only when 'action at a distance' is necessary (i.e. defence or struggle rather than just pleasure or displeasure brought about by immediate contacts) that emotions proper are seen.

Siminov's standpoint is straightforward. We continually strive to attain the tranquillity (behavioural and physiological) of satisfied needs. When we have too little or too much information for this attainment then negative and positive emotions are the respective results.

P. T. Young

Young's (1961) theory is unusual in that it is relatively modern, American and yet somewhat isolated; it differs both in conception and language from many of the other theories summarized here. Although he leans heavily on the concept of arousal, Young distinguishes it from what he terms an hedonic dimension. He seems to be the last of the hedonic philosophers, although simultaneously an experimental psychologist.

Young does not speak of emotion *per se* but rather of affective processes and an hedonic continuum. He regards affective processes as varying in sign, intensity and duration. Thus, if naive organisms develop approach behaviour, he postulates that an underlying positive central affective process is at work; similarly, a negative affective process underlies withdrawal responses. Further he suggests that affective processes can vary from maximally positive intensity to maximally negative—as shown by the development of preferences. And lastly, he maintains that affective processes can differ in duration. Young views these affective processes as spread along an hedonic continuum which ranges from extremely negative through an area of indifference to extremely positive. Hedonic changes can occur in either direction, and from time to time may even be in opposition. This schema leads to four possible types of affective change: increasing positive, decreasing positive, increasing negative and decreasing negative. (In some ways this is similar to Millenson's behaviourist ideas.)

Young proposes that affective processes are quite distinct from sensory processes and that their essential role is motivational, having a regulatory influence on behaviour. He postulates a series of principles and functions concerning affective processes. First the principles. (1) Stimulation has affective as well as sensory consequences. (2) Affective arousal points the organism towards or away from a stimulus. (3) Affective processes lead to motives. (4) The strength of a recent motive is related to various aspects of previous affective arousals (duration, intensity, frequency and recency). (5) Motives also depend on learning—affective processes determine what will and will not be learned, but learning itself is simply practice, neurobehavioural change due to exercise. (6) Affective processes can be conditioned—we learn 'how to feel' in given situations. (7) Affective processes exert their regulatory function by influencing choice. (8) The final principle is very wide-ranging—neurobehavioural patterns themselves follow a pattern of organization which maximizes positive affective arousal and minimizes negative affective arousal.

Young suggests that effective processes have four main functions. (1) They activate, by provoking action. (2) They sustain and terminate behaviour. (3) They regulate behaviour (as to whether or not it will develop or continue). (4) They organize in that they determine the formation of neurobehavioural patterns which usually become learned.

Essentially, Young is speaking of pleasantness and unpleasantness rather than emotion. These are affective processes arranged on an hedonic continuum which itself has an arousal function. The affective processes accompany all behaviour to some degree and themselves work according to a set of underlying principles, and in turn exercise various influences on behaviour.

R. S. Lazarus

Basically, Lazarus stresses the importance of cognitive factors in emotion. However, in addition to this he also considers the significance of factors which stem from biological and cultural perspectives (see Lazarus 1966; 1968; Lazarus *et al.* 1970). Lazarus suggests that although concepts of emotion exist in psychology and are important in the description and classification of behaviour, they are not necessarily much use in its explanation. This idea bears comparison with those of both Duffy and Leeper. Lazarus asserts that the development of the concept of emotion has been hampered by difficulties in description and classification. Since there is no one thing to which emotion can be meaningfully and unequivocally said to refer, Lazarus suggests that it is a 'response syndrome'. This is a directly drawn medical analogy, with emotions viewed as having causes, symptoms and a number of courses. In Lazarus' view, the overall pattern of relationships between causes, symptoms and courses permits the descriptive use of the word emotion and also allows the possibility of classification.

As already mentioned, Lazarus dwells on biological and cultural aspects of emotion. But he finds them lacking. He maintains, for example, that emphasis has shifted away from the role of the viscera and other such peripheral 'biological' structures in emotion and has moved towards more central mechanisms. Even within the CNS, the emphasis has been on the evolutionarily more primitive subcortial structures. He argues, however, that these structures have themselves undergone evolutionary change, as have cortical structures, and that they also play an important part in our cognitive functions. Similarly, Lazarus believes that cultural influences on emotion can be just as easily stressed. He suggests that culture affects emotion in four ways: (1) through the manner in which we perceive emotional stimuli; (2) by directly altering emotional expression; (3) by determining social relationships and judgments; (4) by highly ritualized behaviour such as grief. Should we stress the evolutionary, biological viewpoint or the cultural? Lazarus believes that this problem can be resolved by taking a more individual, cognitive perspective.

To Lazarus we are evaluators; we evaluate each stimulus that we encounter, with a view to its personal relevance and significance. Lazarus regards this as cognitive activity with emotion as part of it. Hence:

'... each emotional reaction ... is a function of a particular kind of cognition or *appraisal*'.

(Lazarus *et al.* 1970, p. 218; their italics.)

Lazarus recognizes emotional reactions at three levels, the behavioural, the physiological and the cognitive or subjective. He views each of these as important in its own right and suggests that the particular pattern which may obtain between them is a distinguishing feature of emotion.

Lazarus extends his ideas with the suggestion that we have dispositions to search for and respond to or attend to particular stimuli, and that these dispositions shape our interaction with the environment. Our cognitive appraisal of these stimuli produces the emotional response. The stimuli themselves are constantly changing and we are continually 'coping' with them; so our cognitions alter, as do our emotional reactions. Lazarus (1966; 1968) argues that there are two sorts of coping process. We may deal with threat or harm by direct action, the urge to which he regards as an important part of emotion. Since the success or failure of this direct action constantly fluctuates, our cognitive evaluations and hence our emotional reactions also fluctuate. Lazarus terms the second type of coping 'reappraisal'. This is solely cognitive, involving no direct action. We may reappraise from positive to negative or negative to positive, and may do so realistically or distortedly. We (and animals) appraise and reappraise all incoming information, each twist and turn of which is shown in emotional reactions.

Lazarus realizes that he has only presented the outlines of a cognitive theory of emotion and that there must eventually be some attempt to point to the detailed cognitive aspects of any individual emotional response. He suggests, however, that a cognitive/phenomenological approach, linked with biological and cultural considerations, will have the effect of putting emotion back into the forefront of psychology.

R. W. Leeper

Leeper (1948) put forward a strong argument against the idea of emotions as having a disorganizing influence on behaviour (see Chapter 4). He maintained instead that emotions pervade all behaviour by organizing and motivating it. More recently (1963a; 1963b; 1965; 1970), he has added considerable refinement to this basic idea.

Leeper (for example 1970) suggests that emotions act as motives since they are mildly aroused most of the time. They control our behaviour without our awareness. He argues that emotions give behaviour (and mental activity) its goal-directedness in, for example, allowing us to choose between alternatives, or solve problems, or endure sanctions to obtain a reward. He believes that the traditional emphasis has been antipathetic to the view of emotions as motives since they have been studied in ways indicated by everyday considerations. As mentioned in Chapter 1, psychologists have given most attention to extreme and sensational (therefore, highly noticeable) aspects of emotion. At present, however, Leeper sees the idea of emotions as motives creeping, almost insidiously, into psychological theorizing, often without appearing as a formal statement.

The most recent idea extended by Leeper (1970) is that emotions function not only as motives, but also as perceptions. By this he means that emotions are cognitive in that they convey information to the organism. In fact, they are perceptions, perhaps long standing, of situations. Again, Leeper suggests that this view is breaking with tradition. He suggests that, in the past, motivation and perception have been regarded as distinct. He puts forward arguments to explain this dichotomy, similar to those which he uses to account for the division between emotions and motives.

Leeper develops his ideas with the assertion that emotional motives depend for their function on a similar mechanism to that of the more obvious physiologically based motives. He believes that there are 'emotional mechanisms' which function through signals that indicate the favourability of environmental circumstances. These mechanisms act like reflexes.

These developing ideas on emotion have sprung from two aims. Leeper has attempted to dispel the more traditional view of emotion as disorganizing, chaotic and interfering in its effects on behaviour. Also, he maintains that emotion is an active force involving motivation and perception, which organizes, sustains and directs behaviour.

D. Rapaport (psychoanalytic theory)

Rapaport (1950) provides a good general introduction to the psychoanalytic approach to emotion. The reader who is interested in pursuing this line of study will find worthwhile analyses of the Jungian idea of emotion in Hillman (1961; 1970) and of the neo-Freudian in Arieti (1970).

As one might expect, Rapaport's first major point is that the Freudian concept of emotion is unclear. On some occasions, Freud considered affects to be *a* or *the* form of psychic energy; on others, he viewed affect as an implied attribute of other psychoanalytic concepts. Hence: '. . . affects regulated from the unconscious are defined as discharge processes of energies of instinctual origin' (Rapaport 1970, p. 29).

Rapaport considers that the old problem of the time sequences involved in feeling and the expression of emotion (see James and Cannon) detracted from the possible idea that 'felt' emotion and physiological changes are both the result of some common variable. Naturally, any investigation of this underlying variable would be difficult, since in Freudian terms it is concerned with the unconscious. For Freud, emotions may be psychic energies or they may be discharge processes associated with these energies, but either way one is squarely within the murk of the unconscious and its instinctual origins. Psychoanalytic theory is not concerned with possible sequences of emotional events. Perception occurs and therefore anything might happen; the emotion 'felt', or the bodily process, or both, or neither.

In his account of the psychoanalytic theory of emotion, Rapaport continues by drawing attention to some of the neo-Freudians and showing how their views on emotion differ from Freud's original ideas. For example, he mentions Brierley (1937) as concluding that affect is some kind of tension phenomenon which leads to an inner and outer discharge. Brierley also believed affect to show what will happen to the basic impulse. According to Rapaport, this notion is in accord with Freud's idea of pleasantness and unpleasantness. These are the conscious parts of decreasing and increasing tension. And further, Rapaport draws from Federn (1933; 1936) to demonstrate the importance of conflict theory in the psychoanalytic consideration of emotion. Affect, or emotions, result when different drive cathexes are in conflict. (A cathexis is an amount of psychic energy which is associated with some idea which may be held by a person.)

This is but a taste of the psychoanalytic theories of emotion. To summarize, as far as this is possible, they assert that the substrates (psychic processes) underlying emotion are unconscious and that affects have been variously viewed as psychic energies, discharge processes of psychic energies, and manifestations of instinctual conflict. It is best to let this discussion rest here, since if it is taken any further the writer will become more lost than the reader no doubt already is.

M. Pradines

A résumé of some of Pradines' ideas has been included for comparative purposes. His work (1958) has become more generally available in translation (Begin and Arnold; see Arnold 1968). Pradines theorizes first in the tradition of distinguishing between feelings and emotions, and second in that of regarding emotions to be disorganizing. Also, in that it is concerned with what is adaptive and maladaptive, Pradines' theory of emotion has biological overtones. However, it is expressed in nonbiological, nonbehavioural terms.

To understand Pradines' ideas on emotion, it is first necessary to appreciate what he means by sentiment. This depends on his assertion that perception occurs not only intellectually but also via various affective states. He views these affective states both as complex feelings and as simple feelings of pleasure and pain. Sentiments involve complex mental images of possible pleasure and pain. But also, sentiment has the effect of breaking down feeling and making the power to act (which is part of feeling) autonomous. Also, Pradines considers sentiment to be a complex feeling because it can absorb strong energies which are aroused by the associations attached to any perceptions. Thus, sentiment can be a simple sensory feeling or a complex feeling following perception.

Pradines argues that sentiments, like perception, are regulators of action; they adaptively guide our actions towards specific objects. In this way he distinguishes sentiments from tendencies, the latter being (unobjective) inclinations which are not tied to specific circumstances. Sentiments, on the other hand, are very much dependent on objective circumstances, which he suggests might give them their agreeable nature; circumstances change. Any stability in sentiment must come from the stability of the object to which it is attached.

Pradines believes that psychologists have often been misled into their ideas on emotion through their observations of disordered sentiments, and it is here that we come to his ideas on emotion. He regards emotion as one of four ways in which sentiments can become disorganized, the others being via what he terms fixation, passion and inversion; these are not worth elaboration here. Pradines maintains that emotions are disruptive in that they reduce sentiments to little more than reflex. Emotions are simply sentiments in extreme, explosive, crisis form. So any situation may produce some sentiment in us (for example anger) without necessarily leading to an emotional outburst.

The key to Pradines' theory lies in the imagination. He suggests that it is through imagination (and belief) that memory images become more affective and active. Both sentiments and emotions spring from imagination, pointing to the adaptive nature of the one and the maladaptive nature of the other. Pradines asserts that it may be that something is imagined as experienced, expected, and then becomes reality. If so, we may react to it in an extreme but simple and effective way. Such an emotional action will squash the more gentlemanly and adaptive sentiment which would otherwise have occurred. 'Emotion is a mental and motor disaster experienced by the subject who is its victim' (Pradines 1958, p. 721; Arnold 1968, p. 200).

E. Duffy

Duffy has expressed her view of emotion many times (for example 1934; 1941; 1962) but probably put it best in her 1941 paper, which she began:

'For many years the writer has been of the opinion that "emotion", as a scientific concept is worse than useless'.

This sets the scene perfectly, for Duffy tries to explain away emotion rather than to account for it, her argument being couched in terms of a behaviourally oriented activation theory. Her views on activation in general can be read in *Activation and Behaviour* (1962).

Duffy's first (1934) reason for suggesting that the term emotion be dropped from scientific usage was that it had been used mainly to refer to the extreme end of a continuum of behaviour, but one which anomalously involved a sharp noncontinuation between emotion and nonemotion. She argued that a behavioural continuum and discrete categories of behaviour are likely to have different underlying constructs. Duffy preferred the idea that emotional phenomena are separate aspects of responses occurring in continua.

In 1941, Duffy developed her argument further. She suggested that emotion as it is commonly conceived refers to how we feel and act towards a situation which we expect to be important; our expectations may be positive or negative. So, we shall feel angry and perhaps afraid only if we are blocked from attaining some goal. Duffy hypothesizes that such a state of emotion must involve a change in energy level; excitement represents a higher energy level and depression a lower energy level. Energy level itself is dependent on the stimulus situation. It will increase either when we are blocked or when a block is removed; conversely, there is a decrease only when a goal is so effectively blocked that we give up altogether.

Duffy then widened her argument to include the idea that all behaviour is motivated. She suggested that without motivation there would be no activity, and that what is called emotion simply represents an extreme of motivation, i.e. energy. But, she then posed the rhetorical question, how do we know when behaviour is extreme enough to be called emotional? Her answer was that there is no criterion for this, since emotion-producing behaviour does not differ in kind from other behaviour—to Duffy other responses follow the same principles. In her terms, *all* responses are adjustive responses which enable the organism to adapt.

From Duffy's standpoint, the second characteristic of emotion as commonly conceived is that it is disorganizing (see Leeper). However, she thought that this apparent disorganization is a function of behaviour which occurs at very high or at very low energy levels. This is not a function of 'emotion' since disorganization is also found at energy levels not extreme enough to be normally called emotions, for example the stammer of an enthusiastic child or the double fault of the over-involved tennis player. This, of course, is representing emotion in terms of the hypothetical inverted U-shaped function relating arousal to performance (see Chapter 1).

Finally, Duffy set out to deal with what she regarded as the commonly proposed fact of its conscious awareness. We tend to feel that our conscious experiences of emotion are different from our conscious experiences of anything else. Duffy argued that such a conscious awareness involves awareness of the environmental situation which leads to the emotional state, awareness of bodily changes, and awareness of a set for response in the situation. Duffy maintained that these factors also make up any nonemotional state of consciousness.

To summarize, Duffy breaks down emotion (and in fact all behaviour) into changes in: (1) level of energy, (2) organization and (3) conscious states, and suggests that each of these occurs on a continuum. The final stage in her argument is that it is meaningless to try to study emotion at all, because it is something which '. . . has no distinguishing characteristics' (1941). Instead, she suggests that *any* response should be considered according to its energy level (activation), how well it maintains goal-direction (organization/disorganization) and the environmental situation in response to which it occurs. Duffy's is a theory of non-emotion.

H. F. Harlow and R. Stagner

It is difficult to categorize Harlow and Stagner's (1933) theory of emotion. It was quite clearly based on a conditioning model and owed much to Watson's behaviourism, and yet retained overtones of Cannon's physiologizing while maintaining a distinction between feelings and emotions. Briefly, they suggested that at the root of emotion are unconditioned affective responses (central physiological changes experienced as feelings). All emotions occur through becoming conditioned to these responses. The effect of this is to modify the original unconditioned affective state in two ways: (1) the range of eliciting stimuli is widened; (2) the violence of the original responses is dampened.

Harlow and Stagner made a number of extensions of their theory. (1) They suggested that although the basic emotional states are feelings, emotions may also reflect other conscious states. (2) Feelings are controlled thalamically, and sensations cortically. (3) Emotions are not innate; Harlow and Stagner simply suggested that there are unconditioned responses from which emotions develop. They believed the innate part of emotion to be the 'four fundamental feeling tones, pleasure, unpleasantness, excitement and depression'. (4) Emotion is distinct from feeling in that in emotion there is cognition of the outside situation. We feel things in such a way that they are connected to external stimuli. To return to the nature/nurture question, we are born with the capacity to feel but have to learn the various emotions.

Finally, Harlow and Stagner suggested a behaviouristic way in which the various emotions become differentiated from the original amorphous mass of feeling states. They argued, via introspective analysis, that the emotion labels which we attach to various experiences simply reflect our cognitions of the external stimuli involved and the meanings which they have for us. Any name which becomes appropriate to describe an affective state must therefore result from social conditioning. Harlow and Stagner viewed fear and rage, for example, as basically the same states. However, the situation which brings them about is one of threat, and if it is appropriate to attack then we call the state rage, whereas if it is appropriate to run we call it fear.

To summarize, Harlow and Stagner suggested that there are innate, undifferentiated, basic feelings. Emotions are the conditioned form of these which we learn to refer to in particular ways. The feelings, the emotional conditioning and the social learning of labels are each mediated cortically and subcortically.

J. R. Millenson

Millenson (1967) provides the closest approximation to a modern behaviourist theory of emotion, although he himself admits it is no more than a model. It is rooted in Watson, owes much to Plutchik and is inspired by Estes and Skinner's (1941) experimental paradigm for studying conditioned emotional behaviour (see Chapter 5).

Millenson's model rests on the fundamental proposition that emotional changes, which he believes come about through a process of classical conditioning, either enhance or suppress other, nonemotional behaviour. He argues that: (1) some emotions differ only in intensity; and (2) some emotions are basic and others are compounds of these. From this Millenson produces a three-dimensional system to describe all emotion, each dimension representing variations in emotional intensity. Dimension 1 is terror, anxiety or apprehension, such emotions sometimes suppressing and sometimes facilitating operant behaviour. Dimension 2 is made up of elation or pleasure which enhance operant behaviour. Dimension 3 is anger; this facilitates some operant behaviour and leads to a greater likelihood of attack and destruction. Clearly, these dimensions are close to Watson's X, Y and Z factors.

Millenson suggests that more complex emotions develop from mixtures of these three dimensions, which he regards as primary. For example, we feel 'guilt' if we steal a book. In Millenson's terms such behaviour would possibly lead to both positive (possession of the book) and negative (being caught) consequences. This is psychological conflict, which Millenson views as often underlying our more complex emotional reactions. Also, he argues that at the human level emotional reactions often become complex due to the very involved history of conditioning and reinforcement which we all have. Occasionally, great changes can be wrought in the mass of interrelated reinforcers which are controlling our behaviour at any time. For example, a friend may die, or we may suffer a loss of status. In either case we have suddenly been deprived of many reinforcers. We label our emotional reaction to this as sorrow. This argument leads Millenson to an interesting conjecture concerning a possible difference between human and animal emotion. He suggests that we may well be correct in believing certain emotions (such as sorrow) to be essentially human. There are simply no conditions in the infrahuman world which are complex enough to produce them—it is not necessarily that animals are incapable of them.

Hence, Millenson's view of emotion is extremely behaviouristic. He concerns himself with little more than observable behaviour and the environmental conditions which he believes to control it. In this singlemindedness, Millenson's ideas are unique amongst the more recent formulations of emotion.

3
The Physiology of Emotion

From the subjective viewpoint it seems clear that different emotions involve distinct bodily changes. It is therefore appropriate that many investigations have been made into the physiological substrates of emotion. However, from its inception, this approach has been bedevilled with problems. Although there is an immense body of relevant research, its techniques and findings are so diverse as to make systematization awkward to impose and conclusions difficult to draw.

There are three basic research strategies within physiological psychology. (1) The most common of these involves the making of lesions in some part of the nervous system and observing any effects that these might have on behaviour. The lesions may be very restricted in extent or may be complete transections or ablations. As will be discussed below, this strategy can lead to great difficulty in the interpretation of any data which derive from it. (2) The second method is that of electrical or chemical stimulation. This type of technique has long been used to record changes in the ANS. However, since the development of a technology which allows the chronic implantation of electrodes, it has also been much used in CNS measurement. (3) The final strategy is fundamental to psychophysiological research (see below). It involves the recording of ongoing changes in such peripheral physiological measures as respiration, heart rate, etc. Each of these research methods has produced a wealth of data. Although this has often shown remarkably little consistency, it has been used as a basis for many theories and models of emotion and for much general physiologizing.

Naturally, physiological studies of emotion often employ behavioural measures. Although the independent variable in such studies is usually physiological, it is always the resultant changes in behaviour which must be of interest. There are two types of behavioural measure of emotion commonly taken in physiologically based studies. The more frequent, and more naive, is the direct behavioural description of 'typical' emotional reactions, usually in infrahuman subjects. For example, fear in cats is thought to be indicated by freezing or by dashing away, rage by violent lashing, arching movements, thrusting, jerking, snarling, biting, and so on, pleasure by purring. Although such measures appear to be simple, on occasion they have been produced in complex systems. Brady and Nauta (1953), for example, developed a six-component rating of emotionality, including resistance to handling, vocalization, startle and flight, urination and defecation. The other behavioural measures used in physiological studies of emotion are considerably more sophisticated. They derive largely from techniques designed to study conditioned emotional responding (CER) and active and passive avoidance. Briefly, the CER technique is based on the indirect recording of the 'emotional' influences of signalled uncontingent stimuli as these affect some ongoing operant baseline. Active avoidance involves the making of a (fear-motivated) response in the presence of a neutral stimulus to avoid some forthcoming aversive stimulus. Passive avoidance can be defined as learning to avoid some aversive stimulus by *not* making a response. (See Chapter 5 for a full exposition of behavioural measures of emotion.)

The first of the behavioural measures mentioned above points to two of the problems encountered in this field. In many studies, although the physiological manipulations are reasonably sophisticated, the behavioural observations are naive, poorly controlled and somewhat subjectively judged. Also, such studies frequently use infrahuman subjects. The difficulty in extrapolating from animals to man has already been discussed. In the search for the physiological substrates of emotion, it is even more of a difficulty. Presumably, the precise functions of, and interconnections between, various parts of the nervous system differ from species to species.

A more fundamental set of problems are an inherent part of studies involving CNS ablation and stimulation. There are a number of technical difficulties: how to separate the brain into distinct areas, how to determine the precise location and extent of a particular lesion, how to confine a lesion or an electrical or chemical stimulation to a given area, to mention but a few. Also, there is the question of localization of function. The majority of studies of emotion which have dwelt on the CNS depend on this concept. Its meaning, however, is difficult to pin down. The implication is that some structurally well-defined area of the brain is (causally) responsible for some well-defined behavioural function. This cannot be so. At best we can say that some area of the brain may be a necessary condition for the occurrence of some behaviour; it cannot be a sufficient condition. Also, even to this extent, we cannot say that function is localized until we understand how the system works, which at present we do not. What can we say if, on removing one area of the brain or stimulating another, we achieve certain behavioural effects? No more than that these parts are necessary to that function. Too little is known about the precise function of the CNS to determine the neurophysiological extent of our manipulations. It may be that the interconnections within the CNS are such that a stimulus or lesion in one area may produce unexpected changes in behaviour. This, of course, could indirectly affect whatever behavioural measure we might be taking. The picture is complicated in at least three other ways. (1) There are large individual differences in behavioural reaction. (2) The effects of a particular ablation may only become apparent under certain criterial conditions. (3) There is some evidence for mass action in the brain, or of a degree of equipotentiality between various areas. At present, there appears to be no solution to this set of problems. However, they should be borne in mind when evaluating the research and theory to be found in this chapter. Most of this research relies unquestioningly on a belief in localization of function.

Those interested in the physiology of emotion have naturally followed diverse paths to the subject. These have frequently been dictated by that part of the nervous system which the investigator believes to be of particular importance. Hence, there is much pertinent information to be found in studies of the ANS, the subcortex and the cortex. The present chapter will cover these approaches systematically and will also include mention of research involving glandular function and neurochemistry. Wherever possible, fact will be presented before theory.

Figure 6. Diagrammatic representation of the limbic system (shaded areas).

Finally, it may be useful to refer to Figures 6 and 7. They represent in simplified form the structural relationships in the nervous system. Much of the text which follows concerns the functional relationships (of emotion) which are hypothesized to cut across these.

PERIPHERAL MECHANISMS

Psychophysiological measures

Psychophysiology is the term which has come to be used to describe the study of peripheral measures of ANS activity, such as respiration or cardiovascular change. It is appropriate to begin a consideration of the physiology of emotion by discussing such responses, since they are basic to the influential James–Lange theory. Initially, the psychophysiological approach looks promising; if there are physiological concomitants of emotion, then introspectively they would seem to be reflected in our breathing or blood flow or sweating, and so on. Subjectively, we can *feel* such changes; when we are angry or afraid our breathing may become

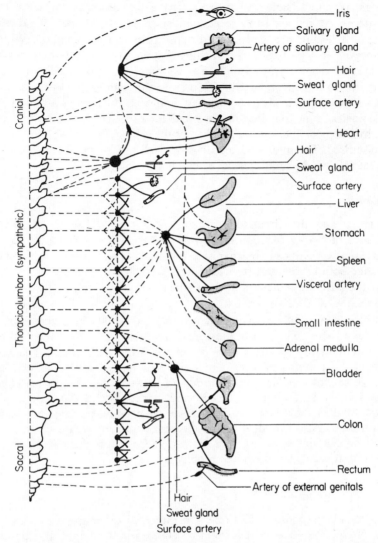

Figure 7. Diagrammatic representation of the autonomic nervous system and the bodily structures that it serves (taken from Morgan 1965).

fast and shallow or we may sweat more profusely. Or, for example, the physiological changes which occur when we engage in some vigorous sport are superficially similar to those which stem from emotion-producing stimuli, but they 'feel' different bodily. Also, it might be expected that any peripheral changes would perhaps occur in orderly patterns corresponding to the various emotions. However, a somewhat disappointing picture has emerged. With a few important exceptions, psychophysiological measures have not produced evidence for any clear patterns. At first sight this seems odd, since, intuitively, peripheral feedback would seem relevant, if not crucial, to our experiencing of emotion. With hindsight, however, it is perhaps less surprising. Psychophysiology relies quite heavily on the idea of general arousal, indeed it is one of the main sources of evidence for its existence. As mentioned in Chapter 1, although arousal is a subjectively reasonable concept, it leads to notoriously imprecise predictions about behaviour or physiological function. Bearing in mind these difficulties, some of the main psychophysiological measures and the results which they have led to will be briefly discussed. The interested reader is referred to Grossman (1967) and Sternbach (1966) for good overall reviews of psychophysiology.

Circulation

Circulation and the circulatory system are important both to the everyday maintenance of bodily function and to any emergency which may arise. There are two equally significant mechanisms involved. (1) The heart, pumping; this may change both in rate and strength and is regulated by central reciprocal links between the parasympathetic and sympathetic nervous systems (PNS and SNS). (2) The relative dilation or constriction of the blood vessels; dilation increases the blood which is available to a particular area and results in a consequent constriction elsewhere. The main measures are blood pressure and pulse rate. Although circulatory changes are correlated with behavioural changes, for example in the patterns of sleep and waking or in reaction to sudden, intense stimuli, we cannot use them to discriminate between the various emotions (for example Landis 1925, but see Lacey and Lacey 1970 below for a possible exception to this). However, cardiovascular changes may represent changes in general arousal. Also, although some circulatory disorders are clearly psychosomatic (for example eczema), there is no evidence for particular disfunctions stemming from particular emotional problems.

Galvanic skin response

Galvanic skin response (GSR) refers to the electrical resistance of the skin to the flow of electromotive current. Skin resistance (or its reciprocal, skin conductance) fluctuates constantly, but any strange or novel stimulus superimposes immediate although transitory changes on these fluctuations. Much research using this measure (as with other psychophysiological measures) is concerned with techniques for recording and although very important is of little relevance here (see Sternbach 1966). As regards emotion, the problem hinges on whether *all* new, sudden or intense stimuli lead to particular emotional reactions or whether these changes in the electrical activity of the skin just reflect general activation. The GSR allows little differentiation between emotions. There are only poor relationships between changes in skin reactivity and (1) the intensity of the stimuli which produced them, (2) reports of emotional reactions, and (3) distinctions between pleasant and unpleasant emotions.

Respiration

The rate and depth of breathing must be quite directly and closely related to our basic needs. Yet again, this indicates that respiration should provide a fair measure of general arousal. By the same token, respiratory changes would appear likely to accompany any emotional reactions, but as with the other psychophysiological measures, no study has successfully used respiratory changes to distinguish between emotions or even between emotional and nonemotional situations. The only exception to this is in two early studies by Felecky (1914; 1916), who reported correlations between measures of respiration and six imagined emotions. However, the research was methodologically inadequate and the results have never been replicated.

Other peripheral measures

The remaining psychophysiological measures present essentially the same picture as that given by circulation, skin resistance and respiration. Muscle potential, for example, providing an index of muscular tension, also simply reflects general alertness or arousal (for example Jacobson 1932; 1951), but no relationships are seen with specific emotions. An early exception to this general rule was seen with gastrointestinal activity and various biochemical measures. Brunswick (1924), for example, showed there to be a loss of gastrointestinal tone during a number of emotional reactions, fear, envy, disappointment, etc. Distress, surprise and startle had the opposite effect of augmenting it.

Electrical activity of the brain

Although the electrical activity of the brain is clearly not a peripheral response like respiration or muscle potential, it is included here because it is often measured peripherally, and recorded as the electroencephalogram (EEG). When a person is at rest or relaxed the brain is characterized by regular 10 per second waves of electrical activity (alpha). This rhythm tends to disappear with the input of sensory stimulation. This is usually termed alpha-blocking; it seems to depend on the novelty of the stimulus and, in fact, may rapidly habituate. (See Coles 1970; Lindsley 1951.)

As with the psychophysiological measures, arousal has a prominent part to play in the thinking of those investigators concerned with EEG activity. For example, it is argued that anxiety may produce nonspecific arousal and in so doing activate electrical activity in the brain (for example Darrow et al. 1946). Also, the stimulation of the brain-stem reticular formation elicits cortical arousal (Moruzzi and Magoun 1949) and the general autonomic and somesthetic responses which tend to accompany emotion (Ranson and Magoun 1939). Such relationships led to

Lindsley's (1951; 1970) activation theory of emotion which is couched sheerly in terms of cortical arousal. Although this theory seems superficially good sense, to be viable it would require fine shadings of cortical arousal; at the moment there is no evidence for these. Also, as with other psychophysiological measures, there is no evidence for relationship between specific emotional reactions and cortical EEG.

Darrow's (1947; 1950) approach also involved EEG. He proposed that particular cortical arousal results from nonsynchronized electrical activity across many cortical neurons. In some way this summates and thereby cancels many of the (electrical) potential differences, so producing the fast, low-amplitude electrical activity characteristic of arousal. Darrow suggests that this could lead to 'cortical anxiety'. He regarded the other emotions as characterized by alpha waves, from synchronized rather than desynchronized activity. There are three main problems with these ideas. (1) It is difficult to see why anxiety should be afforded pride of place. (2) It is odd that an emotion such as rage should be viewed as having the same EEG correlates as relaxation—subjectively they could not be further apart. (3) It is strangely anthropomorphic to regard the cortex as anxious.

Relationships between the ANS and CNS—response patterning

From what has been said so far, it can be seen that work involving psychophysiological measures of emotion has not produced definitive results. However, there is one tenuous line of evidence which looks more promising. This will be described in greater detail. Most of the work in this area has shown only a generalized psychophysiological response to any emotion-producing stimuli. However, Wolf and Wolff (1947) carried out extended observations of a man with a gastric fistula. They found that there were two types of gastric change with emotional disturbance. (1) With reported anxiety and the wish to escape there was a reduction in the output of acid, vascularity and gastric motility. (2) with reported anger and resentment there was an acceleration of gastric functions. This was the first evidence for any form of physiological response patterning in emotion.

The discovery of epinephrine and norepinephrine (adrenalin and noradrenalin) reinforced the idea of physiological response patterning. Both increase systolic blood pressure, but epinephrine by increasing cardiac output and norepinephrine by increasing vascular resistance. These differences led Ax (1953) to devise an ingenious study, the results of which clearly show physiological differentiation between emotions. When connecting subjects to a polygraph recorder, he made them afraid or angry either by handling them roughly and criticizing them or by 'accidentally' giving them mild electric shocks, becoming alarmed and hinting at danger. He found a rise in diastolic blood pressure, muscle potential and in the number of increases in skin conductance; and a fall in heart rate. These effects were all more extreme in the anger than in the fear condition. Also, skin conductance and respiration rate both rose more in the fear condition. The fear pattern was similar to that which follows an epinephrine injection, the anger like that which follows a norepinephrine injection.

The only study to directly confirm Ax's results is Schachter's (1957). Any further attempts, including those of Lacey (1950; 1956) and Lacey and Lacey (1958), although demonstrating that there are various autonomic response patterns, have not shown that any of these correlate with particular emotional responses. However, Lacey and Lacey's (1970) more recent work rests on a far more sophisticated and definitive approach to the psychophysiology of emotion than that of any previous work. Their research depends on the fundamental idea that organs innervated by the ANS are important to emotion and that the various phenomena which they mediate can be brought together by the concept of arousal. Also, they suggest that ANS responses are usually regarded as effector events which may be modified by the CNS. However, they point out that ANS responses are also afferent and affect brain function accordingly.

Lacey and Lacey emphasize the cardiovascular system. They suggest that this provides negative feedback to the CNS, which causes *inhibitory* electrophysiological effects. They quote many studies which show increases in heart rate and blood pressure to cause electrophysiological change—notably those of Bonvallet (for example Bonvallet and Allen 1963). Briefly, the argument is for an inhibitory CNS mechanism which produces an inhibitory control of the duration and course of internally and externally stimulated muscular, autonomic and cortical responses. This hypothesized area (centred on the nucleus of the *tractus solitarious*) is involved with autonomic function and has many cardiovascular afferents. Impulses from this region should suppress any emotional (cortical, motor, autonomic) activity. For example, stimulation of the aortic carotid sinus stops the sham rage usually shown by decorticate cats (for example Baccelli *et al.* 1965).

Lacey and Lacey reevaluated the hypertension (chronic high blood pressure) and tachycardia (chronic high pulse rate) seen in acute emotion as attempts to inhibit an internal 'turmoil' rather than as an index of arousal. Hence, any decrease in blood pressure and pulse rate should lead to an absence of CNS inhibition leading in turn to a corresponding increase in excitation. A test of this proposal involves: (1) a demonstration, following a steady state, of experimental conditions which would *decrease* hypertension and tachycardia whilst other psychophysiological measures are reflecting changes typical of the SNS; (2) an evaluation of whether or not decreases in cardiovascular activity lead to increased behavioural efficiency.

Lacey and Lacey offer four lines of experimental evidence. (1) Lacey *et al.* (1963) gave subjects a series of tasks. Cardiac deceleration was produced by those tasks which required subjects to pay attention to the stimuli. Others which required concentration (for example mental arithmetic) led to cardiac acceleration. A combination of both types of task produced intermediate changes in heart rate. Broadly speaking, 'cognitive' tasks led to a rise in heart rate and 'perceptual' tasks to a fall. Other psychophysiological measures did not reflect this pattern but simply showed the usual arousal. (2) Lacey and Lacey (1970) extended this work in reaction time (RT) studies. They found a systematic deceleration in heart rate during the warning signal. This was accompanied, for example, by wide variation in respiratory responses and preceded by an early, immediate and transient acceleration in heart rate. These heart-rate changes were intensified in more highly motivated subjects. If the actual RT stimulus was omitted, the deceleration continued (subject 'searching' for the target) and with a longer fore-period, the heart decelerated to much the same level but took longer to do so. Also, the greater the deceleration in heart rate the faster the RT. (3) The third line of evidence uses Walter et al.'s (1964) CNVs, a measure of negative EEG variation reflecting the readiness of a subject to respond (RT). Lacey and Lacey (1970) found that the greater the cardiac deceleration, the greater the CNV; this was also related to speed of reaction. (4) Finally, there is some external support. To quote but one example of this, Israel (1969) related cardiovascular change to cognitive style. He regarded people as either levellers (those who make global judgements, do not attend to detail, etc.) or sharpeners (those who do attend to detail). On appropriate tasks, the heart beat of sharpeners decelerated more than that of levellers, a difference not reflected in other psychophysiological measures.

Lacey and Lacey have a more productive approach to the psychophysiology of emotion than have many other investigators. They emphasize the cardiovascular system. They regard this as a specific and delicate response mechanism which does more than just reflect nonspecific arousal. Within a general arousal there appears to be some response patterning and perhaps the possibility of emotional differentiation.

Peripheral theories of emotion

As was seen in Chapter 2, James' (1884) theory of emotion was the first to be couched in psychological rather than philosophical terms. It was also the first of the 'peripheral' theories. Before James, organisms were thought only to react emotionally after having reacted cognitively. James reversed this in saying that emotion (as felt experience) occurs after visceral discharge; we feel 'happy' because we are laughing. In its inherent untestability, James' theory was not satisfactory. On the other hand, in stressing the significance of the viscera it had a far-reaching effect.

In that he regarded the thalamus as the seat of the emotions, Cannon (1927) based his theory more on the CNS than did James. Cannon regarded the thalamus as exerting a continuous inhibitory control which is lifted when emotional stimuli arrive at the cortex. Impulses then released by the thalamus proceed via autonomic motor nerves for behaviour and to the cortex for emotional experience. The research which led to this theory and the various points which can be levelled against it will be discussed later. More importantly, however (see Mandler 1962), Cannon made five major criticisms of James' views. (1) The artificial production of visceral changes does not seem to lead to emotion. (2) There is no evidence for any visceral response patterning in emotion. (3) Visceral organs have little sensitivity; any feedback they give could hardly be used to differentiate emotion. (4) If the viscera are surgically separated from the nervous system by sympathectomy or vagotomy then emotional behaviour still occurs even though no visceral responses can be made. (5) The viscera only react slowly. Emotion could only occur at least one second after external stimulation. Subjectively, it seems to be faster than this.

On the basis of empirical research, Schachter (for example 1964) has effectively argued against Cannon's points (1), (2) and (3) above, at least as they refer to the general role of the viscera in emotion, rather than especially in vitiating James (see Chapter 4). This work clearly shows that the viscera are a necessary, but not sufficient, condition for the occurrence of emotion. Also, Mandler (1962) argues that points (4) and (5) are accounted for by the fact that after the initial formation of emotional behaviour it may become conditioned to external stimuli, and therefore may occur either before visceral change or without its intervention (see Chapter 5).

Two more recent theories also bear on the James–Cannon controversy. Like James, *Wenger* (1950) equated visceral responses with emotion, but also suggested how these could function in a 'hypothetical robot'. To get away from James' introspectionist sort of approach, he concentrated very much on behaviour. He regarded emotional 'states' as in fact emotional 'complexes', which he saw as explaining why we usually have no language which is adequate to describe them. Wenger also suggested that our perception of an emotional stimulus depends on the pairing of conditioned and unconditioned stimuli, following which the arousal of the ANS leads to visceral responses. These in turn lead to drive stimuli which Wenger regarded as perceptions of visceral action. Appropriately enough, the end point in this chain is overt (muscular) response and verbal report.

The essential difference between James' and Wenger's theories is that James' is introspective and therefore essentially untestable. Wenger does at least emphasize behaviour. However, there is a lack of sophistication in his theory; it is a general mixture of behaviouristic and nonbehaviouristic elements, whilst still pointing to the role of the viscera. Some introspective influence remains in that the intervening variable 'drive stimulus' determines both skeletal response and verbal report. It is from the latter that Wenger infers feelings.

If Wenger's theory bears comparison with James', then Freeman's (1948) dynamotor theory was dependent on Cannon's. He suggested a concept of 'neuromuscular homeostasis' pointing to a rapprochement between central and peripheral mechanisms. He regarded emotional experiences as 'peripheral meaning structures'. These come from two sources which interact cortically: proprioceptive impulses from learned responses, and unlearned thalamic reactions. Freeman is proposing a combination between proprioceptive stimuli and hypothalamic processes. This allows him the experiential aspects of emotion via proprioception but keeps emotional behaviour distinct from this. This is different from Cannon's view in that the latter postulated distinct physiological substrates for the two. However, Freeman's theory suffers from the same lack of sophistication as Wenger's, given the complexities of more recent physiologically based findings.

Fehr and Stern (1970) put forward the latest argument for a renewed emphasis on the periphery in studying the physiology of emotion. Moreover, they suggest that the original James–Lange theory still has much to recommend it. James spoke of 'primary feelings', 'immediate reflexes' and 'secondary feelings'. Fehr and Stern maintain that primary feelings and immediate reflexes might *now* be seen as hypothalamic discharges which inhibit the cortex and excite the ANS (the importance of the hypothalamus to emotion will be seen later). Secondary feelings are perhaps afferent feedback from the periphery. This is a similar idea to that of Lacey and Lacey (1970). However, Fehr and Stern deny that there is afferent feedback from the periphery. They argue that behaviour can be produced such that it looks like emotion but without involving visceral mechanisms. Although this may be so, afferent feedback may still occur in 'real' emotion. They also point out that with peripheral feedback cut out there may still be primary feelings and immediate feelings to the object in question. However, as Mandler (1962) suggested, these may be learnt.

Fehr and Stern discuss many recent investigations which lend support to the importance of the periphery in emotion. For example, Hohmann (1966) described the reactions of 25 adult males with lesions in the spinal cord as being consistent with James' theory. Their reported experiences of feelings of anger, sex and fear were decreased. Hohmann showed that although apparently emotional behaviour might still be seen in these patients if and when it is appropriate, no *feelings* are involved.

As might be expected, Fehr and Stern lay most emphasis on the evidence supporting differential physiological responses to different stimuli. They suggest that there are three aspects to this research, these depending on the type of stereotypy involved. (1) They name the first situational stereotypy. Distinct psychophysiological response patterns are related to various empirical conditions, particularly those which simulate various emotions. (2) For a given stress, a given individual shows a reproducible psychophysiological response pattern (intra-stressor). (3) The response pattern for one stressor is similar to that for others (interstressor). This clearly supports Cannon rather than James. But Fehr and Stern argue that all the *different* stress situations which have been studied in this context possibly have fear or anxiety as a common factor. They maintain that any study in this field can be interpreted in this way.

Finally, as an example of Fehr and Stern's argument it is worth mentioning their reservations concerning Sherrington's (1900) and Cannon's (1927) demonstrations of emotional responses in spinal dogs and sympathectomized cats which are often quoted against James. They dismiss this work since: (1) in both the spinal dogs and sympathectomized cats a number of possible pathways from the periphery were not severed; (2) the work was methodologically deficient; and (3) the responses studied may have been as much instrumental as emotional.

Overall, Fehr and Stern put forward a plea, which is endorsed here, that the periphery should not be ignored in any physiological consideration of emotion. The James–Lange theory was sound insofar as it is now clear that the viscera are necessary to emotion. Also, Fehr and Stern's ideas are important to other peripheral theories of emotion (see Goldstein 1968 for a review of these). At present, the significance to emotion of peripheral physiological mechanisms would seem difficult to deny. However, it should not be forgotten that much of the basic work involving psychophysiological measures (including EEG) assigns to them no more than a vague reflection of general arousal.

INTERMEDIATE MECHANISMS

In heading this section, the term intermediate is used very broadly. There have been some recent approaches to the physiology of emotion which concentrate directly on neither peripheral nor central mechanisms. Their methodology differs from that of the more usual research strategies, but their results have relevance for the general physiological bases of emotion.

The endocrines and the ANS

The most interesting recent study of the interrelationships between the endocrine systems, the ANS and emotion has been made by Brady (for example 1962; 1970a; 1970b). His investigations combine standard physiological and behavioural research strategies. Like many others before him, he distinguishes between feelings or affects and emotional behaviour. He bases this distinction on the localizability of the main effects or consequences of the phenomena. Hence, he regards emotional behaviour as part of a class of *effective* interactions, which change an organism's relation to its external environment. He views feelings or affective behaviour as a class of interactions which have their main effects within the organism. He also suggests that feeling has many subclasses, but that emotion is simply a change, an abrupt immediate disruption in the interaction between the organism and its environment.

Brady argues that feelings are associated with autonomic, visceral, proprioceptive and endocrine activity, and quotes many studies as showing such interoceptive events acquiring discriminative control over behaviour (for example Katkin and Murray 1968). He regards any variation in, or proliferation of, feelings as limited only by the conditioning history of the organism and the complexity of the environment. However, he suggests that there is interoceptive participation in some effective response patterns. This does not mean that it is a defining characteristic of emotional behaviour. For Brady, like others who have a behavioural orientation, the defining quality of emotional behaviour is that it is characterized by abrupt changes in an organism's interaction with its environment. This leads Brady to a directly behavioural analysis of emotion, but with an overriding interest in its psychophysiological and hormonal correlates.

Brady, and others working with a similar viewpoint, has followed three strategies. (1) There has been interest in cardiorespiratory changes which result from acute and chronic emotional stress. Such changes have been found mainly in the results of studies involving behavioural conditioning, but ranging from aversive control with physiological stimuli (for example De Toledo and Black 1966) through those including few aversive elements (for example Belanger and Feldman 1962) to those showing transient, situational-bound effects (for example

Ross *et al.* 1962). (2) Brady (1970a) describes a long series of his own studies concerned with visceral-alimentary and endocrine changes; these are more permanent than the cardiorespiratory effects. (3) Finally, some studies have related gastrointestinal and infectious disease to emotional stress. For example, Sawrey and Weisz (1956) produced gastric lesions in rats by placing them for 30 days in a chamber where to get food and water they had to cross an electrified grid floor. Brady (1970a) reviews such studies, which in fact involve the experimental analysis of psychosomatic disorders (see Chapter 8). It is worth noting that a major difficulty in this area comes from the frequent irreversibility of effects that might be produced.

Brady's own studies are of monkeys incarcerated in a complex restraining apparatus. They can be given food, water and foot-shock. They have access to a hand-operated lever, visual and auditory stimuli can be presented to them, and samples of blood and urine collected. Everything is automized, allowing straightforward studies using the CER paradigm or conditioned avoidance, but making it a fairly simple matter to take psychophysiological measures.

Brady's general findings are succinctly summarized in his 1970 papers. Firstly, they demonstrate relationships between autonomic–endocrine activity and emotional behaviour. For example, there is an increase in the output of the pituitary–adrenocortical system during the acquisition of a CER. Some studies have used a Sidman avoidance procedure. The restrained monkey is given footshock every 20 seconds unless it presses the lever to postpone the shock for 20 seconds. This procedure is associated with large increases in corticosteroid levels. Brady suggests that such findings simply reflect the general arousal which is induced by these 'emotional' situations. The time course of steroid and visceral changes has been well observed in these studies. Brady has also shown the importance of the organism's previous history in determining these reactions, behavioural and autonomic–endocrine activity again being closely related.

Brady's investigations point to many interdependent autonomic and endocrine systems as providing broad patterns of change during more prolonged emotional responding. He speculates that there may be a relationship between such physiological activity and broader aspects of emotion, 'mood' or 'affective dispositions' for example. He argues that if autonomic–endocrine response patterning can be established in relation to behaviour then this will be useful in the analysis of many internal consequences of emotion.

In that it provides some further evidence for physiological response patterning in emotion, Brady's approach is interesting. Also the work which it has led to is difficult to fault. However, this evaluation is tempered by the relative artificiality of the experimental procedures on which the approach depends and by Brady's lack of precision when speculating about concepts such as mood.

Intercranial electrical stimulation (ICS)

Apart from the traditional stimulation of various parts of the brain simply to see what behavioural effects this might have, brain stimulation has also been used as punishment, reward and motivation. Its motivating effects seem to be related to emotion. Delgado *et al.* (1954) and Miller (1958) have carried out many studies on the aversive effects of intercranial stimulation. In a typical experiment, cats would receive electric shock through a grid floor. They could terminate this by turning a wheel. Once this response had been satisfactorily learned, the foot-shock would be substituted with electrical stimulation of the CNS through implanted electrodes. Such studies show that animals learn avoidance responses based on CNS stimulation just as fast as those based on external shock. This lends support to the hypothesis that in avoidance learning fear rather than pain is the motivating agent, as it is thought to be in studies involving external aversive stimulation.

The much quoted studies on reward are those of Olds and Milner (1954) and Olds (1955; 1958). Here, an animal, usually a rat, learns to press a bar in a Skinner box solely to receive intercranial electrical 'reinforcement'. This can evidently act as a very powerful drive. With an appropriate electrode placement as many as 2000 responses per hour for 15–20 hours have been observed. This rate picks up again after a sleep. This shows that intercranial self-stimulation may be more rewarding than food, water or sex. Also, with an optimal placement of electrodes, there are very fast rates of acquisition and extinction. The acquisition of responses leading to other, external, rewards may be equally fast, but not so rates of extinction. On the other hand, extended partial reinforcement schedules need much more training; this may mean that self-stimulation is rewarding only when it is activating a structure relevant to some other drive.

Olds has demonstrated the importance both of the positioning of the intercranial electrode and of the characteristics of the shock which it delivers. For example, shock intensity is more important than frequency. There is an inverted U type of relationship between shock intensity and rate of bar-pressing. Of more importance to the present discussion is the locus of the shock. In general, ICS in the neocortex is not rewarding and may be aversive. The most rewarding sites are in the limbic system and its associated areas. There seems to be one main dorsal and one main ventral reward area, although in some locations stimulation can have both rewarding and punishing effects, the lateral and posterior parts of the hypothalamus for example. Thus, self-stimulation studies support the idea (discussed below) that the limbic system is at the physiological core of emotion.

Delgado (1970) describes a recent and important technological development in this field. He argues, with good foundation, that the neurophysiological correlates of emotion may be found more simply with experimental manipulations that disturb the phenomenon in question as little as possible. He suggests that a move in this direction can be made with remote stimulation of the brain with radio waves, whilst recording brain activity telemetrically. So, any subjects are behaving freely. Two research strategies are developing from this basic technique. (1) Using cats, monkeys and chimpanzees a programmed electrical stimulation of the brain has been found to alter behaviours such as pupillary contraction, food intake, grooming, aggression and general instrumental behaviour. (2) A two-way 'communication' has been effected with the brains of people suffering from disorders of the temporal lobe. With the EEG continuously monitored, correlations between electrical activity and behaviour have been observed. As Delgado points out, this is a very new field but it could have far-reaching theoretical and therapeutic ramifications. The type of study described here is based on the general 'localization of function' view that the brain contains groups of functionally related neurons which give experiences the positive or negative bias which typifies each emotion. This will determine the emotional state. Delgado suggests that there is an anatomical and functional differentiation between two groups of neural structures, one related to emotional 'timing', the other to behavioural performance. His results to date support this hypothesis and are suggestive concerning the emotional functions of certain brain areas. In the future, this technique and the hypotheses to which it has given rise could easily assume central importance in the search for the physiological substrates of emotion.

Intercranial chemical stimulation

A technique which has recently been gaining in importance for the study of the physiology of emotion involves the intercranial administration of drugs. In most cases, this procedure simply has reversible effects on function without causing any permanent structural damage. It is therefore useful in delineating the general relationships between the CNS and behaviour. However, in a review of this field, Grossman (1970) points to two problems which have yet to be solved. First, it is difficult to determine precisely either the extent or the rate of diffusion of a drug through the brain. Second, but just as important, the way in which the drug acts is often unknown. For example, it may either affect behaviour directly and/or because abnormal conditions are created at that point where it is injected. Of course, appropriate control groups could, and should, be used to take account of these types of confounding influence.

There has been a great deal of work on carbachol, which is parasympathetic-like in action. Grossman (1963), for example, injected it into the amygdaloid complex of cats. The initial reaction was generalized seizures and convulsions, but the EEG gradually became more normal. Everyday behaviour was relatively unchanged except that the animals remained vicious and unhandleable. In some cases this effect was still in evidence after five months. Similar studies with rats have demonstrated altered reactions to punishment, thus making it difficult to establish CERs and passive avoidance responses. Grossman mentions several studies (for example Grossman 1964; Kelsey and Grossman 1969) which show the involvement of two separate components in the septal region. Carbachol injections cause a radical slowing down of avoidance learning, but not to the same extent if they are given after asymptotic performance. Of course, this *may* be a motivational rather than an emotional effect. Also, injections of atropine (which acts as a cholinergic block and has effects similar to those of epinephrine) into the same area facilitate avoidance behaviour.

Many similar effects on emotionality have been shown with carbachol injections into the hypothalamus and preoptic areas, the thalamus and the caudate nucleus. But more interesting are the reactions which follow injections into the lower brain areas. For example, an injection of carbachol into the brain-stem reticular formation leads to agitation, and inhibition of avoidance responses, reactions which gradually adjust to repeated injections. However, similar injections in the midbrain produce, for example, a marked hyperactivity to all stimuli but no lowering of the threshold to them. This effect does not show habituation. Also, although eating and drinking are quite normal, the acquisition of appetitively based responses is considerably impaired.

Some of the recent studies on spreading cortical depression are also of interest in the context of intercranial chemical stimulation. This technique involves the permanent implantation of cannulae into the skull (usually of rats) such that they can be used to inject small amounts of chemicals (for example potassium chloride) directly on to the surface of the cortex. This functionally depresses cortical activity, the time sequence of the effects being in proportion to the strength of the chemical solution. This technique has mainly been used in the study of the memory trace (for example Bures and Buresova 1960; Russell 1967). However, it has also led to evidence which points to classical conditioning being mediated subcortically (for example Ross and Russell 1967). This has received some support from studies involving surgical rather than chemical decortication (for example Oakley and Russell 1968). If, as is suggested in Chapter 5, conditioned emotional responses come about through a process of classical conditioning, these results have clear significance for the physiology of emotion. They imply that the cortex may be concerned in emotion more on some basis of mass action rather than specific localization of function. Such a possibility should modify any evaluation that is made of the more traditional work on the CNS and emotion.

These then are just a few examples of the recent studies and findings based on intercranial injections. Although the techniques cannot yet be said to have clarified our knowledge of the physiological substrates of emotion, they are providing extra information. As is often the case with a technique which has obvious possibilities, there has been a somewhat hasty proliferation of research. Results therefore tend to be complicated and confusing. This is largely due to: (1) possible species differences, (2) differential responses to different drugs, and (3) the lack of relevant comparative control conditions.

Neurochemistry and emotion

In his review of work on the neurochemistry of emotion, Kety (1970) divides it into two major fields of study: (1) that concerned with peripheral biochemical changes which are related to a possible central emotional state; (2) that concerned with those changes in brain biochemistry which are related to emotion. Peripheral changes have received rather more attention (see earlier) but Kety concentrates on central changes.

This approach gained its impetus from recent Swedish work which indicates the specific locale of those neurons which contain monoamines (mainly norepinephrine and serotonin), and also traces their connection with other parts of the brain. The amines are concentrated at the end of the axons of those neurons and seem to be acting as CNS transmitters. The neurons involved connect mainly with the hypothalamus and the limbic system. This indicates that they probably relate to autonomic control in the hypothalamus and *possibly* relate to emotion in the limbic system. Also, many of the fibres that contain norepinephrine and serotonin pass through the neocortex; Kety suggests that they *may* be important to arousal or learning or consolidation.

Work on the neurochemistry of emotion began with the discovery of lysergic acid diethylamide and of its interactions with serotonin in inhibiting the action of smooth muscle. It seemed as though one function of serotonin was the direct control of mood (see Chapter 4). In addition to this, Kety's (1970) interest was fired by the possible importance of norepinephrine. This will be briefly discussed to exemplify the influence of amines on emotional behaviour. For instance, Thierry et al. (1968) showed that severe and mild stress induce the synthesis and use of norepinephrine in the brain. And Reis and Fuxe (1969) demonstrated an increase in norepinephrine when rage occurred in cats electrically stimulated in the amygdala or with brain-stem lesions. And drugs which promote or inhibit norepinephrine also promote or inhibit rage.

Kety (1966) suggests that drugs which alter man's emotions also affect the amines in a way which indicates that they are involved in emotion. Reserpine, for example, often depresses those who take it to combat hypertension. And antidepressants have the opposite effects on norepinephrine. Of course, depression is only one aspect of emotion, but such results are suggestive. Kety (1970) becomes more speculative when considering electroconvulsive shock (ECS), which is sometimes effective in the treatment of depression but which has an unknown method of operation. Kety proposes that ECS may be effective because it persistently stimulates the brain synthesis of norepinephrine. Animals given ECS twice per day for one week showed a significantly greater turnover of nore-pinephrine than controls for at least 24 hours after the final shock. Kety suggests that ECS may substitute for rapid eye movements or paradoxical sleep and that both act to build up norepinephrine in the brain. These arguments imply that at least one of the amines is involved in depression and may provide the mechanism whereby antidepressant drugs and ECS have their effects.

Kety does not maintain that neurochemistry is the final answer to the analysis of emotion. The research to date is only suggestive. He believes, however, that the amines in the brain possibly provide a system which is 'sluggish, coarse and diffuse' but which parallels the sensory–motor system. He regards it as more primitive and crude but based on survival. It may therefore be influencing all behaviour rather than just emotion.

CENTRAL MECHANISMS

The subcortex

That various subcortical CNS structures are important to the physiology of emotion is axiomatic. However, their precise function and interrelationships in this respect are confusing. This is reflected in both fact and theory. At the lowest level of the CNS, the *spinal cord* and *medulla* provide the first information. Animals with transected spinal cords show some autonomic emotional behaviour, but animals with cuts just above the cord and the medulla show far better integrated autonomic responses—presumably because the medulla probably controls circulatory and respiratory functions.

The *brain stem* (that area above the medulla and below the cerebrum) is more interesting. Studies involving decerebration (i.e. brain-stem transection) tend to rely on observations rather than experimentation and to concentrate on behaviours such as rage in dogs (for example Goltz 1892). Decerebrate animals display some emotion. However, this is usually poorly coordinated and poorly directed (for example Kelly *et al.* 1946). The general rule seems to be the lower the brain-stem transection the poorer the behavioural integration. However, even if it occurs at the highest level, the resultant behaviour is never fully integrated. This suggests that individual emotional responses may be regulated in the lower brain stem, but that the cortex is necessary for their integration. As will be seen later evidence at the cortical level is regarded as supporting this idea.

The subcortical structures most implicated in emotion are the *hypothalamus* and *thalamus*. The classic study was that of Dusser de Barenne (1920), who found that decorticate animals (i.e. with the hypothalamus and thalamus intact) showed violent rage in response to trivial stimuli. This led to the term 'sham rage'. Results of lesion studies are well exemplified by Bard (1928), who confirmed that the threshold for rage is lowered after decortication (pointing to the inhibitory function of the cortex). However, he also demonstrated that a complex emotional reaction was evident only when the hypothalamus was left intact. The general emotional reactions of decorticates do not tend to be directed towards the source of stimulation. This may be partly due to the increased hypersensitivity which is thought to result from the removal of the forebrain.

Evidence on possible hypothalamic involvement in emotion also comes from studies of electrical stimulation and lesions rather than complete transections. Hess (1936; 1949; 1954), for example, has attempted to chart the behavioural responses of cats to systematic electrical stimulation of the diencephalon. His results suggest the presence of distinct systems which mediate attack, defence and flight. In general, electrical stimulation of the hypothalamus produces rage; its destruction should therefore lead to a decrease in emotional behaviour. This was partially borne out by Brady (1960; 1962), for example, with posterior lesions. He also showed, however, that medial lesions may lead to well-integrated but very savage rage and ferocity. And Bard (1950) suggested that emotional behaviour in animals that have been electrically stimulated in the hypothalamus eventually returns to normal.

Work involving the thalamus is even more complex and confusing. For example, stimulation of the posteroventral nucleus elicits a range of emotional activities described as anything from anxiety to attack or defence. And stimulation of the dorsomedial nucleus leads to fear (behaviours such as crouching).

Clearly, the thalamus is well positioned to perform a subcortical integrative function, particularly of afferent input, and there is a wealth of early clinical data bearing on its importance to emotion (for example Dana 1921). Such evidence led to Cannon's usefully straightforward thalamic theory of emotion. However, as mentioned earlier, there would seem to be two main objections to Cannon's theory. (1) The complete removal of the thalamus does not affect the rage reactions of decorticate animals—it is only removal of the posterior and ventral parts of the hypothalamus which does this. (2) Removal of the thalamus should produce a permanent rage reaction, which it does not. In spite of these objections to Cannon's theory, the thalamus must be involved in emotion to some extent. There are also two difficulties in interpreting any experimental evidence which bears on these issues. It should be noted in fact that these difficulties are of general application to this area of research. (1) The thalamus has extensive projections which make it very awkward to confine lesions or electrical stimulation to specific nuclei. (2) The thalamus has important sensory functions. This makes it difficult to separate effects due to a change in emotional capability from those which might be due to changed sensory function. General perception might be altered for example.

To summarize, the subcortex has an important part to play in emotion. This has been indicated with studies involving either complete transections or preparations (experimentally in animals, clinically in humans), lesions or stimulation. The functions and projections of the subcortex are so complex that the overall pattern becomes very confusing. However, in general terms, the higher the position of a subcortical structure within the CNS, the more important to emotion it appears to be. This culminates in the hypothalamus and thalamus.

The cortex and the limbic system

Although there is little doubt that subcortical structures of the CNS are important to the mediation of emotion, it is equally clear that they *alone* do not account for all the facts. The cortex must be involved, particularly those parts of it (i.e. mainly the limbic system) which are interconnected with subcortical areas. For example, general decortication has three main effects on emotion. (1) There is a lowered threshold to those stimuli which usually produce emotion—the organism becomes overreactive. (2) There tends to be little direction to emotional responses—they are very generalized. (3) The timing of the emotion is changed—it has an unusually rapid onset and offset. These effects point to the cortex as having an inhibitory influence on emotion, which is of course removed when the cortex is removed.

The boundaries of the limbic system are ill-defined and, somewhat like those of certain emergent nations, change from time to time. The most recent formulations include all the *allocortical* and *juxtallocortical* parts of the cerebrum. These are the phylogenetically older areas of the neocortex. Structurally, they are both simpler and distinct from the remainder. These areas are formed by: the cingulate, retrosplenial and hippocampal gyri, the island of Reil, the operculum and that part of the fronto-temporal cortex which is not neocortex; also included are the olfactory bulb and tubercle, the diagonal band of Broca, the septal area, the prepyriform and preamygdaloid complex and the hippocampal formation. Finally, the amygdaloid complex is also usually subsumed under the general limbic system heading. This is solely for the sake of functional convenience, since it is actually subcortical. Much of the literature on the limbic system is concerned with its important olfactory functions. However, the main usefulness of this work to the study of emotion has been to point to the extensive interconnections within the limbic system.

Lateral limbic system

From the research viewpoint, the lateral limbic system can be divided into five major structural possibilities. These will be discussed in turn.

1. *Temporal lobe.* It is in the area of the temporal lobe that Klüver and Bucy (1937; 1938; 1939) first made their observations which led to the coining of the term Klüver–Bucy syndrome. They made lesions in the temporal lobe involving the hippocampus, amygdala and pyriform and fronto-temporal cortex. This made previously aggressive monkeys tame, active, hypersexual and very oral, a finding which was supported by Bard and Mountcastle (1948) and Bard (1950), who first ablated the neocortex, leaving the limbic system intact. This produced tame, placid, emotionally unresponsive animals. They then produced an increase in emotionality by ablation of the amygdaloid complex and/or cingulate gyrus, suggesting that these areas may have inhibitory functions.

2. *Amygdaloid complex.* As mentioned above, some studies (for example Bard and Mountcastle 1948) show there to be an increase in emotional activity following amygdaloid lesions. Others do not (for example Schreiner and Kling 1953). Similarly equivocal findings obtain for aggression and dominance. At this point it is perhaps worth reemphasizing the general idea outlined in the introduction that it is virtually impossible to ascertain from one study to the next whether or not the lesions involved were in precisely the same places. The possibility that they were not can always account for discrepancies in results. However, each of the studies on the amygdaloid complex shows some effect, which suggests that this area is sensitive for emotional reactivity without being more specific. This is supported by recent studies involving more sophisticated measurements than the behavioural observations characteristic of the earlier research. For example, Schwartzbaum (1960; 1965) has shown amygdaloid lesions not to interfere with the acquisition of simple discriminations, but to block the formation of CERs and nonreinforced response suppression (see Chapter 5). Also, animals with such lesions are relatively insensitive to changes in reinforcement conditions.

3. *Amygdala–hippocampus.* Both Smith (1950) and Walker *et al.* (1953) carried out studies involving lesions in the amygdala *and* the hippocampus. These produced the tameness and docility part of the Klüver–Bucy syndrome without the hypersexuality and orality. There appeared to be only a *temporary* reduction

in emotional reactivity. Stimuli needed to be far more intense to produce the usual fear or rage.

4. *Hippocampus*. Electrical and chemical stimulation of the hippocampus facilitates emotional responses and autonomic reactions similar to those which are found during normal emotion (MacLean 1954; 1957). Also, the hippocampus influences hormonal mechanisms which may affect emotional behaviour. Whether they have been based on naive or sophisticated experimentation, the results of the many studies of hippocampal influences do not lead to any firm conclusions. For example, at the observational level, Orbach *et al.* (1960) showed monkeys with hippocampal lesions to be highly ferocious, and Mirsky (1960) showed no changes in the social rankings of monkeys with such lesions and described them as being less fearful of man. Similarly, at the more formal level, Pribram and Weiskrantz (1957) showed hippocampal lesions to lead to a decrement in active avoidance responses acquired pre-operatively, although Isaacson *et al.* (1967) showed rats with such lesions to acquire an avoidance response faster than control animals and to be more resistant to its extinction. On the other hand, most studies show hippocampal lesions to produce deficits in passive avoidance learning (for example Isaacson and Wickelgren 1962) and CER responding (for example Brady and Hunt 1955).

All hippocampal studies are difficult to interpret, since lesions and stimulation in this area may have many other effects which could indirectly influence emotional behaviour—such effects could be sensory, motor or motivational. Also, in few studies have the lesions been restricted precisely to the hippocampus; surrounding structures may have been damaged, which again clouds the issue.

5. *Fronto-temporal cortex*. Fulton *et al.* (1949) and Pribram *et al.* (1952) show that ablation of the fronto-temporal cortex leads to much of the Klüver–Bucy syndrome, but excluding orality and hypersexuality.

Reading between the lines of the mass of research findings on the lateral limbic system, it can be tentatively concluded that lesions in this area reduce emotional reactivity, especially where fear and rage are concerned.

Cingulate gyrus

In neodecorticate animals, removal of the cingulate gyrus has effects similar to those following ablation of the hippocampus and amygdala—a *rise* in emotional reactivity. In normal animals, removal of the cingulate gyrus *lowers* the threshold for fear or rage (for example Bard and Mountcastle 1948). But Pribram and Fulton (1954), for example, show such changes to be only temporary. Also, some studies (for example Kennard 1955) report an immediate but transient increase in emotionality following bilateral damage to the cingulate gyrus—there is an increased aggression and viciousness.

Lesions in the cingulate gyrus have often been used in attempts to combat clinical problems of anxiety neurosis and obsession (see Fulton 1951), but reports of such work obscure as much as they clarify. There is the usual problem of ensuring that *only* this area has been damaged and also that of the notorious inadequacy of behavioural testing by many clinicians. However, there have been a few well-conducted analyses of post-lesion behavioural changes. For example, Lubar (1964) showed that rats with cingulate lesions learnt passive avoidance better than normal rats, but were worse at active avoidance. Fortunately, such results have led subsequent work in the direction of greater precision in the siting of the lesion.

Septal region

Much of the experimental work on the septal region has been concerned with avoidance behaviour. Its beginnings can be found in Brady and Nauta (1953; 1955) and Brady (1958a; 1958b; 1960), who made lesions in the ventral portions of this area. Their general findings were quite clear, namely, increases in general emotional reactivity and in the startle response to loud auditory stimuli. But these effects disappeared within a few weeks, behaviour reverting to normal. In the longer term, there is improved performance in the acquisition of active avoidance responses but interference with these same responses if they have been acquired pre-operatively. Performance is impaired whenever appetitive responding is involved. Also, Harvey *et al.* (1961) found general post-septal lesion impairment of CER behaviour. This complex picture is further complicated by equivocal results from passive avoidance studies (see Grossman 1967 for a fuller discussion).

Four possible explanations of the observed changes in avoidance behaviour following septal lesions have been suggested. (1) King (1958) argues that septal lesions result in emotional hypersensitivity. However, this is unlikely, since Brady (1960) showed that any hypersensitivity soon wears off. (2) The weakening of the crouching reflex to electric shock *could* lead to faster active avoidance responses (for example Krieckhaus *et al.* 1964). Perhaps this is so; crouching *may* be a good index of emotional sensitivity. (3) The septal area may be partially in control of motivation; food and water intake are affected by septal lesions. Although this could account for some of the behavioural effects which have been observed, possible changes in drive states would not explain all. (4) Finally, on the basis of many studies showing inappropriate responding in appetitive discriminations following septal lesions, McCleary *et al.* (1965) suggest that behaviour may increasingly perseverate since the lesion has destroyed the mechanism which usually suppresses overt responses to nonreinforced or punished stimuli. Which of these explanations, if any, is correct it is impossible to judge.

Frontal lobes

Although the frontal lobes are mainly neocortex, they are clearly implicated in emotion. There is a straightforward anatomical and functional relationship between them, the limbic system proper, and the relevant subcortical structures. Also, there are no obvious sensory or motor functions mediated by the frontal lobes and they do receive most of the hypothalamic connections to the cerebrum.

The basic work on the frontal lobes began with Ferrier (1875) who carried out frontal ablations in monkeys. This changed their 'character' and 'disposition'. Via the work of such as Fulton (for example 1951) who showed the frustrational responses of chimpanzees to nonreward disappear after frontal ablation, this eventually led to the development of the clinical technique of frontal lobotomy. Many thousands of lobotomies have been carried out. Analysis of these (for example Rylander 1939; 1948) leads to the conclusion that approximately half the cases result in lowered anxiety. However, many individuals also show post-operative intellectual impairment. Different investigators stress the efficacy of the ablation of different areas in the frontal lobes. No further conclusions can be drawn. With the increasing use of drug treatment, interest in frontal operations has declined. The frontal lobes are important to emotion, but how important or in what way is unknown. Arnold (1950) suggests that they are concerned with the sympathetic side of emotion, and (1970a; 1970b) with emotional appraisal (see Chapter 4). But some studies have found (for example Kennard 1955) an increase in emotional responsivity after lobotomy, rather than the more common decrease.

Conclusions

It is as difficult to summarize the results of the more traditional work on the role of the CNS in emotion as it was to summarize evidence from psycho-physiological investigations. Much of the work has been reasonably sophisticated on the physiological side, but there is always the problem of the precise locations and ramifications of the lesions or stimulations. Also, no study has produced unarguable evidence in support of localization of function, although most have simply assumed its existence. On the side of the dependent variable, behaviour, the problem has been the usual one of striking a balance between artificiality and the lack of methodological expertise. It is not easy to fault those studies which have taken measures of avoidance learning or CERs, but how relevant are they to emotion as it is commonly conceived? (See Chapter 5 for a discussion of this.) On the other hand, many behavioural measures taken following CNS manipulation have been little more than observational. Can we rely on the observers? Was their reliability checked? Has the investigator given a precise behavioural definition of 'ferocity' or 'pleasure', etc.? All too often these questions can only be answered in the negative.

We are left in the position of knowing that various subcortical structures, particularly the hypothalamus and thalamus, and perhaps the brain-stem reticular formation, together with parts of the cortex, the limbic system and frontal lobes, are all implicated in emotion. But how exactly they are implicated, or what the functional relationships are between these structures, at the moment cannot be said. Often it is even impossible to say that they are necessary to emotion, simply that they are implicated.

Central theories of emotion

The remainder of this chapter will be taken up with a discussion of six physiological theories of emotion that rely at least as much on hypotheses concerning the CNS as the ANS. The first two are the only truly 'cortical' theories of emotion. The second two have been included to give an idea of recent physiological theorizing in emotion. And the last two represent the more traditional, grander approach to theory.

Papez (1937; 1939) and *MacLean* (1949; 1970) are the two major cortical theorists of emotion. Papez can be discussed quickly. Basically, he suggested that emotional expression and emotional experience may be dissociated and that the experiential aspects require cortical mediation. The physiological details of the theory are not worth describing since they are not supported by empirical data. From this starting point, MacLean suggests that the limbic system in particular integrates emotional experience, although the effector mechanism is probably the hypothalamus. He gives two reasons for this: (1) the limbic system has extensive subcortical connections; (2) it is the one part of the cortex which has visceral representation. This accords with the extensive olfactory functions of the limbic system. MacLean argues that olfaction is of prime importance to motivation in lower animals, from food-seeking to obtaining sexual partners. He suggests that although the sense of smell is no longer involved to the same extent in more advanced organisms, their emotional behaviour may be mediated by the same mechanisms.

MacLean regards the hippocampus and amygdala as having especial significance for the subjective side of emotion. However, as was seen above, much recent empirical evidence simply gives the general indication that the cortex has a critical, complex, but ill-defined role to play in emotion. So, unlike Papez, MacLean does not attempt to trace specific cortical pathways for emotion to follow. All the structures in the limbic system seem in some way to be involved in emotion, but *no* specific mechanisms have been found which mediate particular emotional patterns.

Melzack and Casey's (1970) recent view of emotion rests on the assumption that emotion is so complex as to be virtually inseparable from any other aspects of behaviour. To this extent, rather than providing a theory of emotion, they do away with the necessity for one.

Melzack and Casey are primarily interested in an analysis of pain. They use this to establish some principles which they suggest may account for the main characteristics of emotion. They illustrate their three-part analysis with the example of tickling young children. (1) There is a *sensory input* which invokes emotion—for tickling this is light, repetitive touching. (2) Emotion is always characterized by a high level of *arousal* which in itself has an affective tone and is partially dependent on stimulus intensity. To extend the example, at high intensity tickling becomes unpleasurable and provokes escape reactions. (3) There are *central mediating processes* (perhaps similar to Arnold's appraisals) which are in fact our experience and imagination. The tickle becomes unpleasant if delivered by a scowling stranger.

Although Melzack and Casey regard emotion as complex, their theory is so broad as to either imply that emotion is simple, or to suggest that it is indistinguishable from nonemotion—most behaviour must have as its components input, arousal and central components. To this extent, Melzack and Casey's theory is inadequate. It is based on a mixture of concepts drawn from physiological and phenomenological approaches. It is very difficult to find a firm empirical foundation for concepts such as arousal and central mediating processes. It is hard, if not impossible, to use this theory to make any concrete predictions.

Stanley-Jones (1970) also provides an example of a recent physiologically based theory of emotion, but one which is even more woolly than Melzack and Casey's. He regards love and hate as the two primary emotions. Physiologically, he imagines these to be rooted in lust and rage, which can be used to describe the two primitive emotional reactions of decerebrate animals. Stanley-Jones believes that such animals can express but not feel. Clearly, this can never be more than a belief.

He defines rage as the physiological response of a decerebrate animal, or of a man 'in the solitude of his own company'. It is primarily sympathetic and is characterized by blind, immediate, transient reactions with no cortical control. Its bodily expressions are muscular and cardiovascular, and the affective component, if it occurs, is hate. If rage becomes directed outwards, then it is termed aggression. Lust, on the other hand, Stanley-Jones views as a state which results from decerebration which is followed by a reduction to spinality. The limbs become rigid and the genitals engorged. A similar pattern is seen in spinal man. There is no apparent affective component and it is parasympathetically controlled.

Having established this background, Stanley-Jones turns to what for him is the crux of the emotions, the hypothalamus. He regards the crucial function of the hypothalamus as its homeostatic control over behaviour. Connections of the SNS to the posterior hypothalamus and the PNS to the anterior, balanced controls such as glucostasis, thermostasis and emotional homeostasis are possible. Stanley-Jones argues that the biological origins of the human emotions of love and hate are to be found in the fundamental mammalian defences against heat and cold. This may be described as a *thermostatic* theory of emotion. He suggests that the autonomic centres in the hypothalamus for the SNS and PNS seem to be almost identical to those for temperature control. Also, *both* are reversed in cold-blooded animals, and finally, in some cold-blooded animals, thermostasis is the main control of behaviour. This theory accounts for the immediacy of our emotions—thermal responses could not occur at long range but can only be of use immediately, although of course they could become conditioned.

Up to this point, Stanley-Jones' theory is no worse than many others. Although somewhat speculative at times, it has reasonably firm empirical roots. Hereafter, however, it strays in unjustifiable directions. To take two examples, consider Stanley-Jones' ideas on guilt and will. He regards guilt as expressed by blushing, parasympathetic vasodilation, and sees it as mutually exclusive with lust; there are many obvious sexual examples. When we feel guilty he suggests that parasympathetic lust is being blocked by sympathetic fear. He supports this by pointing out that this 'ethical' sense of guilt is lacking in mania and after leucotomy, but is prominent in psychotic depression. Finally, and without going into more detail, it is perhaps best to allow Stanley-Jones to speak for himself about the will. It is difficult to see what such a comment can do for the physiology of emotion or indeed for the study of emotion in general.

'It has long been known that the principal determinant of human behaviour is emotion, that when the emotions and the intellect are in competition for control of the will, it is usually the emotions that win'.

(1970!)

Gellhorn. Over many years, Gellhorn has made a huge contribution to our knowledge of the physiological bases of emotion. His work, however, both in research and theory, seems to have often been passed over by other investigators. Examples may be seen in Gellhorn (1964), Gellhorn and Loufbourrow (1963) and more particularly and more recently in Gellhorn (1968). The latter gives a good introduction to his erudite approach to the subject and provides a statement of his general theory.

Gellhorn suggests that the basis of emotion is the integration of somatic and autonomic activities, as modified by neurohumours (chemicals liberated at the nerve endings) and hormones, into what he terms ergotropic and trophotropic activities. The former are work-directed and the latter rest-directed. When one of the two systems becomes excited the other is correspondingly diminished, this balance being independent of the stimuli which bring it about. Gellhorn cites the example of the inhalation of carbon dioxide. This increases ergotropic excitability and raises the spindle threshold in the caudate nucleus. This spindle is a series of nervous potentials lasting for a few seconds, and is regarded as a good indicator of trophotropic reactivity. A similar effect is seen if the ergotropic part of the hypothalamus is increased in excitability (for example by electrical stimulation). On the other hand, the spindle threshold in the caudate nucleus drops if the organism receives barbiturates, chlorpromazine or a lesion in the posterior hypothalamus. Also, Gellhorn suggests that both ergotropic and trophotropic effects can be brought about by manipulations of the thalamic reticular system, septum, anterior hypothalamus and medulla—the continuous balance between the two supposedly reflecting emotional reactivity.

Gellhorn evaluates any work on the physiology of emotion in terms of his balance theory. In support he quotes well-established facts; for example, stimulation of the posterior hypothalamus produces rage, whereas lesions lead to somnolence. Or, trophotropic emotion is aroused through stimulation of the touch receptors, the typical picture being a slowing of heart rate, synchronous EEG, pupillary constriction and a tendency to sleep. He also regards broader aspects of emotion, like mood, as dependent on the ergotropic–trophotropic balance. For example, electroconvulsive therapy, like amphetamines, lifts ergotropic activity and mood, whereas the tranquillizers depress mood and diminish ergotropic hypothalamic activity (Gellhorn and Loufbourrow 1963).

Other aspects of Gellhorn's theory of emotion are very broad. He regards emotional arousal and the modification of the ergotropic–trophotropic balance as coming about through afferent impulses, internal environmental changes which act on visceral receptors or the brain stem, and by direct stimulation of the brain stem, the limbic system and some subcortical structures. All the relevant physiological mechanisms are in with a fighting chance, including the possibility that similar effects may be brought about by hormonal change. For example, epinephrine acts on the posterior hypothalamus and increases central and peripheral ergotropic discharge. Gellhorn suggests, in fact, that when emotions are aroused, the ergotropic–trophotropic balance must be altered by *both* neurogenic and hormonal processes.

Gellhorn also argues that there is an increasing cognitive involvement in human emotion, implying that a greater part is being played by the neocortex. To this point Gellhorn's theory is reasonably in accord with the facts, but from here onwards it becomes more difficult to accept. He starts by recouching Schachter's results (see Chapter 4) in his own terms. He regards the euphoria and anger produced in Schachter's subjects after they had been injected with epinephrine and experienced the appropriate environmental conditions as reflecting increased sympathetic activity, increased cortical arousal and, in general, increased ergotropic excitation. Gellhorn extends this by introducing the idea of 'tuning'. He suggests that the hypothalamic ergotropic–trophotropic balance controls the 'group-character' of the emotion, but within this the specific emotion results from cognitive factors and experience. For example, he argues that if we consciously relax then we cannot feel rage. So, we can be ergotropically or trophotropically 'tuned', thereby vastly increasing the likelihood of these types of response. But by now we have probably moved a little too far into speculative realms; a brief quotation will demonstrate how far:

'... facilitation of the activity of sensory projection and association areas of the neocortex as the result of emotion plays a part in man's highest intellectual achievements and in the enrichments of his emotional life'.

(Gellhorn 1968)

Arnold's theory of emotion depends in equal part on physiological speculation and the cognitive concept of appraisal. Appraisal is discussed in detail in Chapter 4. Here it is mainly the physiological side of her arguments that will be covered. At the outset it should be mentioned that Arnold's theory, although quite complex physiologically, is lacking in empirical support and like many other theories of emotion loses power in becoming too speculative.

Arnold's most recent (1970a; 1970b) formulation begins with MacLean's (1970) notion that there are three 'levels' of brain function—reptilian, old mammalian and new mammalian, and Lindsley's (1970) idea that emotional arousal is reflected in the cortex, diencephalon and brain stem. Arnold queries how these levels or areas might be related. To answer this, she suggests that we need identification of '... the relays that mediate the sequence of psychological activities from perception to emotion and action ...'.

Although Arnold's theory is physiological, she clearly states that any physiologizing can only occur after a phenomenological analysis. This will allow us to find out what goes on psychologically in emotion, after which possible neural pathways can be traced. She suggests that there are definite activation patterns for particular psychological activities, rather than any sort of action *en masse*, an idea straightforwardly based on a belief in localization of function within the CNS.

Arnold (1960) defines emotion as a 'felt tendency towards something appraised as good (and liked) or away from something bad (or disliked)'. She regards the limbic system as controlling liking and disliking (i.e. cognitive appraisal) and the hippocampus as the spur to recall of memory and impulse to action. In particular, she suggests that affective recall occurs via a neural pathway from the cingulum, hippocampus, postcommisural fornix and anterior thalamic nuclei, back to the limbic system. Thus the limbic system gives us our experience of liking and disliking both as new appraisals and as remembered affective attitudes. She believes the hippocampus to initiate the emotion in its total form; any pattern associated with a particular emotion (appraisal and affective memory) must be organized before arriving at the motor cortex and being translated to movement. Arnold maintains that action patterns begin at the cerebellum and are relayed to the frontal lobes. When we feel a complete bodily urge to action, then we experience the emotion as an action tendency. Arnold suggests that this experience is mediated by the premotor area in the frontal lobe and that the frontal lobe, in turn, serves motor functions in general. So, any felt urge to action becomes overt action. Arnold proposes that the main function of the cerebellum is that of organization and coordination. Impulses arrive from the hippocampus and are made ready for action—action which includes all the more overt aspects of emotion, namely, movement, facial and bodily expression and autonomic change.

In distinguishing between emotional and nonemotional behaviour, Arnold argues that there are four main patterns of action. (1) Actions resulting from hormonal change; these lead to an approach towards various 'good' objects and are basically instinctual. (2) Emotional action patterns; these arise from positive or negative evaluations of either perceived or imagined objects and lead both to action and emotion. (3) Action patterns based on feeling, which result from evaluations of something which may be beneficial or harmful 'for our functioning'. (4) Deliberate action.

Arnold's instinctive and deliberate actions are of little relevance here; also, she makes little neurophysiological distinction between emotional and feeling action patterns. In analysing particular action patterns, Arnold focuses exclusively on fear and anger. She simply traces neural circuits which could possibly account for behaviours such as anger, fear, rage, escape and avoidance. Thus, for example, she suggests that rage is mediated via impulses from the limbic system to the hippocampus, cerebellum, thalamus, hypothalamus, caudate nucleus and frontal lobe. Similarly, she argues that the desire for flight appears to be mediated by impulses from the hippocampus through the lateral ventral thalamic nucleus to the motor and motor areas and becomes registered in the prefrontal cortex via the anterior and medial ventral nuclei.

Since Arnold engages in even more intricate physiologizing (it is presented here only in brief outline) than most other theorists, it is worth making some discussion of the empirical evidence which bears on her ideas. Grossman (1967) argues that there is not much supporting evidence, and Arnold (1970) herself realizes that hers is a difficult theory to test experimentally. For example, she regards emotion as not only inclusive of a tendency to behave in a particular way but as also incorporating many physiological and hormonal changes. So, cortical stimulation would not be expected to produce any recognizable emotional expression—although subcortical stimulation sometimes has. Also, for example, although Olds' (1955; 1958) studies show 'reward' and punishment' effects from stimulating electrodes placed in the limbic system, as we have seen, the overall evidence from stimulation and ablation studies is ambiguous.

In attempting to account for the confusing results from studies of avoidance learning, CER and emotional reactivity, Arnold's argument becomes tortuous, subjective and mentalistic. She speaks of hungry animals 'wanting to find food'—making possible an active avoidance response. If sated, they are without the food drive which means that the fear drive is gone and that there is a deficit in avoidance; and so on.

Experiments bearing on the concept of affective memory are more supportive. Arnold (1970) quotes several studies in which the basic technique involved training rats in successive discrimination tasks in each of the sensory modalities, and also in some passive avoidance. Electrolytic lesions were made either before or after learning in the proposed affective memory circuit to see which lesions in which areas produce what impairments. These studies support the ideas that, for example, the anterior cingulate gyrus mediates the appraisal of head movements, the posterior insula mediates taste appraisal, and so on.

Arnold has produced an odd mixture of good theory and experimentation with seemingly unnecessary subjective aspects to it, especially when it comes to interpretation and evaluation. She makes an honest attempt to combine all of the bodily structures and functions which have been shown to be concerned with emotion. On the other hand, her main contribution on the theoretical side is perhaps her general notion of excitation (1950). She regards the cortex as having excitatory control over emotion. The cortex supposedly focuses on any stimulus appraising a situation by modifying sensory input to fit in with our expectations. Emotional expression and peripheral changes stem from emotional impulses going from the cortex to the hypothalamus or thalamus. Autonomic changes are then reported back to the cortex, where reappraisals are made.

CONCLUSIONS

The search for the physiological substrates of emotion has produced much research and theory. Inevitably, some of this has been sophisticated, useful and suggestive and some has been naive, poorly conceived and on occasion even obstructive. Unfortunately, however, the better work is inconclusive. The aims of this approach to emotion are straightforward—to further our understanding by studying the relationship between behavioural and physiological responses. For example, it was reasonable to expect that there might be some peripheral response patterning in the different emotions. It is disappointing that such little psychophysiological evidence (except for Ax, Schachter and Lacey) has been found to support this idea. We can say very little more than that the viscera are necessary to emotion. Whether this is an accurate assessment of reality or whether it is grounded in inadequate conceptualization and/or measurement remains to be seen.

The lack of firm, detailed, empirical facts also characterizes the more traditional physiological approach to emotion. We can be certain that the brain stem, the thalamus and hypothalamus, the limbic system and, to an extent, the neocortex are implicated in emotion. We can also say that endocrine changes are important and that the periphery has a part to play and that there are underlying neurochemical changes. However, we cannot say how these possible mechanisms interact. We cannot even assign a relative importance to peripheral and central mechanisms, the ANS or the CNS. We cannot be sure that the idea of localization of function on which most of the CNS investigations are based is valid. Nowadays, there are few psychologists who would argue for a mass action concept of brain function. On the other hand, those who work from the localization standpoint use obviously crude techniques; they can rarely be sure of the precise relationship between structure and function.

Given the confusing mass of empirical data which have come from physiological studies of emotion, it is perhaps hardly surprising that the physiologically oriented theories are of little help. Often, they include far too high a ratio of physiological speculation to empirical fact. This enables them to be twisted in any way and of course lowers their straightforward predictive power. Or they are sometimes too narrow, attempting to generalize from a consideration of but one aspect of emotion. The best physiological theories of emotion are probably Arnold's and Gellhorn's; they at least aim at an overall unification. However, Arnold's physiological speculations are not well supported by the facts and her cognitive ideas are difficult to test. Gellhorn's theory orders the facts consistently, but eventually becomes too speculative.

It may be that this somewhat depressing picture has emerged because enthusiasm for the efficacy of the physiological approach to the study of emotion has run ahead of calmly thought out research and theory. It is easy to think that physiological investigations could do much to simplify and systematize our understanding of a field of this complexity. However, within psychology in general this reductionist approach has not been especially noteworthy in the quantity and quality of any solutions it has provided. It is instructive that the recent neurochemical work on emotion seems to be following the same course. It is interesting and looks hopeful, but at the moment is not producing obvious solutions to any of the long-standing problems. They may simply have been reduced to yet another level of analysis. There is perhaps more hope for our future understanding of emotion at the behavioural level than may come from any sub-behavioural analysis. However, to end on a brighter note, there are some very promising current physiological developments. For example, Lacey's work on individual differences in psychophysiological reactivity stands out, as do research techniques such as Delgado's which reduce the artificiality of physiologically based investigations.

4

Cognition and Emotion

There are a number of cognitively based theories of emotion, some of which are supported by interesting research. However, they are not expressed solely in cognitive terms. Instead, they tend to be part cognitive, part physiological. For this reason some of the work and ideas which are elaborated in this chapter are also mentioned elsewhere in the book, but from a different viewpoint.

Those who have stressed cognitive (phenomenological) aspects of emotion have usually taken one of three starting points. (1) They have regarded the fundamental problem as involving a study of whatever cues—either internal or external—allow us to identify and name our emotional states. Theories (for example Schachter's) which have developed on this basis have been less complex and less far-reaching than others within the field. On the other hand, some of the research which they have inspired is of the most fascinating to be found anywhere in the study of emotion. (2) They have assumed that cognitions cause physiological and behavioural change. Therefore we must study the one to gain knowledge of the others. This proposition typifies the 'appraisal' theorists (for example Arnold, Lazarus) whose ideas, although resting on rather shaky empirical foundations, are widely quoted. (3) They have equated emotions with motives and considered both within a cognitive framework (for example Leeper). These are amongst the most speculative theories of emotion and have generated little research.

INTERNAL AND EXTERNAL CUES IN EMOTION

Schachter (1964; 1965; 1970) is the main exponent of the view that we must study cognitions if we are to gain any understanding of our own emotional states. He drew the impetus for his work from the apparent *lack* of physiological response patterning between the emotions. As was seen in Chapter 3, only Ax (1953) and Schachter (1957) himself had produced any positive support for this idea. And each of these studies merely demonstrated a difference of activation in fear and anger. Also, after several months of testing, even Wolf and Wolff's (1947) man with a gastric fistula had simply shown but two visceral response patterns.

Schachter argues that in any emotion there is a diffuse sympathetic discharge; this becomes named and identified through the situation in which it occurs and through the individual's perceptions of this situation. In other words, the cognition guides the arousal.

In the usual, everyday circumstances, Schachter believes that cognitions and arousal are highly interrelated, one leading to the other, and *vice versa*. Sometimes, however, they are independent. This is exemplified by Maranon (1924—reported by Cantril and Hunt 1932 and Landis and Hunt 1932). He injected 210 patients with epinephrine, which is sympathetic-like in its effects, and recorded their introspections. Seventy-one per cent reported only physical effects and 29 per cent reported in terms of emotion, but the labels which they applied to their feelings were the 'as if' kind. They said they felt 'as if' they were afraid. Maranon could only produce 'genuine' emotional reactions in these people by providing them with appropriate cognitions, by talking of their dead parents for example. Schachter suggests that the 71 per cent who did not show this effect in Maranon's study in fact had a perfectly appropriate cognition to explain their altered state—the injection.

This point led Schachter on to the question which guided much of his subsequent research: what would be the result of a state induced by a *covert* (non-explicable) injection of epinephrine? Schachter (1959) suggests that such a state would bring about the arousal of evaluative needs, which lead to feelings being labelled from whatever can be perceived of the immediate situation. This argument results in three propositions. (1) If we are in a physiologically aroused state for which there is no obvious explanation, then we will label it according to whatever cognitions are available to us. So the same state could be labelled in many different ways. (2) If we are in a physiologically aroused state for which there is an obvious explanation, we are unlikely to use any alternative possible explanations to label it. (3) With the same cognitive condition we would behave emotionally only to the extent to which we are physiologically aroused. That is, there must be physiological arousal for emotion to occur.

With these three propositions, Schachter states his case for the intricate relationship between cognitive and physiological variables in emotion, both of which he sees as being necessary for the occurrence of appropriately labelled emotional behaviour. Much of his work involves ingenious tests of these ideas.

Schachter's basic studies

The experimental test of the three propositions mentioned above requires: (1) the manipulation of physiological arousal; (2) the manipulation of the extent to which a subject has an appropriate explanation of his state; and (3) the creation of situations which lead to possible explanatory cognitions. The first study produced to these ends and that which therefore set the procedural conditions for later studies was that of Schachter and Singer (1962). Subjects were led to believe that the experimenters were interested in the effects of Suproxin (a supposed vitamin compound) on vision. They were persuaded to agree to an injection of this. In fact, they were either injected with epinephrine or a saline placebo. As mentioned above, epinephrine mimics sympathetic discharge in its effects. Systolic blood pressure rises, as does heart rate, respiration and levels of blood sugar and lactic acid. Cutaneous blood flow is decreased. Subjectively, these effects are experienced as palpitations, tremors, flushing, faster breathing, and so on. In the dosage used, these effects lasted for a maximum of 20 minutes.

Just before the injections were given, subjects also received one of three explanations of the effects, differing in appropriateness. (1) *Epinephrine informed.* The gist of this explanation was that Suproxin sometimes has side effects which may last up to 20 minutes. Subjects were actually given a description of the subjective effects of epinephrine. This was all endorsed by the doctor as he was giving them the injections. (2) *Epinephrine ignorant.* Here, the experimenters said nothing. The doctor, whilst giving the injections, said that they were mild and harmless and would have no side effects. (3) *Epinephrine misinformed.* Both the experimenters and the doctor mentioned possible side effects, but these were described as numb feet, body itches and headaches. These are impossible as effects of epinephrine. A fourth control group were injected with the placebo and otherwise received the same treatment as the epinephrine ignorant group.

The second independent variable involved the social manipulation of two emotional states. (1) *Euphoria.* Immediately after the injection, the experimenter took the subject into a room which contained an experimental stooge, supposedly another subject. The naive subject was told that he should wait in the room for 20 minutes to allow the Suproxin to become absorbed, then the vision tests would be run. The room was in a mess, for which the experimenter apologized and left. The stooge behaved in a friendly and extroverted way, engaging in a carefully predetermined sequence of activities: playing basketball with waste paper, flying paper aeroplanes, making a sling-shot, using a hula hoop. The subject's reactions were observed through a one-way mirror. (2) *Anger.* A similar initial procedure was followed as for the euphoria condition, except that both the subject and the stooge were given questionnaires to complete. These were designed such that the questions gradually became more personal and insulting. The stooge paced his answers with the subject's and at predetermined intervals made standard comments. These progressed from innocence to anger and culminated in the questionnaire being torn up and the stooge walking out. The epinephrine misinformed group was not run in this condition as it was decided that one such control group was enough.

Two measures were taken. The first was simple observation aimed at evaluating the extent to which the subject behaved like the stooge. The second involved a self-report questionnaire; this contained many questions hidden amongst which were the two crucial ones. How irritated, angry or annoyed would you say you feel at present? How good or happy would you say you feel at present? There was a five-point scale for each question.

Schachter and Singer's results showed that subjects were significantly more euphoric when they had no explanation of their bodily states. Differences between the epinephrine informed and misinformed groups showed this not to be artificial; the epinephrine informed group was distinct from the other two, which were similar to one another. The placebo group was less euphoric than either the epinephrine misinformed or the epinephrine ignorant, but more so than the epinephrine informed; this, however, was not a significant result. Much the same pattern was found with both the observations and questionnaires. In the anger conditions, the epinephrine ignorant subjects were much angrier than the epinephrine informed, and the placebo subjects were midway.

Except for the awkwardness of the placebo groups, the results conformed to the predictions. Schachter and Singer provided an explanation for the placebo group results in terms of the *injection* itself, by arguing that this must have given a reasonable explanatory cognition to the subjects. (Ideally, of course, they would have liked to produce the physiological state without the injection.) Thus, the fact of having the injection would itself be likely to reduce its effects. From their self-reports it seems that some subjects did in fact explain their feelings in this way, so becoming 'self-informed'. With these subjects removed from the analysis, the differences between the placebo groups and the relevant experimental groups became highly significant. Schachter and Singer continued the argument concerning the placebo groups by pointing out that the injection of placebo does not *prevent* sympathetic activity, even though it might not produce it directly. Sympathetic activity might have come about due to the extraordinary experimental conditions. By good chance, Schachter and Singer took a pulse-rate measure for all subjects before and after the experimental manipulations. Those placebo subjects whose pulse rate rose from before to after could be regarded as showing increased activation. *Post hoc* analysis showed these subjects to be more euphoric and more angry than nonaroused placebo subjects.

Schachter and Singer concluded from these results that they had managed to manipulate, via his cognitions, the feelings of someone physiologically aroused but with no explanation for his arousal. Also, they suggested that if such a person had a satisfactory explanation for his feelings then he would not use any alternative explanations that might be available to him. And, finally, with constant cognitive circumstances an individual will only react if he is aroused. Clearly, these conclusions were somewhat tentative due to the relatively *post hoc* and subjective analyses which were made.

Schachter and Wheeler (1962) took up the point that the differences between the epinephrine and placebo groups had been somewhat obscured. They compared subjects injected with epinephrine with others who were incapable of self-activating their SNS since they had been injected with an autonomic blocking agent. Again, the pretence at a vitamin study was made. Subjects were told that they would receive an injection of Suproxin, a substance high in vitamin C content, after which effects on their vision would be observed by presenting them with black/white stimulation—a film. There were three main groups, injected with: epinephrine, a placebo, or chlorpromazine (a sympathetic depressant, or tranquillizer). It was predicted that when watching a comic film the epinephrine subjects would show more amusement than the placebos, who in turn would be more amused than those injected with chlorpromazine.

Three subjects, one from each group, simultaneously watched the film each time it was shown; they were unable to see one another. Every 10 seconds each subject was observed by two independent observers ignorant of the subject's experimental group. They used five categories to record behaviour: (1) natural, (2) smile, (3) grin (smile with teeth showing), (4) laugh and (5) big laugh. The amount of amusement shown under the three experimental conditions generally confirmed Schachter and Wheeler's predictions. However, there was no overall statistically significant difference between the epinephrine and placebo groups, although these groups were clearly different when just the stronger reactions were analysed (laugh and big laugh).

Further support for Schachter's original formulations comes from two animal studies. Singer (1961) gave rats injections of epinephrine or of a placebo and observed subsequent behaviour in 'frightening' situations. For example, the rats were put in a box and suddenly and simultaneously subjected to a bright flashing light and to the sound of a doorbell and a buzzer. Usual measures were taken of defecation, urination, etc. Singer showed that the fear state was related to sympathetic activity in that the epinephrine rats were more afraid than the controls. This was supported by Latane and Schachter (1962), who demonstrated that rats injected with epinephrine were better able to learn to avoid noxious stimuli than control (placebo) animals.

Schachter's conclusions

Schachter's (1964; 1965; 1970) first and most important, although tentative, general conclusion from this series of studies is that there may indeed be very little physiological differentiation between emotional states. How we label such states may be largely a cognitive matter. He also suggests that his results would be generalizable to *any* internal states for which there would otherwise be no good explanations. This is partially supported by Nowlis' (1965; 1970) somewhat similar studies of mood, and by Valins' (for example 1970) work on the giving of false information about bodily reactions. However, Schachter also maintains that his results do not support an activation theory of emotion. He suggests that aroused subjects are not necessarily emotional. If the determinants of emotion are cognitive to the extent which Schachter believes, then they should be manipulable by factors similar to those which are known to affect opinions and attitudes. This idea gains some support from Wrightsman (1960), who put 'anxious', 'fearful' or 'calm' subjects together in groups and observed their social interactions. Interaction affected emotion in the direction of conformity; also subjects who were too anxious were rejected by the remainder of the group. Similar support again comes from Nowlis' studies on mood.

Schachter (1964) devotes some time to a consideration of whether or not his 'cognitive' ideas allow one to deal with the limitations of the visceral theory of emotion. He suggests that three of Cannon's criticisms of James' formulations are overcome by his (Schachter's) ideas. (1) If visceral changes typical of strong emotion are produced artificially then the emotion is not produced. This seems reasonable when Maranon's results are considered. However, Schachter's work shows that if a 'cognitive' approach is adopted then conditions can be specified in which an injection will produce an emotional state. (2) The same visceral changes occur in different emotional states. Although this seems to be the case physiologically speaking, Schachter's ideas bypass it, since they suggest that cognitive and situational factors determine the labels applied to any state of physiological arousal. He argues that it may well be that emotions are characterized by high sympathetic arousal with little physiological differentiation. (3) The viscera are insensitive. This, although a relevant criticism of any purely visceral formulation of emotion, is not relevant to the cognitive ideas.

Schachter views Cannon's final two points as being awkward for the cognitive interpretation of emotion as well as for James. Visceral changes are too slow to provide any emotional feeling and if the viscera are separated from the CNS then emotional behaviour is not altered. Both James' view and Schachter's need visceral arousal as a necessary condition for emotional arousal. Wenger (1950) and Mandler (1962) argue that any emotional behaviour seen in sympathectomized subjects is very well learned, having been acquired long before. This has two implications: that sympathectomized subjects only *act* emotionally, they do not *feel*. Clear support for this idea comes from Wynne and Solomon (1955), who showed that sympathectomized dogs learned an avoidance response much more slowly than controls; they also extinguished faster than controls. Two dogs sympathectomized after learning behaved like control animals during extinction. This more recent evidence would suggest that Cannon's criticisms of James' analyses are not so cogent as they first appeared to be.

To support these general ideas, Schachter also draws on a study by Hohmann (1962). He divided 25 paraplegics into five groups depending upon where they fell on a dimension of visceral innervation and sensation; the higher up the spinal cord the lesion, the less the sensation. Schachter would predict decreasing emotional behaviour with high lesions. The subjects were intensively interviewed in an attempt to make comparisons of their remembered reactions to emotionally arousing events both before and after their injuries. Hohmann's data were somewhat clumsy, nevertheless they were fairly clear in showing that the higher the lesion the greater the decrease in emotionality, at least in fear, anger and sexuality. Subjects described themselves as acting emotionally, but as 'feeling' nothing. This result adds breadth to Maranon's. His subjects described the visceral correlates of emotion (as produced by the epinephrine), but as they had no relevant cognitions, reported that they 'felt' nothing. Hohmann's subjects described appropriate reactions to emotional situations, but with no visceral arousal did not 'feel' emotional.

From considerations of this kind, Schachter concludes that autonomic arousal facilitates the acquisition of emotional behaviour, but if this behaviour is acquired beforehand, autonomic arousal is not necessary for its maintenance. Also, without autonomic arousal, behaviour which appears as emotional will not be experienced as such.

As a final point in support of his general position, Schachter draws on some imprecise but interesting observations concerning marihuana. He argues that his central idea, namely that when an individual is physiologically aroused with no explanation for this he will label his state by recourse to the cognitions open to him, suggests the presence of a drive state. He regards this as similar to Festinger's (1954) evaluative need, which pushes or pulls us to label and understand any new feelings. Marihuana is of interest since its physical effects are quite well defined, but the feelings associated with it are not so easy to describe.

Becker (1953) described a sequence which he believes is typically involved in learning to use marihuana for pleasure. The smoker has to learn to label his physiological symptoms as 'high'. The effects themselves are not enough for this; the smoker has to recognize them and connect them with marihuana before he can have the experience. In other words, the new user must *learn* to notice his feelings and that other people label them in certain ways, i.e. he must notice that he is 'high' and that this is pleasant. In passing, it is worth noting that such an idea gains support from Skinner's (1957) argument that we learn to differentiate emotional states through others labelling them for us by observing the environmental stimuli which brought them about.

Schachter's applied research

To complete this discussion of Schachter's analysis of internal and external cues in emotion, some of his more recent, applied investigations will be described. Schachter and Latane (1964) began this research with a consideration of the implications of Schachter's previous work for the study of criminal behaviour. Briefly, they suggested that given a criminal impulse and the inhibiting conditions which usually surround it, the probability of the crime being committed should be manipulable by altering sympathetic activation. Thus, it should be possible to either encourage or discourage crime with the judicious use of drugs. They undertook two studies as a test of this hypothesis.

Cheating

Schachter and Latane regard cheating as crime in microcosmic form, and argue that it should vary inversely with the fear of being caught. They describe a study by Schachter and Ono in which the physiological component of fear was manipulated. From the subjects' point of view, this was a study first of perception and then of the evaluation of university courses. In the latter part, subjects were told that they would get extra grade points if they did well on the test that they would be given.

Having heard the usual talk about the effects of vitamins (Suproxin) on vision, subjects took, in pill form, chlorpromazine or a placebo. Schachter was thus attempting to reduce fear physiologically. They were given 55 minutes of fairly trivial tests and a questionnaire and were then asked to help out the experimenters by scoring their own test papers. The main test was of multiple-choice items which they were given too little time to complete. Also, some items on the scoring key from which they had to mark were wrong. Clearly, both of these conditions would encourage cheating. The effects of the drugs were measured by pulse rate and questionnaire.

It was found that more subjects who had had chlorpromazine cheated than did those who had had a placebo. This was not a strong effect. It became more powerful when, in his usual but nonetheless meaningful inquest, Schachter argued that chlorpromazine taken orally has weak effects. He then analysed data from only those subjects whose completed questionnaires and records of pulse rates showed them to have been affected by the drug. The relationship then became statistically significant.

Psychopathy

Schachter and Latane (1964) go on to distinguish two types of crime: (1) where motivation or passion becomes unbearably high, and (2) where fear is weak. They suggest that if the second condition becomes chronic, psychopathy results. Psychiatrists usually describe psychopaths as emotionally flat, and Lykken (1957) found by questionnaire that they were relatively anxiety-free. He also showed that they were almost incapable of learning an avoidance response, which is often thought to be based on fear.

Schachter and Latane had their subjects selected by prison authorities using Lykken's procedures, including his anxiety scale—on which psychopaths should score very low. The selection procedures were rigorous. In the experimental situation, subjects faced an arrangement of lights and switches which represented a 20-choice point mental maze, a correct switch leading to the next choice, and so on. All errors were accumulated on a visible counter; some of these were punished with shock, which, however, could be avoided by the appropriate selection of switches. Epinephrine or placebo was injected just before the experimental run, and pulse, heart rate and questionnaire measures were taken. All subjects were given a variation on the usual pre-experimental talk but were told to expect no side effects from their hormone (Suproxin) injection.

Results comparing normals and psychopaths showed them to learn the positive maze tasks at the same rate. Also, this measure did not distinguish between epinephrine and placebo groups. However, normal subjects steadily learned to avoid shock, psychopaths did not. Avoidance seems to be mediated by fear, which is not present in psychopaths—a replication of Lykken's result. On the other hand, after epinephrine injections psychopaths learned the avoidance task very well, in comparison with normals. There was also a marked relationship between the degree of psychopathy and the post-epinephrine avoidance learning.

The obvious explanation of these results is that psychopaths are less sympathetically responsive, the implication being that they have a different physiological system from nonpsychopaths. But this was not supported by the pulse-rate data. Further analysis showed that the greater the psychopathy the higher the pulse rate. Valins (1963) showed this to be due to *greater* autonomic reactivity in the psychopath, a result supported by Landis (1932) on delinquents and Jones (1950) on adolescents. Schachter and Latane also make the point that the best predictor of avoidance learning in their study was whether or not the subject was sensitive to epinephrine. They also argue that psychopaths are more sensitive to epinephrine and that epinephrine sensitives should tend to behave psychopathically.

In discussing their results, Schachter and Latane conclude that high autonomic reactivity characterizes both those that are high in anxiety (cf. Duffy 1962) and those that are low. Schachter's other studies show that cognitive and situational factors determine whether a given physiological state will be labelled as an emotion. Hence, the psychopath, although ultra-sensitive autonomically, also reacts to stimuli to which others would not. For him, little stands out from his environment. It may be that he has not learned to apply emotional labels to his states of arousal. On the other hand, the anxiety neurotic *constantly* interprets his world in emotional terms and gives cognitive explanations of what is occurring. Returning to the original idea of two types of crime, the psychopath would be expected to commit the 'cool' unemotional crimes, the 'normal' the passionful ones.

Valins (1970) interprets Schachter and Latane's results somewhat differently. His first suggestion is that the psychopath may simply not perceive his own bodily changes; there is no evidence to support this. Alternatively, he maintains that the psychopath may experience and perceive his bodily changes but nevertheless ignore them; not use them to appraise an emotional situation. In support of this interpretation, Valins quotes one of his own studies (1967a) in which psychopaths were chosen by questionnaire and subjected to his usual false heart rate, nude picture, procedure (see below). They were not much affected. Also Stern and Kaplan (1967) gave subjects true feedback on their GSR and asked them to produce decreases in their own skin resistance. They found a significant correlation between GSR reactions and scores on Lykken's (1957) psychopathy scale. Psychopath-like subjects could not produce GSR changes, although their usual GSR responding was normal.

Obesity

The most recent extensions of Schachter's work are in a series of studies on obesity. Schachter (1967) found that the labelling of internal cues of hunger seem to be important in determining obesity. He suggests that the eating habits of the obese are independent of bodily changes from hunger. This is supported, for example, by Schachter et al. (1968), who set up an experiment that from the subjects' viewpoint was concerned with the interaction between food and taste. Normal and obese subjects were required to miss a meal and were then given either beef sandwiches or no food at all. After this they had to rate many different types of biscuit on various measures of taste. During these ratings they had electrodes attached to their ankles. Some were given low shocks through the electrodes, others were given higher shocks. Before eating the biscuits they completed short anxiety questionnaires. Normal subjects ate more when calm than when frightened and more when they had been deprived of food than when they were sated. Obese subjects ate the same amount under all conditions.

This result gains generality from three further studies. Schachter and Gross (1968) showed the eating of obese subjects to be dependent on the passage of time; if they believed it to be later than it actually was since their last meal, they would eat more. Nisbett (1968) found that underweight subjects were highly responsive to internal, visceral cues of deprivation but not very responsive to external, food-related cues of taste. The picture was reversed for the obese. Finally, Goldman et al. (1968) carried out three confirmatory field studies. They found that fat Jews were more likely to fast on Yom Kippur than those of normal weight; that fat students were more intolerant of dormitory food than normal weight students; and that fat fliers more easily adjust to time-zone changes than normal weight fliers.

Schachter has successfully broadened his analysis of emotion, producing a clear link between the reactions of psychopaths and the obese. However, as Valins (1970) points out, there are still many unanswered questions. For example, is responsiveness to bodily change an important dimension of emotion in its own right? And/or does an individual have many independent responsivities to different internal states?

Veridicality and bodily change—Valins

Breadth is added to the analysis of internal and external cues in emotion by Valins' (for example 1970) investigations of what he terms veridicality. Valins' general research strategy is based on a very similar proposition to that of Schachter. He suggests that when studying the relationship between bodily change and emotional behaviour, any effects due to the subjects' perception of the changes should be separated from effects based on the changes themselves; they may be reasonably independent. Valins divides work in this field into two broad categories: (1) the general cognitive/physiological approach, and (2) the approach which is concerned with the modification of established emotional behaviour. Within these categories, he subdivides the research into that which deals with (1) veridical bodily perceptions, and (2) nonveridical bodily perceptions. The latter division will form the basis of the discussion which follows.

Veridical perceptions

The 'veridical' approach is best exemplified by Schachter's work. Valins views this as dependent on the idea that we try to understand and label any unusual bodily symptoms that we may experience. If we latch on to certain stimuli in our explanations then emotional behaviour will result. Valins argues that although Schachter and Singer (1962) and Schachter and Wheeler (1962) provide reasonable experimental support for this idea, they leave at least two possible criticisms unanswered: (1) their results may be specific to artificial and extreme autonomic arousal; (2) they make no suggestion as to how a cognition about an external emotional stimulus becomes emotional behaviour. These problems are partially solved by Nisbett and Schachter (1966), who gave their subjects painful electric shocks. One group believed the shock-induced sensations to be the effects of a placebo capsule which they had taken. Another group attributed their sensations to the shock itself, since as far as they were told their placebo capsule had different 'side effects'. Subjects in the first group thought that the shocks were less painful and withstood more of them than those in the second group. Thus, subjective and behavioural reactions to shock were affected by the perception and labelling of artificially induced bodily sensations. This result clearly broadens Schachter's original results and also suggests the possibility that an emotional stimulus becomes reevaluated (Lazarus' reappraisal? see later). It is this reevaluation which perhaps leads the cognition to affect the emotional behaviour.

Other work on the manipulation of veridical bodily perceptions has already been discussed. The best example comes from Schachter and Latane (1964), who were interested in the modification of established emotional behaviour in the psychopath. This was achieved by the external manipulation of bodily perceptions and labelling.

Nonveridical perceptions

Valins' own work has usually involved deceiving subjects about their bodily reactions and observing the effects of this on their subjective responses to emotional stimuli. Subjects have been led to believe that their heart rates are being recorded on somewhat archaic equipment; equipment that is so old and crude as to be audible. They are therefore instructed to ignore the sounds from the equipment and simply to look at some slides that they will be shown. In fact, the subjects hear prerecorded heart beats. The presentation of emotional stimuli is carefully timed so that the experimenter can control the subject's perception (audition) of the apparent size of his reaction to them.

Valins (1966) showed subjects slides of female nudes. One group 'heard' their heart beats increase from 72 to 90 per minute (bpm) when viewing five of the slides, but heard no change when viewing another five. A second group 'heard' their heart beats decrease (from 66 to 48 bpm) to five of the slides but not to the other five. Two control groups experienced the same conditions except that they knew that the sounds were recorded. All subjects rated the attractiveness of each nude, chose copies of five of the slides as a reward and in a disguised interview one month later again ranked the attractiveness of the nudes. Results showed that nudes to which subjects had heard their heart rate change were liked more than others; this was independent of the direction of the change. No consistent preferences were shown by the control groups.

In general, this again points to our apparent need to account for our own bodily changes in some meaningful way. In Valins' *post hoc* interpretations he points out that other than their apparent change in heart rate, from the subjects' viewpoint all other stimuli in the experimental situation were nudes. They could hardly do otherwise than focus their attention on these nudes, and as they (the nudes) were all attractive had little choice but to analyse their apparent sensations in the way they did. The interviews carried out afterwards suggested that to try to explain what their hearts were telling them, subjects looked more closely at those in the presence of which they heard their heart rate change. This was supported by Valins (1967a), who had his subjects rate specific features of the nudes which they were shown. They rated particular features as 'nicer' in those nudes to whom they heard their heart rates react. This perhaps points to some process of selective attention, or perhaps, it should be said, to experimenter bias. It is impossible to be sure which from the study.

These results were extended by Valins (1968) in a study which differed from the previous ones in that it contained a debriefing session. Preferences which the subjects had expressed previously were maintained after debriefing. Their heart beats had made them aware of the positive features of particular nudes; these features had been unnoticed before. From such results, Valins emphasizes the cognitive aspects of the perceptions of bodily changes and suggests that this sort of manipulation does not have important physiological consequences. In passing, it is worth noting that under the usual conditions of Valins' experiments, actual heart rates did not change. This is perhaps an unfortunate finding, since it calls into question the extent to which the slides which Valins used had any 'emotional' effects. However, a recent study (Bloemkolb et al. 1971), although somewhat naively presented, does add generality to Valins' work. The same basic method of study was followed but slides of positive stimuli other than nudes (attractive food, scenery, etc.) were presented to subjects, as also were slides of negative stimuli (for example wounded people). General results were similar to Valins' and clearly pointed to the possibilitly that internal cognitive events can be used to evoke or reduce emotional experience.

As before, the other aspect of nonveridical bodily perceptions comes from studies involving emotional behaviour which is already established. Valins (1970) suggests that Wolpe's (1958) techniques of systematic desensitization for the treatment of anxiety can be construed in these terms. (See Chapter 8 for a discussion of this, and Davison 1968 for a review.) The technique is based on the assumption that anxiety depends on ANS response patterns. If these are inhibited by some antagonistic response pattern, then the anxiety will disappear. The patient is generally taught to relax whilst thinking of stimuli at some point within a hierarchy of anxiety-provoking stimuli. Valins makes a cognitive rather than physiological interpretation of this technique. He suggests that the individual may be anxious because he thinks: 'that stimulus has made me react'. Desensitization leads him to think: 'that stimulus no longer makes me react'. It is this which Valins thinks reduces anxiety—a subjective idea which it would seem difficult to test.

In an attempt at an empirical investigation of systematic desensitization, Valins and Ray (1967) instructed subjects so that they thought they were having their heart rates measured in response to (1) slides of snakes and (2) to a slide of the word 'shock', followed seven seconds later by a shock to the finger tips. They heard what they believed to be their heart rates increasing to shocks and to shock slides but not to snake slides. Valins and Ray argued that these subjects should approach live snakes more than would control subjects, since they presumably were not affected internally by snakes. Control subjects were put through the same procedure but as usual knew that the heart beats were recordings.

Each subject was then put into a room with a small caged boa constrictor and had to: (a) enter the room and look at the snake, (b) take the cover off the cage and look down, (c) reach his hand in so that the wrist was below the cage top, (d) touch the snake once, (e) pick up the snake a few inches, (f) take the snake out for as long as possible. Experimental subjects approached significantly nearer to the snake and significantly more of them completed each of the six stages. This result was repeated with subjects who were selected because they were generally more frightened of snakes. Valins suggests that this result supports a cognitive analysis of emotion by implying that there is no evidence for any physiological substrate to systematic desensitization. However, there would have to be more information concerning actual physiological changes during this study before such a conclusion could be drawn with any confidence. In general, Valins' work does add to our knowledge of the interaction between internal and external cues of behaviour. However, he sometimes claims more from his data than they warrant, and sometimes is perhaps not dealing with emotion at all. In his study with Ray, for example, it is by no means clear in what way emotion might be involved.

Mood—Nowlis

A line of research which is related to internal and external cues in emotion involves the study of mood. Since 1953, Nowlis and Nowlis have been making a conceptual and empirical analysis of mood, their results partially endorsing Schachter's view of emotion. Nowlis (1953; 1959; 1963; 1965; 1970) regards mood as a 'multidimensional set of temporary reversible dispositions'. It refers to some constancies in behaviour and experience which endure over some time. Nowlis believes the 'entire' individual to be involved in mood. He also suggests that the determinants of mood are often obscure or inaccessible although its main function is to monitor or control behaviour. Hence, in its breadth, the concept of mood is more or less equal to that of emotion. However, it is discussed here since it also overlaps with emotion. In Nowlis' terms, some moods may be emotional, while others are not. In general, though, he regards emotion as shorter than mood. When both are involved in some behaviour and experience, he views emotion as the onset and mood as the continuing steady state. In this sense, emotion is seen as more intense and explosive, whereas mood is less intense but more available for inspection. Clearly, Nowlis has a somewhat restricted view of emotion. Also, although he suggests that the determinants of mood are obscure, he also maintains that it follows three types of experimental manipulation. (1) Those that bring threat, pain, frustration, reward, etc., which he regards as eliciting emotional responses, and therefore, indirectly, mood. (2) Those that cause persistent intraorganic changes such as illness, shock, fatigue and brain injury. (3) Persistent environmental stimulation or deprivation.

Basic studies

Nowlis and Nowlis have used one basic procedure throughout most of their analyses of mood. This involves the giving of drugs such as dramamine, benzedrine and seconal to groups of four men interacting in various laboratory settings. Regularly, over a five-year period, such groups would meet for lunch in the laboratory, where their interactions were observed and recorded and they were given questionnaires and tests. This was repeated three hours later following the administration of drugs (or placebo). During each session, subjects had piles of envelopes labelled by time and containing instructions for tasks, check lists to complete and capsules to take. There was further study or recreation during the evening and further observations during the following morning.

There are a number of significant points about this general design. (1) Students were used as subjects because of the apparent reliability with which they would arrive for experimental sessions. (2) Only a few subjects were studied over many occasions in order that they should be maximally relaxed in the experimental situation. (3) Records were made of a wide range of behaviour. (4) Only moderate oral doses of drugs were administered. (5) Double-blind procedures were used throughout.

Of the various measures which they took, Nowlis and Nowlis emphasize the adjective check list (ACL) for self-report of mood. They state that there are 'good' and 'fair' agreements between this and their observational ratings. Also, they suggest that verbal report is the best index of mood since we learn to assign verbal labels to the self-regulatory responses of mood. (This verbal behaviour may then influence more behaviour.) A description of how the mood ACL was devised is given in Nowlis (1970).

The general results showed that dramamine increased the amount that adjectives such as tired, detached, lazy and sluggish were checked, and decreased the use of businesslike, genial, cheerful, etc. Benzedrine produced approximately the reverse of this. Benzedrine plus seconal led to increases in generous, cheerful and expansive for example; whereas in larger doses they produced adjectives such as assertive, confident, decisive and fearless. However, these results were all dependent on how many of the four interactants received a drug, and of course on whether or not they all received the same or different drugs. For example, Nowlis reports one study in which there was systematic variation of which man in the group was given dramamine whilst different numbers and combinations of the remainder of the group received either dramamine or seconal. ACL data showed that dramamine had its usual effect of increasing scores in the cluster of adjectives concerning inactivity whilst decreasing those concerning activity. Also, seconal had the general effect of increasing the checking of words describing control and elation (for example mischievous, wilful) and like dramamine decreased responses to the active/industrious words. However, although they were dependent on task and individual differences, the results also demonstrated subjects on seconal to be far more influenced by the mood swings of their partners than those on dramamine.

Conclusions and recent developments

Nowlis (1970) rightly argues that the concept of mood is awkward because it is basically nontechnical. It is therefore difficult to say whether or not his analyses of behaviour in terms of mood are helpful. Although the experimental techniques used are similar to Schachter's and sometimes the behaviour studied falls under the head of emotion, their precise relevance is difficult to determine. Some recent studies by Kamiya and his colleagues are important in this context (Kamiya 1969; Stoyva and Kamiya 1968; Tart 1969). These put together reports of subjective states and EEG alpha rhythms. The techniques used are based on feedback systems and allow a simultaneous concentration on private events, verbal reports and neurophysiological processes. Nowlis suggests that Kamiya's work provides two solutions to the problem of how to observe states of mind. (1) Training subjects in awareness, discrimination and verbal reports of subjective states. (2) Focusing on interrelationships between subjective variables, physiological responses and verbal report. The eventual outcome of this approach could be the autoregulation of mood rather than its manipulation by drugs.

Be this as it may, it remains to evaluate the extent to which Nowlis' work is relevant to our understanding of internal and external cues in emotion. Given his broad definition of mood, it is fair to say that he demonstrates that it depends on an interaction between internal factors (manipulated by drugs) and external factors (the tasks being performed and the behaviour of the other people in the situation). To the extent that some of the behaviour displayed by Nowlis' subjects must be emotional, although not specifically described as such, his results and general propositions add breadth to Schachter's. The techniques of study are similar but the behaviours involved differ; that in Schachter's studies is clearly emotional (aggression, euphoria) whereas that in Nowlis' is more concerned with the complexities of social interaction.

EMOTION AS APPRAISAL

The second major 'cognitive' approach to the study of emotion has the concept of appraisal at its core. For theorists with this orientation, appraisals are the cognitions which intervene between environmental stimulation and physiological and behavioural responses. Essentially, appraisals are evaluations of the personal worth of any incoming stimulus. We appraise any stimulus as to whether it is 'good' or 'bad' for us, i.e. whether it is worth our while to approach or avoid it. An appraisal is a hypothetical construct which allows us to give some 'meaning' to our environmental situation. Both Arnold and Lazarus believe appraisals to be essential to the generation of emotion.

Arnold

Arnold's (for example 1960; 1970a; 1970b) theory of emotion is a mixture of the cognitive and physiological approaches to the subject. As was seen in Chapters 2 and 3, her theory depends very much on the concept of appraisal as a determinant of emotion, itself a felt tendency to action. It will be remembered that Arnold regards correct appraisals and consequent actions as requiring: (1) memories of sensory and motor events; (2) memories of previous positive and negative attitudes; and (3) the rehearsal in imagination of the appropriate actions. She also spends much time in neurophysiological speculation as to the substrates of these hypothetical processes. Enough space has been given to a description of Arnold's theory, so at this point a few words of evaluation will suffice.

Arnold's (1970a; 1970b) latest starting point is that we know little about brain function, particularly in emotion. To obtain this knowledge, she suggests that we need to identify the physiological mediation of the process which runs from perception to emotion and action. She argues that this is best achieved at first by a cognitive analysis. Before pursuing this argument, it is worth pointing out that it is to some extent arbitrary whether or not we *need* to search for the physiological substrates of emotion; this idea will be explored further in Chapter 9. Assuming for the moment that it would be helpful to do this, then one may also question why Arnold should place importance on perception. Again, it may be perfectly possible to study emotional processes without once considering perception.

In support of her plea for a cognitive analysis of emotion, Arnold maintains that if we can find out what is going on psychologically between perception, emotion and action, then we are in a better position to hypothesize about possible physiological substrates. This may well be so. However, if we find out in enough detail what is going on psychologically in emotion, then surely this would be enough to make the necessary predictions. Arnold would argue, though, that knowledge of the physiology would provide a useful check on the psychology. This cannot be denied, as long as it is clear what is meant by psychology in this context. Arnold seems to use the word in the somewhat old-fashioned sense of being synonymous with 'cognitive'. If this is so (and there are many that would argue that it is not), then it is difficult to see how a knowledge of possible physiological mechanisms would allow us to check it. It would seem that cognitive notions such as appraisal can basically never be more than subjective. It is unlikely that physiology will enable us to say how an appraisal occurs or where an affective memory is stored and in what way our imaginations allow us to rehearse appropriate emotional actions.

It is perhaps on the cognitive side that Arnold's theory is found most wanting. Although her physiologizing has led to a number of testable predictions and in that way has furthered the study of emotion, it is difficult to see what predictions can be made from her concept of cognitive appraisal, especially as it is a process which she regards as occurring almost instantaneously.

Lazarus

Other than Arnold, the main proponent of the appraisal view of emotion has been Lazarus (see, for example, Lazarus 1968; Lazarus *et al.* 1970; Lazarus and Opton 1966). His theoretical contribution consists partly of an attack on motivational theories of emotion; this will be discussed later when reviewing Leeper's recent ideas. Lazarus regards emotion as a response, but suggests that this does not deny emotion as an intervening variable. It simply places a different emphasis on it. Like Arnold, his basic viewpoint is that cognitive processes are causes which arouse coping processes to deal with an appraised situation; a cognitive/adaptive argument. Before discussing the details of Lazarus' theoretical approach to emotion, his research strategies will be briefly described.

The four research strategies which Lazarus has followed have been mainly concerned with an analysis of the possible determinants of appraisal.

1. *Direct manipulation.* The work for which Lazarus and his coworkers are best known is that involving stressful films. The basic technique is to show subjects stressful films with various soundtracks added to them, or to compare the effects of these films with those of more benign films. (See Lazarus *et al.* 1965 and Spiesman *et al.* 1964 for reviews of this work.) The main film to be used has been on subincision—'a ritual performed by men of an Australian stone-age culture in which the penis and scrotum of male adolescents are cut deeply with a sharpened piece of stone'. In comparison with benign films, the subincision film typically generated far more emotional disturbance. This disturbance was enhanced or reduced as a function of the type of soundtrack added to the film. Lazarus interprets these results as demonstrating that emotional appraisal can be directly manipulated, the different degrees of emotional reaction being regarded as dependent on appraisal. These results were reflected in both autonomic and subjective measures.

2. *Indirect manipulation.* This strategy has involved the manipulation of those variables on which Lazarus believes cognition to depend rather than on 'direct' manipulation of the cognition itself. The main emphasis has been on anticipation. Generally, stress (emotional) reactions increase as confrontation time approaches, although this effect is modified by factors such as the duration of the anticipation, prior experiences, and so on. For example, Folkins (1970) made subjects wait either 5 sec, 30 sec, 1 min, 5 min or 20 min for an electric shock. Control subjects waited during similar lengths of time for a light to come on. There was a large, obtrusive clock on which time could be counted off. Folkins found a complex relationship between physiological measures, stress and time of anticipation. For instance, physiological reactions were at their height in the 1 min group, they fell in the 3 and 5 min groups and rose again in the 20 min group. Lazarus argues that these physiological reactions result from *cognitive* attempts at coping, an idea, of course, which leads to unlimited speculation about the nature of such appraisals.

3. *Self-report.* There are obvious disadvantages to a methodology which depends on the self-report of thoughts after some stressful experience. However, it may

be indicative of other hypotheses which could be tested, or act as support for results gained from other strategies. Folkins (1970), for example, found data from affect-rating scales, word association and interviews to run parallel to his physiological data. Lazarus *et al.* (1962) in a film study showed there to be three response patterns observed in self-supports: (1) an emotional flooding, (2) an intellectualized detachment, and (3) a denial (I'm not bothered). However, there were no concomitant autonomic differences in people who typically gave one of these types of report. Clearly, this result is not in line with those from the direct manipulation studies. Lazarus suggests that this discrepancy is due to subjects only developing appropriate responses when they have time to prepare them or when they are provided with a ready-made way of coping.

4. *Dispositional variables.* The final strategy involves the selection of subjects with different emotional dispositions. For example, Spiesman *et al.* (1964) in their film study chose deniers and intellectualizers. Stress reactions were more reduced when deniers heard a film-track expressing denial and when intellectualizers heard an intellectualizing track superimposed on the same film.

Appraisals

As a cautionary note before discussing Lazarus' theoretical analysis of emotion, it should be borne in mind that a common theme to his research is stress. Many of his studies have been based on comparisons of the effects of stressful and nonstressful stimuli. It is not appropriate in this context to spend time attempting to define stress. It is enough to say that it is probably more interrelated with the extreme types of emotional reaction than with the mild. Strictly speaking, Lazarus' views should only be regarded as applying to the 'strong' emotions. Empirically, he does not much concern himself with the 'weak' or 'mild' emotions.

Lazarus suggests that there are two broad types of appraisal: benign and threatening. Benign appraisals have three possible adaptive consequences.

1. Adaptive, *automatic* coping may occur without the emotion. This is in fact some sort of automatic self-protection, the type of response we may make when crossing the road. The evidence for this is shaky; Berkowitz (1962) and Buss (1961) both cite many examples of the inhibition of aggression, but it is impossible to tell whether it is aggressive behaviour or the emotion of anger which is being inhibited. Lazarus seems to be saying that appraisal is involved. It is only if we appraise something as dangerous, for example, that we will experience a negative emotion. But he is also saying that under some conditions we can adaptively and automatically avoid things without making such appraisals; we simply do not consider harm as a likely outcome. From this analysis, however, it is difficult to say when any particular stimulus will lead to an appraisal and when it will not.

2. A benign stimulus may provide us with more information such that it requires reappraisal. A simple example might be the sight of his favourite dish to a hungry man being reappraised when he discovers that it has been burnt. In

fact, a benign stimulus may be reappraised as benign or threatening and a threatening stimulus may be reappraised as benign or threatening. This is pointing to a continuous interplay between emotional reactions and appraisals.

3. Positive emotional states may follow from benign appraisals, although Lazarus can cite no evidence for this. He suggests that such states follow from three nonthreatening conditions, each of which involves the absence of serious threat (when it has been overcome). If this occurs by itself there is elation. If it occurs with an unusual sense of security, there is euphoria. And if it occurs with a sense of identity, belonging and warmth with another, there is love. Lazarus describes a complex interaction between these possibilities, which can be summarized by people apparently seeking danger to experience the pleasure of overcoming it. At best, these notions are extremely subjective and lean heavily on undefined concepts. Lazarus makes little attempt to operationalize concepts such as belongingness or love and can offer no empirical support for these ideas. They are highly speculative.

Lazarus suggests further that threatening appraisals involve two possible processes. The primary process deals with an evaluation of threat or nonthreat and the secondary deals with how to cope with the threat. This has two consequences, each representing a way of coping with the threat. (1) Direct action; impulses or tendencies to remove the threat. This is essential to emotion since its success or failure or any feedback from it changes the cognition and hence the emotion. Lazarus regards these tendencies to direct action as leading to the usual classifications which are made of emotional behaviour. (2) Benign reappraisal; this is entirely cognitive, might or might not be realistic, and occurs when the stimuli suggest that no direct action is possible. Again, fluctuations in emotion are seen as reflections of this continuous cognitive appraisal and reappraisal. The basic problems then are those of describing the cognitive factors in particular emotions and of attempting to describe the empirical conditions which lead to them. Without such a description, any theoretical system of the sort proposed by Lazarus is circular in that cognitive factors can only be inferred from behaviour, both verbal and nonverbal.

Emotional response patterning

Difficulties which Lazarus sees both for his theory and for any other are those of defining emotion and of establishing satisfactory criteria for distinguishing between different emotions. He believes, however, that ultimately emotional states will be distinguished from one another by the identification of specific physiological, cognitive and behavioural patterns, and eliciting events. On the other hand, he realizes that at present this is not possible.

More particularly, Lazarus does not think that Schachter's approach to these problems is justified by his research. He rightly summarizes Schachter's viewpoint as regarding all emotion as characterized by sympathetic arousal—a common, one-dimensional state. Thereafter, labels resulting from cognitions give emotions their particular qualities. Lazarus agrees with Schachter on the importance of cognitive processes in emotion but argues against emotions being a single state of physiological arousal to which a cognitive label has been applied. He suggests that in reality emotions do not depend on epinephrine injections, but on appraisals of situations; arousal follows. Schachter, though, would surely not disagree with this. Lazarus also criticizes Schachter for overemphasizing the labelling of emotion whilst placing little importance on the possible steering functions of cognitive activity. However, his alternative is not very different. He suggests that physiological patterns might be associated with the various adaptive tasks which follow directly from cognitive appraisals. He also argues that what he regards as each emotional response system—the cognitive, behavioural, physiological—has its own adaptive function. This implies that there are special transactions between a person and his environment on each of these levels. He suggests from this that we may learn most about emotion where we find apparent discrepancies between the various response systems. It should be pointed out, however, that these may not be different response systems. It could be argued, for example, that physiological responses in emotion are simply an underlying substrate to behavioural responses and that the cognitive aspects of emotion do not lead to any predictions which cannot be made at the more overt level.

Be this as it may, it is important to describe what Lazarus regards as causing any lack of agreement between response indices or measures of emotion. He suggests two possibilities. Such discrepancies might be due either to methodological inadequacies in experimentation and/or they might simply reflect an individual's various attempts to cope with the situation. The second possibility is again based on the idea that each dimension of response has its own adaptive functions. Ekman and Friesen (1969, see Chapter 7) provide good examples of this in an analysis of 'nonverbal leakage', in which they stress the importance in emotion and social interaction of bodily and facial movements of which we are often unaware. Everyday examples of discrepancies between the dimensions of emotion are easy to imagine: no, I'm not angry—with clenched teeth, fists and legs. Lazarus maintains that these apparent contradictions should be expected and that they give us much extra information about emotion.

EMOTION AS MOTIVATION/PERCEPTION

There are two other theories of emotion which are best considered within this chapter. They both depend on an analysis of emotion in motivational terms, but regard motivation as a perceptual or cognitive process. In so doing they provide the third major cognitive approach to emotion.

Leeper

Leeper's (1948) original formulations were as much a critical attack on previous theories as they were positive suggestions. He argued that experimental psychologists usually stressed disorganization when discussing emotion. At that time the concept therefore had little application to other, more applied, fields. Depending on the basic standpoint, emotion was seen either as disorganized behaviour or as having a disorganizing effect on behaviour. Leeper suggested that the idea of emotions as disorganizing sprang from an everyday and psychoanalytic and technological background which placed (and probably still does) value on intellectual processes and denigrated anything that detracts from them. Emotion was regarded as something that did detract; it simply impeded the higher activities of man—a slightly more modern conception of the rationalist doctrine.

Leeper extended his critical argument in two ways. First, he quoted from writers such as Munn (1946) to demonstrate that the concept of disorganization had been ill-defined. For example, he asked, is the disorganization the emotion, or does it produce the emotion, or both? Second, he set out to look more closely at the concept of disorganization and then to demonstrate that the facts of emotion did not fit it. He maintained that disorganization must depend on whether functional changes in the organism can be random and chaotic or whether they tend to mesh in with any ongoing function. He tested this idea in three ways: according to the 'facts' known about visceral processes, behaviour and conscious experiences.

Leeper argued that viscerally, during fear for example, a person is in an overall state of organization (for flight perhaps). However, he may seem disorganized because, amongst other things. his heart rate is speeded up and his digestion is slowed down. Leeper believed that changes in behaviour and in conscious experience are consistent with the organizing visceral changes. So the behaviour involved in fear tends to include running away; and associated with this is a persistent series of thoughts. He also argued that it is not appropriate to say that emotion disorganizes whatever behaviour precedes it since any sort of stimulus may do this. Unless emotions are seen just as 'foolish and inappropriate responses' then he urged that it is not meaningful to suggest the change to be a disorganization because it involves a switch from constructive activities to useless ones. However, in cases of extreme emotion he did believe that disorganization can occur. A man may become so angry that he cannot retain any skill whatsoever.

As mentioned above, Leeper was not just critical of earlier ideas. He first made out a reasonable case against emotions as disorganizing and suggested instead that they are organizing. In fact, he viewed emotional processes as motives which both arouse activity and also give it direction and persistence. For example, if we arouse love in someone, this makes it more likely that certain behaviour will be energized and maintained in particular directions. And except in extreme cases, the more it is aroused the more likely the behaviour will be.

More recently, Leeper (1963a; 1963b; 1965; 1970) has updated his motivational/organizational theory of emotion. He first puts forward a case against separating emotions and motives, the traditional division of which he thought to be dependent on preferences to think in terms of categories rather than hierarchies. He suggests that emotions should be seen as part of a continuum of motivational processes ranging from physiological motives through to clearly emotional motives. He also considers that dichotomy which puts emotions and physiological motives together and distinguishes them from perceptual/cognitive processes. The former tend to be viewed as lower processes, evolutionarily, phylogenetically and ontogenetically. Recently, exponents of such theories have seen the role of motives as arousing and energizing, not directing (for example Bindra 1959; Brown 1961; Duffy 1962; Hebb 1955).

Leeper suggests four reasons for this viewpoint: (1) motivation is relatively old, phylogenetically; (2) the influence of the arousal theories of motivation; (3) traditional studies have shown perceptual processes to be transient, brief, end products which are tapped via verbal report; (4) the assumption that the brain only operates rapidly, its short-term consequences being the domain of perception; motivations/emotions are long-sustained.

Against these points, Leeper argues that (1) is simply not so. Many so-called older parts of the brain also serve 'higher functions and the responsibility for emotion/motivation is cortical as well as subcortical. Second, he maintains that arousal theorists do in fact emphasize that behaviour has directional properties but that these can only be predicted when we know an organism's motivation. They circumvent this difficulty by focusing on 'drive stimuli' as directors of behaviour, but Leeper states that these are simply some sort of intervening variable whose workings we do not know. He suggests that this view is little different from the older one that motives both arouse and direct behaviour. Third, Leeper believes that the more traditional ways of studying perception are changing. For example, there is less reliance on introspective report and more emphasis on material such as speech which is extended in time. He therefore suggests that it may be appropriate to subsume motives under the general heading of cognitive processes. Finally, he maintains that the idea of the brain as a transmission device and brain processes as only short-term is being gainsaid by modern work.

Leeper's alternative viewpoint is that it is reasonable to look on motives/emotion as perceptual processes. He puts forward three propositions. (1) There was evolutionary advantage in animals responding perceptually to situations in which crucial features stood out. Also, behaviour would be guided by perceiving such situations in terms of anticipations of other perceptual effects which might occur if particular actions were followed. (2) There would be biological advantage in such perceptions being fast. (3) For maximal advantage such perceptions should have some effects on activity. For example, rapid perceptual processes might sometimes make the organism forego present satisfaction to escape impending danger—it is far more adaptive to have the *fast* perceptual mechanism also as a mechanism of motivation.

Leeper is not saying that all perceptual processes are also motivational, but that the perceptual domain is large, complex and contains many dimensions. Clearly, motives/emotion have much in the way of autonomic and 'older' brain involvement. But even the simplest perceptual processes are dependent on cortical arousal, from the lower brain stem. Leeper argues that subcortical processes and the viscera influence thought through the contributions they make to cortical

88

processes. He regards such *representational* processes as motivational. Thus, perceptions range from motivationally/emotionally neutral to motivationally/emotionally very powerful processes.

Finally, Leeper proposes that his organizational/motivational/perceptual theory of emotion has three important implications. (1) Our emotional life should become very diverse as time goes on. (2) We must often create our own objective realities, since our perceptions allow us to recognize these and our emotions involve perceptions of life situations. (3) Leeper suggests that man has been through two great ages, tool-using and technology/scientific or endeavour/education, and that these have each deemphasized the emotional aspects of life. He believes that his theory might occasionally edge us towards dwelling on emotional experiences—perhaps leading to the third great age of man. Such speculation requires no comment.

Taken at its face value, Leeper's analysis of emotions as motives and of emotions and motives as perceptual or representational processes would seem to be parsimonious. However, this apparent parsimony is perhaps little more than the replacing of one nebulous concept with another. As Bolles (1967) points out, motivation has not proved to be a particularly helpful explanatory or predictive concept. It is merely taking a further step in the same direction to then speak of emotion/motivation as aspects of the even broader concept of perception.

In evaluating Leeper's theory, it is worth bearing in mind some of Lazarus' (1968) criticisms of emotion as motivation. He suggests that this idea has five disadvantages. (1) It takes emphasis away from emotions as substantive states in their own right. (2) It takes attention away from the causes and antecedents of emotion. (3) It leads to a theory of behaviour in which one emotion (anxiety/fear) does most of the work. (4) It artificially separates some components of emotional states. (5) It is not predictive of adaptive responses, although given the terms in which he speaks, Leeper would presumably debate this last point.

Finally, Leeper's theory can be criticized on the grounds that it has led to little experimental work; it does not have very much general empirical support. Indeed, it is difficult to derive any testable predictions from it. Having read Leeper, one is left with two ideas. (1) Mild emotions have organizing characteristics. (2) Anomalously, emotion does not really exist.

Izard and Tomkins

Izard and Tomkins (1966) suggest an entirely different analysis of emotion (which they refer to as affect) as motivation from that of Leeper. Nevertheless, they rely quite heavily on phenomenological/cognitive considerations. They base their theory on four main ideas. (1) Affect is motivation (Tomkins 1962; 1963). (2) Positive affect provides the background motivation to effective functioning and to creativity (Izard 1960; Izard et al. 1965b). (3) Positive affect is important to learning, perception and personality (Izard 1965; Izard et al. 1965a; 1965b). (4) Negative affect is disruptive and suppressive (Izard 1964; Izard et al. 1965a; 1965b).

Their general theory starts with the suggestion that personality is made up of five interrelated *and* autonomous subsystems: homeostatic, drive, affect, cognitive and motor. By this they presumably mean that these subsystems sometimes function together and sometimes independently. The first two subsystems mainly concern biological maintenance and the remaining three provide the foundation for more complex human behaviour. Affect is the primary motivational system, cognitive is the primary communication system and motor is the primary action system. Under different conditions any one of these subsystems can dominate and then become the main determinant of behaviour. If affect becomes dominant, they suggest that behaviour will probably be maladaptive. Affect itself can only be fully understood by looking at personality as a *process* of communication both with and within a social and physical environment.

The aspect of this theory which is of interest here dwells on affect as the inherent primary motivational system. Izard and Tomkins suggest that it has three components: (1) neurological—concerning density of neural firing; (2) behavioural—facial, bodily and visceral responses; (3) phenomenological—affect as a motive. The affect system is seen as relatively independent of the others and as laying down cognition, decision and action.

Izard and Tomkins postulate three neurological activators of affect: (1) an increase in stimulation, leading to surprise, fear and interest; (2) a stable level of stimulation, leading to distress and anger; (3) a decrease in stimulation, leading to enjoyment. Hence, there is emotional sensitivity to novel stimulation, enduring stimulation or waning stimulation. By intensifying neural messages, affect is regarded as slowing all the motivational systems.

Behaviourally, Izard and Tomkins place more emphasis on facial than bodily or visceral responses, although they view feedback from any of them as making us aware of our response patterns and therefore of our affects. They define eight innate affects which are expressed facially. Three are positive: (1) interest/excitement: eyebrows down, stare fixed; (2) enjoyment/joy: smiling; (3) surprise/startle: raised eyebrows, blink. And five are negative: (4) distress/anguish: crying; (5) fear/terror: eyes frozen open or moving away, sweating, trembling, piloerection; (6) shame/humiliation: head and eyes lowered; (7) contempt/disgust: sneer; (8) anger/rage: frown, clenched jaw, red face.

Phenomenologically, the picture is even more complicated. Izard and Tomkins state that an individual's purpose is an image (of an end state), often of doing or achieving something. The affects involved and what is being done may be quite independent. For example, in any habitual action affect definitely has no place. Also, they suggest that on occasion affects do not join with cognitions to form purposes. We sometimes may not act on our preferences for positive and against negative affects. On other occasions we may be unaware of the affect that is driving us. When affects compete, that with the greatest density of neural firing becomes conscious and there is a complex relationship between intensity of stimulation, novelty and the likelihood of the consciousness of affect. The affect system with its learned and unlearned aspects is the main provider of the blueprints for cognition, decision and action. This phenomenological analysis must be seen to be lacking in that it provides for any contingency in a highly speculative way. It is impossible to unravel any firm predictions from it.

Izard and Tomkins use fear/anxiety to exemplify their position. They regard cognitive processes as the most general and pervasive instigators of fear. We have purposes, achieved through feedback. These are mainly conscious images of possible end states made up of the memories and perceptions that must govern behaviour. Feedback from the cognitive constructions that make up the image activates affect; this in turn initiates and maintains any behaviour that will close the gap between the achieved state and the image. Specific fears may occur through cognitive constructions (which may often be wrong). Or the memory of anticipation of fear may itself instigate fear.

Fear also strongly determines what we perceive, think and do, and thus has a very constrictive influence. From this point of view, anxiety is often considered to be the most important and basic pathological emotion (see Chapter 8). However, there has been little experimental work on the phenomenology of anxiety. An exception to this is Bull (1951), who induced 'fear' hypnotically in her subjects. Afterwards, but while still in a trance, they described their experiences. The same pattern was mentioned by her seven subjects. This was a conflict between tensing-up or freezing of the body and a desire to get away. Finally, Izard and Tomkins suggest that in the face of a fear-producing object, adaptive behaviour requires a cognitive appraisal, cognition also being needed for a plan of action. Basically, they are proposing the sequence: fear (emotion), cognition, action, and in so doing are not far away from Arnold, Lazarus and Leeper, although the terms they use in getting there are far looser. The criticisms which were levelled at Leeper can also be levelled at Izard and Tomkins' theory. The main point against it is that it covers too much ground at too many levels of analysis. It is impossible to anchor it to concrete empirical possibilities.

CONCLUSIONS

The first conclusion that can be drawn from the ideas discussed in this chapter is that there have been sufficient cognitive approaches to emotion to ensure that this type of analysis is firmly entrenched. Schachter's views are probably the most important in this field, namely, that there is scant physiological differentiation between emotional states; rather, distinctions between emotions are made on the basis of cognitive labelling. This notion gains support from Valins' investigations of the perception of bodily change as distinct from the bodily change itself. Breadth is also added by Nowlis' work on the effects of drugs on mood. In general, the studies of these three investigators point to an interaction between internal and external cues in emotion. However, the suggestions made by Nowlis, and to a certain extent Valins, apply to a wider sphere of behaviour than just emotion.

A significant effect of Schachter's approach to the study of emotion is to have given greater credence to James' ideas. Schachter deals convincingly with a number of Cannon's criticisms of James and points forcefully to the importance of visceral arousal in emotion.

The other cognitive analyses which have been made of emotion have less to be said in their favour. Arnold's and Lazarus' idea of appraisals is difficult to evaluate since, empirically, it tends to be a somewhat elusive concept. At best, appraisals can only be inferred from behaviour, although Arnold engages in much neurophysiological speculation. Similarly, those theories which reduce emotion to a mixture of motivation and perception are so speculative as to be able to account for any contingency with ease. They have little predictive power.

Overall, it is a hard matter to determine whether or not the cognitive approach to emotion is worthwhile. It leads to hypotheses which are difficult to test directly. On the other hand, it has inspired some ingenious and interesting research, which is meaningful and worthwhile in its own right: specifically, Schachter's drugs, Valins' nudes and Lazarus' stressful films. The main problem is that with a cognitive or phenomenological emphasis we are not simply dealing with one level of discourse, as is the case, for example, with the physiology of emotion. Instead, we are faced with hypothetical processes, intervening between stimuli and responses. These are believed to be produced by the former and to affect the latter. Such ideas will further our knowledge only to the extent that they lead to testable predictions which do not emerge from noncognitive theories. At the moment the problem cannot be resolved. It may well be that a purely behavioural (or physiological) analysis of emotion is possible. If so, parsimony would suggest that we accept it.

Assuming that cognitions are important determinants of emotion, then it should be pointed out that even then they may only apply to certain types or classes of emotion. The usual emotions discussed by the cognitive theorists are the milder ones. Although Lazarus, for example, speaks of investigating stress, this is very much stress in the laboratory and as generated by films. Stress in real life may be quite differently determined. In fact, it would seem likely that if cognitive factors do have significance, then this will be for the milder forms of emotion. More extreme emotion may be better analysed in some more direct way.

5

Emotional Behaviour

The content of this chapter is summarized by its title—emotional behaviour. For the most part, research and theory in this area has focused on what is directly observable and directly measurable. Those interested in emotional behaviour usually see emotion as a response, or a large class of responses, which is basic to life and survival, rather than as a state of the organism. They make no attempt to say that emotional states or feelings do not exist, but simply take the emphasis from them and put it instead on what is (at the moment) more open to sound investigation. Viewed in this way, emotion can be easily defined in terms of the operations necessary to bring it about, an approach which is of obvious importance to science, but which may seem too restricted to apply to as broad an aspect of behaviour as emotion.

There are three main lines of research into emotional behaviour; although often conceptually related, these have progressed fairly independently of one another. (1) The first is based on the straightforward observation and measurement of 'emotionality'. Investigators of emotionality have tended to centre their interest either on behaviour in the 'open-field' situation or on the perseverative effects of noxious stimuli. Such an approach has its roots in Hullian theory, which in fact provides an important background to the study of emotional behaviour in general. (2) The second line of research has grown out of the central theoretical emphasis laid on the general role of emotion in conditioning and learning by such as Miller and Mowrer, and recently culminating in Amsel's frustration theory. (3) The final approach could just as well be called 'behaviouristic' as behavioural, stemming as it does from Watson and, later, Skinner. It owes much to an ingenious experimental technique developed in the early 1940s by Estes and Skinner. In the last decade, this technique, for studying the conditioned emotional response (CER), has produced a proliferation of research.

As implied above, much of this chapter is concerned with recent work which depends on developments of Hullian theory made by N. E. Miller and Mowrer; their ideas will be briefly discussed now. Drive theorists such as Miller have tended to view fear (or anxiety) as the salient emotion; they regard it as a necessary part of theoretical accounts of avoidance learning. In such a context, fear is an acquired drive. To Miller (1951), fear (or emotion in general) is: (1) an unconditioned reflex, mainly an ANS reaction which can be brought under stimulus control; (2) a discriminative stimulus; and (3) a drive—new responses can be learnt by the reduction of fear. This formulation leads to two basic hypotheses: (1) that learnable drives such as fear follow the same laws as overt responses; and (2) that they have the same drive and cue properties as strong external stimuli. This in turn suggests a two-factor theory of avoidance learning. For example, a painful shock produces fear (an unconditioned response as an interoceptive stimulus). Fear then acts as a drive which motivates behaviour. In avoidance learning, a neutral stimulus is paired with shock; by classical conditioning this will come to elicit fear, which will bring about avoidance via drive reduction.

Although having the same type of Hullian background, Mowrer's (1960) theory differs from Miller's. Mowrer regards emotion as being of central importance in learning, viewing emotions as drives which have particular eliciting conditions. He suggests that there are four fundamental emotions; fear, hope, relief and disappointment. Fear occurs with the onset of some environmental stimulus which signifies that danger will follow. When this same stimulus ends, there is relief. With the onset of some stimulus which indicates that a period of safety (from noxious stimuli) will follow, then hope is experienced. When the safety signal ends, there is disappointment. A more detailed discussion of Mowrer's ideas appears later, but for the present it should be noted that although there is a reasonable amount of evidence which supports his operational definitions of fear and hope, there is less to support relief and disappointment. In general, Mowrer believes that sensations from an organism's own behaviour may signify these four states. This enables emotion to come under instrumental control.

As must be implied by this brief introduction to the more behavioural study of emotion, much of the work it has led to has been with infrahuman subjects (mainly rats, pigeons and monkeys). Arguments for and against 'animal' studies of emotion were mentioned in Chapter 1. From these arguments, it is clear that many techniques of study *must* be developed with animal subjects and thereafter applied to humans. We still do not know whether or not the determinants of emotion are similar in man and animals; for the moment, perhaps it is more parsimonious to work as if they were. But it is of obvious importance that any techniques developed with animals should as far as possible be refined for human study. Fortunately, investigators in the field of emotional behaviour have realized this necessity and where they have produced relevant work it will be discussed.

EMOTIONALITY

Open field

The study of emotionality in the open-field situation began with Hall (1934a). (The basic procedure consists of placing an animal, usually a rat, in a large open space which it has not previously experienced. To begin with, this produces in the animal what, at the everyday level, would be called fear—urination, defecation, crouching, freezing in one position, high-pitched vocalization, etc. The floor of the field is usually marked off in squares, and observational tallies are made of the animal's movements and various other behaviours which might be considered relevant.)

Hall (1934b) defined defecation and urination as *the* measures of emotionality (fear, anxiety) in the open field, presumably because they have the physiological respectability of dependence on the ANS. The main questions to have arisen from this are: whether or not eliminative behaviour is a valid index of emotionality, and how does it compare with other possible measures? Hall (1934a; 1934b) found that eliminative signs habituated with repeated testing and suggested that they did seem to give a reasonable measure of emotionality. However, there are a number of objections to this. For example, Hunt and Otis (1953) found no correlations between the number of boli produced in the open-field situation and in the emergence-from-cage test. Using a classical conditioning procedure with rats, they paired a neutral stimulus with electric shock. During the study, they compared changes in the rate of defecation with other possible behavioural indices of fear conditioning (for example crouching). They found a rise in the number of fecal boli produced during acquisition when the conditioned stimulus (CS) was presented, and a fall during extinction. But crouching appeared earlier in the sequences than defecatory changes and disappeared later. Also, Broadhurst (1957a; 1957b) found no increase in the amount that an animal would walk about with repeated experience of the open field, whereas elimination habituates. Ambulation may, of course, be dependent on many factors other than those concerned with emotionality.

In addition to this, emotionality, as indexed by elimination, can be inherited (Broadhurst 1960; Hall 1941). Although Tryon *et al.* (1941) originally found support for Hall's results, this did not hold good for male rats, and they also found that their criteria of emotionality (defecation, hiding, vocalization) did not generalize across situations. Billingsea (1942) in a factor analytic study of many 'emotional' responses found three factors, emotionality, timidity and freezing, and also suggested that the responses shown by his animals were situation-dependent. This was endorsed by O'Kelly (1940) and Tobach and Schnierla (1962) who concluded that defecation is situation-specific rather than a characteristic general reaction of an animal.

One measure which does appear to stand out from the rest is that of the latency of the approach to food and its consumption in the open field. The argument is that if emotionality is high then this should be reflected in a failure to eat food which is easily available. Hall (1934) found a high negative correlation between approach to food and defecation and urination scores. Animals which scored highly on eliminative measures were slow to approach food and *vice versa*. Weiskrantz (1968) suggests that the open-field situation has two main effects: (1) it leads to specific respondents such as defecation; (2) it interferes with behaviour such as eating. These effects are correlated and show habituation with repeated exposure to the situation. This conclusion, however, ignores the apparent situation-specificity of defecation.

If the open-field situation can be regarded as a reasonable testing ground for emotionality, then a further problem is evident—do differences in emotionality as measured in the open field have anything to do with behaviour in general and, more particularly, with drive strength? (Emotionality was, at first, thought to be indicative of drive strength.) Broadhurst's results (1957a; 1957b) have most bearing on this. He found (1957a) that animals bred for emotionality (measured by elimination) are more responsive to situational stimuli than are animals bred for nonemotionality. Motivation being 'bred in' may simply add to energy rather than to emotionality in certain situations. Broadhurst (1957b) forced emotional and nonemotional rats to swim and make brightness discriminations to escape from an underwater alley. They were held under water for varying lengths of time before being allowed to swim. The response was the correct solution of one of three brightness discriminations differing in difficulty. This study supported the Yerkes–Dodson (1908) law, i.e. as the discrimination was made more difficult so the optimum deprivation of air for the best performance decreased. More relevant to the present discussion, Broadhurst also found that the supposedly emotional and nonemotional rats failed to differ as they should have. Thus, genetically determined emotionality does not add to total drive in the same way that air deprivation does. There has been no demonstration that the extra 'motivation' in animals bred for emotionality in any way energizes behaviour.

It is difficult to assess whether or not the idea of emotionality is a useful one in accounting for the behaviour of animals placed in open-field and similar situations. It is probably fair to say that the two main criteria of emotionality which have emerged are reasonably good. In that one is a respondent (elimination) and the other an operant (approach-to-food) at least there is breadth. However, Broadhurst's work has demonstrated that emotionality cannot be explained by using the Hullian concept of drive. Open-field emotionality does not energize behaviour, as was at first believed. Thus we are left with a concept which is more descriptive than explicative. In certain novel situations, there are alterations in behaviour which habituate with time, i.e. as the situations become less novel. Such changes can best be described as dependent on emotionality.

Also of relevance in this context are studies of the effects of early experience on later emotionality (see Chapter 5 for a discussion of these). They have usually involved giving young animals electric shock or systematic handling by the experimenter, and testing them as adults in open-field situations. The most general finding (for example Levin 1962) has been that increased stimulation of any sort during infancy produces more robust, less emotional adults. Or, to put this another way, that an exposure to stress early in life increases a later resistance to it.

Perseverative effects of noxious stimuli

There have been various studies concerned with the effects of prior or contemporaneous but noncontingent aversive stimuli on ongoing behaviour, either consummatory or instrumental. (See Myer 1971 for a review of this work within the context of noncontingent aversive stimulation in general.) This area sprang up in an attempt to provide supportive evidence for the hypothesis that fear is a drive which will facilitate behaviour which is based on other drives (Hull's idea of the summation of relevant and irrelevant drives). Thus, if fear could be produced independently of other behaviour then it should lead to facilitation. When considering the studies which have devolved from this original idea, there are two problems which sometimes make evaluation difficult. (1) Slightly different experimental procedures have been followed in different studies; the use of shocks of differing intensity and/or duration for example. (2) There has been some doubt as to how to describe and explain the effects obtained. For example, the perseverative effects of shock have sometimes been labelled as the perseverative effects of shock, as 'anxiety' or as 'emotionality'. Basically, however, most of the studies have been concerned with the unconditioned effects of aversive stimuli measured indirectly on a behavioural baseline; they seem to be dealing with 'emotionality' in some form.

Consummatory behaviour

Siegel and Siegel (1949) deprived rats of food and water on a regular regime and measured their water intake. On the test day, just before their normal time of access to food and water, the experimental group were shocked at a 'fairly intense' level. The rationale for this procedure was that shock inhibits salivation which should promote drinking. A control group remained unshocked. There was a tendency for the experimental group to drink more than the controls. However, this effect was provided mainly by one animal.

At the time of this study, the facilitatory effect of prior shock on consummatory behaviour was explained within the Hullian framework of an irrelevant drive (produced by shock) summating with a relevant drive (produced by food or water deprivation). Conversely, the effects could have been due to some immediate and perseverative emotional effects from noxious stimuli. Studies by Amsel and others added complexity to this picture. Amsel (1950) measured the running speeds of rats in a straight alley. They had to leave the start-box in order to escape shock. They were also either 0 hours or 22 hours food deprived, although they were not fed in the runway. By the third day, the irrelevant hunger group were running significantly faster than the controls. Amsel explained this as the summation of the hunger drive with the residual effects of shock. Amsel and Maltzman (1950) allowed rats 10 minutes' access to water every 12 hours. Having established this regime for 14 days, they then shocked the rats in a different situation immediately before they were due to drink. All animals were shocked in this way for three days. Then followed two further days in which half the animals were shocked on the first and half on the second. Although water intake rose significantly during the first three days, at this point there were no unshocked control animals. Also, when shocked and unshocked animals were compared on the last two days, there were no differences. Amsel and Cole (1953) extended this result by showing that the degree to which shock interferes with consummatory behaviour depends on the similarity between the shock and the test situations. There was no facilitation observed in this study, nor in that of Levine (1958) delivering shock in a different situation to the drinking cage. At this point, it was difficult to assess the status of the emotionality-drive sort of hypothesis. Amsel and Maltzman (1950) had made the only definitive statement when they distinguished between pain: a reaction to noxious stimuli; anxiety (fear): a conditioned pain reaction; and emotionality: a continuing reaction following pain. However, the mainly suppressive results at this time could be explained as a generalization of the usual suppressive effects of shock on ongoing behaviour.

More recently, it has been clearly shown that 'emotionality' does facilitate drinking. Moyer and Benninger (1963) demonstrated that intense pre-shock facilitated drinking in rats whose water intake had previously been depressed for some time by handling. Moyer (1965) suggested that novelty effects of emotionality might overcome any facilitatory effects. Hence, only animals that had previously experienced emotionality in the drinking situation would be likely to drink more. He confirmed this in a very full study involving the production of emotionality by handling, shock or placement in a shock-box. His results were significant and showed facilitation of drinking to occur in those animals who had had some prior experience with emotionality; the novelty of emotionality must have habituated.

Levine (1965) also showed clear evidence for a facilitation of drinking in a pre-shock group (0·8 mamp for 20 sec) and in a group simply placed in the shock-box before drinking. Suppression was shown in groups either shocked for four 20 sec durations separated by 10 minute intervals or simply placed in the shock-box for these durations. Although these results add to Moyer's, it is not at all clear what determines the contrasting effects that they show.

The generality of these findings on pre-shock and water intake has been extended in a number of ways. Siegel and Brantley (1951) placed rats on a 22 hour food-deprivation schedule. On the sixth day of this regime, the experimental group were taken to a different situation and shocked just prior to eating. They ate more than an unshocked control group. Strongman (1965) provided evidence of a similar facilitation of eating. He placed rats on a 23 hour food-deprivation schedule until intake had stabilized. On the test day, in a shock-box completely different from the home cages, they were given one of three durations (3, 30 or 300 sec) of shock (2·65 mamp). This occurred immediately before their usual time of access to food which, on the test day, was for some subjects adulterated with quinine. With normal food the 3 sec shock group showed significant increases in intake in comparison with unshocked controls, while the 30 sec and 300 sec groups showed decreases. When the food was adulterated with quinine there was a monotonic decrease in intake with increasing shock durations. The results were interpreted as reflecting an interaction between 'anxiety'—the perseverative effects of shock (emotionality)—and the incentive value of the food. It was also argued that the shock effects were temporally biphasic at the higher levels: immediate suppression of eating occurred, followed by a gradual recovery for the groups receiving normal food. With the quinine groups there was an initial suppression which as it dissipated would allow the quinine to exert its effects and keep intake down. The time course of the effects supported this interpretation.

Myer (1971) suggests an alternative interpretation of Strongman's results which is in accord with Moyer's discussion of the novelty of emotionality. Thus, it is possible that the food intake of the quinine groups was depressed after low shock because of the novelty of the quinine. Any change in the test situation should therefore magnify possible *suppressive* effects of prior shock. As Myer points out, this should even be so if the food is sweetened rather than embittered. Further light is thrown on this by Strongman *et al.* (1970) in a parametric study which also confirmed the facilitatory effect of pre-shock on eating. The intake of food-deprived rats was measured until it had stabilized. They were then subjected to 3 or 30 sec of shock at intensities of 0, 0·5, 1·5, 2·5 or 3·5 mamp immediately before their time of access to food. On the test day the food was adulterated with 0 per cent, 10 per cent or 25 per cent sucrose. Shock intensity was found to be insignificant, there being a general enhancement of intake after 3 sec and a general suppression after 30 sec. There was no interaction between sucrose adulteration and shock, a result at variance with the earlier quinine findings, but also not quite in line with the novelty hypothesis.

Instrumental behaviour

A second line of research into the generality of the effects of prior aversive stimulation has dwelt on instrumental rather than consummatory behaviour. However, there is little evidence for facilitatory effects. Baron (1963) and Baron and Antonitis (1961) found respectively that pre-shock in one situation suppressed subsequent exploratory behaviour and unconditioned responding in other situations. Similarly, Ellis (1957) and Anderson *et al.* (1968) found that pre-shock either has no effect on, or interferes with, the subsequent running of alleys to food. And studies by Bevan *et al.* (1967) and Strongman (1967) each demonstrated pre-shock to suppress subsequent lever-pressing for water or food. The only study which goes against the general finding that pre-shock suppresses instrumental behaviour is that of Ducharme and Belanger (1961). However, the information available concerning response rates before shock was introduced does not permit the conclusion that other factors were not involved.

Also relevant in this context are those studies in which aversive stimulation has been administered *during* ongoing behaviour. The most dramatic results in this field come from Webb and Goodman (1958) and Siegel and Sparks (1961), who showed that flooding a Skinner box with half an inch of water increased the response rate of rats previously working at a stable rate. This again brought attention to the idea that emotionality somehow energizes behaviour. These studies are at one extreme of a fairly large literature on the effects of unconditioned aversive stimulation on behaviour such as aggression (for example Azrin *et al.* 1966) or eating (for example Pare 1965; Sterritt 1962). (See Myer 1971 for a review.) The general finding has often been of enhancement of whatever behaviour is occurring at the time of or immediately after the aversive stimulation. It may be that moderate shock (the usual aversive stimulus to be used) simply facilitates whatever behaviour is predominant at the time, or there could be some special (and unknown) relationship between shock and consummatory behaviour.

Finally, it is worth describing in some detail the work of Deaux and Kakolewski (1970), since they suggest further factors which should be taken into account in any research into the basic facilitatory effects of 'emotionality' on consummatory behaviour. They investigated the effects of handling rather than shock, initially to ascertain whether or not rats that had only been rarely handled would differentially increase one or other consummatory response (eating or drinking) after stress-inducing activity. To test this they handled previously unhandled rats for $1\frac{1}{2}$ min and at the same time seven days later rotated the same rats on scales for $1\frac{1}{2}$ min each. On each occasion and at the same time after a further seven days they observed the rats for a subsequent two hour period. There was a significant increase in drinking but not in eating after both handling and rotation. If the stressful experiences had simply had a general energizing effect, then an increase in both eating and drinking would have been expected.

In their second study, Deaux and Kakolewski deprived rats of water, allowing them 4 ml per day. $0\cdot5$ min after this each rat was removed from its cage, half were returned immediately, the other half were handled for $1\frac{1}{2}$ min. Handling eliminated the *eating*, which in the control group began within the first minute after they were returned to the cages. (On schedules such as this, eating habitually occurs *after* drinking.) This was confirmed in a further study with rats that were less used to water deprivation. Deaux and Kakolewski's basic hypothesis was thus supported, i.e. that handling raises body-fluid osmolality by raising 'emotionality'; an hypothesis based on supportive biochemical analysis. Their argument is that: (1) in food-deprived rats an increase in body-fluid osmolality leads to the emergence of thirst during food intake; and (2) in water-deprived rats a decrease in body-fluid osmolality induces hunger during water intake. Their studies show that anxiety or emotional excitement (i.e. emotionality) increases body-fluid osmolality which induces thirst, which in turn leads to drinking and delay or elimination of eating. This clearly points to the necessity for considering both types of consummatory behaviour in any future study, even though deprivation may have occurred in only one of them; food and water intake interact at a basic level, any emotion-induced changes in one possibly being due to changes in the other.

Conclusions

It is difficult to draw a definite conclusion from the studies reviewed in this section. Aversive stimuli affect subsequent behaviour. When any effects are suppressive, as is often the case, they can be easily explained in terms of 'fear' conditioned in one situation generalizing to another. However, studies which have demonstrated facilitatory effects are now too numerous to be ignored and are not in any way accounted for simply by recourse to the emotionality-drive idea. It would seem improbable that experience with noxious stimuli leads to some sort of autonomous 'emotionality'. Explanations for both the facilitatory and the suppressive effects of prior aversive stimulation are far more likely to be found by a more detailed consideration of the general testing situations. Such variables as amount of deprivation, type of reward, the relative novelty of the shock-box (if shock is used) or experience with emotion-producing stimuli need careful investigation before anything further can be said. It may well be that exploration of these variables would undermine the usefulness of any explanation in terms of general emotionality. Which, of course, is not to say that they would deny that some form of emotional responses follow aversive stimulation.

FRUSTRATION—A NEO-HULLIAN APPROACH TO EMOTION

The most recent line of Hullian inspired research into emotional behaviour comes from Amsel (for example 1958; 1962). It is based on a technique which Amsel developed for investigating frustration and also on the theoretical ramifications of the so-called frustration effect (FE). However, frustration was a broad topic before Amsel's contribution. Thus, before discussing the FE and the theories of frustrative nonreward to which it has led, brief mention will be made of earlier research into frustration.

Early theory and research on frustration

Excellent summaries and discussions of the earlier work on frustration can be found in Yates (1962) and Lawson (1965). As the present purpose is merely to provide a background against which to view Amsel's contribution to the field, the surface of the earlier work will only be skimmed. In the 1930s and 1940s four major theories of frustration appeared. They each depended on Freud, but also saw frustration as a unique topic, attempted to define it operationally, and produced definite hypotheses about behaviour. In regarding frustration as unique they differed considerably from the more recent theories.

Rosenzweig (1934; 1938; 1944) viewed frustration as an obstacle which prevents the satisfaction of a need; in other words, it somehow blocks motivation. This definition and its various riders generated little research and was significant only in its position as a progenitor of those which followed.

The frustration–aggression theory of Dollard et al. (1939) contained two basic propositions. (1) Frustration increases the tendency towards aggression. (2) Aggressive behaviour is sufficient evidence to conclude that frustration must previously have occurred. Again, frustration was seen as an interference with any behaviour which would normally lead to a goal or reinforcement. This theory was tied to both Freudian and commonsense notions of frustration. It has led to a reasonable amount of empirical work and ideas (for example Berkowitz 1962; Miller 1948; Sears 1950). However, Yates (1962) summarizes the criticisms that may be made of it. (1) Aggression is not unitary. (2) Frustration situations are not all alike. (3) Aggression could occur for reasons other than frustration.

A similar theory was proposed by Barker *et al.* (1941). On the basis of rating children's 'constructiveness' with toys, they suggested that frustration results in regression, i.e. produces behaviour which is characteristic of an earlier level of development. However, they also thought that frustration could have effects other than regression and their theory generated very little research. Also, two fundamental objections can be made to their original investigations. (1) The intelligence range of the children they studied was very limited. (2) Data were gathered by experimenters who were aware of the experimental conditions and who might therefore have shown bias.

Maier (1949; 1956) was the final theorist to view frustration as a unique concept. He suggested that any behaviour which follows frustration becomes fixated, an effect which he believed to have nothing to do with normal processes of learning or motivation. He based this idea on results obtained from training rats to make discriminations from a jumping-stand for a food reward. When they could do this satisfactorily, Maier presented them with a series of insoluble problems, reward positions being at random. At first, the rats refused to jump; they were encouraged further by blasts of air from the rear or raps on the tail. They began to jump, but always to one side or to one stimulus, irrespective of whether or not this led to a reward or a bump on the nose. Their behaviour remained fixated even when the problems were made soluble. Since it has possible applications to neurosis, this is an attractive theory. However, again, there are two objections to the data on which it was based. (1) Given the air-blasts and tail-raps, it is likely that the rats in Maier's studies were jumping to escape punishment rather than in any positive sense. (2) As their jumping gained them access to reward on roughly 50 per cent of occasions, they were in fact on a partial reinforcement schedule, which of course tends to strengthen behaviour.

Lawson (1965) describes the next stage in the development of frustration theory and research as being characterized by: (1) far more experimental work; (2) closer connections with general concepts of behaviour; (3) a recognition that many independent variables are involved in studies of frustration; (4) a belief that there is no unique behaviour which is characteristic of frustrating situations. This more general approach is of clear importance to the broader study of emotional behaviour, and these developments have been mainly productive through Amsel's theory of frustrative nonreward. However, there are two other theories which should be mentioned, since they are each important to Amsel's ideas.

Child and Waterhouse (1952; 1953) extended the theory of frustration–regression. They suggested that a frustrating situation, or its emotional consequences, arouses responses which (1) interfere with ongoing behaviour, and (2) bring about changes in motivation. This idea of frustration denied the concept any unique qualities. In situations which could be defined in a general way as frustrating, goal-directed behaviour is interfered with, motivation changes and other responses become more likely. Thus, in Child and Waterhouse's view, there is no one reaction which is typical of frustration.

Brown and Farber (1951) regarded frustration as a higher-order hypothetical construct—a construct integrating several interrelationships between antecedent and subsequent events. This is a very Hullian formulation. A response tendency is interfered with and other response tendencies are therefore aroused. This results in conflict between the original tendency and the alternative. Frustration is the relationship between these two tendencies. Brown and Farber argue that the effects of this frustration are mainly to increase drive; and responses which are already strong (more probable of occurrence) are strengthened further. Also, internal 'emotional' stimuli are aroused. Other than this they mention no specific outcomes of frustration. Besides helping to set the scene for Amsel, the importance of this theory is that it strengthened frustration as a technical rather than an everyday term.

Amsel: the frustration effect (FE)

It has been known for some time that an animal will often respond with momentarily increased vigour when extinction conditions are first instituted, i.e. when reinforcement is witheld (for example Marzocco 1951; Miller and Stevenson 1936). This is the basic FE and has frequently been taken as evidence for an increase in drive. However, there is not much hard evidence that frustration has the functional properties of a drive. As Bolles (1967) points out, an increased response rate is by no means an increased vigour of response; the initial increase in response rate during extinction may be due to an elimination of eating. Also, Marx (1956) and Lawson and Marx (1958) doubt many of the supposedly demonstrated FEs, and where they do exist attribute them to associative relationships. They suggest that blocking of behaviour produces a frustration state. This state will elicit either innate and/or learned responses, one of which may be an increase in vigour. This word of interpretative caution should perhaps be borne in mind throughout the discussions below.

Amsel's first and most important contribution to this field was to define frustration operationally. He suggested that it is what occurs when an organism experiences nonreward after previous experience with reward. This definition was based on a study by Amsel and Roussel (1952) which has proved prototypical for much of the recent work on frustration. Their apparatus consisted of a two-unit runway with a goal-box at the end of each alley. Rats were trained to run the first alley (A1) to the first goal-box (GB1) where food was available, and then run A2 to GB2 where there was further food. Each trial ended after food had been eaten in GB2. This procedure was followed until running speeds had stabilized. On 50 per cent of the trials during the subsequent period, food was no longer available in GB1. Measures were taken of the start time from GB1 and the running time in A2. Rats showed significantly faster start and run times during those trials when food was witheld in GB1 than during those trials when it was not. This is the FE.

Two refinements were soon made to this basic procedure. (1) Amsel and Ward (1954) and Amsel and Prouty (1959) replaced A2 with a choice situation. To obtain food in GB2, the animals had to make one response on frustrated trials and another on rewarded trials. Such a discrimination was rapidly learned and seemed to be dependent on the immediate effects of nonreward. (2) Seward *et al.* (1957) suggested that the FE might be due to response suppression—a comparative depression in A2 running speed on rewarded trials due to relative satiation with food. Wagner (1959) overcame this objection by running three groups of animals. The first was never fed in GB1, the second was fed during test on a 50/50 basis in GB1, the third was always fed in GB1. Wagner found that on nonrewarded trials the second group ran faster in A2 than animals in either of the other groups. Similar controls for possible response suppression have usually been incorporated in more recent runway studies of the FE.

Frustrative nonreward

One interpretation of the effects of reward and punishment has been based on the Hullian notion of fractional, anticipatory goal responses (for example Miller 1959; Mowrer 1960a; 1960b; Spence 1956). For example, in a food-deprived animal, the stimuli in a stimulus–response sequence which ends with food elicit fractional components (r_g - - - s_g, hope) of the primary emotional responses to food. The elevating effects of a food reward on behaviour are then attributed to the energizing influences of these fractional (hope-elicited) responses which can either be regarded as hypothetical constructs or more concretely as actual responses such as salivation. Similarly, the depressing effects of punishment on behaviour can be attributed to fractional fear-elicited responses which are incompatible with the criterial response. Amsel (1958; 1962) suggested that nonreward could also be viewed in this way. After reward, nonreward will elicit a primary aversive emotional reaction—frustration—which is related to the magnitude of anticipatory reward. (For discussion of the relationship of extinction to magnitude of reward see Wilton and Strongman 1967.) Amsel regards the components of such frustration as becoming conditioned to antedating stimuli, resulting in anticipatory frustration. If this is so then the decrement in instrumental behaviour which results from the witholding of reward may be due to: (1) suppression effects of incompatible responses, which are learned via anticipatory frustration; (2) the acquisition of avoidance responses reinforced by a reduction in frustration-associated cues.

With the development of the double-runway technique and the theory of frustrative nonreward, Amsel has made two important contributions to the study of frustration. (1) Frustration is defined using one basic operation: nonreward after experience with reward. (2) The idea of anticipatory frustration has been used extensively as an explanation for other problems in learning and motivation: extinction, the partial reinforcement effect and discrimination for example (Amsel 1958; 1962; 1967). The theory contains three fundamental generalizations. (1) Frustration is defined solely by nonrewarded trials in conjunction with rewarded. (2) Anticipatory frustration is seen as being conditioned to specific stimuli within the environment. (3) Anticipatory frustration affects response strength by increasing overall drive strength (motivating immediate behaviour), by acting as a drive stimulus the reduction of which is reinforcing and to which other responses become conditioned, and finally by inhibiting overt behaviour (cf. Brown and Farber 1951; Miller 1959). To date, this is the most rigorous analysis to have been made of frustration. It has generated a great deal of research and thought, some of the more interesting aspects of which will be discussed below.

The aversiveness of frustrative nonreward

Wagner (1966; 1969) offers an alternative theory of nonreward in terms of aversive events—events that an organism will terminate or avoid. He argues that the transition from nonreward to reward is reinforcing and that this is due either to the initiation of reward or to the termination of nonreward. The same is true of avoidance; it can be seen as the avoidance of nonreward or as the prolonging of reward. This is doubtless a logical possibility, but there is some question as to its usefulness. Leitenberg (1965), for instance, finds the concept of aversiveness unnecessary when accounting for the effects of time-out (TO) from positive reinforcement (see below).

Wagner's view implies that nonreward is frustrating and aversive in proportion to the degree to which reward has been anticipated. The usual double-runway studies support this idea by showing increased running speed in A2; nonreward is more aversive and better motivating of escape behaviour in GB1 (for example Amsel and Roussel 1952; Wagner 1959). Anticipatory reward extinguishes as a function of experience with nonreward. McHose (1963) demonstrated that in turn this leads to a reduction in the aversiveness of nonreward. Of course, many studies (for example Amsel 1958; Amsel and Ward 1965; Peckham and Amsel 1967) show that the active properties of nonreward are dependent on the previous history of reward. But Wagner (1969) argues that it is impossible to deduce from such studies whether or not the *escape* from GB1 is reinforcing in that it may increase the probability of some new contingent response. Frustrative nonreward theory simply points to a nonspecific energizing effect of frustration, just assuming by exclusion that escape is unimportant.

There are few studies which are directly relevant to Wagner's basic view of frustration and even these can be criticized on methodological grounds (for example Adelman and Maatsch 1956; Church 1969). However, they support the idea that nonreward has active properties as a result of previous history of reward, and that these properties are aversive in that their reduction or avoidance is reinforcing. The best of the studies is Wagner's (1963) in which frustrative nonreward was associated with distinctive cues. These cues motivated new learning (hurdle-crossing) far better than in control groups.

Wagner extends his argument with a parallel between fear and anticipatory frustration. He suggests that if fear and frustration are capable of similar 'anticipatory' explanations then the effects of punishers (with fear presumably responsible) will not be very different if frustrative nonreward is the aversive event. In support of this, Barry et al. (1962), for example, showed a disinhibition of the

FE in rats with alcohol and sodium amytal, both of which are known to disinhibit responding which has been inhibited by punishment (fear).

Further, Wagner maintains that if there is some similarity between the anticipatory stimuli produced by fear and those stemming from anticipatory frustration, then behaviour learned in the presence of one emotional response should generalize to occasions when the other is aroused. Rescorla and Solomon (1967) support this idea by showing that any stimulus which would elicit anticipatory frustration would enhance avoidance responding based on fear, whether the cue came from Pavlovian or instrumental conditioning. Also, Amsel (1958; 1962) argues that, during partial reinforcement, frustrative nonreward is less decremental in its effects when the animal has been trained such that anticipatory frustration will elicit responses compatible with the ongoing instrumental response. Fear would seem to be similar. Miller (1960) showed that rats receiving gradually increasing shocks at a rewarded goal are more resistant to the decremental effects of intense shock than are rats without such experience. This is supported by Brown and Wagner (1964).

Wagner, then, puts forward a convincing argument that frustrative nonreward may have properties which make it, like punishment, a response-contingent aversive event, and also that fear and anticipatory frustration appear to have much in common.

Frustrative nonreward in humans

At the human level, Amsel's idea of frustrative nonreward has usually been applied to children—it has implications for learning, the building of frustration tolerance, and so on. This work has been thoroughly reviewed by Ryan and Watson (1968). They bring together the literature concerned with the FE and the partial reinforcement effect in children, consider the relationship between nonreward and failure, and mention subject variables such as age, sex and personality. Some of their conclusions will be briefly discussed.

From studies on children, it is clear that nonreward leads to increased vigour of performance at some tasks, and also that frustration may become conditioned to previously neutral stimuli. In forming discriminations, nonreward may have a greater effect on learning than reward. All of which is in line with work on infrahumans. The reaction of a child to nonreward appears to depend quite heavily on individual variables. For example, reward expectancy is related to both chronological and mental age, but not necessarily directly. Thus it is possible that older children and brighter children react to nonreward by devising various strategies for 'solving the problem', rather than by simply showing increased vigour of responding. Also, nonattainment of social reward has similar effects on performance to those of the nonattainment of more concrete rewards.

Such conclusions are important to any behavioural study of emotion since they suggest that in the end there may be implications for behaviour outside the laboratory. With the FE, however, this is not surprising since it probably originated in commonsense notions; one's own reactions are instructive when, having put money into a cigarette or chocolate machine and pulled the drawer, nothing happens.

The FE in the Skinner box

There are two recent developments which add some generality to Hullian derived analyses of emotional behaviour. The first extends the idea of frustrative nonreward in the double runway by demonstrating similar effects in the Skinner box. The second analyses another 'emotion' using similar techniques.

Staddon and Innis (1966) trained pigeons to respond on cyclic presentations of two identical fixed-interval (FI) schedules separated by a brief TO period (delay in GB1 of a double runway). During test trials, omission of reward after the first FI component led to FEs in the second component—a higher than baseline rate of responding. These results were extended by Staddon and Innis (1969) using blackout rather than reinforcement at the end of 25 per cent of the first components of two linked FI schedules. For both rats and pigeons they reported FEs in the second component, which were largely attributable to a decreased latency of the first response. Blackout duration was inversely related to start latency.

These results are clearly similar to those from double-runway studies of the FE. However, a third operant study obtained somewhat discrepant findings. Wilton et al. (1969) showed that, if the reward which normally followed responding in the second component of a two-part chain was sometimes omitted, then immediately subsequent responding was sometimes elevated and sometimes depressed. This result is difficult to account for other than in the broad terms that rate of bar-pressing may be a measure of behaviour which is more sensitive to emotional disruption than that of running an alley. Be this as it may, the important feature of this study is that responding was measured *immediately* following nonreward. This is not so in the double runway, where a delay in GB1 on nonrewarded trials is usually instituted to control for the time taken by eating on rewarded trials; nor in the Staddon and Innis experiments where TO responding was largely suppressed. Amsel, however, clearly points to the FE being an increase in response vigour immediately following nonreward (1958, p. 103).

The most recent study of frustration in the Skinner box again provides support for the runway studies. Wookey and Strongman (1971) showed that responding during the 10 sec TO between two linked fixed-ratio (FR) schedules increased following nonreward on the first FR. This was the case during the test period for a group of rats previously rewarded at this time but now only receiving reward on a 50/50 basis, and also throughout training for another group never rewarded at the end of the first FR, but, again, experiencing 50/50 reward/ nonreward in test. Little effect was seen on subsequent instrumental responding. Wookey and Strongman argue that the results from the increased reward group were due to 'comparative frustration', a notion first put forward by Karabenick (1969, see below). Thus the effect of an introduction of reward after the first FR on 50 per cent of the trials was to reduce intercomponent TO response rate following reward below that of the baseline rate of the other group rewarded after the first FR from the start of training.

As well as adding generality to the double-runway effects, operant studies of frustration also emphasize the importance of looking in detail at the behaviour which immediately follows nonreward (or reward—see below) in the first goal-box.

'Elation' in the double runway

The other 'emotion' which has been studied within this empirical framework is elation. Work on this has developed in an attempt to outline the effects of a reward increase rather than decrease in GB1. Intuitively, this might be expected to have an 'elation' effect in A2, which, like the FE, is reflected by an increased running speed. However, with one exception, results from the relevant studies do not point in this direction.

The first study to contain a reward-increase group was that of Bower (1962) using a triple runway and rewards of eight, eight and one pellets in the three goal-boxes during a long period of training. During test an increase in GB1 up to 12 or 16 pellets on a 50/50 basis led to a *suppression* of running speed in A2 in comparison with normal trials. However, there was no unshifted control group in this study, i.e. no group to receive the larger reward throughout. Meyer and McHose (1968) used a standard double runway, their experimental groups receiving either one or four food pellets in GB1 throughout 48 training trials. For each of these groups, reward in GB1 was raised to seven pellets during testing. This was, surprisingly, on a one in six basis. Meyer and McHose found that A2 running speed and starting speed were *lower* after seven pellets than during the training, but *greater* than those of a control group always receiving seven pellets in GB1. They refer to these results as demonstrating an 'apparent elation effect', although the within-subject analysis showed a suppression.

Strongman and Wookey (1969) gave the relevant group in their study 80 training trials with one pellet in GB1. During testing this was increased to two pellets on a 50/50 basis. A2 running speed was faster after one pellet than after two. Also, there were no differences between running speeds on trials with increased reward and those of controls always receiving the larger number of pellets. On the other hand, test trials where the reward was as in training produced faster A2 speeds than in any of the control or experimental groups during training. The authors interpreted this as a rapidly developing frustration effect.

Karabenick (1969) gave rats 30 trials with either 15 pellets or one pellet in GB1 and GB2. Then, for a further 30 trials, half of the subjects in each group were shifted to the other reward magnitude in GB1. Increased reward led to decreased A2 running speed, although this was still faster than that of unshifted control animals—'apparent elation'. Within subjects there was frustration following decreased reward, but this was not upheld with the control animals.

Karabenick developed the concept of 'comparative frustration' to account for his results, an FE building up during acquisition due to the different reward in the two goal-boxes. This would also tend to obscure any effects in studies involving reward increase which used different levels in GB1 and GB2. As mentioned above, this result was borne out in a Skinner box study by Wookey and Strongman (1971) and also by Prytula and Braud (1970) in a double runway.

Taking a somewhat different look at this problem, Wookey and Strongman (1972) increased GB1 reward qualitatively rather than quantitatively. After training rats with two standard pellets in both goal-boxes, on 50 per cent of the test trials the reward in GB1 was changed to two sucrose pellets for the experimental group. This produced no change in A2 run times, but start times tended to be greater than those following normal food pellets. So subjects remained longer in GB1 after a preferred food than a normal, but this was a transitory effect and one which did not extend to performance in A2.

In spite of the very different parameters used in these studies of reward increase in GB1, it is possible to draw two conclusions. (1) An increase in reward in GB1 of a double runway after training at a lower level of reward leads to within-subject performance decrement in A2. (2) Under some conditions A2 performance does not fall as low as that of unshifted control animals always receiving the larger reward.

CONDITIONED EMOTIONAL RESPONSE (CER)

The other behavioural approach to emotion developed from two important advances made by Watson (1929). (1) He asked questions about the *external* causes of emotional behaviour rather than speaking in the necessarily more speculative terms of emotional states. (2) His study with Rayner (Watson and Rayner 1920) laid the groundwork for the present large and increasing literature on CER. Watson and Rayner demonstrated that a young child who had previously shown only approach responses to a white rat could be conditioned to 'fear' it. They associated the rat with a sudden loud noise—a stimulus which leads to crying, moving away, etc., in a young child. This 'fear' of the rat was long-lasting and generalized to similar animals and objects. (It is worth noting that although this study formed the background to the Estes and Skinner (1941) CER technique, the two procedures differ in one important respect. Watson and Rayner measured 'emotional' behaviour directly, whereas the CER procedure measures it as indirectly expressed in changes in ongoing operant behaviour. See below.)

Through a long chain of empirical research and theoretical discussion, Watson and Rayner's finding has led to the general behaviouristic viewpoint that emotions are names that we can give to the disruptions and enhancements of behaviour which occur as immediate consequences of presenting organisms with positive or negative stimuli (S+ and S−). It is argued (for example

Millenson 1967) that there are two operations that bring about such alterations in behaviour. (1) The presentation or termination of primary reinforcers. (2) The presentation of previously neutral stimuli which have been associated with primary reinforcers by a process of Pavlovian conditioning. Emotion is regarded as changing the reinforcing value both of primary reinforcers and of general activity. In this it is like motivation, but Millenson (1967) argues that its antecedents are different; for motivation they are deprivation and satiation, for emotion they are abrupt stimulus change.

After Watson, the next major (technological) step was taken by Estes and Skinner (1941) and Hunt and Brady (1951; 1955). It mainly involved the development of a technique for studying conditioned emotion in a methodologically 'tight' manner. The basic procedure consists, for example, of having thirsty rats in a Skinner box bar-pressing for water on a variable-interval (VI) schedule of reinforcement. When their response rate is steady, an occasional conditioning stimulus (CS), a clicker for example, is presented for five minutes, at the end of which the rat receives a brief shock (unconditioned stimulus— US). Initially, the CS has no effect, but the US results in a lowered response rate. After a few pairings of CS and US, the response to the US becomes adapted and response rate is lower only during the CS. 'Fear' responses originally made to the US have become conditioned to the CS. When these effects were first observed, they were termed conditioned anxiety reactions.

The basic CER paradigm

The basic experimental paradigm for studying CERs can be expressed by the notation: CS - - - US, where CS is neutral at first, US is an unavoidable, inescapable, aversive stimulus, and - - - is a short time interval. This procedure is superimposed on an ongoing operant baseline. Since, typically, there is a suppression of operant behaviour during CS, this basic procedure has recently become known as conditioned suppression (Lyon 1968). However, the CS - - - US paradigm *may* lead to acceleration during the CS. Sidman (1960), for example, superimposed a CS linked to unavoidable shock on a baseline which was maintained by negative reinforcement. He found an increase in response rate during the CS.

From this it may be seen that the basic CER paradigm leads to a number of logical possibilities for the study of conditioned emotion (see Strongman 1969 and Weiss 1969 for a fuller exposition).

	CS - - - S−	CS - - - S+	CS - - - $−	CS - - - $+
Positive baseline	Anxiety	Elation	—	Anger and aggression
Negative baseline	Anxiety	Elation	Relief	—

In this analysis, positive baseline refers to a steady ongoing operant response maintained by positive reinforcement (for example food), and negative baseline refers to a steady ongoing operant response maintained by negative reinforcement (for example shock avoidance). Superimposed on these can be CSs which

110

precede four types of emotion-producing event: S— (for example shock), S+ (for example food), $— (for example TO from shock) and $+ (for example TO from food). This leads immediately to the six possibilities which are shown; such a breakdown brings about the four 'human' emotional possibilities of anxiety, elation, relief and anger, although Millenson (1967) collapses elation and relief into one. (Of course, no great claim can be made for the validity of these particular 'emotion' names in this somewhat rarified context. However, intuitively, they seem to be reasonably appropriate and they can at least function as shorthand descriptions of the basic procedural operations.) The two remaining sections have been left blank since at first sight they appear difficult to establish empirically. However, as will be discussed at the end of this section on CER, they can perhaps be regarded as other aspects of relief and anger. A discussion of how this scheme can incorporate the more complex human emotions will be reserved for later. First, the research which can be fitted under each of the four headings will be briefly reviewed.

Anxiety—conditioned suppression

There has been a great deal of work on conditioned suppression. It has already been well reviewed and analysed by Davis (1968), Hearst (1969), Hoffman (1969), Kamin (1965) and Lyon (1968), for example. By comparison, what follows will inevitably be brief.

Conditioned suppression is defined as a decrement in response rate during a pre-shock stimulus which has been superimposed on, and is independent of, ongoing operant behaviour. This superimposition is achieved by a classical conditioning procedure. This distinguishes it from 'punishment' procedures where the noxious stimulus is response-contingent (Azrin and Holz 1966) Also, the US in conditioned suppression is believed to have its effects on respondents, heart rate for example (De Toledo and Black 1966) Changes in responses such as these are incompatible with the continuation of normal operant performance. Usually, an appetitive baseline has been used, with shock as the US; its effects are reasonably reliable When they are used in CER studies, other aversive stimuli, TO for example, sometimes produce an acceleration of responding (for example Leitenberg 1966).

An alternative procedure which has sometimes been followed (for example Hunt and Brady 1951) to overcome possibly post-US disruptions of the baseline is to give the animal CS - - - shock pairings in a 'grill-box' which has no bar and from which there is no escape. Then the CS alone is superimposed on the operant baseline in the Skinner box. Here, of course, the disadvantage is that acquisition is not measurable.

The species used to study conditioned suppression have varied considerably. They have mainly been rats and pigeons, but also include fish, mice, guinea pigs, cats, dogs and monkeys. Results obtained from these species have shown marked variations (for example Valenstein 1959). Conditioned suppression has rarely been investigated in human subjects, perhaps largely for ethical reasons.

Recently, however, other CER procedures have been studied at this level (see below). A final general point is that once it has been established conditioned suppression seems to be very stable over time. The most extreme demonstration of this stability is Hoffman *et al.* (1966), who showed pigeons to retain suppression after a five year period.

The major variables which affect conditioned suppression are those which stem directly from operant conditioning. For example, the type of reinforcement is important. Gellar (1960) showed that the acquisition of conditioned suppression was slower and its extinction faster with a reinforcer of higher incentive value. Also, Brady and Conrad (1960) demonstrated complete suppression in monkeys working for sugar pellets but no effect in those working for inter-cranial stimulation (ICS). Rats, on the other hand, showed similar effects with water reinforcement and ICS. (In fact, the work involving ICS and conditioned suppression is far from clear, perhaps because the ICS is usually sited in the limbic system, which is imprecisely implicated in the substrates of emotion—see Lyon 1968 for a good résumé of this work.)

Schedule and frequency of reinforcement are the other operant variables which affect conditioned suppression. Brady (1955), for example, demonstrated that conditioned suppression could be established in eight pairings on a VI schedule and that it would extinguish faster when superimposed on ratio schedules than interval schedules. Also, Stein *et al.* (1958) showed that response rate within the CS increased as the length of the stimulus increased in relation to the interstimulus interval; but this was so only to the extent that the suppression did not much reduce the overall number of reinforcements received during the experimental session (the 'reinforcements lost' hypothesis—see below). However, this idea was refuted by Carlton and Didamo (1960), who achieved the same result with the overall number of reinforcements held constant. Conversely, Lyon (1963) and Blackman (1966; 1967) show local reinforcement rates to be important. The higher the frequency of reinforcement the greater the resistance to suppression, although higher rates of responding lead to greater suppression.

Lyon (1964) suggests that conditioned suppression on VI or variable-ratio (VR) schedules is determined largely by reinforcement frequency, while suppression on FI or fixed-ratio (FR) schedules is determined more by the interval between the onset of the CS and the scheduled reinforcement. There is some support for this notion (Lyon and Felton 1966a; 1966b).

Apart from obviously relevant variables such as CS duration and US intensity, deprivation is the only other significant variable to affect the course of conditioned suppression. Estes and Skinner (1941) showed that suppression is reduced as deprivation increases, a result supported by Hoffman and Fleshler (1961).

At this point, mention must be made of the main study of conditioned suppression on a negative baseline. Sidman (1960) gave rats and monkeys signalled unavoidable shock on a baseline response which was maintained by a Sidman avoidance schedule. The rate of bar-pressing increased during the CS.

This is perhaps another line of evidence to support the idea that 'emotionality' may have bidirectional effects. Comparisons can be made with Amsel and Maltzman (1950), Levine (1968), Moyer (1965), Strongman (1965), Strongman et al. (1970) and Weiss (1968), who each showed shock to enhance behaviour.

There have been four main interpretations of conditioned suppression. The first and most obvious is the interference hypothesis. For a long time there was a general consensus of opinion that suppression was caused by the interference of conditioned respondents with ongoing instrumental behaviour. Any conditioned suppression study can be interpreted in this way. However, the important question, to which little attention has been paid, then becomes: what are the respondents? The only good study to attempt an answer to this is De Toledo and Black's (1966). They measured changes in heart rate and showed them to occur independently of the course of conditioned suppression. The study of overt behavioural measures such as defecation and urination have been no help in this context.

The punishment hypothesis suggests that the results of conditioned suppression can be explained by an adventitious contingency between the behaviour and the aversive stimulus; early in the procedure, there is a high probability that shock will be delivered while the animal is operantly responding. Hunt and Brady (1951) found no differences in suppression in rats with response-contingent and conditioned-suppression procedures. But in their contingent group it seemed that only terminal bar-pressing was punished. With pigeons, the results of this comparison are equivocal. Azrin (1956) found punishment superior in suppressing behaviour, Hoffman and Fleshler (1965) found conditioned suppression superior, and Leitenberg (1966) found no differences. Cohen (1967) resolved these apparent contradictions by using a procedure which involved discrete trials, a retractable bar so the subjects could not be responding while being shocked, and a response–shock delay interval. With increasing shock intensity he found the complete range of effects from no suppression to severe suppression. When the response–shock delay interval was increased, to achieve the same degree of suppression the shock intensity also had to be increased. The explanation is more complex than a simple reliance on shock intensity. Although the punishment hypothesis has a certain amount of face validity, it cannot easily account for: (1) the rapid acquisition of conditioned suppression observed by some investigators (for example Annau and Kamin 1961); (2) results from studies using the 'grill-box' procedure (for example Hunt and Brady 1951); (3) Cohen's (1967) findings.

An 'invariant reinforcement rate' or 'reinforcements lost' hypothesis was proposed by Stein et al. (1958). The gist of this is that suppression is constrained to the extent that only up to 10 per cent of baseline reinforcement density would be given up. This would not seem to have enough generality to account for all conditioned suppression effects. Finally, Millenson and de Villiers (1971) regard conditioned suppression as a negative drive which might be expected to detract from other, positive drives, particularly that which is maintaining baseline performance. This is similar to an idea proposed by Estes (1969). This hypothesis brings together many apparent discrepancies in the CER literature but has at least one basic difficulty. It would lead to the prediction that a *positive* US would produce CS facilitation for all *positive* baselines. This is not necessarily so (see discussion below of Pliskoff 1963 and Azrin and Hake 1969).

This brief summary of some of the research and theory in the field of conditioned suppression permits a number of conclusions. (1) Conditioned suppression is not a straightforward effect; it is influenced by many variables, including those from the underlying baseline. (2) The theories which have been put forward to account for it all suffer from some deficiency. (3) However, it is a useful procedure for the study of 'negative' emotion in that it allows the definition of stimulus conditions which suppress many forms of behaviour at once. (4) It offers a useful way of systematizing the other approaches which have been made to emotional behaviour.

Elation

Referring back to the basic CER paradigm, it will be recollected that the term elation was used to describe the superimposition of a signalled positive stimulus (free reward) on either a positive or negative operant baseline. For the most part, the empirical research within this area of conditioned emotion has only accrued very recently. It began with Herrnstein and Morse (1957). They established pigeons on a DRL five minute schedule of reinforcement. (Such a schedule differentially reinforces a very low rate of responding by requiring one response to be separated from the next by five minutes.) Then, independently of the animals' behaviour, key light changes for one minute signalled access to food for five seconds. This led to an overall increase in response rate which gradually became restricted to the CS. However, Herrnstein and Morse's procedure did not control for the possibility (albeit an unlikely one) that this effect could have been maintained by adventitious reinforcement of superstitious behaviour. Brady (1961) established a positive VI baseline in rats and superimposed on this a CS leading to ICS in the septal region—where it is generally believed to have positively reinforcing effects. There was an acceleration in response rate during the CS. The final report to give impetus to the behavioural investigation of elation was that of Longo *et al.* (1964). They took baseline measures of activity in pigeons and demonstrated increased activity during a CS which signalled free food.

The last two or three years have produced a small crop of animal investigations of elation within the CER paradigm. Unfortunately, comparisons between them are made difficult since they differ on background variables such as species, baseline and CS length. Azrin and Hake (1969) established rats on a VI one minute schedule. They added to this a 10 sec CS which led to a US of free food, free water or ICS. For each animal the reinforcer used in the operant baseline was qualitatively or quantitatively different from the US used in the classical conditioning pairings. They found CS *suppression* in almost all subjects under all conditions; they termed this *positive* conditioned suppression. Henton and Brady (1970) established monkeys on a DRL 30 sec baseline schedule. With an 80 sec CS leading to free food they found an acceleration during the CS, but no effect with shorter CSs. Meltzer and Brahlek (1970) showed suppression in rats during a 12 sec CS on a VI baseline, no effect with a 40 sec CS, and an acceleration in rate with a 120 sec CS. This was partially confirmed by Miczek and Grossman (1971). They found suppression in monkeys with a short CS but no acceleration with a longer CS. Finally, Remington and Strongman (1972b) showed CS facilitation, but with pigeons classically conditioned off the baseline in a separate box and only when they were tested during extinction. Similar effects were seen following both VI and DRL schedules.

In spite of the apparent discrepancies between these results, Azrin and Hake (1969) do show positive conditioned suppression to be the general case when short CSs are used to signal free reward. A more general suppression effect was found by Pliskoff (1961). He established pigeons on multiple VI VI schedules which alternated every 15 min, the alteration being signalled within the last three min of each component of the schedule. For one group, the baseline condition was mult VI 1 VI 1, for the other it was mult VI 10 VI 10. All animals were tested on mult VI 10 VI 1. These conditions, although complex, do consist of a noncontingent signalled change in reward. All subjects showed a downwards shift in response rate during the CS which signalled the more favourable schedule and an acceleration during the CS which signalled the less favourable schedule. This result, together with those from other parts of the study, led Pliskoff to conclude that transition in reinforcement schedules from high to low produces effects which are like those of signalled TO–acceleration (see below), whereas a shift from low to high reinforcement density has suppressive effects. Pliskoff (1963) added generality to this result with a study in which signalled changes to higher or lower reinforcement schedules were superimposed randomly over a VI baseline. Results were essentially the same as in the earlier study.

Azrin and Hake (1969) argue that, like the conditioned-suppression procedure, the elation paradigm produces 'emotionality' and that this depresses response rate. Pliskoff's data support this. But it is also apparent that signalled low payoff VI reinforcement schedules or extinction tend to produce rate increases. Further, all studies which have completed classical conditioning out of the experimental situation have shown facilitatory effects during the CS (Bower and Grusec 1964; Estes 1948; Hyde et al. 1968; Morse and Skinner 1958).

From this work it is clear that at least four variables are important in the conditioned elation paradigm: (1) whether the CS - - - US pairing takes place before or during responding on the instrumental baseline schedule; (2) whether the CS is presented against an ongoing operant or during extinction; (3) the nature of the operant reinforcement schedule; (4) CS duration.

Breadth is added to these results by some recent studies on standard conditioned suppression. Blackman (1968b) showed that extinction of conditioned suppression is a function of schedule-dependent response rates (with reinforcement held constant) and reinforcement density (with response rate held constant). Also, Blackman (1968a) showed that on DRL schedules with low levels of shock as the US, rate of bar-pressing increased during the CS and decreased for higher shock levels. The Azrin and Hake and Herrnstein and Morse studies differ on both schedule and rate. Blackman also observed disruption of timing responses, leading to increases or decreases in response rate; such an interpretation could be made of Herrnstein and Morse's results.

Up to the present, there has been only one study where a CS leading to free reward has been set against a negative baseline. Coulson and Walsh (1968) superimposed a one minute CS leading to 10 sucrose pellets on a VI Sidman avoidance baseline with rats. They used a Rescorla (1967) control condition (discussed at the end of this section) and incorporated a delay in the procedure to prevent adventitious reinforcement. With rats at 70 per cent of *ad lib* weight (they are usually run at 80 per cent or 85 per cent) they found response facilitation during the CS. However, as their subjects had *not* to respond for 10 sec in order to get the US (the normal control procedure for the effects of adventitious reinforcement) this may have led them to be shocked on their baseline schedule, so bringing about a superstitiously maintained increase in response rate.

From these studies on animal subjects it can be concluded that a CS which signals free reward almost invariably produces a change in response during that CS; this may facilitate or suppress criterial responding. As yet there is no one explanation of these effects.

Finally, there is one study which demonstrates the application of conditioned elation techniques to human subjects. Remington and Strongman (1972a) established students on a lever-pulling response. They were working for points linked to a monetary reward. Reinforcement schedules were either VI 30 sec or DRL 15 sec. Superimposed on these were half minute CS presentations leading to either one or 10 free points. Each of these experimental conditions was also followed in other groups but with the CSs and USs presented randomly and independently (Rescorla 1967). There was a response facilitation during the CS, mainly within the experimental groups. This was independent of magnitude of free reward, and primarily within the group working on the VI baseline. DRL experimental subjects showed no effects. Other studies, with infrahuman subjects, have tended to show an acceleration on DRL schedules, and a suppression on VI schedules. Kaufman et al. (1966) showed instructional control to outweigh any schedule effects with human subjects, a result supported by Remington and Strongman (1970). In Remington and Strongman (1972a), subjects working on the DRL schedule obtained almost maximal reinforcements. Accurate responding in DRL produces positive feedback, the controlling effects of which may overshadow those of a small monetary reward.

(A note on the Rescorla (1967) control procedure. In some of the earlier CER studies, the CS alone was presented to subjects during pretest baseline measurements. If the subject has not had previous experience with both the US and the CS, then any effects during testing may be simply due to the introduction of the

US rather than to its contiguity with the CS. This, and other considerations, have led to the Rescorla control conditions in which the CS and US are both presented randomly and independently. With rats and pigeons this is clearly a useful procedure. But Remington and Strongman (1972a) show that it may be less straightforward with human subjects, with whom, to avoid boredom, experimental sessions must be short. The Rescorla control procedure requires *many* random independent CS and US presentations to avoid any possible effects of trace conditioning (Kamin 1961). Human subjects may well form some associations between the CS and US in short control sessions, thereby negating the control.)

Anger and aggression

Anger and aggression are used to describe the procedure in which, following a signal, positive reinforcers are withdrawn from or are no longer available to a subject working on a positive baseline. This is generally known as TO. With the exception of one or two more recent studies, what little work there is under this heading is reviewed and discussed by Leitenberg (1965). The general finding is that during the presence of a stimulus which signals TO from positive reinforcement there is an increase in response rate. This has been demonstrated by Ferster (1958) with chimpanzees, and Herrnstein (1955) and Leitenberg (1966) with pigeons. There is some confusion in Ferster's and Herrnstein's studies between punishment and TO, but Leitenberg's is quite clear-cut in showing the facilitatory effect with either response-free *or* response-contingent TO. However, using the same procedure, Leitenberg et al. (1968) show a pre-TO stimulus to produce a suppression in response rate in rats. At present, the reason for this discrepancy between species is unknown.

Before discussing two recent human studies on the effects of signalled TO, it is worth mentioning an investigation in which Azrin et al. (1966) showed the aversiveness of TO, rather than conditioned TO, and also demonstrated what might reasonably be termed 'anger'. They established pigeons on a key-pecking response where continuous reinforcement alternated with extinction. Meanwhile, strapped in one corner of the conditioning chamber was another pigeon. Rapidly, with the onset of extinction conditions, the experimental bird immediately began to attack the 'target' bird. (The everyday parallels to this are too numerous and too near home to need mention.)

Trenholme et al. (1969) demonstrated that signalled TO leads to CS facilitation in human subjects working for a monetary reward. Their procedure began with a long period of baseline (CS only) training, followed by a DRL 20 sec schedule and then a VI 1·33 min schedule with a concurrent DRL 5 sec. They ran their subjects for 12, 50 min sessions, but the effect of the first DRL schedule on response rates caused the observed response facilitation to be associated with greater reinforcement frequency. This obscured their results.

Remington and Strongman (1970) used a VI 30 sec schedule and a Rescorla control procedure to obtain a comparative baseline. Subjects worked for points linked to a monetary reward. Also, instructions varied, either verbally establishing the TO discrimination, or not. Facilitation of response rate during the CS was found to be mainly a function of instructions, being much greater following those which did not specify the significance of TO. This study showed a clear facilitatory effect on response rate during a pre-TO stimulus which was independent of any increase in reinforcement density.

Relief

This refers to that procedure which would involve allowing subjects signalled TO from a negative baseline. Any disruption of the ongoing operant could be termed relief and would probably be predicted to take the form of an increase in response rate. At present there is no work on this within the CER framework, but see later for a discussion of Hammond's (1970) ideas with reference to Mowrer's concept of relief.

Relief and anger—other aspects

There are two sections of the schema for the logically possible studies of CER which have not yet been discussed: (1) signalling TO from a negative stimulus on a positive baseline; (2) signalling TO from a positive stimulus on a negative baseline. With appropriate controls, studies involving these procedures could take the form of:

1. Establishing subjects on a VI baseline for food reinforcement until they had reached a stable response rate and then superimposing on this a continuous aversive stimulus (for example loud white noise) which would lead to an overall reduction in response rate. A CS would be used to signal TO from the aversive stimulus.

2. Establishing food-deprived subjects on a Sidman avoidance schedule independently of which they occasionally and unpredictably receive free food. Once a stable response rate had been established, then an occasional CS would be superimposed signalling a period of TO from the possibility of free reward.

Such procedures could be regarded as aspects of relief and anger, and studies along these lines are currently in progress in the author's laboratories.

To summarize, within the CER framework, there has been a great deal of work on conditioned suppression (anxiety) but as yet its determinants are far from clear. The basic technique has been extended to the study of conditioned elation and conditioned aggression and has led to some straightforward human investigations. Conditioned relief is an unknown quantity. Clearly, there is much scope in this field, particularly for parametric studies systematically manipulating variables such as CS length, US intensity and baseline schedule. However, the CER procedure has been extensively used in other fields of research and provides a good structure for the study of emotional behaviour.

THEORETICAL CONSIDERATIONS

There are no completely behavioural theories of emotion. This is perhaps not surprising since many thoroughgoing behaviourists would adopt an anti-theoretical attitude to psychology in general. There are, however, a few primarily behavioural theoretical syntheses of some aspects of emotion.

Millenson

Millenson's (1967) theory or, more properly, model of emotion is one of the most recent and perhaps most extreme formulations of the behaviouristic approach to emotion. It owes a great deal to Watson and is directly dependent on the CER technique. Basically, he takes Watson's X, Y and Z factors and puts them within a CER context. He suggests that CS leading to an S− produces some degree of anxiety which suppresses positively maintained operant behaviour whilst sometimes facilitating that which is negatively maintained. A CS leading to an S+ or to the removal of an S− invokes some form of elation which enhances some operants. And a CS leading to the removal of an S+ produces anger which can increase both the strength of some operants and the frequency of aggressive behaviour.

Millenson recognizes that anxiety, elation and anger do not provide an exhaustive list of human emotions. He extends his ideas by making two fundamental assumptions. (1) Some emotions only differ from each other in intensity, for example joy and ecstasy. (2) Some emotions are basic, others are compounds of these. Millenson regards the three basic patterns of emotion as those described above. Again, his reasons are twofold. (1) He believes that in their unconditioned form, fear, elation and anger cover all the logical possibilities for the presentation and withdrawal of positive and negative reinforcers. (2) In their conditioned form, they cover all the conceivable simple classical conditioning paradigms.

This reasoning leads Millenson to a three-dimensional 'emotional coordinate' system, as shown in Figure 8. It can be seen from this figure that Millenson's three primary emotions are represented as vectors and the various emotions are portrayed as dependent on different intensities of the reinforcer which forms their basis (this model is only representative—many more terms could be fitted to it). The emotions at the extremes represent extremity in every way. The convergence of the three vectors on one point is meant to indicate that as the emotions become less intense they become more difficult to distinguish behaviourally.

A point of awkwardness in this model is that it is based on only three primary emotions, but there are four possibilities for the basic manipulation of reinforcers. Millenson overcomes this difficulty by suggesting an equivalence between the withdrawal of a negative reinforcer and the presentation of a positive reinforcer —he terms both of these elation. In the schema presented earlier, the withdrawal of a negative reinforcer was termed relief. Whether or not this collapsing of the likely effects of the two procedures is justified remains to be seen. As the pro-

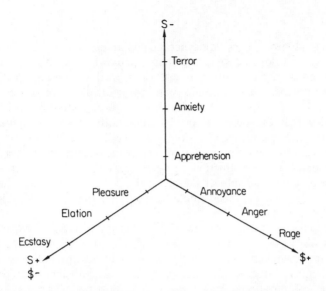

Figure 8. Millenson's three-dimensional model of emotional intensity.

cedures themselves are easily distinguishable, the answer is likely to be an empirical matter.

Millenson is aware that his three-dimensional system does not include all the 'human' emotions. However, he argues that those which it excludes are simply mixtures of the primary emotions. A neutral stimulus can become paired with two or more primary emotions or with a US that contains more than one primary reinforcer. Millenson cites the example of a child stealing a cookie. The cookie is a CS for the S+ of eating it, *plus* a CS for the S− of punishment. He suggests that this combination is usually called guilt. Where a CS is paired with a US that has both positive and negative characteristics there is conflict, of the kind seen in experimental neurosis. Also, Millenson suggests that what we usually term sorrow or despair or depression is the result of removing a generalized reinforcer, such as would be involved in the death of a close friend.

Finally, Millenson extends his ideas on emotion by commenting on emotional control and pathological emotion. He proposes, from the behavioural viewpoint, that we use three methods of controlling our emotions. (1) Adaptation to the continual presentations of emotion-producing stimuli; this leads to the building of a tolerance to frustration and also to 'good' things losing their effect. (2) Masking respondents with opposed operants, for example keeping a 'poker face' or a 'stiff upper lip'. (3) The avoidance of emotion-producing situations. Millenson's view of pathological emotion is straightforward but oversimplified. He simply regards prolonged 'anxiety'-producing situations as leading to neurosis, and psychosis as due to the more extreme, normal positive reinforcers being either drastically disrupted or absent altogether.

Weiskrantz

Weiskrantz (1968) ranges idiosyncratically across many of the behavioural approaches to emotion, drawing together a somewhat selective set of evidence. His basic view is that if reinforcers can be defined as stimuli which are consequent to responses, then emotion can be defined as responses which are consequent to reinforcers. He indicates that reinforcing stimuli can be positive or negative; also that the onset of one is often difficult to distinguish from the offset of the other in its effects. For these reasons, he defines responses very widely and speaks of emotion as a *state* which includes many responses. He also follows Skinner's (1938) distinction between operants and respondents and points to the latter as being the subject matter of the study of emotion. That they may be difficult to distinguish (for example Miller 1969; Rescorla and Solomon 1967) he views of little account.

Weiskrantz discusses the problem of stimulus stability and then, more importantly, gives his view of specific respondents. He suggests three reasons for not accepting autonomic activity and EEG as straightforward indicants of emotion. (1) Sympathetic activity or EEG activation are not sufficient conditions to infer the existence of emotional states—cognition may be necessary, as Schachter argues. (2) There are many problems and opposed viewpoints on the relevance of autonomic responding; the questions these have raised have so far only produced theoretical answers. (3) Autonomic and EEG changes cannot yet be differentiated to discriminate different emotional states. As an alternative view, Weiskrantz regards it as necessary to study respondents in general. He places these on a 'practical' dimension depending on the extent to which instrumentation has been used in their study. Within this framework, he reviews some of the literature on respondents.

Finally, before a brief discussion of fixation and conflict, Weiskrantz makes a number of useful points about emotion in general, taking illustrations from the CER literature. He suggests that in an everyday sense emotion often refers to alterations in characteristic *patterns* of behaviour, for example not smiling, shoulders drooping, not eating. This implies that the effects of emotion-producing stimuli are to make ongoing behaviour either more or less vigorous. He regards this as supporting the idea of emotion as a state, or perhaps a collection of responses.

Studies on conditioned emotion lend some weight to this view. In particular, Weiskrantz raises the interesting notion that if conditioned suppression, for example, can be seen as similar to a conditioned respondent such as heart rate, then it should be able to be used to monitor emotional states. However, it should be borne in mind that De Toledo and Black (1966) found this not to be so. On the other hand, Kamin *et al.* (1963) provide evidence which is more positive. They trained rats in a shuttle-box either by giving them pairings of tone and shock which they could neither avoid nor escape, or by giving them conditioned avoidance trials. They had all been trained previously to bar-press in a Skinner box. They were later returned to the Skinner box and presented with the CS which had been used in the shuttle-box. For the CER group, suppression in response rate was found to be a monotonic function of the number of CS - - - US pairings they had received, but for the avoidance group it was a U-shaped function relating suppression to the number of consecutive successful avoidance trials. Also, when the avoidance response had extinguished, the CS still produced strong suppression. This result suggests that if suppression is a (conditioned) respondent then the operant and respondent aspects of conditioned aversive stimuli are somewhat independent.

In summary, Weiskrantz regards emotion as respondent behaviour, and suggests that emotional states are reflected by alterations in large classes of behaviour. He argues that to speak of emotional states has an heuristic value, as long as the 'situational context' is not forgotten. There is much to be said for this view of emotional behaviour. It is clear, based on few assumptions and gains reasonable empirical support. However, there are some areas of study which it does not easily encompass. Amsel's FE for example; Weiskrantz makes no mention of this. Also, it is surprising to find a behaviourally oriented theorist speaking of emotional states. This might have a convenient, shorthand value, but also carries confusing implications. Perhaps Weiskrantz's main contribution is to emphasize the respondent aspect of emotional behaviour and to remind us that, at best, changes in operant behaviour can only be an indirect index of this.

Conditioned emotional states

Hammond (1970) provides the best recent synthesis of behavioural work on emotion. This will be described in detail since it brings together some of the Hullian based research with some of the Skinnerian. Hammond regards emotion as a central state (CES) of the organism, which is elicited by both learned and unlearned stimuli. The unlearned stimuli may be rewards and punishments (or their absence); the learned are those which signal the unlearned and which, through classical conditioning, acquire similar properties. Broadly, this is emotion within a motivational framework.

Hammond begins his argument by reviewing Mowrer's (1960) contribution to the CES concept. Mowrer's main idea was that rewarding events lead to decremental processes (drive reduction) and punishing events lead to incremental processes (drive induction). These are correlated with pleasure and pain and represent unlearned emotional states which motivate the organism. If a neutral stimulus occurs just before an incremental event it is a 'danger' signal; if it precedes a decremental event it is a 'safety' signal. Also, the nature of the emotional state which is produced depends on whether the signal is turned on or off:

Danger signal: on - - - fear, off - - - relief
Safety signal: on - - - hope, off - - - disappointment

The CESs are learned through classical conditioning with the signals as predictive of reward or punishment.

Such a schema provides a straightforward way of specifying the development of the signals, with behaviour being simply measured as approach or withdrawal. Motivational behaviour within a test situation gives a measure of whether or not the CES has been produced; hope and relief should elicit approach and fear and disappointment should elicit avoidance.

Fear and hope are easily dealt with. The conditioned suppression paradigm has provided a mass of supportive evidence for fear. Wike (1966) reviews studies of hope, more traditionally called secondary reinforcement. Stimuli preceding reward increase the probability of new responses being made when such responses are followed by the onset of that stimulus. Also, the onset of such safety signals can have facilitatory effects on ongoing behaviour. Relief and disappointment are less clear; they depend on the idea that stimulus offset produces a qualitatively different state from stimulus onset. As mentioned earlier, because of the difficulty in distinguishing between these in many studies, Bolles (1967) believes relief and disappointment may be redundant. However, Hammond goes on to suggest that Rescorla and Solomon's (1967) argument has revitalized these concepts.

Rescorla and Solomon reemphasize Pavlovian inhibition and excitation. Pavlov distinguished two types of conditioned reflex. (1) Excitatory; signals followed by reinforcement. (2) Inhibitory; signals not followed by reinforcement. Most Pavlovian studies have been on excitation, but Rescorla (1967; 1968) makes the idea of inhibition more plausible. He suggests that the important relationship between a CS and a US is *predictive*. The *value* of the CS in predicting the US leads to conditioning. If the likelihood of shock, for example, is independent of the CS then no conditioned fear will develop, whereas if the likelihood of the shock increases after the CS, then conditioned fear will develop. So, if the probability of shock (or some other noxious stimulus) *decreases* after the CS then this is inhibitory Pavlovian conditioning. This points to the possible importance of the absence of reinforcement where reinforcement existed before. A CS which predicts a decrease in the occurrence of shock is similar to Mowrer's relief condition.

If these excitatory/inhibitory ideas are applied to Mowrer's original formulations, they change the defining operations for his conditions:

1. Stimuli predicting an increase in the occurrence of an aversive event lead to fear—excitatory.
2. Stimuli predicting a decrease in the occurrence of an aversive event lead to relief—inhibitory.
4. Stimuli predicting a decrease in the occurrence of a rewarding event lead to hope—excitatory.
4. Stimuli predicting a decrease in the occurence of a rewarding event lead to disappointment—inhibitory.

Given this general framework, there are many studies which become relevant to relief and disappointment. For example, Rescorla and Lolordo (1965) trained dogs on an (unsignalled) Sidman avoidance schedule until they had established a high rate of jumping from side to side of a shuttle-box. They were then penned in one side of this and given pairings of a CS and unavoidable shock. One tone signalled shock, another its absence. They were tested in the avoidance situation. The excitatory stimulus led to an increase in the jumping rate but the inhibitory stimulus to decreased jumping. This inhibition of behaviour is 'relief'. Similar results are reported by Hammond (1966) with rats in a CER procedure. Also, Hammond (1967) combined fear and relief signals during testing. There was less conditioned suppression than was seen with the fear stimulus alone. And Hammond (1968) showed the acquisition of fear to be comparatively retarded when a relief stimulus was changed so that it signalled shock. Both the latter results are supported by Rescorla (1969). So, there are many studies which show that stimuli which predict the absence of punishing events acquire conditioned properties akin to relief.

Given Hammond's (1970) reconceptualization, Mowrer's disappointment is supported by the many studies on the FE—this fits the paradigm as described, it is operationally similar. The properties of the stimuli which produce conditioned, anticipatory frustration are seen as based on Pavlovian inhibition.

Finally, Hammond engages in some interesting physiological speculation. He maintains that CES theory is useful for the physiological investigation of emotion. He believes this to be supported by the emotional interpretation which can be given to the limbic system (see Chapter 3). For example, septal lesions facilitate shuttle-box avoidance learning (for example King 1958) but bring about deficits in passive avoidance learning (for example McCleary 1961). Therefore the suggestion is that limbic lesions produce response perseveration in such situations (for example Douglas 1967; McCleary 1966), leading to the prediction that animals with septal lesions will be temporarily unable to learn to withhold high-probability responses. Also, Beatty and Schwartzbaum (1967; 1968) and Schwartzbaum et al. (1967) showed that rats with septal lesions overreact to the incentive value of reinforcement. For example, when water was adulterated with quinine, rats with septal lesions drank less of it than controls, and when adulterated with saccharine they drank more.

Hammond suggests that it is possible that lesioned animals perseverate due to an enhanced emotionality. However, the studies which support the idea of response perseveration can also be interpreted in terms of enhanced frustration. For example, passive avoidance animals with lesions show a deficit in performance since they are more persistent; it may be that primary frustration from the shock is enhanced, so they continue to approach rather than to avoid. But Hammond argues further that septal lesions do not enhance all emotional responses; frustration is differentially affected. He suggests that, if this were not so, then in passive avoidance an increase in fear would cancel the increase in frustration.

Hammond provides an illuminating setting of more recent work on emotional behaviour within a framework of Pavlov and Mowrer, particularly as he is also able to accord this an interesting although speculative physiological basis.

Elation—broad aspects

A similar although not so far-reaching attempt at synthesis within the field of emotional behaviour has been made by Strongman *et al.* (1971). They concentrate on elation, which they define as a noninstrumental change in the vigour of responding which is brought about by upward shifts in the conditions of reward. They argue that any change in reward has both instrumental and Pavlovian components, the latter being immediate, unconditioned effects which can be conditioned associatively, usually with a baseline of ongoing instrumental behaviour as a reference point.

As mentioned previously, there have been other behavioural conceptions of elation. For example, Millenson (1967) suggests that it is the change in responding brought about by a signalled or unsignalled noncontingent reinforcer; and Meyer and McHose (1968) see elation as an increase in response vigour (in comparison with control groups) brought about by an increase in contingent reward. However, given the definition proposed by Strongman *et al.*, then the various forms of elation depend on parameters of reward change. Reward change can be: (1) contingent or noncontingent; (2) signalled or unsignalled; (3) the same or different in quantity or quality from that which went before. In combination, these three possibilities lead to eight methods of changing reward.

Strongman *et al.* examine studies which appear under each of these eight conditions, and which have used ongoing instrumental baselines against which to assess any emotional effects. These include investigations of the CER using the 'elational' paradigms and those within an Amselian framework but involving upward shifts rather than downward shifts in GBI reward. Also discussed are CER studies of anger and behaviour contrast (for example Reynolds 1961).

On the basis of their analyses the authors can show only putative conclusions. An upward shift in reward does have immediate emotional effects on ongoing behaviour, but sometimes this takes the form of an enhancement or facilitation (for example Herrnstein and Morse 1957) and sometimes impairment or suppression (for example Bower 1962; Wookey and Strongman 1971). However, they also argue that the depressive effects sometimes produced by these procedures may be in accord with everyday notions of elation, since excitement and euphoria can be facilitatory *or* disruptive. They suggest that the term elation should be restricted to procedures and not to effects; then the effects produced by the individual procedures should be studied—a view which points to the need for parametric studies in this field and indeed in the area of emotional behaviour in general. As has been constantly evident in this chapter, many of the existing studies are difficult to compare since they have varied in so many experimental or procedural details.

CONCLUSIONS

Finally, it should be apparent that the topic of emotion studied from a behavioural viewpoint is a relatively new area which at present is producing a great deal of empirical research. It is progressing on three fronts, which can be broadly conceived as emphasizing: (1) emotionality and perseverative effects of various (usually aversive) stimuli; (2) further research within a Hullian framework which has recently become narrowed to an analysis of effects found in the double runway and its analogues (although with ideas such as Hammond's this narrowing tendency may reverse); (3) Skinnerian based studies on conditioned emotional responding. However, it is equally apparent that behavioural analyses of emotion have added little in the way of theory. Any theories which have appeared do not apply to the whole field and are deficient in one or more respects. Other than Millenson's model, there is no general theory of emotion which places emphasis on behaviour. There is clearly scope for one.

6
Emotional Development

Research into emotional development is a mixture of very well conceived and very poorly conceived studies. Broadly, the division is between investigations and ideas involving animal subjects and those involving humans. For the most part, the recent animal studies are well controlled, methodologically reliable and provide interesting ideas. Equally, with some exceptions, the human studies are of questionable methodology and illuminate very little, often being not much more than slight extensions of commonplace ideas.

Generally, human-based studies of emotional development are characterized by a lack of definition and precision. Terms such as anxiety, fear, love, aggression and emotionality are bandied about with few attempts to operationalize them. They are used mentalistically and come to connote a great deal—denotatively they are lacking. Even with the better quality animal research, one question always intrudes—how relevant for the important issue of human emotional development is an analysis of infrahuman emotional development? Few would deny the inherent importance of research with animals, but on theoretical or practical grounds an understanding of the emotional development of children would seem to take priority.

There is far more animal than human research into emotional development. This has created a double-edged situation. Were the work with children better, it would be useful to have more of it; as things are, its proliferation would be of small benefit. One reason for the paucity of work at the human level, presuming it is not simply due to a lack of interest, may be concerned with the difficulty of study. It can be argued that emotion is simply one aspect of all behaviour; at the level of everyday observation, this would seem likely. Emotional development then becomes difficult to study in any way distinct from the remainder of development. Investigations with children have often been from the viewpoint that changes in emotional behaviour may account for other developmental phenomena. Rather than dealing satisfactorily with the problem, this may just be pushing it one stage further back.

Overall, the field of emotional development is in a mess. It is unsystematized and, indeed, it is difficult to impose any system on it. Unfortunately, an attempt at integration is not a matter (as was once thought) of considering in turn each of the 'emotions' and what we know of its development. It is a question of putting together some widely differing approaches involving a broad range of species and including research strategies ranging from abysmal to, if not exactly ideal, then quite good. One way of achieving this is to retain the human/animal distinction and to discuss representative samples of the work and ideas within each category.

CHILDREN

Apart from Watson's (1930) observations of fear, rage and love in children, Bridges (1932) set the scene for the study of emotional development. Her analysis is summarized in Figure 9. She considered that a child is born capable of showing

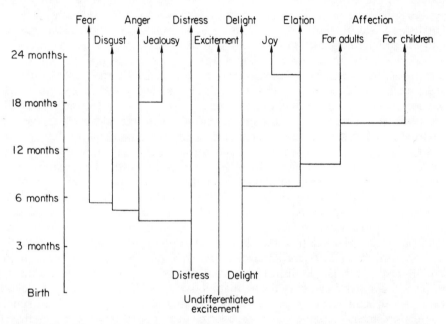

Figure 9. Bridges' scheme of emotional development (adapted from Bridges 1932).

only undifferentiated excitement, which by the age of three months or so has become differentiated into positive and negative aspects—delight and distress. Following this, she suggested that there is increasing differentiation until about two years of age, when the child displays most of the complex adult emotions. Although this seems to be a very neat schema, Bridges' data were based on observations rather than experimentation, her definitions were inadequate and she paid scant attention to neonate behaviour. This last point is well made by Schneirla (1959), with whom it is worth comparing Bridges (see below).

In spite of these objections to Bridges' work, it provoked a series of similar investigations. Some good examples of these are summarized in Singer and Singer (1969), who build their discussion of emotional development on the reasonable if subjective foundation that a child experiences pleasure and displeasure which are caused either by internal processes or by external stimuli. However, it is in considering the relevant empirical evidence that confusion is met.

Smiling and crying

The two emotional responses most studied in young children are smiling and crying. These are presumed to be representative of pleasure and displeasure. Research into smiling has mainly been concerned with the degree to which it is learned or innate. If a very young infant is handled he will usually smile; this is thought to point to some innate component. On the other hand, at a fairly early age he will smile when he sees a human face, which seems unlikely to be an innate response. Salzen (1963) provides a good example of the typical research into the smiling response. In observing one child he found that it first smiled to an external stimulus at seven weeks of age ('smiles' which appear earlier than this are usually regarded as facial grimaces caused by internal discomfort). By eight weeks, Salzen's subject was smiling quite distinctly and to a human face; this may, of course, have been due to a maturational process. However, the child was then shown three, 13 inch cardboard ovals, one white, one black and one white with a black rim. The child smiled at them all, particularly if they were moved about, a response which was maintained over many presentations, independently of the order in which the child was shown the stimuli. After the eleventh week, he was more likely to smile in response to speech or to noisy, moving stimuli than to anything else. Salzen concluded that smiling in infants can be produced by any type of change in contrast or brightness. (In passing, it is interesting to conjecture whether or not this response is in any way akin to the following response which forms the basis of imprinting—see below.)

Both Ambrose (1961) and Brackbill (1958), for example, suggested that the smiling response is largely learnt. Ambrose showed that smiling tends to appear earlier in children raised at home than those raised in institutions. Brackbill extinguished smiling in three-and-a-half to four-and-a-half year olds by simple nonreinforcement—although this, of course, does not *necessarily* mean that it was learnt to begin with. On the other hand, Spitz and Wolf (1946) argued that the smiling response is innate, since an infant will smile at face-like configurations from a very early age. There is a good deal of this sort of research and conjecture —it has only been sampled here—but it allows little in the way of definitive statements. However, as with all heredity/environment questions, the conclusion is that they interact.

Research into infant crying has followed much the same course as that for smiling, with the general conclusion that there is a large innate component to it, but one which is capable of easy modification by experience. At one time it was thought that crying in the very young would only occur to noxious (pain-producing) stimuli. However, a number of studies have shown that from quite an early age various nonpainful stimuli which are presumed to bring about anxiety and fear may also instigate crying. West and Farber (1960) provide a good example. They investigated a girl who was congenitally analgesic. Her disability was such that at the age of two she was breaking limbs with equanimity and by the age of seven she was almost blind from rubbing her eyes whilst they were open. No sources of what would normally be regarded as extreme stimulation made her cry. However, she did show negative emotional reactions to a tongue depressor, which had often made her gag; and she would cry when spanked by her mother. Presumably she was not physically hurt by the spanking, although it may have represented a discriminative stimulus for the withdrawal of positive reinforcement.

Thus the negative, displeasure side of infantile emotion also allows no definitive statements to be made. Like the positive aspects, it has necessarily been bedevilled by the nature/nurture question. Indeed, in the case of crying it would seem likely that two distinct responses are involved. The first to appear is respondent crying—a reflexive type of response to stimuli of pain or discomfort (for example hunger). Operant crying would seem to appear a little later in the course of development—here the response is clearly dependent on its consequences (for example receiving adult attention). Many parents believe that they can easily distinguish between the sounds of these two types of crying. It is reasonable to suppose that respondent crying is innately determined. Also, although it never entirely disappears, it would seem to lead to the development of operant crying which is then under environmental control.

Deprivation

Throughout the last 25 years many comparisons have been made of the development of children raised in institutions and that of children raised under the usual family conditions (for example Bowlby 1951; 1953; 1960; Spitz and Wolf 1946; Yarrow 1964). This work is clearly related to that of Harlow on chimpanzees (see below). It has generally been claimed that in comparison with their more fortunate peers, institutionalized children are often intellectually impaired and emotionally flat, even to the extent of showing 'anaclitic depression'. However, these claims are often not justified by the research on which they are based, and the studies themselves are frequently of dubious methodology. Be this as it may, there have been various proposals to account for the possible effects of early deprivation. Some of these ideas and investigations are relevant to an understanding of emotional development.

The most frequently suggested aetiological argument in this field stresses the significance of breaking the social/emotional tie which exists between a parent (particularly the mother) and a child. This tie is regarded as rooted in the initial feeding situation, although Harlow's (for example 1970) work extends the limits of this idea where ethically it would not be possible with human subjects. Schaffer (1958), for example, demonstrated what he termed over-dependency in infants who by chance had been removed from their homes and then returned after varying periods of time. If removal occurred before they were seven months old then they were simply depressed, staring 'anxiously' at everything. Similarly, Yarrow (1964) suggested that by six months of age, 86 per cent of the infants he studied were showing serious emotional disturbance following permanent separation from their mothers. Bowlby (1960) went further and suggested that an emotional reaction may occur within a few hours if separation is experienced within the latter half of the first year of life. He argued that this is expressed by frequent crying and depression, and even happens to a limited extent if the parents go out for a few hours and the child remains with babysitters. Bowlby maintains that the child in this situation has been emotionally hurt by his parents and may therefore be hostile to them when they return.

A permanent separation quite commonly experienced by young children results from adoption. Scott (1968) suggests that any adverse effects of adoption depend more on breaking the old relationship than beginning the new. He believes, basing this largely on evidence from animal studies (see later), that once the primary social relationship has developed—by about seven months in children—then there is a fear reaction to strangers. This in turn increases the likelihood of a more severe reaction to adoption. Thus, adoption is best pursued before this age, since, according to Scott, if it is not maladaptive 'emotional damage' may occur.

There is then support for the idea that emotional disturbance may result from the breaking, even temporarily, of ties with familiar individuals and places. It is likely that temporal factors are important in this, but it is as yet unclear in exactly what way. Any effects must also depend on such variables as the type of relationship which existed beforehand. At the animal level, the significance of early experience for later emotional development has led to the emotionality hypothesis (Levine 1956; Denenberg 1962—see later).

Aggression

In recent years, there has been much speculation about childhood aggression. The viewpoint of the ethologists has been frequently taken over: that within us there are reservoirs of aggression which build up due to certain environmental circumstances. If this is not given expression, then it may well overflow in an apparently pointless direction. This is speculation and is perhaps best ignored. On the other hand, aggression is one aspect of emotion and its development must be of significance. As an example of the type of investigation which has been made into the development of aggression, the relevant parts of Sears' *et al.* (1957) famous study on child-rearing will be discussed. (For a good general analysis of the concept of aggression, see Singer 1971.)

Sears *et al.* define aggression in mammals as behaviour intended to hurt or injure someone and suggest that this may take the form of fighting or the expression of rage. Their definition emphasizes *intent*, which places it outside the realms of objectivity. However, given this definition, it is clear that aggression will be modified and attenuated by the process of socialization.

In particular, Sears *et al.* stress the place of anxiety in the development of aggression in children. They suggest that a common parental response to a child's aggression is to meet it with more aggression. In fact, from their surveys they gained the impression that children are punished more for aggression than for any other behaviour. Sears *et al.* suggest that one of the consequences of punishment is anxiety, and that throughout childhood anxiety *may* therefore become attached to aggression. This, in turn, will become modified to a 'mental sensation' of unease whenever an aggressive impulse is felt. Hence, by adulthood, we willingly tolerate neither our own aggression nor that of others—which, of course, is highly appropriate to the smooth running of society. In parallel to this, the child develops techniques for dealing with punishment. Thus, punishment does not stop the impulse to aggression, it simply makes it more selective. Finally, Sears *et al.* suggest that extreme punishment *increases* aggression since it is thought to induce more frustration in the child.

As an adjunct to this analysis, Sears *et al.* studied the effect of maternal permissiveness towards aggression, and found, not surprisingly, high permissiveness to be associated with high aggression. However, although these ideas are interesting and fit well with intuitive ideas of childhood aggression, as Sears *et al.* admit, they are based entirely on ratings of punishment, aggression, etc., made by mothers; such ratings might be open to any kind of bias. Also, in their theoretical analysis, Sears *et al.* make use of many concepts such as anxiety and frustration which, if anything, are more difficult to define than aggression itself. However, in spite of this, the general approach to the development and socialization of aggression is well worth pursuing.

Internalization and emotional development

The concept of internalization embodies an even more mentalistic approach to human emotional development than those considered so far, and also extends Sears' work on aggression. It rests on the idea that anxiety becomes associated with punished behaviour. On future occasions, this anxiety may suppress the behaviour (thereby reducing the anxiety). If a child learns to suppress some aspects of his behaviour without any obvious external intervention, then he is said to have internalized the behaviour of stopping himself from doing something. Hence, emotional changes mediated by cognitive evaluations are believed to form the basis of self-regulatory behaviour through internalization.

Internalization refers to a child's learning of what we normally term self-control through the cognitive aspects of emotional changes (cf. Skinner 1953). From the subjective point of view, this means that either pleasure or fear and anxiety become attached to everyday acts, which of course lead to reward and punishment. It is thought that these positive or negative emotions can then become associated with a child's understanding, i.e. cognition, of a situation. In putting forward this argument, Aronfreed (1968) concludes that the child may become happy or afraid when he *thinks* of doing something, before he actually does it.

Some aspects of the results of a well-conducted experiment by Parke and Walters (1967) are regarded as bearing on Aronfreed's ideas. They divided six to seven year old children into four main groups depending on the time and manner in which they were to be punished. Punishment consisted of verbal castigation and unpleasant noise for choosing a toy which they were led to believe was actually meant for another child. Punishment either occurred early (when they started to reach for the toy) or late (after they had picked it up). After training, the toys which had been associated with punishment were placed on a table and covered with a cloth; the child was left alone with them for 15 minutes. Those children who had been punished early picked up the toys from the table less often, waited longer before they did so, and if they handled them at all did so for less time. This can be interpreted as supporting the hypothesis that early punishment leads to greater internalized suppression of behaviour. However, all that can be firmly concluded is that suppression of behaviour occurred. It is a result similar to that obtained from conditioned suppression studies in animals.

Aronfreed (1968) extends his theory by emphasizing that for internalization to come about all a child need do is experience some emotional change in connection with some behaviour; this may happen simply through observation. In stressing the importance of imitation he suggests that a child imitates as a result of the pleasure he has gained from observing the model. Hence, feeling good becomes associated with his perceptions and cognitions of the model. Aronfreed considers cognitions to be crucial since they allow the self-control which the child exerts over his own emotions to expand. He can remember his social experiences and those memories will have emotional components. So he comes to be able to represent to himself, and hence anticipate, reward and punishment. In the end, he is acting to produce 'good' feelings and to avoid producing 'bad' feelings. This general thesis is very similar to Arnold's (for example 1970a; 1970b) ideas of appraisal and affective memory.

Another aspect of Aronfreed's (1968) concept of internalization accords well with the possible significance for emotional development of initial social attachments. Internalization is thought to presuppose an initial attachment to some person (although, in passing, it might be noted that such was not the case in Parke and Walters' study). This implies that the threat of withdrawal of love or nurturance from the child is important to emotional change and development. Self-criticism is the internalization of this; the child is taking away 'love' from himself. A study by Grusec (1966) exemplifies the empirical approach to self-criticism. Five and six year old children were divided into three groups. Initially, an experimenter either: (1) played with them and was friendly and approving (i.e. showed a high degree of warmth); or (2) mainly ignored them (i.e. showed a low degree of warmth); or (3) showed a high degree of warmth and then withdrew it. A game was rigged to go wrong. Each child was led to believe that it was his fault, after which he was then questioned to determine the extent to which he was self-critical. In general, the children were judged to be more self-critical if the experimenter had been warm towards them, but this self-criticism only generalized to a new situation if the experimenter had also shown withdrawal of affection.

In a final extension of his argument, Aronfreed suggests that a child learns to reduce the cognitive force of unpleasant emotions by being self-critical. Thus, the rejected or neglected child will have no love to lose, will not become self-critical and may therefore end as a delinquent. In Aronfreed's terms, a child behaves so as to maintain his emotional bonds.

To summarize, Aronfreed suggests that emotional development is dependent on the process of internalization. Thus, the child learns to control his own behaviour by paying attention to the cognitive aspects of his emotion. Emotional change may come about through direct experience or by the child's imitations of rewarding models. So, internalization is more likely to occur if the young child has formed a good social bond with some adult. This way of analysing emotional development is an odd mixture of a concentrated cognitive approach and a somewhat dilute behavioural theory. The cognitive elements are often untestable and the behavioural aspects are often undeveloped. It would perhaps be more useful if the cognitive arguments gave way to a clearer behavioural exposition.

The biology of emotional development

It is appropriate to complete this consideration of the emotional development of children with a brief analysis of the biological or physiological approach to the subject, since in many ways it is representative of the most interesting ideas and best-conducted research in the field. Again, the tendency has been, and still is, to build on somewhat shaky foundations. To take an example from a modern and supposedly psychobiological psychologist:

'... early childhood is a time of feeling rather than knowing.'

'Emotion is, indeed, the driving force that enables the organism to overcome or circumvent a block to dissatisfaction.'

(Nash 1970, pp. 327 and 307.)

In fact, the biological approach to emotional development rests on the idea that to begin with emotion is only associated with physiological need—the infant cries when it is hungry or cold. In other words, emotion (or at least negative emotion) is said to be experienced when a drive state is blocked.

Bousfield and Orbison (1952) appear to have initiated two quite profitable lines of speculation concerning the ontogenesis of emotional behaviour. These rest on two assumptions. (1) A neonate is functionally decorticate; cortical control becomes increasingly apparent throughout development. (2) They suggest that infants are partially lacking in hormones which are important to stress reactions.

The cortex and its interrelationships with the thalamus have often been implicated in emotion (see Chapter 3). There is little 'downwards' inhibitory influence in the brain at birth. This should mean that the emotional responses of children are similar to those of animals, since as adults the latter are comparatively lacking in cortex. In turn, this suggests that emotions in children, although quickly aroused, do not stay aroused for long. They dissipate rather than persisting or reverberating. This certainly is in accord with everyday observations. Bronson (1965) even goes to the lengths of seeing infantile emotions as mediated mainly in the brain-stem reticular activating system, thus resulting in a generalized arousal which is not oriented towards any particular goal, a view which is reminiscent of Bridges (1932) and also of Schneirla (1959). (It should be noted here, however, that there are 'downward' CNS influences in animals and there is little evidence that their emotions are easily aroused.)

Emotional states are thought to increase in vigour with age (cf. Hebb 1949), and this vigour is thought to be largely due to the influence of the adrenal glands. The development of the adrenal glands themselves seems to follow an odd course. By the time the child is two they have decreased to half their weight at birth, following which they rapidly increase in weight up to about five years, increase more slowly until 11 and then accelerate until 20. It is not until the age of about 16 that they are back to their birth weight. Presumably, output is associated with weight. Although it is mainly the adrenal medulla which is growing throughout this time, the adrenal cortex is known to be essential to life and important for controlling prolonged reactions to stress. Also, there are differences in the secretions of the adrenal cortex between childhood and adulthood, although what exactly these differences are is unclear. Overall, this relationship can only be tentatively suggested.

Funkenstein et al. (1957) provide the most detailed hormone-based ideas on the development of emotion. From the fact that the adrenal medulla secretes both epinephrine and norepinephrine, they suggest that the former is related to passive, nonaggressive reactions to stress (and predominates in the rabbit for example) and the latter to solitary, aggressive reactions (and predominates in the lion for example). On the basis of their studies, Funkenstein et al. also argue that amongst humans there are two sorts of anger. There is that of the anger-inners (who bottle up everything and blame themselves—a predominance of epinephrine), and that of the anger-outers (who show anger and blame others—a predominance of norepinephrine). They also claim that in childhood there is always a preponderance of norepinephrine, which by adulthood has either balanced out with epinephrine or still carries greater weight. It should be pointed out that, although of considerable interest, these ideas are highly speculative.

Cleary, Funkenstein et al. seem to be stressing physiological maturation and individual differences in their account of emotional development. They are tracing much the same line as Aronfreed, although in a different manner and with different emphases. However, they also argue that anger-inners and anger-outers tend to experience different upbringings, which of course puts us more squarely into the learning camp. They regard anger-outers as having parents with whom they identify. Their mother provides them with affection and their father is an angry authoritarian. The anger-inners have good relationships with both parents; there is little difference in parental authority, but the mother is again the more affectionate. These ideas are all based on retrospective, questionnaire studies, the results of which have led Funkenstein even further into speculative realms. An acceptable way of testing them is not immediately apparent.

Conclusions

From this sample of the literature on emotional development in children, one can say that there is more discussion than hard data and that any empirical information has often been gathered in ways which are open to criticism. Although there are some common threads, systematization is difficult. However, it is possible to draw a few tentative conclusions. (1) Emotional development depends on a combination of genetic and environmental factors. The genetic factors seem to be reflected in the maturation of the cortex and endocrine system. A central environmental influence would appear to be the child's first relationships with significant adults in its life. (2) Throughout childhood, there may be increasing differentiation of the emotions. This might simply involve the continuous refinement of the labels which a child is taught to use in describing his emotional states. (3) Like any other aspect of emotion, its development can be viewed from a cognitive and/or a physiological and/or a behavioural viewpoint.

ANIMALS

Research into the emotional development of infrahuman species is more abundant than human research and more capable of systematic discussion. The approaches which have gelled over the years range from investigations of genetic factors and heritability, through ethological and physiological analyses of the nature/nurture problem, to theories, research and applications of the concepts of early emotionality and infantile affection.

Heritability and emotionality

Research into heritability and emotion rests on two assumptions. (1) There are differences in emotionality or emotional reactivity between individuals. (2) Some variations in behaviour are due to genetic variation. Here, the term emotion is in a context of biological adaptivity, referring to processes concerned with both self- and species-preservation, these being the usual fighting, escaping or avoiding, eating, reproducing and caring for the young. The emphasis is on 'instinctual' species-typical behaviour. Bruell (1970) distinguishes between the genetic determination of a behavioural trait and its heritability. Some inter-species differences in behaviour are genetically determined. But whether or not behavioural differences within a species are due to genetic variation, namely, heritability, is a question which must be answered empirically.

This argument has led to the development of two procedures designed to investigate the effects of heritability on emotionality. Each of these will be exemplified by one study. First, there is that strategy which involves breeding animals selectively so as to minimize or maximize particular behavioural characteristics. Hall (1951) placed each of 145 rats in a bright circular enclosure for two minutes per day. Any urination or defecation in this enclosure led to a score of +1 for that day. After 12 days, high-scoring animals were mated with one another, as also were those with low scores. Similar separations were made in succeeding generations. In the original sample, the mean defecation score was 3·86. After 12 generations, the mean score for the group of 'emotional' rats was 10·4 and that for the 'non-emotional' group was 1·65. Clearly, if defecation in a strange environment is accepted as an index of emotionality, as it sometimes has been (see Chapter 5), then emotionality must have been heritable in Hall's original rat population.

The other main research strategy in the study of heritability involves comparisons between inbred strains of animals. Bruell (1965), for example, investigated 'timidity' in 1500 mice by using a tunnel-emergence test. The mice would be placed singly into a narrow, eight inch long tunnel which opened into a rectangular, lighted, open box. Bruell found significant differences in the times which it took different strains of mice to emerge from the tunnel to the box. He interpreted this as indicating that one strain was more timid, or emotional, than the other and that in consequence it is possible to infer that timidity must have been heritable in the original parent population. Although Bruell (1970) supports this with closely reasoned genetic/mathematical arguments, his data are open to other possible interpretations. His mice may have been fortuitously bred with different visual capacities for example, which might lead them to show behavioural variations such as those described.

The use of these two fundamental techniques has produced research into the heritability of many types of behaviour. For the present three of these will be mentioned to illustrate the point. In their analysis of aggressive behaviour, Scott and Fuller (1965) maintain that there are huge differences between the aggressiveness of various breeds of dog, which for centuries have been bred more or less selectively. Also Guhl et al. (1960) found differences by the second generation when selectively breeding aggressive and nonaggressive chickens. Secondly, with respect to what might loosely be termed affection, Hess (1959) managed to selectively breed in one generation high and low imprinters. (See below.) Finally, Hale and Schein (1962) found a sevenfold difference in the frequency with which turkeys mated after nine generations of selective breeding. As Bruell (1970) points out, this last is an odd result (although it does not stand alone) since sexual behaviour might be expected not to be heritable. Natural selection must work in favour of the better reproducer, and time should therefore have dispensed with any inappropriate sexual behaviour generations ago; any variation should by now be of environmental origin. On the other hand, such a result is less surprising if it can be assumed that one mating every so often is enough to produce all the eggs that a female turkey can lay.

There has been much research demonstrating the heritability of many different forms of emotional behaviour; those mentioned here have simply been examples. However, one overall point is that all the studies have shown quantitative differences. The same emotional behaviour has been observed within a species but at different thresholds. Emotional reactions appear to be species-typical; within any species any differences are never qualitative.

Innate fear

The problem of innate fear is given special mention for two reasons. (1) Because there is always much conjecture (although little useful research) about built-in fears in children. (2) It highlights the broader controversy over the nature/nurture question which existed for many years between ethologists and psychologists. Recently, however, there has been something of a rapprochement in that heredity and environment are seen as interacting, one being clearly unable to exist without the other.

The discussion of innate fear began with reports from a number of ethologists (see Thorpe 1956) that many birds that are nest-reared show fear if a cardboard shape representative of a flying bird of prey (usually regarded as a hawk) is passed over them. When its direction of 'flight' is reversed, that is it becomes long of neck and short of tail, no fear is shown. The usual argument has been that this apparent fear remains intense over some time during the birds' early life, in the absence of any obvious reinforcement. Stress has most commonly been put on an 'innate' explanation (i.e. there exists a 'blueprint' for a hawk) but with little information on the precise conditions of the early environment.

In order to clear the ground a little, Melzack et al. (1959) carried out a more exact study of this phenomenon. They raised a group of mallard ducks in a very restricted environment for 25 days after hatching. They were housed in individual cages with the only visual outlet being upwards. Throughout this time they were presented with 'hawk' or 'goose' models. In a series of tests conducted after day 25, it was found that ducks which had had such experiences were *less* fearful than those which had not. (Fear was defined as either high-level excitement, short jerky movements, wing-flapping and shrill sounds, or avoidance, running as far as the cage space permitted, flapping and vocalizing as they went.) When the object was moving fast, there was more fear of the 'hawk', otherwise there was not. The exception to this was that ducks raised in restricted conditions initially showed more fear of the 'hawk'. However, under all conditions, any fear tended to dissipate (habituate) rapidly.

It is worth noting that Schneirla (1959) suggests that these effects are due to differences in the intensity of the stimulation generated by the two directions of travel. However, Melzack et al. interpret their results as generally supporting the idea of some innate component to the fear. But they also suggest that *any novel* stimulus produces fear. They regard the 'hawk' fear as emerging from what is initially a great variety of fears of new objects, with inherited mechanisms favouring the continuation of this fear whilst others habituate more rapidly. Their results, however, definitely point to the importance of environmental factors.

Critical periods

By now, there is an extensive literature on critical periods in development, imprinting and early experience in general, although not all of it is relevant to emotional development. Moreover, these three topics are intertwined; for example, it is impossible to consider the evidence concerning critical periods without going on to the broader question of early experience. However, for the sake of convenience, they are separated in this discussion.

Scott (for example 1967; 1968) has done much to further the importance of the concept of the critical period in development. The evidence from his work with dogs revolves around the notion of there being, early in life, a critical period for socialization, during which the animal is maximally sensitive to social stimuli. Scott maintains that a young puppy shows 'distress vocalizations' when it is removed from the objects and/or situations which it has experienced during its critical period. This emotional distress can only be relieved by the presence of other puppies or familiar surroundings. Scott regards this as a simple innate response. More important, he views it as a response which *maintains* an attachment to another member of the species. This thesis leads to the prediction that if other negative emotions are produced an intensification of the attachment should result.

Scott takes his argument one stage further by suggesting that many animals form emotional attachments to certain familiar physical surroundings—a phenomenon he terms *primary localization*. For example, he suggests that young puppies form these attachments very soon after their eyes open. Support for this is derived from marked changes in their 'yelp' rate if put into a strange environment. Scott believes this also to be the case with human infants, although any evidence for human critical periods is sketchy to say the very least.

Scott is more tentative when discussing the possible effects of these early emotional experiences on later behaviour. He supposes that safety and security might be felt when a return is made to a familiar area or individual. If a young human infant is put into a strange locality for a time, then he may (1) always associate this locality with unpleasantness (which could, of course, be straightforwardly seen as classical conditioning), and (2) become even more positively attached to his more familiar environment.

The concept of critical periods will be evaluated later, when exploring the general effects of early experience.

Imprinting

Imprinting refers to the formation of specific attachments by young precocial birds. It is generally regarded as developing from approach and following responses and not to be simply explicable by recourse to the principles of conditioning. (Although it should be noted that the capacity to be reinforced is greatly enhanced by proximity to the source of reinforcement.) The usual example of imprinting involves a young chick which follows the first moving object which it encounters—normally the mother. However, in numerous studies the young of various species have been induced to follow virtually anything, from wooden blocks to rows of lights that become illuminated in rapid succession. In the limiting case, even approach and following do not seem to be crucial for imprinting to take place; it is merely necessary for the young animal to see an apparently moving object. However, the basic conditions are as have been outlined, immediately suggesting the (biological adaptivity) conclusion that under 'natural' conditions imprinting is a highly appropriate way for the young of a species to become attached to older members, on whom they are anyway dependent.

Imprinting is regarded as occurring during a critical period. Much of the creative endeavour which has been put into the study of imprinting has been directed towards providing theories to account for the *end* of this sensitive period. These theories can be reduced to four main possibilities. (For a fuller analysis of these theories and a description and analysis of imprinting in general see Sluckin 1964.) (1) Sensitivity ends with maturation. (2) Sensitivity is inhibited through socialization. (3) Sensitivity ends with the growth of timidity. (4) Sensitivity ends because a state of low anxiety also ends. The first theory simply suggests that the ending of the critical period depends on innate, internal factors. This is difficult to refute entirely, although some studies have shown that critical periods can be extended (see Sluckin 1964). The second theory is perhaps more self-evident. It implies that the sensitive period for imprinting ends when imprinting has occurred. This has some support. However, the last two theories are of more relevance to emotion and will therefore be considered in more detail.

Timidity/fear

Within the context of imprinting, fear is variously viewed as immobility or flight, or as a response to sudden, intense stimuli or to particular species-specific stimuli. There is evidence from studies on young birds that some objects (for example food) sometimes produce approach responses, others (for example humans) sometimes produce fear responses, and others (for example other members of the species) sometimes produce both (see for example Hinde *et al.* 1956). Often the birds have been observed to be apparently in the throes of an approach/avoidance conflict.

This sort of fear is not seen in a newly hatched bird but only appears after a day or two, gradually developing thereafter. It is this which led to the view expressed by both Hinde (1955) and Hess (1959; 1962a; 1962b) that this fear gradually inhibits any approaching and following, since the overwhelming responses to new objects become freezing or flight. However, it is not as simple as this.

Sluckin (1960) suggests that an animal may develop a fear of fluctuating stimulus patterns and a fear of a static environment. Together, these lead him to conclude that strangeness is the main determinant of fear (cf. Salzen 1962; Schaller and Emlen 1962). Thus, new objects or new grounds are accepted to the extent that an animal is familiar with them. Also, the longer spent in any environment, the stranger will be any new environment. If the environment is strange and one part of it (the figure) is familiar, then Sluckin (1964) regards the environment as 'pushing' the animal to the figure. If the figure is unfamiliar, following is inhibited, while fear of the ground promotes following. Fear of the environment can either occur through strangeness or can be conditioned. Either way, the animal fearing the environment will move towards the figure. In support of this, Moltz *et al.* (1959) showed that shock-conditioned fear of a runway increased the strength of an already imprinted following response. Fear may also arise from too intense or insufficient stimulation—loud noises, bright lights or darkness, solitude—otherwise early fears are of novel or strange stimuli (for example Melzack 1952; Salzen 1962).

Sluckin (1964) suggests that the recognition of strangeness depends on experience rather than simple maturation; to run from something strange there must have developed enough 'knowledge' to perceive it as strange. There are many reports in the imprinting literature that initially there is no fear in very young birds, for example for the first 24 hours in chicks. Hence, imprinting can take place before objects are strange enough to be feared. Also, there are many observations that a bird will later follow an object which was originally feared, although Hess (1959) does not believe that animals become imprinted to such objects. In fact, fear seems to develop with imprinting and then, after imprinting is complete, to lead to the development of withdrawal from strange stimuli.

Anxiety

In this context, to distinguish it from fear, anxiety tends to be defined as a general fearfulness in the absence of any obvious stimuli. Not surprisingly, the proposed indicants of anxiety are difficult to distinguish from the proposed indicants of fear—perhaps the concepts themselves are not easily or usefully separated.

Moltz (1960) is the main exponent of the anxiety view. He suggests that the young imprinting bird is in a state of low anxiety, but at the same time is very receptive to the sight of moving objects. In Moltz's terms, this may lead to the object in question inducing a drive state. (This follows from Mowrer's (1939) view of anxiety being acquired in an avoidance-learning situation and then its subsequent reduction motivating new learning.) Moltz argues that a newly-hatched chick comes to associate a (rewarding) state of low anxiety with a moving object. In turn, the object comes to act as a reinforcer which can mediate new learning. Following and imprinting occur because they bring the chick nearer to this reinforcer. So Moltz maintains that the critical period for imprinting ends when the state of low anxiety ends.

Salzen and Tomlin (1963) take a slightly different view; they suggest that the sight of the moving object *produces* the state of low anxiety—there is an initial fearlessness simply because imprinting has not yet occurred. This question is not yet resolved, nor is it known whether or not imprinting is explicable in emotional/learning theory terms or is a quite independent process. However, as can be seen above, some facts and ideas about some aspects of emotional development have emerged from its study.

Early experience and emotionality

The typical procedure in studies of the effects of early experience on later emotionality involves subjecting animals as young as possible to conditions such as handling by the experimenter or electric shock. After this, they are reared individually under standard laboratory conditions. As adults they are tested in situations believed to allow a measure of emotionality, the 'open-field' test for example (see Chapter 5). The degree to which they behave emotionally is compared with that of untreated control animals. The degree to which control subjects are untreated is a determinant of how firmly any conclusions can be drawn.

An important theorist in this field is Denenberg (see particularly 1964). His thesis begins with an attack on Scott's (1962; 1968) ideas concerning critical periods. Scott implies that there are *limited* periods during development when certain stimulation has profound effects. Before and after this period the effects are more restricted. However, studies designed to test this idea (mainly involving mice, rats and dogs) have not often shown positive results. Denenberg maintains that the only hard evidence in support of the critical period concept comes from studies which used physiological measures (for example Levine and Lewis 1959). His argument is based on an analysis of many studies, including his own. He suggests that any purported critical period is an artifactual result of stimulus intensity, both within the early experience and during the adult tests. Consequently, by chance or by a conscious manipulation of stimulus intensity as an independent variable, an investigator could easily find evidence for what looks like a critical period but which is, in fact, not. Experiments involving shock in infancy and later avoidance learning (in mice) and handling and gentling and later emotionality (in rats) do *not* support the critical period hypothesis. Denenberg suggests the advisability of concentrating on the relationship between various classes of independent and dependent variables between birth and weaning, rather than trying to isolate critical periods—a view reminiscent of Yarrow's (1961) on maternal deprivation and Anastasi's (1958) on the nature/nurture problem.

Denenberg then considers the problem of finding a common factor in studies of the effects of early stimulation. He suggests that any stimulation between birth and weaning reduces 'emotional reactivity'. The greater the infantile stimulation, the less the emotionality in adulthood. Thus Denenberg's main hypothesis:

> '... *emotional reactivity is reduced as a monotonic function of amount of stimulus input in infancy*'

(1964, p. 338, italics his.)

There are a number of lines of evidence which support this general proposition, although they are usually concerned with either handling or shock. For example, rats that are handled more in infancy, as adults are more active and defecate less than control rats in open-field tests (for example Denenberg and Smith 1963). Rats handled and shocked in infancy and later deprived of water (such deprivation being a novel situation) drink less than controls (Levine 1957; 1958; 1959). (Of course, an increase in water intake would also have supported the 'emotionality' argument.) Or rats stimulated in infancy are bolder than unstimulated controls as adults in emergence-from-cage tests, and handled rats are less emotional than nonhandled on measures of avoidance learning. Also, in general, rats given early shock are less emotional than controls in open-field tests (Denenberg and Smith 1963). This evidence suggests that stimulation in infancy reduces adult emotional reactivity. Further, various studies imply a monotonic relationship between amount of early stimulation and later reduction in emotionality (for example Denenberg and Smith 1963; Lindholm 1962).

Denenberg (1964) takes the argument a stage further by equating emotionality with motivation, that is, the more emotional animal is more highly motivated. He also suggests that there should be an optimal level of emotionality for efficient performance. This puts us squarely in the inverted U country, which Denenberg represents as in Figure 10. This suggestion is supported by evidence from Karas

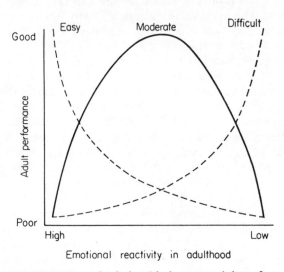

Figure 10. The proposed relationship between adult performance and emotionality for tasks of varying difficulty (taken from Denenberg 1964).

and Denenberg (1961), Denenberg and Morton (1962) and Denenberg and Kline (1964). Set against this should be the lack of more general support for this hypothetical relationship between motivation (arousal) and performance, and the inappropriateness of motivational accounts of emotion.

Finally, Denenberg admits that his data have been usually restricted to rodents that have been stimulated before weaning; weaning has been the cutoff point since all a rodent's senses are functioning by then. This would naturally make the effects of handling and shock quite different (an idea which suggests a critical period).

It is clear that Denenberg, and others such as Levine, has shown that early experience affects late behaviour. Also, emotionality appears to be a reasonably useful hypothetical construct to account for the mediation of these effects. However, the generality of early experience effects, particularly at the human level, is an open question. Few species have been studied and few sources of stimulation used. Intensity of early stimulation is likely to be an important variable, but it has appeared in few investigations and then has provided scant support for Denenberg's hypothesis suggesting a monotonic relationship between stimulus input and emotional reactivity. Finally, Denenberg argues that intensity of infantile stimulation is a major parameter affecting later differences in 'chronic' (i.e. general) level of arousal. Again, however, this is simply trying to explain one rather unwieldy concept (emotionality) by another, and in the absence of more precise definition and firm evidence should be treated with caution.

Affection, fear and aggression—Harlow

Harlow (for example Harlow and Harlow 1962; 1970) is accorded a section to himself in this discussion of emotional development, since: (1) his approach is unique; (2) he normally studies rhesus monkeys, results from which can perhaps be more meaningfully extrapolated to the human level. Harlow regards social and emotional development as being intimately connected. He suggests that there are three fundamental patterns of social response, which make their developmental appearance in the sequence: affection, fear, aggression. Anything which distorts this sequence may distort social–sexual development.

Affection

Harlow and Harlow (1962) suggest that the initial reciprocal attachment between mother and infant lays the groundwork for later social development both in subhuman primates and to a large extent in humans. At birth, rhesus monkeys reflexively cling to their mother's body, and move up it—root and suck. Harlow and Harlow believe emotional attachment to develop in the first month or two of life due to the satisfaction of hunger and comfort, warmth and support from the mother. They suggest that the grooming and caressing of their young by adult females is a reflection of reciprocal emotional satisfaction.

By the second month of life, infant monkeys evince interest in their peers. The contacts between them lengthen, turn into play and lead to the development of emotional attachments. Harlow regards this new type of attachment as growing with the decline of mother–infant attachment; it is not simply generalization. Alexander (1966, quoted by Harlow and Harlow 1970) showed that infant monkeys that have been deprived of peers are very wary when first exposed to them and never develop any strong ties with them. Harlow and Harlow (1970) then argue, but with only discursive, observational support, for the ubiquitous nature of peer affection in primates, including humans. Early on, sexual differentiation is unimportant, but after three or four months, male monkeys become progressively more dominant and females more passive. In the juvenile period (one to two years in monkeys) friendship pairs are usually like-sexed—the human parallels are clear. Harlow and Harlow suggest that culture merely emphasizes and moulds sex differences which already exist. They view peer affection as a main factor in learning effective adult social and sexual adjustment—learning the appropriate place in the group.

Fear

Harlow and Zimmerman (1959) affirm that fear in rhesus monkeys only begins after the first two months of life. They scream, cling to or run to their mothers if shown unfamiliar places, objects or humans, objects moving towards them, or unusual and loud noises. If they are separated from their mothers they cry and clasp themselves. Harlow and Harlow regard the development of fear as partially dependent on experience, since it involves perception of potential danger.

Aggression

Harlow and Harlow state that playful *attacks* are obvious from the start of social play. Free aggression towards peers does not appear until about ten to twelve months in monkeys raised in a group, but earlier in those raised in isolation. The latter also inflict worse injuries on one another. Once the dominance hierarchies have been established in socially raised monkeys, there is relative peace. Monkeys raised in isolation often show uncontrolled or undiscriminated aggression, or sometimes incapacitating fear. Harlow and Harlow conclude that affectional relationships are necessary precursors to normal social aggression, which keeps physical injury at a minimum.

Much of Harlow's research has involved social isolation. Monkeys are raised from birth in stainless-steel chambers with diffused light temperature and air control and food, water and cleaning accomplished remotely. Typically, the monkeys see *nothing* living for either three, six or twelve months, after which they are placed in individual cages and a few days later they have their first social experiences. Often, they are put together in a playroom with another isolate plus two cage-reared monkeys for half an hour per day, five days per week, for six months.

The main response to removal from isolation seems to be fear. This fits well with work on imprinting. The three-month isolates recovered (became normal) in a few days or weeks. In the six-and twelve-month animals the fear remained predominant. They did not defend themselves against attack and they did not form social attachments. In the six-months group, minimal play was observed, in the twelve-month group none. When six- and twelve-month animals of the same age were put together, the twelves were attacked by the sixes with very accentuated aggression. After these tests the monkeys spent two years in standard laboratory cages, and were then tested with strangers, either large, powerful adult monkeys, normal peers, or normal one year olds. All the experimental monkeys were terrified, but this was punctuated by isolated, extreme, violent, suicidal, aggressive attacks. It seems that the fear and aggression had intensified with time. These results perhaps point to the three-to-six-month period being critical in a monkey's development.

Further support comes from Harlow's observations that even monkeys reared with their mothers but whose peer experiences were somewhat delayed showed a measure of this fear and aggression. Also, very immature, long-lasting clinging was seen in monkeys raised with no mothers but continually in contact with peers. If four monkeys are reared together with no mother, they spend most of the time sitting clinging in a line, like carriages in a train, to use Harlow's analogy.

The emotional inadequacies in monkeys reared in isolation also extend to their sexual behaviour. The separate behaviours involved in copulation are evident, but they never become integrated into a whole unless the monkeys are taught by an 'experienced' adult. The sex drive seems to be as strong as in normal monkeys but the behaviour is typically autistic and onanistic with short bursts of aggression.

On the basis of this and similar work, Harlow and Harlow (1970) draw a number of conclusions. They believe the absence of mothering to be partially surmounted by peer associations. Also, given a mother's presence, peer deprivation can occur without much harm for quite long periods. Hence, they suggest that there are two independent but interchangeable affectional systems—that which is based on peer socialization and that which is based on mother–infant socialization. Finally, they maintain that for fear and aggression to develop 'normally', then the positive affectional system must develop *first*.

SCHNEIRLA'S THEORY OF EMOTIONAL DEVELOPMENT

Before drawing any conclusions, it is appropriate at this point to include a theory; a theory which is of emotion in general but which is clearly relevant to emotional development in particular, and which even depends on the concept of development for its structure.

Somewhat similarly to Leeper (1970), Schneirla (1959) regards perception, motivation and emotion as intricately bound together, but in ontological development. He defines emotions as:

'(1) episodes or sequences of overt and incipient somatic adjustment, (2) often loosely patterned and variable, (3) usually with concurrent exciting sensory effects, perhaps also perceptual attitudes characterisable as desirable or undesirable, pleasant or unpleasant, (4) related to the intensity effects or perceptual meaning of a stimulus, (5) synergic with organic changes of A- or W-types.'

(1959, p. 26)

Schneirla's A- and W-types are fundamental to this view of emotion. They refer to *biphasic* mechanisms of receptors, central and auxiliary nervous systems and effectors which Schneirla regards as basic to *all* ontogeny. A-type arousal is caused by weak-intensity stimuli and leads to local or general approach to the source of stimulation. W-type arousal is caused by strong-intensity stimuli and leads to local or general withdrawal.

Schneirla argues that a James–Lange type of theory may be useful for studying the early ontogeny of animals when these A- and W-type patterns overwhelm behaviour, depending on stimulus magnitude. Equally, he suggests that a Cannon–Bard approach is more germane to the later stages of emotional development, which are far more perceptual and motivational in nature.

Quite differently from Bridges (1932), Schneirla weighs the evidence concerning very early emotion and believes that it warrants the conclusion that the reactions of neonates are essentially biphasic, although the evidence which Schneirla draws on at this point is very early and quite obscure (for example Peiper 1926). Schneirla also argues that emotion and motivation are fundamentally related. He suggests that there are physiologically prescribed biphasic states, which in maturing lead to the advancement of emotion and motivation. He supports these contentions by detailed analyses of smiling and reaching. For now it is sufficient to describe his analysis of smiling.

Schneirla maintains that in mammals there are two antagonistic systems of facial muscles, one pulling the lips downwards, the other pulling them up. He cites Koehler (1954) as representing the view that the smiling pattern is innate in man, but argues that any very early smile is in fact a grimace, physiologically determined by low-intensity stimulation (see Dennis 1935; Spitz and Wolf 1946). Also, the studies cited do not suggest any unconditioned stimuli which may bring this response about. Schneirla opines that it is elicited by a *class* of stimuli, their common characteristic being low intensity. Thereafter, he believes that smiling develops through a gradual conditioning process. As noted previously, Spitz and Wolf (1946) report that the smiling response occurs to visual stimuli after three months, in particular to faces and face-like objects. Initially, smiling is general and diffuse, but gradually becomes more refined. By six months there is more definite expression which is under stimulus control, after which it indexes a discrimination between familiar and unfamiliar faces. Hence, in Schneirla's terms, there is an initial biphasic substrate which makes possible an 'approach' response to many types of low-intensity stimuli. This gradually becomes conditioned and refined to specific social situations, thereby suggesting the increasing importance of motivation and perception to emotional development.

CONCLUSIONS

The wide range of research strategies which have been used to study emotional development make it difficult to draw any firm conclusions. There has been too little research with human infants and much of what has been done is too subjective to permit concise evaluation. The biological approach perhaps provides an exception to this. On the other hand, conclusions drawn from infrahuman investigations are more justified by the less criticizable research techniques on which they are based. However, the relevance and extrapability of this work to human emotional development can only be tentatively pursued.

In general, work on animal species has been concerned with the effects of early experience, either appreciated or depreciated, on later (adult) behaviour. Often any effects have been accounted for by the idea of emotionality. It is argued that the effects of early experience ranging from handling to electric shock cause the animals involved to be less emotional (fearful) later on. Such work has pointed to the possible importance of critical periods (of maximal sensitivity to certain stimuli) to these effects. And also to the significance for emotional development of early attachments or bonds between an animal and other members of its species (usually adults). It may be that human emotional development is equally dependent on initial familial attachments. Perhaps there are critical periods which are also important at the human level, and of course a form of imprinting may even take place. There is no direct evidence for these ideas, but it is clear that those who postulate internalization as a necessary part of human emotional development rely on the quality of the early mother–child interaction in their explanations. Also, Harlow's work has done much to bridge the gap between human and animal studies based on these ideas.

At both levels of investigation, emotional development is seen to depend on an interaction between genetic and environmental influences. This is implied by studies of smiling and crying in children, and of critical periods in animals. Of course, this is little different from the position found with almost any aspect of development; there is a nature–nurture interaction. Indeed, it is often difficult to distinguish emotional development from development more broadly conceived, social development for example. It would seem likely that we are born with the capacity to respond to certain stimuli with increased general activity. From this, more specific emotional responses become refined by experience (learning). However, this may involve little more than learning to use and name (culturally) appropriate expressions in particular situations. Such learning could well be dependent on our initial social attachments and on periods of increased sensitivity in our development.

These rather speculative conclusions have some resemblance to Bridges' original ideas on emotional differentiation. It is important to bear in mind that as yet there has only been direct support for them at the observational level. However, Schachter's work with its emphasis on situational cues allowing us to label physiologically undifferentiated states has obvious relevance. Finally, it is clear that a first priority in the general field of emotional development must be for a rapprochment of the observational techniques used with children and the more experimental strategies used with animals.

7

Emotional Expression and Recognition

Since a social psychologist's main concern is with social interaction, his interest in emotion tends to be limited to its communication within a social context. He spends little time in broad considerations of emotion, but instead focuses on emotional expression on the one hand and the recognition of emotion on the other. One result of this is that he is rarely in the position to produce a grand theory of emotion, although, as we shall see, he sometimes does. However, the problems with which any study of emotional expression and recognition is fraught, and the attempts which have been made to solve them, are instructive for more general analyses of emotion. Also, of course, they are interesting in their own right.

Whenever we interact with another person, whether face-to-face or otherwise, we are continually expressing emotion. Simultaneously, we are monitoring and interpreting the other person's emotional expressions. He (or she) is doing the same. It is fair to say that it is this complex and possibly often unconscious process which gives social interaction much of its subtlety and depth. Our emotional expressions are providing stimuli to anyone with whom we might be interacting. He in turn responds to these stimuli. He observes, judges and classifies, and then perhaps engages in some 'answering' expression. It is with how we express ourselves emotionally and with how accurately we identify such expressions in others that the social psychologist has been concerned. It is worth noting here that the identifying response is not made to the emotional expression itself, but to the *meaning* behind it. For example, a frown can be an expression of emotion. It is the state which is underlying the frown which we try to interpret. A thought about the complexities of this will show that in this chapter we are dealing with a particularly awkward and difficult area of research.

Frijda, who has produced excellent reviews and analyses of this field (for example 1960; 1970), suggests that the recognition of emotion may be broken down into three aspects. He means that when we express emotion we refer to three events , and when we recognize emotion we use three systems of identifying response. (1) We recognize emotions by the *situations* in which they occur. If we are asked to describe fear, for example, we refer to some recent situation in which we 'felt' afraid. (2) Emotional expression *anticipates action*. We observe an emotional expression in another person and ask what behaviour is likely to follow it. (3) We *experience* emotion. The meaning of any expressive behaviour may be bound up in our subjective emotional experiences or attitudes. The observer may represent this experience to himself in some empathetic way, or even make fractional empathetic expressive movements himself.

The first part of this chapter will survey the major work in this area, drawing attention to some of the difficulties which have beset it and highlighting some of the better research and theory. Following this, some recent promising approaches will be mentioned. There are two points which should be borne in mind when appraising this field; in a sense they are both methodological. (1) Although we are directly within the sphere of the social psychologist, emotional expression and recognition is only one aspect of communication, and communication is also of concern to others, notably the clinician and the ethologist. Often, the research methods of such people differ from those of the social psychologist. This sometimes makes evaluation and comparison difficult. (2) The problem which any social psychologist has to face somewhat more squarely than does the 'individual' psychologist is that of artificiality. Do results gleaned from laboratory studies of social behaviour tell us very much about social behaviour in real-life settings? This problem is intensified for the investigator of emotional expression. How does he produce 'real' emotion in the laboratory? How does he measure the way in which it is judged? Is the identification process the same as that which we use from day to day? And so on.

Finally, attention is drawn to several interesting reviews of emotional expression and recognition; each has its own emphasis. Davitz (1964)—social psychological; Frijda (1969; 1970)—social psychological; Knapp (1963)—clinical; and parts of Vine (1970)—human ethological; although the thorough reader should begin with Darwin's (1872) *The Expression of Emotions in Man and Animals*.

FACIAL AND VOCAL EXPRESSION OF EMOTION

Basic research and problems

The facial expression of emotion has been studied in many ways, the main problem being the choice of stimulus material. The solution to this has varied from posed photographs (more typical of the early studies, for example Frois-Wittman 1930) or schematic drawings (for example Frijda 1956) through fully acted live expressions (for example Osgood 1966; Thompson and Meltzer 1964) to spontaneous expressions (for example Coleman 1949; Frijda 1953). Typically, during recognition, subjects have been asked to provide verbal labels for the emotions expressed, or they have been given rating scales to complete or have had to match the photographs of emotional expressions to stories. Laboratory studies using animals report even more ingenious measures (for example Miller *et al.* 1959a; 1959b, see below). Another difficulty concerns the number of responses which have been required of a subject. In describing the emotion he has seen, he may have two adjectives to choose from, or a hundred. He may have a check list or be asked for a free description. He may be asked to respond strictly in terms of the emotional expression or be allowed to concentrate on the situation as well.

Similarly, various strategies have emerged for the study of the vocal expression of emotion. Here, the main problem has been to devise a method for cutting out the verbal content of speech while leaving nonverbal aspects. There are three solutions to this. (1) Subjects have been asked to express various emotions while reciting the alphabet (for example Davitz and Davitz 1959a), which on the face of it seems an awkward task. (2) Or they have been asked to express the same few neutral sentences in different ways (for example Polack *et al.* 1960). (3) Or, finally, electronic filtering techniques have been used on recorded speech (for example Soskin and Kaufman 1961). Again, as with studies of facially expressed emotion, the task set to the subject and the number or type of responses required of him have varied enormously.

Any evaluation of investigations into emotional expression and the degree to which its recognition is accurate is made difficult by this multiplicity of factors. Studies vary according to the task the subjects are given, the selection of response which they are allowed, and the type and number of stimuli with which they are presented. This means that no definitive statements can be made about the accuracy of emotional recognition. Also, it is instructive to consult Brown's (1965) discussion of accuracy in this context. He 'explains away' the concept by suggesting that it may simply be the result of fortuitously appropriate projection, knowledge of the group to which the other person belongs and/or a fortunate response bias. However, some general statements can be made. For example, most studies based on spontaneous emotional expression in adult subjects lead to the conclusion that the performance of judges of the emotion is better than chance (for example Coleman 1949; Dittman 1962; Ekman 1965a; 1965b; Frijda 1953). Also, most studies of the vocal expression of emotion agree that emotional meanings can be communicated by vocal expression. For example, Davitz and Davitz (1959a) instructed eight speakers to express 10 different feelings by reciting parts of the alphabet. These were tape-recorded and played back to 30 subjects, who were each given a list of 10 feelings and asked to use them to identify what they heard. Results were significant but showed marked variation within listeners, speakers and feelings—a lack of coherence which, incidentally, accords well with other work on vocally-expressed emotion (see Davitz 1964 for review).

Examples of earlier research and interpretation

Coleman (1949) provides an exhaustive study of facially expressed emotion. His two basic procedures involved the elicitation and recording on film of facial expressions of emotion and the subsequent identification of these from the eye or mouth regions or from full face. He filmed 12 subjects while they were either responding 'naturally' or acting out the 'appropriate' response to squeezing a dynamometer, hearing a horn blast, receiving an electric shock, being threatened with an electric shock, treading on a snail, being told a joke, and being 'natural'.

From the overt responses and introspections of his 12 filmed subjects, Coleman concluded that emotional feelings had been elicited but with marked individual differences. Films of two subjects (one male, one female) were chosen and shown to 379 students with either the mouth region, the eye region or the full face in evidence. These judges were provided with a list of the situations used and in each case were asked to identify the situation which led to the expression. Although identifications were no better from the mouth region or the eye region, some expressions were identified better from one than the other. Identifiability depended on the subject, the facial region viewed and whether the expression was acted or natural. From subjective report, Coleman concluded that the method used for identification could best be described as empathy, a point which will be picked up later in a consideration of Stotland's (1969) work.

Frijda (1953) provides further examples of similar work. He took 68 short film sequences of two women, each sequence showing some emotional movement. He showed these sequences and photographs taken from them to 40 subjects and asked them for free descriptions. These descriptions were then scored on a five-point scale according to their judged correspondence to the 'true' emotion. This true emotion was based on Frijda's evaluation plus the introspections of the person filmed. This was a weakness in methodology, but no other method seems obviously better. Frijda's results showed that recognition of emotion had occurred, but not at a high level.

This would seem to be the right point to introduce the important work of Woodworth and its development by Schlosberg. Woodworth (1938) reanalysed data from earlier studies, and proposed a six-point scale of emotional recognition. (1) Love, mirth, happiness. (2) Surprise. (3) Fear, suffering. (4) Anger, determination. (5) Disgust. (6) Contempt. Woodworth and Schlosberg (1955) turned this into a circular rather than linear scale with contempt alongside love, mirth and happiness. Finally, Schlosberg (1952; 1954) proposed a dimensional representation of emotional expression and recognition. This implied that all emotional expression could be represented according to the three dimensions of: (1) pleasantness/unpleasantness; (2) attention/rejection; (3) activation level (sleep/tension). These analyses all seem quite reliable and have led to considerable developments in the study of emotional recognition. They will be discussed in detail later.

By the 1960s the investigations described above, and many similar studies, although providing useful information, had raised more questions than they had answered. Then, with a series of basic studies, Davitz (1964) broke much new ground. Further, R. E. Miller and his coworkers produced a series of investigations which, with an interesting technology and animal subjects, lent support to the human studies.

Davitz—earlier work

Having reviewed previous work on facial and vocal expression of emotion, Davitz (1964) devotes the remainder of his book to a description of the research undertaken by his group. He suggests that the field of vocally expressed emotion is an open one, research having shown little more than its probable occurrence. He poses two basic questions concerning facially expressed emotion. (1) To what extent is it innate or to what extent acquired? (2) To what extent does it depend on individual differences? Two earlier research strategies had been directed at the nature/nurture question in emotional expression. There had been a few studies based on the proposition that if learning is important to expression then cross-cultural recognition of emotion should be poor. May's (1938) study, although methodologically weak, did demonstrate some similarities between the recognition of emotion from photographs by Chinese and American subjects. Cross-cultural similarities were supported by Triandis and Lambert (1958) with Greek college students. The other type of study had concentrated on subjects blind from birth. Both Goodenough (1932) and Thompson (1941), for example, had found strong similarities between the emotional expressions of the blind and the sighted (innate influences), although the range and extent of the expressions of the blind were not as great (acquired influences). Also relevant were studies by Jeness (for example 1932b; 1932c) which showed that brief periods of training increased the accuracy of recognition of emotion.

Previous work on individual factors had been more or less restricted to sex differences (for example Coleman 1949; Jeness 1932a), with no general effects being found. Also, other than a few studies (for example Weisberger 1956) which had shown low positive correlations between intelligence and the ability to identify facial expression, there had been very little work on personality variables.

In describing the contribution of Davitz's group to this area, Beldoch's (1964) work will be mentioned in detail as it provided the basis of many of the other studies. He constructed tapes of male and female speakers reciting an emotionally neutral passage in ways expressive of various emotional states. He presented these tapes twice to 58 subjects. From their responses he produced a final tape containing those items most often correctly identified and representative of 10 emotional meanings. He followed the same procedure with musical tapes created by musicians in the same way—i.e. aimed at the expression of 10 emotions—and also with abstract art created for this purpose. All this stimulus material was then presented to 89 subjects with an adjective check list (ACL), a questionnaire concerning their general background in these three media, a self-report scale of sensitivity to the emotional expressions of others and a simple test of verbal intelligence.

Beldoch found significant correlations between the ability to make correct judgments in all three media, and also with vocabulary scores. Background training and interest contributed nothing and the ACL did not distinguish between high and low scorers. However, scores of sensitivity to emotional expression on the self-rating scale were positively related to those on the speech and graphic art material.

Levy (1964), using 'content-standard' material derived from Beldoch, studied the ability to express feelings vocally, the ability to identify such expressions and also the ability to identify one's own vocal expressions of feeling. Subjects had to judge vocally expressed emotion, to record similar items which were then judged by others and finally to try to recognize their own tapes (i.e. feelings) one to two weeks later. Levy found significant correlations between each of these measures, which still held when controlling for intelligence (although she only used graduates as subjects). There were no sex differences. Since self-perception, other-perception and expression each contributed significantly to the variance in Levy's results, she considers them as implying a general 'communication factor' which underlies at least three specific abilities.

Davitz himself takes up this idea of a general communication factor. In his first study, again using Beldoch's tapes and 33 personality variables derived from a number of tests, he found no reliable correlations between personality and the ability to identify vocal expressions of emotion. But in a further study, he found that this ability did correlate with general auditory ability, abstract symbolic activity, verbal intelligence and knowledge of the vocal characteristics of emotional expression. Putting these together, he found a multiple correlation of 0·60 with emotional sensitivity and tentatively suggested that general emotional communication is perhaps some sort of symbolic process. He is, however, well aware of the dangers of reading too much into purely correlational results.

The other studies reported in Davitz (1964) each make a cogent contribution, but there is little point in itemizing them in detail here, since the interested reader will find Davitz's book rewarding in its own right. However, two particularly relevant findings will be mentioned. Levitt (1964) studied the relationship between the ability to express emotional meanings vocally and facially. He made films of 50 subjects portraying six emotions through both voice and facial expression. The judges of these films were presented with sound alone, film alone, or both. Levitt found significant correlations between facial and vocal expressive abilities. However, full (vocal/facial) presentations were no better than facial communications alone. It may be that the vocal cues in the full presentations contributed little information. These results again provoke conjecture as to whether emotional communication is a matter of a general factor and/or a number of specific factors.

In what is probably the most interesting paper presented in the book, Blau (1964) devised a test of various commonly held hypotheses about the ability of the blind to communicate. For example, that the blind differ from the sighted in their ability to identify feelings from nonverbal cues, that blind females are better at this than blind males, that the blind pay more attention to 'affect' than the sighted, and that they can make much fuller descriptions of sounds and are more confident in their judgments of feelings and sounds. He studied 57 blind adolescents and 66 sighted adolescents, both groups being comparable in other ways. The blind were significantly better than the sighted at judging sounds, but controlling for this ability, the sighted groups were found to be better at judging feelings. In fact, where members of the blind group sometimes scored better than the sighted, this was later shown to be dependent on differences in mental age. There were no sex differences, but the blind paid significantly more attention to affect and were the more specific reporters of sounds. However, they were not

154

more confident than the sighted in the judgment of sounds and feelings. Blau concludes that sensory compensation exists to an extent, but not sufficiently to make the blind any better at judging emotion.

Although the research techniques reported by Davitz have resulted in such interesting exploratory findings, he is aware that they are not above criticism. The main question is whether or not they lead to results which are at all representative of real life. Most of the studies he describes rely on experimental instructions rather than actual emotional states; nevertheless, the overall findings are reasonably consistent. Also, he sets a fairly stringent operational definition of what he means by communication, and sticks to it. It requires 'many' listeners to agree with the intent of the speakers and within this agreement the number of 'correct' responses being beyond the 0·01 level of significance. But Davitz does not make too strong a claim; he simply regards this work as a start and not necessarily representative of fine-grained, sensitive, everyday nuances of the communication of emotion.

Davitz is also aware of the need for theory. At the basis of his approach was an association between words like anger or joy and their expressive, behavioural referents. From the consensus of opinion obtained from judges, there is clear evidence of communication in Davitz's investigations, but words such as anger and joy also refer to 'felt' rather than expressed emotions. Some theory is needed to bring the two together. Although Davitz has recently proposed his own theory (see later), in 1964 he suggested that Schachter's physiological/cognitive ideas could best account for his results. He argued that the verbal aspects of speech might affect the cognitive determinants of emotion and that the vocal aspects might be a function of activation. This is a crude analysis but it does lead to definite predictions for any work involving the use of the semantic differential, where one of the three main factors is activation.

Davitz (1964) also engaged in somewhat vague speculation as to the relationship between emotional sensitivity and intelligence. He suggested that emotional sensitivity involves both perceptual and cognitive variables. Also, that there may be some general factor which influences the many behaviours involved in non-verbal emotional communication, although overlaying this there may be special factors. Finally, he argued that emotional sensitivity may be a sort of intellectual ability which is made up of a type of 'g' factor (intellectual), plus various non-intellectual variables. However, other than saying that it is not necessarily related to intelligence, he did not specify the nature of this intellectual factor. Although Davitz's early research was stimulating, his theoretical speculations were confused and added little to our understanding of emotion.

R. E. Miller

Miller has produced a very different, but equally interesting, series of studies to those of Davitz. These began in 1955, when Murphy et al. conditioned rhesus monkeys to make instrumental shock-avoidance responses using other monkeys as conditioned stimuli. This was followed by Mirsky et al. (1958), who first conditioned and then extinguished an instrumental shock-avoidance response in monkeys. After extinction was complete, they exposed the experimental monkeys to a stimulus monkey who was behaving apprehensively. Even though they received no further shock, the monkeys immediately began to make the instrumental response. This was described as the perception of affect and empathy, and was confirmed by Miller *et al.* (1959a; 1959b) using coloured photographs of calm or apprehensive monkeys as their stimulus material.

As part of a more complex series of studies, Miller *et al.* (1962), for example, trained three rhesus monkeys to bar-press to avoid shock within six sec of the presentation of a light. After acquisition training any two of the monkeys were placed opposite one another, one with a bar but no light, the other with a light but no bar. As each had incomplete information, Miller argued that the only way in which they could avoid shock was by the communication of affect. As a control condition the monkeys exchanged roles, and also, except for their faces, were often hidden from one another by a screen. Results showed significant evidence for cooperative avoidance; the monkeys must have been giving and receiving visual auditory emotional cues. In a further extension of this procedure, Miller *et al.* (1963) trained six monkeys in the usual instrumental avoidance response and tested them in pairs as in the previous study; the stimulus animal had only the conditioned stimulus, the response animal had only the bar. The responder could observe the face of the stimulus monkey via a television screen. Under these conditions, what Miller describes as the emotional expressions of the stimulus monkey elicited avoidance responses from the observer monkey. This suggests that different, specific expressions of affect may be learnt in this way. As a final example of this procedure, Miller *et al.* (1966) studied positive affect and took physiological measures. They trained monkeys to press a bar for food and then presented the conditioned stimulus to one of a pair. The other, with the bar, could see the face of the first on a television screen. In six of the 12 pairings responses showed the communication of what might be positive affect, accompanied by changes in heart rate. They suggested that their six failures were of recognition rather than expression.

Clearly, this is a most promising line of research, using highly controlled but to some extent 'natural' situations, and one which might provide useful suggestions about emotional expression. However, it should be borne in mind that at best these studies can only be said to deal with the first two of Frijda's (1969) aspects of emotional recognition—the situation and the anticipation of action. It would be going too far in the direction of anthropomorphism to speak of animals having emotional attitudes and inner empathetic representations.

CONCEPTUALIZATION OF EMOTIONAL EXPRESSION AND RECOGNITION

There are at least three ways in which emotional expression and recognition may be conceptualized. (1) Categories: emotions as expressed could be classed into any number of distinct, unrelated events. Tomkins and McCarter (1964), for example, assume that there are eight primary 'affects': interest, enjoyment, surprise, distress, fear, shame, contempt, anger. They also assume that each of these is primarily a facial response which is under the control of some innate subcortical programme. The main point about any categorization system is that the classes are unrelated and unordered. (2) Dimensions: from the dimensionality viewpoint, expressed emotions can be regarded as mixtures of pleasantness, activation, etc. (Statistical techniques based on factor analysis lead to the enumeration of distinct factors underlying behaviour. These may be conceived as occupying hypothetical n-dimensional space, each dimension being orthogonal to the remainder. Although this is easily understood with three dimensions, we need mathematical or philosophical analysis to conceive of more. Emotional expressions can be conceptualized in terms of such underlying dimensions.) This type of analysis can account for some of the more surprising similarities between emotional expressions (for example between contempt and mirth). Equally well, it can account for differences and the various nuances of emotional expression in general. However, it quickly becomes unwieldly if too many dimensions are proposed. (3) Hierarchy: this refers to a combination of categories and dimensions. In a particular region of n-dimensional emotional space there may be differentiation between emotion in terms of the dimensions especially pertinent to that region. Emotions may be comparable as regards dimensions both within and between categories, although each category may have its own distinguishable qualities.

Are these ideas sufficient to define emotional expression? The answer must be no. Ideas of categories, dimensions or a hierarchy are abstract. And emotions as they are distinguished in the language cannot be distinguished in the same way from their expression. They are confused by observers. Frijda's (1969) analyses show that subjects use many different labels for any one expression (this is also implicit in Davitz 1969), all of the labels frequently being quite wrong. Also, different emotions can produce the same expression. This strongly suggests that there is something more or perhaps finer than is given by possible dimensions of emotion. The necessary richness could come from cognitive factors, as is suggested by Schachter. However, if cognition is important, then emotion could not be fully recognizable from expressive behaviour.

Frijda (1969) suggests that those aspects of emotion which are expressed can be called 'positionality'. He defines this as: (1) tendencies to approach, withdraw and attend; and (2) the degree of control of activity. He regards these as usually but not necessarily being combined with possible cognitive determinants of emotion and argues that the naming of emotion follows from the recognition of positionality. Finally, Frijda suggests that there may be a sort of balance between cognitive and behavioural factors in emotion; when one is high the other will be low and *vice versa*. However, why the behavioural components are sometimes well differentiated and sometimes not is unclear. Also, for any one emotion, there are numerous behaviours and expressions which are considered to be appropriate. The problem really is that many different states may share one expressive pattern, and that many different expressions may characterize one emotion. Analysis and conceptualization become difficult.

DIMENSIONALITY

The idea of dimensionality in emotional communication, relatively quiescent since Schlosberg (1954), has recently begun to assume more importance. The basic hypothesis is that errors in the recognition of emotion run parallel to similarities between expressed emotions, and these similarities are in fact proximities in multidimensonal space. Thus, emotional recognition becomes a matter of placing emotions in this multidimensional space. This is extended by the similar idea that *named* emotions are also reducible to combinations of fewer dimensions than are immediately apparent; a notion which is important to Davitz's (1969) more recent work (see below). The concept of dimensionality has led to a search for the number of dimensions which will describe hypothetical emotional space more simply. Although Schlosberg set the scene, the three dimensions he proposed appear arbitrary and unsatisfactory. Other studies have found evidence for the pleasantness/unpleasantness (P/U) dimension and the sleep/tension (S/T) dimension, but often the attention/rejection (A/R) dimension has been missing (for example Abelson and Sermat 1962; Shepard 1963).

There have been two approaches to the study of dimensionality. (1) Judgment of the meaning of emotional expression through the use of ACLs or rating scales. (2) Judgment of similarity using paired comparison techniques or their extensions into triads or groupings.

Osgood (1955) provides a good example of the former. Subjects had to select one from 40 emotional-state labels which, in their estimation, best charaterized a live, motionless expression portrayed by an actor. From an analysis of the frequency of usage of each label for each expression, Osgood plotted his results on three dimensions. There was a P/U dimension, an 'intensity' dimension (corresponding to S/T) and a 'control' dimension. Control can be regarded as a dimension peculiar to Osgood's experimental technique, since it distinguished expressions started by the 'actor' from those simply coming from the environment.

Frijda's (1969) methodology was a little different. He reanalysed his own earlier work (Frijda and Philipszoon 1963) using factor analytic techniques. Originally, he had gathered 27 seven-point scales which were representative of 400 terms used by 30 subjects in a free-labelling of expression study. The scales were then used by 12 judges for rating photographs of an actress portraying various emotional expressions. Frijda found six main factors which were accounting for 92 per cent of the variances: (1) P/U; (2) activation—but Frijda described this as corresponding to intensity rather than S/T since the low end was a lack of expression rather than sleep; (3) similar to Schlosberg's A/R, but more like what might be called interest since the low end was disinterest rather than rejection; (4) Frijda found this dimension difficult to label, but suggested social evaluation or something akin to Osgood's control; (5) and (6) smaller factors, the first being described as surprise, the second as simple/complicated. Frijda draws particular attention to factors (2) and (3) since they are both to do with activity. He regards (2) as emotional intensity or activation as Duffy (1962) might use the term; it refers to the mobilization of energy. (4) concerns the arousal of attention; it is akin to the orienting reflex. It is worth noting that these results are supported by a similar study which used Schlosberg's original photographs as stimulus material (Karsten 1965, quoted in Frijda 1969).

If emotional expressions can be reduced to dimensions, two questions require answer. (1) Do the dimensions delineate the 'meaning' or 'real' emotion which underlies expression, or, more mundanely, do they simply reflect the words used to describe emotional expressions? Frijda maintains that at least his first four dimensions correspond to expressive meaning; to support this he quotes a study by Elshout (1967) correlating expressive meaning and facial features. (2) How many dimensions are there? The only study to point to as large a number as Frijda's six factors is Osgood's (1966), which involved semantic differential-scale responses of judges. He found that his usual three dimensions could be divided further into nine interpretable clusters or factors, a number almost large enough to bring us back to a list of primary emotions: anger, amazement, boredom, quiet pleasure, disgust, sorrow, interest (expectancy), joy and fear.

Typically, studies using matching techniques for the judgment of similarities between photographs of emotional expression have found far fewer factors (for example Abelson and Sermat 1962 who found two, or Gladstones 1962 who found three). However, such studies have normally used only a few posed expressions. An exception to this is Stringer (1967), who used the same 30 photographs as in Frijda's original study. His subjects were allowed to group them freely and then label each one. A great deal of data manipulation only yielded three factors.

From the standpoints of their experimental requirements, the major difference between these two sorts of study is that when endeavouring to label an emotional meaning a subject has to make a discrimination, whereas when he is estimating similarities between emotions he must overlook any differences. From this point of view, Frijda (1969) maintains that pleasantness and interest are more important to the estimation of similarity than are intensity or artificiality.

It can be concluded that the search for dimensions of emotion has proved to be an important influence in the study of emotional expression. However, this is due more to the research which it has generated than to any fundamental theoretical contributions. Clearly, the parsimony implicit in the idea of dimensions could be significant in any analysis of emotion, but any economy is lost when, as has often been the case, too many dimensions are proposed. Also, it is sometimes difficult to compare dimensions between studies. Various research strategies and techniques of data analysis have been used and difficulty is often met with in describing and naming the dimensions when they have been found. Of course, naming is perhaps not important since dimensions are anyway mathematical/philosophical abstractions. Finally, it should be remembered that, given the research techniques most often used in this area of study, any dimensions of 'emotion' may simply be reflecting verbal behaviour.

OTHER ASPECTS OF EXPRESSION

So far, only studies involving the facial expression of emotion have been discussed. However, behaviour may reflect emotion in many ways; before considering other factors which might influence emotional expression in general, some of these will be mentioned.

When reviewing studies each of which has used still photographs, it is easy to forget that in real life emotional expression extends in time. Again, it is Frijda (1953) who has shown the importance of the temporal extension of expressive behaviour. He found an increase in accuracy of almost 50 per cent when comparing judgments of emotion from 10 sec films with judgments made from stills of the culminating points of the same films. He also showed that the effects of single expressive movements are mainly due to their onset and offset. He found that: (1) a rapid onset of an expressive movement was usually interpreted as being caused by a sudden change in stimulus leading to a voluntary change in the direction of behaviour, or simply as a spontaneous impulse which disrupts control; (2) a gradual onset of response suggested a spontaneous, integrated emotional response; (3) a very slow onset indicated a lack of energy or inhibition; (4) a rapid offset of the response implied a disruption of continuity; (5) a gradual offset indicated that the emotion had followed its natural course. Frijda regarded this as a dimension of voluntariness versus spontaneity. This is perhaps going too far from data that are anyway oversubjective. Clearly, more research is necessary in this field.

Recently, some interesting investigations have been made of body movements in emotional communication. Ekman (1965a; 1965b), Ekman and Friesen (1967a) and Dittman et al. (1965) have all shown that bodily posture and movement contribute to the recognition of emotion, particularly its intensity. Body cues do not seem to be especially important for the P/U dimension. In extending this idea, Ekman and Friesen (1969) provide a novel slant on emotional communication. They suggest that nonverbal behaviour escapes the efforts that we make at deception and in fact allows our 'real' feelings to leak out. They propose that there are two types of deception, each of which contains much simulation. (1) We attempt to deceive others about our feelings. Even if we are discovered in our deception we may carry it through, with subtle changes, since open verbalization might prove embarrassing. (2) We may deceive ourselves. This is a somewhat 'clinically' viewed blocking from self-awareness of feelings that might arouse anxiety if they were given free expression.

Ekman and Friesen regard these deceptions (which we all make) as having three dimensions. (1) Saliency—the degree to which the deception is of obvious importance to the interactants; clearly a function both of the situation and the personality of those involved. (2) The roles adopted by the interactants—i.e. whether they are both deceiving and/or detecting, or one adopting each role, etc. (3) Collaboration or antagonism—an implicit or explicit pact (or lack of it) about the discovery and/or the continuation of the deception (psychotherapy is a collaboration to discover deception). They also suggest that each of us has a certain sending capacity for nonverbal signals; we can send them quickly or slowly, we can send many or few and we can make them easily visible or not. Ekman and Friesen maintain that according to each of these measures, the face is the best sender of nonverbal information, the feet and the legs are the worst and the hands and arms fall somewhere in between. Further, they stress the importance of external feedback. Nonverbal behaviour from B is perceived by A as in response to his own nonverbal behaviour. Even so, it may be inappropriate to openly comment on this. For example, although we may comment if someone frowns in our presence, we shall probably not mention his squeezing his legs together. Finally, there is internal feedback—conscious awareness of what we are doing. Again, there is the progression face, hands, feet, this time in terms of the amount of nervous system feedback we obtain from these areas.

Ekman and Friesen's concluding suggestion is that the legs and feet are the worst senders of messages, they are the least responded to, they are the least in self-awareness and *therefore* they provide the best source of information about leakage or clues to the deception that is being practised on us. From this point of view, the face is the worst source of information and the hands and arms are again in between. Ekman and Friesen provide some support for these ideas with studies involving ratings of filmed interactions; the raters see only the head or the hands and arms or the feet and legs.

There is self-evidently an unfavourable ratio between speculation and hard data in Ekman and Friesen's work. Their ideas, however, certainly appear to have face validity and point to the possibility of an interesting field of research.

The final more 'living' aspect of emotional expression to be briefly described is eye-gaze, a topic which is engendering a great deal of research at the moment (for example Argyle 1967; Argyle 1969; Argyle and Kendon 1967; Strongman 1970; Strongman and Champness 1968). With eye-gaze we are back to facial expression, but often with procedures based on the systematic observation of ongoing social situations by trained observers or on the study of filmed inter-actions. The fundamental concern has been with the patterns of looking towards and away from another's eyes during a conversation. For obvious reasons, emphasis has fallen on mutual gaze. Typically, this is expressing social sentiments and social attitudes. Clearly, the length of time we spend looking into another's eyes, how often we do so and who breaks eye contact first have importance for the communication of emotion, although as yet few definitive statements can be made. (For reviews of such work see particularly Argyle 1969 and Vine 1970.)

THE CONTEXT

During our normal, everyday lives we perceive expressive behaviour in context; this would seem to be an important aid to our judgment of the emotion. We make evaluations on the basis of information about body type, facial charac-teristics, purposive action, the situation, behavioural constants, personality, age, sex, cultural group, and so on. These are all contextual cues. A two-stage process appears to be at work: (1) an evaluation of (Frijda's) general positional activity pattern; this is made from the actual emotional expression; (2) the more precise specification of this pattern from contextual cues. Cline (1956), for example, demonstrated the possible importance of context in judging emotional expression. He manipulated the context by making schematic drawings, unarguably a very artificial technique but nevertheless one from which putative conclusions can be drawn. He found, for instance, that the drawing of a face was perceived as angry, jealous and unhappy when paired with a smiling face, but aloof, independent, domineering and unafraid when paired with a frowning face. Out of context it was judged to be glum.

It was once thought that the context was the only way in which we can recognize emotion and at best the expression itself was secondary (for example Landis 1929). However, it is now clear that expression does give important cues, although perhaps when there is an obvious context available such expressive cues may become less important. This point implies that contextual cues may possibly conflict with expressive cues.

If contextual and expressive cues are dissonant, which is dominant? Flores d'Arcais (1961) gave the first answer to this by using films with either correct or incorrect soundtracks. Expressive cues were dominant. This finding has been confirmed in a series of studies by Frijda. His basic experiment involved the use of photographs with either concordant or discordant descriptions. The design called for free ratings of the photographs and also ratings including the information given by one or other of the descriptions. Ratings shifted in the direction of the expression rather than the situation. Interestingly, the discordant description seemed quite acceptable to the subjects, a point made by Luchins (1958) in a different context. It may be that in real life such apparent paradoxes are not uncommon. Frijda (1969) quotes two further studies (Jaanus 1966; Warries 1963) which support the dominance of expression over context. They showed, for example, that if a person behaves happily or sadly when from the context we expect something different, then we believe his behaviour. However, both studies also showed the situation to be important to the recognition of emotion.

It is simple to suggest factors that might influence the dominance of expressive over contextual cues when the two conflict, for example, ambiguity in the cues, the nature of the expressive cues, the nature of the contextual cues, and so on. It is more difficult to specify the process of judgment when there is such conflict. The obvious answer is a sort of compromise. But, as usual, it is Frijda (1969) who provides the more subtle and more interesting explanation. He suggests that the person making the judgment forms various hypotheses until he has an aggregate of them. He believes that 'gap-filling' hypotheses are often produced, i.e. possible additional factors are hypothesized to have their effects between a particular situation and a facial expression which may be gibing with it. If the discordance persists, then Frijda posits four possible ways of reducing it. (1) Divorce the emotion from the situation. (2) Divorce the emotion from the situation and accept the situation. (3) Divorce the expression from the emotion.

(4) Deny the situation. There are obvious resemblances between these ideas and those proposed by Festinger (for example 1957) for the reduction of cognitive dissonance.

OTHER LINES OF RESEARCH

Movement

There has been little follow-up of Michotte's (1950) work on the emotional significance of movement. This is odd since the research technique looks as though it has reduced the communication of emotion to an elemental level. Michotte's experiments are based on one simple paradigm. There are two small coloured rectangles which can be moved along a horizontal slot. They can be stopped or started at any moment; they can have their direction, extent and speed of movement altered. The observer of these moving rectangles tends to invest them with emotional significance; certain conditions produce compelling impressions. For example, A 'runs away from' B, A 'goes to find' B 'and take it away', A 'pushes' B, and so on.

Michotte argued that these impressions are very primitive phenomena rather than emotional 'meanings'. The observers often drew analogies with human action when they were describing the 'behaviour' of the rectangles, the descriptions often implying emotional states, attitudes and tendencies. Michotte accounted for this by suggesting that fundamentally any human interaction involves these same elements: two people move in relation to one another.

More theoretically, Michotte divides emotions into two groups, according to whether the 'interactants' imply an integrative or segregative relationship to one another. In more usual terms, this is simply 'positive' or 'negative'. Motor reactions include either approach and contact or escape, withdrawal and avoidance. Michotte extends this idea to suggest that the physical expressions of emotions produce similar impressions of movement to those of the rectangles. He also believes that, in different situations, integration and segregation take on different characteristics. Speed seems to be particularly important. For example, rapid movement often implies violence, whereas slow movement implies gentleness. On this basis, Michotte lists a whole range of impressions.

Via similar speculations to these, Michotte eventually comes to the view that motor reactions *per se* are fundamental to expressive behaviour. However, it is difficult to pin down the emotion in Michotte's arguments. His studies, although related to emotional expression, are vague and subjective. And his theoretical analysis goes far beyond his data.

Empathy

Stotland (1969) puts together social and physiological aspects of emotion in a similar way to that in R. E. Miller *et al.*'s recent (for example 1966) studies.

Stotland's work rests on the intuitively reasonable assumption that we share other people's feelings. This sharing of feeling does not necessarily imply any sympathetic *behaviour* on the part of the observer. Stotland defines empathy as '... an observer's reacting emotionally because he perceives that another is experiencing or is about to experience an emotion'. He regards emotion as a state of physiological arousal, with strong subjective concomitants. He is not unaware of the problems which such a notion carries with it, but relies on Lacey (1950) to support the idea that psychophysiologically people show arousal in different ways. However, the subjective aspects of emotion as Stotland sees them are unreliable for the usual reasons; physiological arousal is broader than emotional arousal—the latter only exists when there is also some affective component. Stotland realizes that the foregoing might imply that the observer and the observed are experiencing different emotions. But he suggests that even if emotional response patterning has not been convincingly demonstrated physiologically, it exists subjectively. Thus, he goes no further than to dichotomize emotions into positive and negative and then make any further differentiations via subjective report. It is then a little difficult to see why he brought physiology into the picture at all.

Stotland distinguishes empathy from those situations in which a person's experiences may carry implications for the welfare of one who might observe them. For example, when his father frowns a child might expect unpleasantness to follow. This is not empathy; the other's perceived emotions are acting as discriminative stimuli (sources of information) about the observer's possible or probable fate. Stotland also distinguishes empathy from predictive empathy. In the latter he suggests that the observer does not have to *experience* the emotion he is perceiving to predict what it may be. However, he also argues that predictive empathy and nonpredictive empathy must share any factors which influence the perception of another's emotional state. Also, they may interact.

Stotland distinguishes between his own work and that of Schachter (for example 1964); his distinction relies on the hypothesized direction of influence. Schachter proposes that we use the behaviour of others to interpret our own, perhaps amorphous, feelings. Empathy is the reverse of this; we perceive another's emotion and then change our own emotional state—both physiologically and subjectively. Rather than contradicting one another, these directions of influence may happen in sequences or in different conditions.

Stotland's (1969) experimental procedure typically involves five or six subjects observing another, pseudo-subject, undergoing some positive or negative experience. The observers' reactions are measured by palm sweating and vasoconstriction; and also by self-ratings of their feelings immediately after the emotion-producing stimulus has ceased (a limited but inevitable measure in such studies).

In the first study, subjects observed another, with instructions to either (1) imagine how they would feel in his position, or (2) imagine how he felt, or (3) watch his physical reactions closely. The pseudo-subject was treated to one of three possible experiences in a 'diathermy' machine—pain or neutral or pleasant heat to the arm. There were various baseline controls taken of the physiological measures. The confederate subject acted his part. Stotland's general findings were of differences in physiological measures between pain, neutral and pleasure conditions for the two 'imagining' sets of instructions, but not for the 'watch him' one. He concludes from this that 'set' is important to empathy and that an interpersonal process which leads us to *imagine* ourselves in the position of another leads us to empathize.

Finally, Stotland describes a series of experiments in which the main independent variable was the relationship between the observer and the observed. Such relationships presumably alter empathetic responses by altering perception. The most important variable Stotland mentions seems to be birth order. For example, later-born people empathize more with someone similar to themselves than with someone different; the empathy of first borns remains unaffected by similarity. This is extended to later borns empathizing more with those with whom they have interacted, although first borns do not.

Such results are interesting and the general research strategy is promising. However, the findings often show a lack of consistency between the physiological measures and the self-ratings. And, as often seems to be the case with investigators of emotional expression and recognition, Stotland goes further than is justified by his data.

The language of emotion

Davitz (1969; 1970) makes one of the more fruitful recent approaches to the social psychology of emotion. He deals with a problem which sprang from the final stages of Davitz (1964)—'What does a person mean when he says someone is happy or angry or sad?'. Davitz believes that this should be answered descriptively—a belief which characterizes the social psychology of emotion in general. His answer leads him, by a completely different route, to a concept of dimensionality reminiscent of Frijda's.

Davitz (1969) suggests that the meaning of the various emotions depends on our experience. He argues for a study based on language. A problem which all psychologists must face is having to use everyday terms in a more rigorous, restricted context; the everyday connotations of words simply cause confusion, 'anxiety' perhaps being the best example. Davitz therefore aimed to produce a dictionary of emotional terms, drawn from what he calls 'commonalities of meaning'—verbal descriptions of emotional states. Clearly, such an aim is likely to result in enormous subjective confusions. Davitz is aware of this but hypothesizes that any common ground may appear in mathematical abstractions from the basic data.

Davitz asked 30 people to imagine a time when they experienced a given emotion and then to describe it. From this and from judgments about information relevant to the emotional experiences, he ended with 556 statements which referred to (in decreasing order of frequency) physical sensations (for example 'I feel soft and firm'), relations to the external world (for example 'Everything seems unimportant and trivial'), cognitive events (for example 'My thinking is rapid'), relations to others (for example 'I feel outgoing'), self-reference (for example 'I feel aimless'), impulses to behave or to control behaviour (for example 'I want to be tender and gentle with another person') and formal aspects of the experience (for example 'It's a steady, ongoing feeling').

Terms for labelling the emotions were taken from *Roget's Thesaurus*. The 400 words obtained in this way were read to 40 subjects who were asked to say which of them they would use to label an emotion; 137 of these were well agreed on, of which 50 were chosen on the basis of their coverage of the vocabulary of emotion. Each subject was asked to think of a critical experience for each of these emotions, describe it and then use the check list to find each statement which agreed with the experience. Next, 50 subjects used this large check list, each describing a range of emotional situations. Although these subjects were taken from both sexes and from negroes and whites, they were all highly verbal graduates; this is a clear limitation to the generality of Davitz's findings. Arbitrarily, Davitz included in his final definition of a term any statement which had been checked by at least one-third of the subjects in their descriptions. Finally, each of these definitions was given to 20 judges with instructions to rate (on a four-point scale) their adequacy in describing both the emotion and their own experience of it. Davitz then presents his reader with the actual list of phrases and his resultant dictionary of emotional meaning.

One obvious advantage of Davitz's dictionary is that it gives a vocabulary which can be simply used for phenomena which are normally very difficult to describe. On the other hand, as Davitz shows himself to be well aware, it must represent an oversimplification. He oversimplified further by carrying out an analysis of 215 items that each appeared in the definitions of at least three emotions. He found 12 clusters to which, with caution, he assigned labels: (1) activation, (2) hypoactivation, (3) hyperactivation, (4) moving toward, (5) moving away, (6) moving against, (7) comfort, (8) discomfort, (9) tension, (10) enhancement, (11) incompetence/dissatisfaction and (12) inadequacy. These clusters were then factor analysed, and the results led Davitz to suggest four dimensions of emotional meaning. Working from the clusters, (1), (2) and (3) concern levels of *activation*, (4), (5) and (6) concern *relatedness* to the environment, (7), (8) and (9) concern the *hedonic tone* of an emotional state, and (10), (11) and (12) refer to a sense of *competence* in relating to the environment.

Davitz gathers some background support for his four dimensions of emotional meaning. Activation and hedonic tone have often appeared in the literature on emotion. Many writers have discussed both (activation: for example Block 1957; Duffy 1962; Schlosberg 1954; hedonic tone: for example Block 1957; Harlow and Stagner 1933; Schlosberg 1954). However, support for the other two factors comes more from Davitz's interpretation of what others have said than from their actual words. For example, he changes Duffy's (1941) 'direction' to his own 'relatedness'. And stretches Sartre's (1948) existential theory and Plutchik's (1962; 1970) notions of adaptive emotional behaviour to fit his concept of competence. Although similar terminology provides broad support for Davitz, it can in no sense be considered validation.

Davitz's (1969) tentative theory of emotion can be reduced to six main propositions. (1) Emotion is partly concerned with private (experienced) events—a clear, phenomenological, subjective viewpoint. (2) Emotion embraces specific states which are labelled, and each label refers to experiences about which there is reasonable common ground within a culture. This proposition comes more directly from Davitz's dictionary. (3) The language of emotion reflects experiences but is also directly influenced by linguistic considerations; people make mistakes in their descriptions of emotion, and, in fact, learn to label the emotion from the situation (see 5 below). (4) Definitions of emotional states fall into 12 clusters, which can fit into four dimensions of emotional experience: activation, relatedness, hedonic tone and competence. (5) Labelling emotion depends on experience. Any change in experience will change the label and the state. (6) Emotional states come about from stimuli which are psychologically relevant to the four dimensions of emotional meaning.

Davitz is aware that these propositions fit neither phenomenology, a psychoanalytic approach, nor behaviourally oriented ideas. In fact, as a theory it leaves much to be desired, since it is both lacking in formal properties and is not well anchored to empirical fact. However, he believes that his proposals do lead to productive research. For example, he quotes Farmer (1967), who with interview techniques studied the development of the language of emotion in 64 children from the ages of seven to 14. He found that as children grow older their reports of emotional experiences become more like those of adults. Also, that those clusters of emotion most emphasized by adults appear earlier in the children's reports. These results are hardly surprising. Also, Allerand (1967), for example, argued that as there is a physiological basis to emotion, those who are genetically similar should also be more similar in their verbal reports of emotion than those who are genetically dissimilar. He carried out a study involving 24 pairs each of monzygotic twins, dizygotic twins and siblings aged 13 to 18. He recorded their descriptions of some emotions and found a significant difference between the monozygotes and others in the similarity of their emotional reports. These are just two examples from a number which Davitz quotes in support of his approach to emotional language.

In making an evaluation of this work, one must conclude that the experiments are weak and the implications of the theory on which they are based are not expanded sufficiently to be useful. Davitz's (1969) main contribution is clearly the dictionary of emotional meanings. It is a fresh approach to the social psychology of emotion and may provide the impetus for some fundamental descriptive research.

Ethology

Recent advances in the ethological approach to emotional expression bring us back full circle to the Darwinian starting point. Interestingly, modern ethology has been extended to man as well as animals. However, the study of animals is instructive since it perhaps points to the origin of emotional expression. Tail-wagging in dogs and purring in cats are obvious examples of this. Ethologists believe such responses to have a communicative function; to act as releasers for the coordination of social behaviour.

Eibl-Eibesfeldt (1970) argues that, evolutionarily, expressive behavior is often derived from other behaviour that had been accompanied by frequent arousal or activity. For example, in many species social grooming always indicates that social contact may proceed. Sometimes it has become ritualized into expressive movements. The lemur, for instance, greets other lemurs with the movements it uses to comb its fur. Similarly, Eibl-Eibesfeldt maintains that behaviour which once led to attack has evolved into gestures of threat. It may, for example, be reduced to preparing to jump, or to jumping and falling short. One unfortunate aspect of such evolutionary arguments is that they tend to lead to useless specula-tions about similar mechanisms in man. To take the last example, a man stamp-ing his feet in anger can be said to be showing incipient, but ritualized, attack movements.

The ethological suggestion is that ritualization—the modification of behaviour to make it communicative—is the main process underlying the evolution of expressive movements. The changes that it produces in behaviour are regarded as all-important to signalling. Eibl-Eibestfeldt (1970) describes eight changes in behaviour which accompany ritualization. (1) Behaviour changes in its function. (2) Ritualized movements change their *apparent* motivation. (3) Movements become simpler but exaggerated both in frequency and amplitude. (4) Movements 'freeze' into postures. (5) The actual behaviour occurs to a greater range of stimuli. (6) Orientation changes. (7) The behaviour becomes stereotyped and occurs with a constant intensity. (8) The variability of behaviour is suppressed. He also suggests that these changes are often accompanied by the development of conspicuous bodily structures. Although these ideas may appear good sense from the viewpoint of biological adaptivity, it is difficult to see how they may be substantiated. They are speculative in the extreme. However, at the descriptive level, there are many possible examples of the process (see Eibl-Eibesfeldt 1970 for review). For instance, many carnivores feed their young by pushing food into their mouths, and also often greet one another by pushing together their muzzlès and rubbing them. (In this case, the ethologist would maintain that the latter has evolved from the former by a ritualization process.) Also, both apes and man sometimes feed their young with a mouth-to-mouth method and greet one another by kissing. More interestingly, Eibl-Eibesfeldt suggests that ritualization may begin to occur within ontogenesis as well as phylogenesis. He supports this by the exaggerated, rhythmic and stereotyped behaviours seen in zoo animals; these often seem to be directed towards 'begging' food for example. The alternative explanation for this is that it is just superstitiously maintained operant behaviour and has little to do with emotional expression. Such superstitious behaviour is usually seen when animals are interacting with man; dogs 'shaking hands'.

Modern ethologists also provide classifications of expressive behaviour. Again, to take Eibl-Eibesfeldt's (1970) work as an example, he classifies expressive movements according to their function. His major division is between intraspecific and interspecific releasers. The intraspecific group are: (1) signals that promote group cohesion; these are precise signals which regulate interaction and attraction, for example courtship behaviour, submissive gestures and behaviour which establishes and maintains contact; (2) communication about the external environment; for example, warning and distress is signalled in squirrels and birds, and chemically in some fish; also there is the famous bee language (for example von Frisch 1950; 1968; Johnson 1967; Wenner 1967) in which the direction and distance of a food source from the hive is communicated; (3) intraspecific threat signals; for example certain bird songs, a gorilla's chest-beating, various ritualized attack behaviour. Eibl-Eibesfeldt subdivides interspecific expressive releasers into two: (1) contact readiness, in which many members of different species live near to one another to mutual advantage; (2) threat postures, for example back-arching in cats.

An important (although implicit) thesis in recent ethology is that an obvious way to overcome the difficulty of laboratory studies of emotional expression in man is to study them using more 'naturalistic' techniques. Brannigan and Humphries (1971) exemplify this approach. They criticize the more traditional photograph-based studies of emotional expression by pointing out that their validity depends on the correctness of the basic definitions of the emotion on which they are based. Also, of course, the expressions are not occurring within their usual dynamic context. They suggest further that the actual expressions which have been studied have not received enough ethological analysis. Such analysis is complex, but they argue that a sound ethological description of an emotion should be the starting point.

Brannigan and Humphries discuss the descriptive breakdown of behaviour into units and describe in detail changes in facial expression. For example, 'Smiles are characterized by an upward and outward movement of the mouth corners, and may be clarified into various categories according to the degree and form of mouth opening and tooth exposure'. Each smile occurs in a characteristic situation.

A further problem that Brannigan and Humphries consider is that of 'what do the signals signal?'. Subjective projection makes it easy for man to judge man, but by the same token it is difficult to be objective. Of course, the broad answer to the question is that the signals are expressions of emotion. But Brannigan and Humphries feel that this is too vague and too difficult to separate from the 'behaviour patterns themselves'. Instead, they argue that as well as expressing emotions, communicative signals give information about likely behaviour and also give feedback on the receipt of one's own behaviour. They consider that it may be wrong to try to give each signal some specific emotional context; a frown may occur in several different situations although it looks the same in each. In general, they are saying that the traditional approach to the study of emotional expression is oversimplified.

CONCLUSIONS

There is only one conclusion which can be drawn from the many different approaches to the social psychology of emotion: there exists some immediate and, to use an everyday term, intuitive perception of expressive meaning. But this by no means accounts for all the findings in this field. Although the recognition process occurs very quickly, much knowledge and experience must intervene. Clearly, the recognition of emotion is determined by a very complex process. This process depends on the integration of many cues, from facial expression through body movement to the situation and the more static features of the interactants; whilst at another level, the process depends on any hypotheses which we may hold about life. Frijda (1969) offers the most complete formulation. (1) The understanding of a situation and its implications. (2) A store containing factual and emotional implications; many possible emotions connected with varying probabilities assigned to each situation. (3) We are 'set' for a person in a situation to experience a particular emotion. (4) A store of emotional knowledge; emotions and their scale values—from which we also get our own emotional expression. (5) The system must be able to register expressive behaviour and code it. (6) A working out of expressive meaning. (7) A comparison of expressive meaning and situational suggestions. (8) A combination of (4) and (6). (9) An emotion is selected from the store in (4). (10) An adjustment is made if the selected emotion does not conform to expectations. (11) A mechanism to resolve any continuing discordance. (12) The selected mechanism then defines a new emotion. (13) Finally, there is the construction of situational components to fit with the selected emotion.

Frijda (1970) simplifies this formulation to three main points. (1) Categorizing an observed behaviour pattern in terms of a set of general dimensions of emotion. (2) Further differentiation. (3) The specification of probable emotion from situational cues or suppositions. Theoretically, Frijda (1970) suggests that his view of emotional expression is also applicable to emotion in general. But the relationship between expressive behaviour and emotion is too complicated for this sort of direct inference to be made. It is clear that every emotion can occur in many different expressions, sometimes with very little in common, and often with little hope of its recognition out of context. On the other hand, all the complex combinations of expression make sense in their situational context.

Finally, it should be said that in spite of the various attempts to define dimensions of emotional meaning, the process is much more complicated than simply inferring the dimensions of emotion directly from the dimensions of the recognition of emotional expression. And in real-life situations with all their other cues, our recognitions and even the recognition process itself *may* be quite different from those suggested by laboratory studies.

8

Pathological Emotion—Anxiety

The topic of pathological or morbid emotion can be said to cover the whole field of psychopathology. For example, as the term suggests, all of the affective disorders are implicated in emotion, schizophrenia can be regarded as involving emotional change, the neuroses are largely characterized by problems of anxiety, the emotional problems of old age can become pathological, and so on. *Any* abnormal behaviour can be viewed as an emotional disturbance or at least as involving abnormal (unusual) links between stimuli and emotional responses. The abnormality lies not in the emotion itself but in the interaction between the individual and his circumstances. Be this as it may, there is little profit in attempting to cover the whole sphere of mental illness in one chapter. Any understanding that this might bring would be severely limited by its lack of depth. In delimiting the area to be considered, the one concept which there is no justification for excluding is anxiety. It is a ubiquitous concept, the definition of which escapes precision, and yet one which has been much used in the description and explanation of abnormality. The problems which it embodies reflect many of those to be found in the study of both emotion and abnormality. The present chapter will therefore be restricted mainly to a discussion of anxiety.

More particularly, there will be discussion of (1) the definition of anxiety; (2) the measurement of anxiety; (3) the aetiology of anxiety. The related topics of psychosomatic illness, experimental neurosis and the treatment of neurosis by desensitization will also be discussed.

Even though it is impossible to provide solutions to them, it is worthwhile mentioning some of the problems which make this field difficult. The most obvious is that of definition. There are numerous definitions of abnormality, each of which has its good points. There are far more of anxiety, all of which leave unanswered questions. For example, is anxiety simply a convenient shorthand way of describing certain behaviours typically found in particular circumstances? Or is it an internal state which causes abnormal behaviour or leads to mental illness? What is the distinction between normal and abnormal anxiety? A second problem is that some of the studies in this area have been carried out on animals. If there is debate about the relevance of animal investigations to normal human behaviour, then there is surely even more with regard to abnormal human behaviour. Do animals become neurotic and psychotic as we know it? Is it meaningful to apply a concept such as anxiety to animals and then extrapolate to man? Finally, of course, there is the problem of how generally useful the concept of anxiety can be. Does it lead to predictions that would not otherwise be made, or does it simply add confusion to an already confusing field?

THE DEFINITION OF ANXIETY

Anxiety from the clinical viewpoint

General reaction (see Mayer-Gross *et al.* 1969 for a fuller description)

From the clinical viewpoint, anxiety reactions are regarded as normal adaptive responses which carry unpleasant emotional overtones. They are described as involving a strong expectation of danger, threat and distress for which an extra effort will be needed, but about which nothing can be done at the time. Physically, there is increased ANS activity, a rise in the output of adrenalin and a rise in blood pressure and heart rate. The skin becomes sweaty and pale and the mouth dry. Respiration is deep and frequent and the muscles lose tone. Rate of defecation and urination increases. If this state continues for some time, then fidgety movements begin to appear and digestion and sleep are affected.

From such a description it is difficult to decide whether we are dealing with a bodily state, a complex of feelings, or a set of behavioural and physiological responses. However, anxiety is recognized not only as the most common neurosis but also as basic to the other neuroses. It is often believed to occur as a secondary reaction to depression and it is implicated in specific phobias which tend to develop after stress in someone already suffering from an anxiety neurosis. Prolonged anxiety inevitably leads to physical debilitation, which in turn will often lead to hypochondriasis; an hysterical reaction may then result. Sometimes 'depersonalization' is seen in those anxiety states which are also symptomatized by agarophobia.

Anxiety is regarded as coming about through organic conditions or as an accompaniment to involutional melancholia and the depressive psychoses. Genetic and constitutional factors become implicated when it is seen as associated both with immaturity and advanced age. For example, tendencies to anxiety are usually described as lessening markedly when the normal individual moves from adolescence to adulthood. Also, in any anxiety neurosis there is usually some precipitating factor. This may vary from organic stress to psychological stress. It is thought to be more likely to occur in those who are unsure of themselves; they are doubtful of their own ability to achieve and to cope; they magnify their own failures, worries, tensions and apprehensions. At best, they are people who need a great deal of support from others; they are immature, dependent and sexually cool. After the precipitating event, there is fearful anticipation, tension and restlessness. Relaxation is replaced by fidgety, stereotyped movements. The emotional state is unpleasant, often with depression. Sleep and concentration are each broken and poor, and the person becomes irritable, short-tempered, frustrated and impatient.

Simple anxiety

Simple anxiety is usually described as characterized by 'free-floating' effects; although very evident, the anxiety is not attached to specific stimuli. There is a preponderance of somatic symptoms. The responses of the cardiovascular system become heightened and unstable. There are palpitations, feelings of faintness, pressure on the chest and feelings of suffocation in close and cramped conditions. There is also a general alimentary dysfunction with a lack of appetite, a dry mouth and dyspepsia. Bowel actions are disturbed and frequency of urination rises. Sexual functions are impaired. These 'symptoms' tend to become worse in any crowded situation which offers no obvious, inconspicuous egress.

Phobic anxiety

Gelder and Markes (1966) suggest a classification which distinguishes mono-symptomatic phobias from those which are more complex. They regard the former (mainly animal phobias) as often beginning in childhood and being fairly well contained, specific to the one object. The latter tend to appear between the ages of 25 to 35, mostly in young married women, and are agarophobic. They suggest that the main cause is the stress produced by the loneliness of early marriage after being used to a wide family circle. These more complex phobias often begin as simple anxiety states on which agarophobic or depersonalized anxiety becomes superimposed. They are at their most intense in enclosed spaces and crowds. The anxiety phobic may not be able to leave home, or may not be able to stay in it alone, or may only be able to go out wearing dark glasses or at night. There are usually intermittent feelings of depersonalization and unreality.

Another recent classification (Markes 1967) is into: (1) specific animal phobias; (2) specific situational phobias; with these there is no generalized anxiety, the symptoms persist but are treatable; (3) social anxieties, which are not very different from (4) anxiety based on agarophobia and depersonalization. Markes again regards women of 25 to 35 as being the main class of people likely to suffer situational and general anxieties.

Diagnostically, it is often thought to be difficult to separate the anxiety neuroses from the depressive disorders; they tend to be heavily linked. Gurney and Roth (1969) allocated 145 patients to one or other of these categories. Analysis showed that those classified as anxious were more unstable than the depressives and that they more often came from a neurotic or unstable family background. They were poorer socially and were more immature and dependent. Gurney and Roth managed quite clear differentiation on 13 diagnostic features.

Some theories of anxiety

The theories of anxiety which are summarized below have been chosen because they seem to be representative of the general field, but it must be added that this is according to my own interpretations which, in such a vast and amorphous area of study, are somewhat arbitrary. For more comprehensive reviews see: Fischer (1970); Hoch and Zubin (1950); Lader (1969); Lazarus *et al.* (1952); Malmo (1957); Spence (1958); Spielberger (1966); Taylor (1956).

A natural starting point for a theoretical consideration of anxiety is with Freud, who regarded anxiety as an unpleasant affective state and sought to distinguish between *objective* anxiety and *neurotic* anxiety. At first, he described anxiety as resulting from a discharge of repressed, unrelieved, somatic sexual tension. Such libidinal excitation produced dangerous mental images which were therefore repressed. The blocked libinal energy built up and turned into anxiety. Freud's revised analysis was more general. He regarded anxiety as a danger signal, and differentiated between objective anxiety, with its sources in the external world, and neurotic anxiety, with internal causes. This is an obvious parallel to reactive and endogenous depression. In more detail, he viewed objective anxiety as dependent on external danger; this leads to the perception of the danger and then the anxiety. The intensity of such anxiety would vary in proportion to the size of the external danger. Freud's proposed aetiology of neurotic, internal, anxiety was more complex; here, he described four stages. (1) Aggressive or sexual impulses in childhood for which the child is strongly punished. (2) Objective anxiety; the apprehension of punishment for the acts in (1). (3) An attempt to reduce this objective anxiety by repressing whatever stimuli are associated with the punished impulses. (4) Finally, neurotic anxiety as representing a partial breakdown in this repression, the anxiety seeming objectless to the individual since he is not conscious of the repression. Although Freud believed that we all show some neurotic anxiety, he also regarded it as basic to the neuroses.

Other anxiety theorists have usually made things no clearer than this. There is simply lack of agreement. For example, and in brief, Spielberger (1966) quotes *Mowrer* (1950), who has a theory of guilt. In this, anxiety comes from those acts which the individual has committed but which he also regrets. Thus neurotic anxiety comes from not paying attention to one's conscience; irresponsible, self-indulgent behaviour. And *Sullivan* (1953), who regards anxiety as intensely unpleasant tension resulting from experiences of interpersonal disapproval. And, finally, *May* (1950), who believes anxiety to result from an apprehension brought about by a threat to any value which an individual might regard as essential to his personality. He views neurotic anxiety as disproportionate to the objective danger and as involving no repression.

Or, in more detail, consider a different view of anxiety put forward by Prick (1969), who is primarily concerned with the place of anxiety in the psychoses. He describes endogenous manic depression as basically compulsive and implying a moral/ethical sensitivity. Thus there is continual moral anxiety from feelings of failure. He does not attempt to define moral anxiety but states that it implies to the person involved that it is right that he be harshly punished for his failures. This makes him more anxious. So the anxious depressive is guilty, scrupulous and despondent. Prick also argues for an even more complex role for anxiety in schizophrenia, again without the luxury of a definition. At first, anxiety warns the person that his existence is in danger, but with a worsening of the disorder the anxiety becomes 'mortal anguish'. Anxiety constricts the schizophrenic and therefore to some extent protects him from his threatening environment. Prick regards anxiety as an instinctive response to threat, but a response which makes things seem even more terrifying than they are—then it becomes obsessive. The schizophrenic has both 'normal' and pathological anxiety. The latter eventually overpowers his ego and he may kill himself. The weaknesses in definition, conceptualization and testability in a thesis such as this are too obvious to be worth further elucidation.

One of the most extensive theories of anxiety to emerge in recent years is that of Epstein (1967). He bases his ideas on a series of investigations involving parachutists. On the days of their jumps he took three measures from novice and experienced parachutists: (1) physiological reactions to parachute-relevant words in word-association tests; (2) subjective ratings of fear; and (3) physiological reactions at all stages of aircraft ascent. His general, and very consistent, findings were that novices show a steep monotonic gradient of both expressed fear and physiological arousal as a function of time or of the four levels of parachute-relevant stimuli in the word-association tests. Experienced jumpers, on the other hand, provide inverted V-shaped curves relating fear and arousal to time and relevant cues; with increasing experience, the peak of these curves nears the remote end of the dimension. These findings were established in both cross-sectional and longitudinal studies. It was also noted that differential functional relationships obtained for physiological arousal and self-reported fear. Rising fear and its inhibition regularly preceded rising physiological arousal and its inhibition.

 These results led Epstein to put forward a general theory of anxiety, or more properly of the mastery of anxiety. He proposed that two developments accompany any increasing experience with some threatening stimulus: (1) a generalization gradient of anxiety heightens, steepens or broadens; (2) an inhibition gradient develops and becomes increasingly steeper than the anxiety gradient. Epstein also argues that psychological and physiological inhibitory reactions are organized into a system of defence in depth. He suggests that there are three lines of defence, each of which allows an organism to maintain an appropriate level of arousal: (1) fear and its inhibition; (2) physiological arousal and its psychological inhibition; and (3) physiologically mediated (i.e. reflexive) inhibition.

Epstein goes on to a comparative analysis of fear, arousal and anxiety. Briefly, he views fear as an avoidance motive and arousal as a nonspecific excitation which underlines all motives and reactions. Anxiety is an undirected arousal state which follows the perception of danger. He characterizes it as extremely noxious and as therefore often channelled into direct motives (fear), so allowing the possibility of action. This is clearly an adaptive function, implying as it does an increased likelihood of direct action as the situation (threat) worsens.

Epstein regards these ideas as resulting in a system for keeping high arousal within reasonable limits. He sees this as part of a general system for modulating the *intensity* of all stimulation. As a theoretical substrate for this view, he provides a set of postulates. These relate excitation and inhibition to stimulus intensity, the time since stimuli were presented and the numbers and rate of stimulus inputs. Although these postulates are very speculative, Epstein believes that they apply to a wide range of phenomena (for example, the working through of extreme grief, and GSR adaptation). Finally, he suggests that his basic unifying assumption regarding anxiety should qualify as a law of excitatory modulation. This states that '. . . the gradient of inhibition as a function of increasing (or decreasing) excitation is steeper than the gradient of excitation that it inhibits' (1967, p. 86). He believes that this law describes how the intensity of any stimulation is modified, allowing the organism to function at appropriate (i.e. efficient) levels of arousal.

Epstein extends his basic theory (law) by freely speculating on its implications for psychology in general. For example, he argues that experimental psychologists should most profitably concentrate on analyses of unconditioned stimuli before analysing conditioned stimuli. Or, in a very different area, Epstein suggests that the implication for the schizophrenic is that with his relatively high and low levels of arousal any further stimulation is noxious. The schizophrenic therefore learns to protect himself from this stimulation, thereby inevitably restricting his contact with the world.

Clearly, Epstein has made a very broad attempt at theoretical unification in this difficult field. Although many of his ideas are highly speculative, they are also useful in that they lead to testable predictions. His studies with parachutists are interesting, well conducted and informative, and, resting on them as it does, his basic theory of anxiety is more firmly grounded than most. However, in extending his theoretical arguments he strays a long way from his original data. Although it is worthwhile and stimulating, Epstein's 'unified' theory of anxiety perhaps suffers from being a little too grandiose.

In his very useful attempt at theoretical clarification of anxiety, Spielberger (1966) suggests that conceptual ambiguity has surrounded the term because it has been typically used in two different ways. (1) As a complex response—a fluctuating state, varying in intensity. (2) As a personality trait, in which there are individual differences. On the basis of factor analytic studies, Cattell and Scheier (1958; 1961) identified two distinct anxiety factors, which they labelled (1) trait anxiety and (2) state anxiety. Trait anxiety refers to stable, individual differences in relatively permanent personality characteristics and state anxiety to a transitory, fluctuating state.

In the field of transitory anxiety, most work seems to have focused on delineating the state and outlining the conditions which may invoke it. Krause (1961) concludes that it can be inferred from six types of evidence: introspective reports, physiological signs, gross behaviours such as bodily posture, speech, etc., task performance, clinical intuition, and responses to stress. However, he suggests that the most important of these is introspective report, since most researchers argue that all one needs to be satisfied that anxiety is present is this plus some physiological or behavioural indices. Martin (1961) describes anxiety as a complex response pattern which should be carefully distinguished from its eliciting internal or external stimuli. This concentrates attention on physiological/behavioural patterns which distinguish anxiety/fear from other emotions. This formulation also carries the implication that it is important to differentiate anxiety from the cognitions and behaviours which are learnt to reduce it.

Work on personality anxiety has mainly centred around subjects chosen because they differ in measured anxiety level. For example, patients with high chronic anxiety have been compared with nonanxious controls in stressful and nonstressful conditions. Using this method of investigation, Malmo (1950; 1957; 1959) has concluded that the chronically anxious show much more reactivity and variability than normals, irrespective of stress. Also, many questionnaire-based studies have been carried out on normal populations. Recent instances of these (for example Spielberger and Smith 1966) suggest that subjects with high manifest anxiety scale scores have higher than average responses in situations involving some stress, but not otherwise. Trait anxiety may therefore be measuring anxiety proneness. However, in more general terms, state anxiety is seen as an empirical reaction occurring *now* at some given intensity. Trait anxiety is a latent disposition for a certain type of reaction if this is cued by the necessarily stressful stimuli.

Spielberger (1966) proposes an interesting trait-state conceptualization of anxiety. He suggests that anxiety as a state is characterized by subjective, conscious feelings of apprehension and tension, with ANS rousal. Anxiety as a personality trait is more like a motive or an acquired behavioural disposition, predisposing the perception of a threatening environment and also predisposing disproportionate responses to these threatening situations. He suggests further that the arousal of anxiety states involves a series of events. (1) An external stimulus or internal cue. (2) If there is a cognitive appraisal of danger or threat, then an anxiety state develops. (3) The sensory and cognitive feedback may make the anxiety state act as a signal which initiates a behaviour sequence to deal with the danger or avoid it. (4) Also, cognitive or motivational defence processes have been effective in reducing past anxiety states by altering appraisals. (There are clear similarities between this view of anxiety and Arnold's, for example 1960, more general view of emotion.) Anxiety traits, on the other hand, reflect residues of past experiences which have determined individual differences in anxiety-proneness, the most important aspect of this probably being during childhood and involving parent/child punishment situations. Finally, he suggests that anxiety-trait level will only affect some anxiety-state responses, depending on the stressfulness of the situation.

Spielberger's ideas have been described in some detail since they represent a worthwhile attempt at synthesis in a very woolly theoretical field. They gain impetus because they were suggested by two distinctly developed areas of enquiry. Even so, they are speculative and the lack of a general definition is very apparent. Also, whether or not we are considering transient anxiety as well as anxiety as a more permanent characteristic, the status of the concept remains obscure. We cannot say if it is best to regard it as a state of the organism or as a set of physiological and behavioural responses. If we define it in terms of responses, then it is difficult to say whether it is best left there or whether these responses should be seen as symptomatic of some underlying (causal) condition. Also, the distinction between 'normal' and pathological anxiety remains hidden. The differentiation implicit in much of the foregoing discussion is one of degree; the more extreme forms of transitory or personality anxiety are considered abnormal. The difficulties with this viewpoint are: (1) the arbitrariness involved in drawing the demarcation line; (2) the question of whether or not different determinants might underlie normal and abnormal anxiety. In an attempt to illustrate some of these difficulties, the topic of psychosomatic illness will be discussed. This is clearly pathological and anxiety is obviously implicated.

Psychosomatic illness

Psychosomatic disorders have medical, organic symptoms, but an aetiology closely bound up with psychological variables. Although there have been many models and definitions of psychosomatics, most of them include specific reference to emotional disturbance (particularly anxiety) since the symptoms are seen in structures innervated by the ANS, the stomach, bronchioles and skin for example. (Instances of the more common disorders are asthma, peptic ulcers and hypertension.) However, it should be said at the outset that it is impossible to determine the extent of the emotional involvement, the degree to which emotion is a causative factor. Sternbach's (1966) view is that *all* illness is psychosomatic, but that some diseases have more obvious emotional aspects than others.

There have been many explanations offered for psychosomatic illness. For example, one viewpoint is that, biologically, emotions have come to energize us for survival. Nowadays, however, violent physical responses gain social disapproval. Hence, we experience emotion from physiological change, but have no opportunity to discharge our energy behaviourally. Organic changes persist and pathology results. Alternatively, it has been argued that psychosomatic disorder results when physiological responses in emotion are either too great or too small. This leads to excessive or inadequate adaptation. Finally, from the psychoanalytic viewpoint, it is said that if a person regresses for example, the inappropriate emotions associated with an earlier stage in his development lead to specific symptoms and pathology results.

These various ways of accounting for psychosomatic disorder can be categorized into two major groups, the biological and the psychological. A more detailed example will be given of each of these and the work of Grinker will be covered, since he has done much to aid our understanding of psychosomatic disorder, both conceptually and as regards measurement. Moreover, his views rely heavily on the notion of anxiety. (For a full summary of theories of psychosomatics see Buss 1966.)

The biological theory of psychosomatics most relevant to emotion suggests that

patterns of autonomic reactivity are inherited. This is based largely on the work
of such as Lacey *et al.* (1963) and Lacey and Lacey (1958), which shows consistent individual variation in automatic reactivity. They demonstrate that there are
hierarchies of autonomic reactivity which are maintained whatever the stress
might be. Of course, it could be that such differences are learned. But Mirsky
(1958) showed fairly conclusively that physiological overreactivity, which is
probably inherited, is an important determinant of ulcer formation.

There are many psychological theories of psychosomatic disorder, but they can
be exemplied by Mahl (1950). He points to the importance of fear (anxiety) in
this context, and sees it as usually preventing the expression of behaviour. For
example, a conflict between dependency and anxiety will lead to ulcers, between
anger and anxiety to hypertension, and fear of separation or crying in children
will lead to asthma. Mahl's theory is specific to ulcers and is based on studies
with dogs, monkeys and students. For instance, he compared students who were to
sit an examination later in the day with those who were not. He found more free
hydrochloric acid in the 'anxious' than the 'nonanxious' group. Confirmation of
this comes from Brady's (1958b; 1963) studies on 'executive' monkeys. Monkeys
were studied in pairs, one being trained to respond to shock for both of them.
Only the executive monkey developed ulcers. Mahl suggests that acute anxiety
leads to sympathetic dominance and therefore a decrease in stomach acid, but
that in chronic anxiety the parasympathetic nervous system becomes dominant and
acid is secreted. This is supported by research which shows that acid is only
secreted after prolonged anxiety. To account for some individuals developing
ulcers and others not, such a theory must also depend on the inheritance of
physiological dispositions.

In making observations during World War II, Grinker and Spiegel (1945)
showed that, in the field of battle, moderate anxiety facilitated performance. On
the other hand, excessive anxiety resulted in inefficiency. Perceptions were distorted and the men became overreactive. They described this as tending to lead
to psychological and physical regression and dependency, which often became
intensified towards the end of stressful stimuli. Various post-war studies (for example Harrower and Grinker 1946) confirmed these observations. Grinker also
developed a test of stress tolerance which provided an index of the capacity to
tolerate stress and recover from it.

Grinker (1966) argues that he chose to measure anxiety because it is ubiquitous and because it spirals; in his terms, inadequacy leads to anxiety leads to
inadequacy leads to anxiety... He regards mild anxiety as a useful signal for
threat, but extreme anxiety as leading to a great disorganization in behaviour. He
suggests that psychopathological defences often develop against this extreme
anxiety. Thus he regards anxiety as a fundamental mover in behaviour. He believes this to be evident in any form of therapy; when defences are penetrated
there is the underlying anxiety. Grinker *et al.* (1961) go further and say that
anxiety as a feeling indicates that an individual is moving into or out of a depression; any other factors are mere defences against the presence of anxiety. The

problem is worsened if we attempt to provide an external cause for our anxiety but cannot; it then becomes impossible to explain it away by calling it fear.

Although he basically regards anxiety as a danger signal, Grinker also views it as being associated with many interrelated but often individualistic somatic processes. As the anxiety increases so the somatic components become more diffuse. Anxiety also colours interpersonal behaviour with inexplicable feelings of the foreboding of danger or disintegration. The basic problem as Grinker sees it is that we are all prone, but we need to establish what makes this proneness become realized.

At the start of his work, Grinker was unable to find freely anxious people, so he had to manufacture anxiety. He did this in terms of four phases: alertness, apprehension, free anxiety and panic, the last two being seen as neurotic or pathological. His first studies were conducted on the liver (for example Persky *et al.* 1950; 1952). Substances which needed to be broken down in the liver were injected and a measure taken of the amount of hippuric acid secreted. The rapidity and degree of the breakdown was used as an index of the extent of the anxiety. As anxious patients were treated, so the amount of hippuric acid which they secreted fell. Grinker (1953) then moved on to an analysis of what he called 'system anxiety', i.e. he attempted to break down anxiety into its parts. He gradually developed what he believed to be reliable measures. These were based on: (1) observing patients diagnosed as anxious and developing specific verbal descriptions of their various degrees of anxiety; (2) interviewing the patients and taking statements as to their levels of anxiety; (3) having the patients rate their own anxiety. After this, anxiety was manipulated individually, this being determined by what the interviewer had found to be most likely to disturb the patient. The best method was usually to block dyadic communication. There were various problems with this technique—ranging from the anxiety produced by the comparative strangeness of the experimental set-up and the consequent difficulty in the first few stages of the experiments, to the slowness involved in the experimental production of anxiety. Also, it is ethically impossible to subject someone to anxiety-provoking experiences for more than two to three hours, and, of course, responses such as anger and depression were also often unwittingly invoked.

Grinker's analysis points to anxiety as having a central place in the aetiology of psychosomatic disorders. Initially, there was excitement over Alexander's (1950) idea that there are specific emotional factors involved in degenerative diseases not associated with bacterial infection—such as migraine. Thus, if people suffer from a particular emotion for a long time then psychosomatic symptoms will develop. However, Grinker (1966) argues that it has been long observed that various psychosomatic diseases do *not* have specific emotional aetiologies, but instead ones that are characterized by specificity of response. Hence, he suggests that the main causative factor is likely to be anxiety. Grinker (1953) also proposes that it is the individual conditioning of responses in the young organism that is critical in psychosomatics, rather than specific emotional constellations.

Grinker has clearly made a considerable contribution both to the study of psychosomatic disorders and to the study of anxiety, but again it is obvious from this description of his work and ideas that he is dealing with an obscure, nebulous concept that he can do little to clarify.

MEASUREMENT OF ANXIETY

If we assume that anxiety is a state of the organism, then at present it cannot be measured directly. However, it is presumably safe to regard it as being reflected both physiologically and behaviourally. In a discussion of the measurement of anxiety, one might also expect to see subjective report mentioned as a separate category. However, for the sake of simplicity, this will be regarded as a measure of verbal behaviour.

Anxiety and behaviour

At the behavioural level, anxiety has frequently been analysed in learning theory terms. It is regarded as denoting a secondary drive and a source of secondary reinforcement (see Chapter 5). The primary drive is pain. Neutral stimuli which are associated with this produce fear, which has drive properties; that is, it will motivate new behaviour. This conditioned fear is defined as anxiety. The reduction of such anxiety is reinforcing and therefore brings about learning. Miller (for example 1948; 1951) was the first to propose this idea. He demonstrated that neutral stimuli which have been associated with noxious stimuli become both motivating (an animal will escape from them) and reinforcing if they cease (they produce new learning).

Eysenck is the major advocate of the usefulness of this view of anxiety at the human level. He argues (for example 1969) that if anxiety is a drive then it should be governed by the laws which apply to drives in general. These are best seen via the Yerkes–Dodson law (cf. Broadhurst 1959). This proposes a curvilinear relationship between drive and performance, intermediate drives leading to optimal performance. Also, optimal drive level depends on the difficulty of whatever task is being performed, simple tasks having a high optimal drive level and complex tasks a low optimal drive level. There are many examples of this relationship in the psychological literature (see Easterbrook 1959 or Eysenck 1964 for review), although they are somewhat lacking in clarity. For example, no study has shown the inverted U relationship to exist within one subject.

With respect to anxiety, these propositions have two main implications. Anxiety may be produced by particular situations and have its effect on virtually anybody who experiences it. Studies on this tend to support the Yerkes–Dodson law. However, such anxiety-producing stimuli do not have similar effects on everybody; some individuals are habitually more anxious than others; they react more strongly to situations which would not be productive of anxiety in others. The parallel between this, Eysenck's view of anxiety, and Spielberger's is clear. However, Eysenck believes that studies on the personality variable of anxiety are best conducted via his own two-dimensional model of anxiety, with neuroticism (stability/unstability) and extraversion/introversion as the two orthogonal dimensions. He suggests (1967; 1969) a strong hereditary basis for these dimensions and also argues that they accord well with psychiatric classifications. For example, dysthymic neurotics are introverted and unstable, whereas psychopaths are extraverted and unstable. He believes that the dimensions have a firm physiological basis.

Eysenck regards anxiety (conditioned fear) as typifying the dysthymic personality. The evidence he regards as supporting this is exemplified by: (1) introverts are easier to condition than extraverts; (2) those with higher 'emotionality' show stronger responses to pain-producing stimuli. However, there would seem to be a basic confusion in the studies from which these results are taken, since they could have been due to differences either in extraversion/introversion or emotionality/stability. Also, it is not clear in what way emotionality (neuroticism) is related to anxiety. They may or may not be synonymous.

A further criticism of Eysenck's approach to anxiety is made by Pichot (1969), who argues against equating a disposition to anxiety with pathological anxiety. He reasons that pathological anxiety tends to be reduced when the anxious person is exposed to an objectively threatening situation. Also, he suggests that schizophrenics are often markedly anxious, but at the same time they are able to withstand extreme stress. He suggests that it may be that 'anxiety disposition' is the proneness to respond to real danger maladaptively, and that anxiety state is the result of nonobjective danger, a psychological conflict for example.

Some light is thrown on this general area by Cattell's (for example 1963) factor analytic studies of anxiety. His work is based on the idea that anxiety is an underlying state which is manifested in many ways, introspective, behavioural, physiological. He lists many 'typical' measures, for example hand steadiness, muscle tension and tendencies to see threatening stimuli in ink-blots. He took many such measures from large groups of people over a 12 year period. Factor analysis of these produced strong evidence for one main factor which he suggested could best be labelled anxiety.

In his original analysis, Cattell pointed out that he was clearly studying anxiety as a personality variable. However, by taking many measures of anxiety from one person over many days, he was also able to investigate anxiety as a fluctuating state. Again, factor analysis showed the importance of one factor. Cattell argues that this factor analytic conception of anxiety helps to locate the physiological patterns which are related to it and also separates them from those related to stress, of the type studied by Grinker (see above). In general, Cattell believes that factor analysis sorts out anxiety from neuroticism and stress reactions.

Anxiety and psychophysiology

Psychophysiological studies of anxiety in pathological form are in fact extensions of clinical observations—the clinician observes the sweaty palm, the psychophysiologist measures PGR. Reviews of such work may be seen in B. Martin (1961), I. Martin (1960) and Lader (1969b). There have been two main approaches to the subject, further variations on Spielberger's ideas. (1) Stimulation has been used to induce anxiety in normal subjects or psychiatric patients. (2) Differences have been measured between the anxious and the normal. As before, this implies two different conceptions of anxiety—as a predisposition and as a chronic, morbid, affective state. With anxiety seen as a predisposition, the stimuli used to produce it can be regarded as stressful, in the sense taken by Lazarus and Opton (1966). Usually, psychophysiological ANS measures, plus EEG and electromyograms, have been taken.

The best results come from cardiovascular measures. For example, in patients with anxiety states there is a general raising of heart rate (for example Lader and Wing 1966), although sometimes blood pressure has also been shown to be raised (for example Malmo and Shagass 1952). Large increases in the flow of blood into the forearms often accompany emotional stress. In a series of important studies, Kelly (1966; 1967) has shown that there is a greater flow of blood in the forearms of anxious patients at rest than there is in normal controls. Kelly and Walter (1968) go further, and show an increasing blood flow from normals through phobics, obsessionals, chronic schizophrenics and agitated depressives to chronic anxiety states. Other measures have not been especially productive, with the exception that, at rest, skin conductance levels are lower in anxious patients than in normal controls (for example Howe 1958). The typical finding for muscle activity is that, recording from the frontalis muscle, the EMG is reliably higher in anxious patients than in normals (for example Malmo 1950).

Lader (1969a) points to the problem of reactivity. If the 'resting' levels of various physiological measures are studied there is no consistent relationship between anxious patients and normal subjects. When stimulation is added there are more obvious differences, but these go in *both* directions. For example, Lader and Wing (1966) and Kelly (1966) find anxious subjects less reactive than controls, whereas Malmo and Shagass (1952) and Martin (1956) find them more reactive. One consistency is that anxious subjects adjust much more slowly to the experimental situation than do normal subjects. This is shown in two ways. First, the more anxious individuals are slow to adapt to a changing stimulus situation and slower to return to a pre-stimulation level of response (for example Martin 1956; Kelly 1966). Second, anxious subjects show impaired habituation to repetitive stimuli (for example Howe 1958).

In his review, Lader (1969) de-emphasizes arousal, but also suggests that anxiety can be seen as one of many arousal states that can be distinguished as arousal becomes more intense. Hence, he argues that psychophysiological measures reflect the level of arousal and therefore the intensity of emotion. But, of course, he is forced to say, as has already been mentioned several times, that there are no *definite* physiological patterns yet delineated for different emotions—with the usual three exceptions (i.e Ax 1953; Schachter 1957; Wolf and Wolff 1947).

Lader also provides four reasons for the relative unimportance of psychophysiological measures of anxiety to psychiatric considerations. (1) Very broad groupings tend to have been used in the studies which have been completed, for example 'neurotics'; to be meaningful the divisions must be smaller than this. (2)

The methodology of the studies has often been poor. (3) There are obvious intrinsic limitations to the measuring techniques which have been used. (4) It is not *anxiety* which has been measured. This, of course, is the most cogent criticism; it rests on the argument that a high level of physiological reactivity is not necessarily an indicator of anxiety. The increased physiological activity may be a secondary reaction to increased physiological needs and/or high arousal may accompany other states of intense emotion.

The best work in this field is probably Lader's. He has tended to use a standard set of stimuli, for example 20, 1 kHz, 1 sec tones at 100 db presented randomly but on average once every 45 to 80 sec. He has found that the best measure of the effects of these is PGR. Using such a procedure, Lader and Wing (1964), for example, showed that anxious subjects exhibited higher physiological activity than normal controls and hardly habituated at all to the stimulus. Lader (for example 1967) has also extended this same type of technique to other, more fine-grained classifications of abnormality.

THE CAUSATION OF ANXIETY

Again, leaving aside the question of whether anxiety is a state or a set of responses, many different accounts have been given of its possible causation. In this section, two very distinct but representative aetiological hypotheses will be described. The view of anxiety causation which relies on learning theory has already been mentioned. Some of its more practical extensions into the field of experimental neurosis will be considered below. Finally, this presents a good opportunity for a brief discussion of the efficacy of desensitization as a method of alleviating anxiety neuroses.

Anxiety and affection

Bowlby (1961; 1969) discusses the role of affectional bonds, particularly those between mother and child, in the formation of pathological anxiety. Freud proposed the idea with his suggestion that anxiety in children is caused by the loss of some loved person. He extended this idea to consider anxiety as the reaction to the possibility of the loss of the loved object, and to argue that the reaction to the actual loss be termed mourning. From this basic viewpoint, pathological anxiety arises from disturbed interpersonal relationships. Bowlby maintains that there is much evidence at both human (Bowlby 1961) and animal (Schneirla 1965) levels that supports this hypothesis.

Bowlby suggests that two sorts of behaviour are related to subjective feelings of anxiety: escape and attachment. Escape is the result of sudden and strange events; attachment occurs when the members of a 'bonded pair' become separated from one another. Without discussing all the evidence and theories of such separation anxiety, it can be said with reasonable conviction that some children with an unsettled early home life are far more anxious than control children who have had more settled home lives. Also, some of these children are more aggressive and more antisocial. Separation anxiety only becomes pathological when it is extreme, although of course it is difficult to define what is meant by extreme. Clinicians such as Bowlby believe that proneness to this more extreme anxiety is caused by childhood exposure to long or repeated separations in strange surroundings—or at least exposure to threats of this. An adult who has had such experiences will tend to be overreactive to loss. The most extreme reactions are likely to occur if a parent threatens to commit suicide, or possibly when a grandparent dies.

Bowlby's ideas have clear importance for the genesis of anxiety and perhaps provide a base for attempting to alleviate pathological anxiety in children. However, although the idea of separation anxiety is intuitively reasonable, the evidence in support of it is somewhat shaky, again due in part to difficulties in definition.

Anxiety and genetics

Slater and Shields (1969) provide a review of studies designed to assess possible genetic influences on anxiety. Various well-controlled selective breeding experiments with mammals (for example Broadhurst 1967) have shown that emotional reactivity (which is presumed to be akin to anxiety) depends on multiple genetic factors. Twin studies in man have shown ANS function to have hereditary components (for example Lader and Wing 1966). This result is supported by questionnaire studies on mono- and dizyogotic twins, at least for the dysthymic aspects of neurotisism (cf. Vandenberg 1967). Further support comes from family studies (for example Cohen 1951) which show that about 15 per cent of the parents and siblings of anxiety neurotics are also highly anxious. A large-scale study by Slater and Shields (1969) showed that 50 per cent of the co-twins of anxiety neurotics had the same diagnosis, and 65 per cent showed marked anxiety traits. The equivalent figures for dizygotic twins were 4 per cent and 13 per cent. Slater and Shields suggest that the evidence gathered from twins reared apart militates against any environmental explanation of the hereditary twin studies, and in fact argue that a predisposition to anxiety is best accounted for by some interaction between heredity and environment.

Although work such as this is suggestive of possible genetic involvement in anxiety, as usual the lack of definition makes interpretation difficult. Even in this brief description, the terms emotional reactivity, ANS function, dysthymic neuroticism and anxiety have been used. Although there must be considerable overlap between these expressions, they are by no means synonymous. However, it is not possible to be precise about the similarities and differences between them.

Experimental neurosis and densensitization

For reviews of experimental neurosis and the various behaviour therapy techniques which have developed from it see Kimble (1961), Lazarus (1972) and Wolpe (1961; 1966). The basic problem is implicit in the question—if neuroses are learned, then how does this learning occur? The psychoanalytic answer is either that there are learned habits of repressing painful complexes, or that the ego is the locus of anxiety in its attempts to suppress the antisocial desires of the id. Wolpe, on the other hand, suggests that neuroses occur through simple conditioning. In discussing this, he focuses on conditioned anxiety, which he regards as central to the neuroses.

The background to this approach was laid by Pavlov (1928) as an outcrop of his research into the conditioned reflex, and was extended by such as Liddell (1944) and Masserman (1943). Pavlov found that some of the dogs used in his experiments began to behave irregularly and became difficult to handle. He described such 'experimental neuroses' as occurring when: (1) either the excitatory or inhibitory processes in conditioning were overstrained; (2) these processes followed one another too closely in time; (3) there was a conflict between emotion and drive; (4) a very rigid time schedule was followed during conditioning. These observations led to the development of two methods for producing experimental neuroses. (1) Subjecting animals to ambivalent stimuli when they are under the influence of a powerful drive. This is exemplified by Pavlov's circle and ellipse study. These stimuli were presented to hungry dogs, the circle being linked with food, the ellipse with shock. Subsequently, the semi-axes of the ellipses were altered such that they increasingly approximated to the circle. This produced an increasing and generalized anxiety in the dogs, i.e. they whined, froze, increased eliminative responses and would not work in the experimental situation. (2) Presenting animals with aversive stimuli in confined spaces. Liddell and Masserman originally suggested that experimental neurosis produced in this way is the result of conflict, but Wolpe (1952) and Smart (1965) have shown that it simply depends upon the shock. Experimental neuroses can be excitatory or inhibitory in their effect, leading to large general increases in activity or to hypnotic, sleep-like conditions. Either way, both cortical and subcortical changes are evident. On the one hand, any ongoing, learned behaviour is interfered with; on the other, there are changes in responses such as respiration and heart rate. The degree of the neurosis seems to depend on predispositional factors—the previous 'emotionality' of the animal.

If the work on experimental neurosis can be meaningfully generalized to the development of neuroses under 'natural' conditions in humans, i.e. if neuroses are learned, then according to Wolpe (1966) they will show three common features of learning. (1) Neurotic behaviour will be similar to that which occurred in the precipitating situation. (2) The neurotic responses will occur in the presence of the original stimuli. (3) There will be stimulus generalization; neurotic responses will be strongest to those stimuli which are most like the original ones. Each of these features was shown in Wolpe's neurotic cats—the same ANS responses were evident as produced by the original shock, the reactions were always strongest in the experimental cages where the shock had been given, and there were many types of stimulus generalization. From the human point of view, anxiety, as we have seen, is thought to be at the forefront of most neuroses and in the background of others. The starting point for a neurosis is usually regarded as a single or recurrent anxiety-producing event of a chronic anxiety situation. The stimuli present at this time are those which are most likely to become conditioned to neurotic anxiety responses, although second-order conditioning may occur. Also, stimulus generalization is clearly evident in neurotic anxiety.

Wolpe (1966) argues that neurotic anxiety is very persistent, even though in the long term it is maladaptive and in the short term it is unpleasant. For example, if the phobic patient is forced into contact with the feared object he does not improve and may in fact worsen—the neurosis may even spread in this way. However, it can easily be eliminated by counterconditioning: presenting the anxiety-invoking stimuli when anxiety-inhibiting responses are present. To return to the animal studies, Masserman, using cats, conditioned anxiety to a buzzer. They were then made hungry and required to eat food pellets 40 feet away from the original situation. Anxiety gradually disappeared. Then, by degrees, the distance was diminished. Food-approach responses systematically weakened the anxiety. In humans many responses other than eating have been used as reciprocal inhibitors of anxiety (see Wolpe and Lazarus 1966). Wolpe (1966) describes three of the more common responses.

1. *Assertive* responses involve the overt expression of feelings other than anxiety. The therapist encourages the person to be assertive in the appropriate situations; each assertion reduces the anxiety a little, leading to easier assertion the next time, and so on.

2. *Sexual* responses are used mainly against neurotic reactions to sex, often impotence or premature ejaculation for example. The patient is persuaded to restrict his sexual advances to the point in time where he experiences minimal anxiety. He only allows himself to move on to the next point when the anxiety is entirely gone. Again there is a slow build-up, but of course this technique usually requires the aid of another person (or persons).

3. The idea of *deep relaxation* is probably the most important in this context; it began with Jacobson (1938; 1939; 1940). If a person is taught to relax deeply, then this involves him in ANS responses which are the opposite to those seen in anxiety. Bodily processes are at rest, rather than mobilized for some nebulous action. Clearly, these two states cannot be simultaneously evident, i.e. the PNS and SNS cannot be simultaneously dominant. Relaxation has been mainly used in the treatment of phobias. Wolpe (for example 1961) introduced the notion of *systematic desensitization*. This requires the construction of a hierarchy of situations which are increasingly threatening to the individual. Over the course of about one and a half hours of 15 minute sessions, the deeply relaxed patient is asked to imagine these situations. The weakest scene is presented first and repeated until it is reported that no anxiety is experienced while it is being thought of. The hierarchy is gradually worked through in this way. With any one patient, several hierarchies may be involved.

The learning theory approach to neurotic anxiety has produced an interesting therapeutic technique, but what of its success? Eysenck (1965) suggests that *any* therapy is successful in about 40 per cent of cases. Using techniques such as have just been described, Lazarus (1963; 1965) and Wolpe (1958) have achieved remission in 90 per cent of unselected neurotics. Although this is a very promising result and Wolpe asserts that the effects are lasting and that there is no symptom substitution, it has been largely confined to specific phobias; it has not been successful in cases of general anxiety neuroses.

CONCLUSIONS

The coverage of this chapter has been restricted and somewhat biased. A rough systematization has been given to the topic of anxiety and in particular pathological anxiety. In this way it was hoped to highlight some of the problems which typify the field of abnormal emotion, and indeed of abnormal behaviour in general. If these problems cannot be solved with respect to the centrally important concept of anxiety, then it is unlikely that they will be solved more generally.

It is clear that much of the theory and research into anxiety is poor. It tends to be descriptive rather than explanatory, with the descriptions themselves being made at very different levels, from the psychoanalytic to the physiological. When anxiety is used as an explanatory concept, then it suffers from a lack of definition. From a reading of this chapter, I am sure that it is impossible to give a precise definition of anxiety or to distinguish 'normal' anxiety from pathological anxiety. This is simply a reflection of the general field. There is a vast literature on anxiety, the surface of which has been barely scratched here, and it represents work carried out from many different standpoints and according to many personal whims and idiosyncracies. A similar problem is met with in any attempt to define abnormal emotion in general or to distinguish it from 'normal' emotion.

One conclusion that can be drawn is that there would seem to be two sorts of anxiety: (1) trait—enduring, a personality characteristic; (2) state—transient, situational-bound. In the extreme, either of these may be described as pathological, or as having pathological effects. Of course, the definition of 'extreme' is arbitrary. However, this conclusion is somewhat similar to Freud's ideas of neurotic and objective anxiety and has a parallel with endogenous and reactive depression. Other than this, we can say that it is impossible to measure anxiety directly, but that there are many indirect measures, that it has genetic and environmental causes, that it is important in certain illnesses and that in some form it can be produced experimentally.

In extending these conclusions, such as they are, to pathological emotion in general, their relative triviality becomes even more obvious. Sometimes abnormal emotion springs from what, to the individual, are abnormal and extreme external situations and sometimes it *seems* to come from within. The problem is further complicated if one considers that in psychopathology the anxiety (or the emotions) need not be particularly abnormal—if comparisons are made across individuals, it is not even an extension of 'normal' anxiety. It is the interaction of the person and his circumstances which is unusual. This may stem from an abnormal environmental situation and/or from an abnormal constitution which predisposes extreme reactions to relatively mild stimuli. So-called pathological or morbid anxiety (or emotion) is then little more than a corollary to this.

Overall we are in a state of ignorance; much remains to be done, particularly from an aetiological viewpoint We simply do not know what makes one person anxious or depressed and another not. We do not know whether (pathological) anxiety (or emotion) is best understood as a series of behavioural or physiological responses, or as an internal state which affects overt behaviour. We do not even know what *type* of definition is most appropriate. However, to end on a somewhat brighter note, Gellhorn and Loufbourrow's (1963) general analysis of pathological emotion will be described. Although, like any theory, it can be disputed in part, it does represent a well-conceived attempt to pin down pathological emotion and to relate it to 'normal' emotion.

Initially, Gellhorn and Loufbourrow (1963) review fields such as experimental neurosis, sensory deprivation (for example Solomon *et al.* 1961) and stress. In each case they argue that the hypothalamus is crucially involved. For example, they suggest that the hypothalamus is unable to cope with the reduced sensory input characteristic of sensory deprivation or that prolonged stress produces hypothalamic changes which may ultimately prove pathological. They maintain that in neurosis and experimental neurosis the two divisions of the hypothalamus are simultaneously activated; this produces autonomic imbalance, which in turn leads to neurosis. The premorbid balance determines the extent of the reaction, in some cases there being no neurosis at all. They suggest that such effects occur following exposure to severe and unexpected pain, 'emotional excitement', particularly where life is threatened, and strong conflicts. Each of these will change behaviour, via their effect on the hypothalamus; the autonomic changes may persist for years with the behavioural aspects varying from stuporous to manic, convulsive to compulsive.

Gellhorn and Loufbourrow support the role of the hypothalamus in emotion by their analysis of the physiological mechanisms involved in such states as hypertension, peptic ulcers, nausea and fever. They believe that all evidence points to the importance of the hypothalamically-controlled autonomic balance. For example, the SNS is predominant in sympathotonics, so disposing hypertension. Gellhorn and Loufbourrow argue that the experience of different moods is the reflection of various states which exist between the extremes of hypothalamic action on the cortex, from emotional excitement (sympathetic—ergotropic) to sleep (parasympathetic—trop' opic). Also involved are positive feedback systems, such that if the skeletal muscles are somehow relaxed, then emotional reactivity and possibly neurotic symptoms will be reduced (as in some aspects of behaviour therapy). Finally, they suggest that the physiological and pathological states of altered hypothalamic balance are characterized by changes in autonomic reactivity and by changes in the whole personality. These effects will result partially from altered hypothalamic–cortical discharges. This picture is complicated further by the influence of the hypothalamus on the endocrine system.

Gellhorn and Loufbourrow extend their argument with the suggestion that there is an interrelationship between emotional disturbance, autonomic changes and behaviour disorder. At this point their thesis weakens. They maintain, for example, that the fact that many investigators have emphasized the emotional aspects of psychoses and neuroses also points indirectly to the hypothalamus. Also, they suggest that perception depends on emotion and hence on the various links which exist between the hypothalamus and cortex. Anxiety modifies perceptual thresholds and perceptions are distorted in psychoses and neuroses. They argue that psychosis is characterized by two symptoms, which again point to the hypothalamus. (1) The psychotic will often not react to physical pain—the hypothalamus is pain-sensitive. (2) The catatonic schizophrenic state known as waxy flexibility can be produced by bilateral hypothalamic lesions (Ranson 1939).

In outlining the possible role of the hypothalamus and emotional responsiveness in the functional mental disorders, Gellhorn and Loufbourrow stress Walther's (1956) idea of the autonomic–affective syndrome, which shows fluctuations in mood, restlessness, anxiety and various autonomic disturbances. They argue that this syndrome is the response of a labile hypothalamic system to acute emotional stimuli and bodily stress and that a gradually developing imbalance from similar circumstances will produce hypertension or gastric ulcers. Walther also observed the autonomic–affective syndrome to precede functional psychoses and to occur transitorily during remission from a psychosis and on awakening from an insulin coma. This all supports the idea that 'mood' is determined by the state of the hypothalamus and its autonomic balance. Mood is determined by the hypothalamic–cortical discharge, and by the rate of secretion of various hormones.

Gellhorn and Loufbourrow's theory is best illustrated by a brief description of their analysis of battle fatigue and abreaction. They suggest that in combat fear is the first reaction. Those who are exposed to such fear for long periods of time and are unable to conquer it react with nervous fatigue, irritability and tenseness—an overreaction. They then become emotionally exhausted, dull, listless, apathetic, anxious and depressed. Sargant (1957) draws the parallel between this change from overreactivity to emotional exhaustion and some of the phenomena seen in experimental neurosis. Prolonged excitation of the SNS leads to a basic change in autonomic reactivity—the usual level of sympathetic dominance is increased. If this goes too far there is a reversal in autonomic balance and the general emotional state swings.

Abreaction involves reviving a memory of supposedly repressed unpleasant experiences and expressing the emotions related to them. This is believed to relieve the pressure on the personality: a release of emotions through reliving the experience. It is usually brought about by the administration of cortical depressants. Again, there is strong emotional excitement, then exhaustion, and then finally the disturbances disappear. Gellhorn and Loufbourrow suggest that the hypothalamic action which typifies intense excitement is enhanced by a cortical depressant since this releases the hypothalamus from cortical inhibition. After an abreaction there is some evidence for a physiological oscillation until the balance is restored; this is supported by the alternating laughter and crying which is seen at this stage. Thus, to Gellhorn and Loufbourrow, an abreaction consists of an intensive hypothalamic–cortical discharge, lessened hypothalamic–cortical interactions and the reestablishment of normal relations and excitability.

This has only been a brief description of some of Gellhorn and Loufbourrow's (1963) fundamental arguments. They range far wider than it is possible to show here. However, whatever the topic they touch on, it is with the same guiding principle: the conviction that the hypothalamus, its interactions with the cortex and the balance between its ergotropic and trophotropic systems are crucial to all aspects of emotion, particularly pathological emotion. At times they become highly speculative, but nevertheless provide a reasonably solid theoretical starting point for the future study of pathological emotion.

9

Overview

The aims of this final chapter are: (1) to summarize the current position in the various approaches which have been made to the study of emotion; (2) to discuss some of the problems which remain unsolved; (3) to present a framework within which any analysis of emotion could be made.

The search for a physiological substrate to emotion has shown both the CNS and the ANS (plus hormonal and chemical change) to be implicated. However, their relative importance remains unclear. Within the CNS, it is the evolutionarily 'older' parts of the brain (mainly the limbic system) which appear to be necessary to emotion. Their precise function and mechanism of action are still obscure. The indirect measures of psychophysiology have led to some well-conducted research on the ANS. However, the evidence for any physiological response patterning is disappointingly slight. All that can be definitely concluded is that the viscera are necessary to emotion.

There are many reasons for the absence of more precise conclusions at the physiological level. As mentioned in Chapter 1, there is the problem of reductionism. It may be inappropriate, particularly in our present state of knowledge, to attempt a reduction of the study of emotion to the physiological level. Also, of course, there is the more obvious reason that emotion may not have an easily interpretable physiological basis. Two more subsidiary but nevertheless cogent reasons are, firstly, that physiological research into emotion has run ahead of theory. It is comparatively more sophisticated and expert. Secondly, with a few exceptions, there has been little rapprochement with the behavioural approach. It is possible, and indeed likely, that a closer working relationship between these two levels of study would be highly productive.

The best that can be said of the more cognitive or phenomenological study of emotion is that it has led to some of the most interesting research in the whole field. However, the theorizing which lies behind this research is more open to question. The usual position has been based on a hypothetical interaction between physiological factors and cognition. Schachter's work, which is clearly the most significant in this area, suggests that although there is no physiological response patterning, patterns in emotion occur through cognitive labelling. This is possibly an illuminating point, but the general theorizing which backs it up is too speculative. It is difficult to decide whether or not it is useful to consider possible cognitive elements in emotion (this will be discussed further below). It may be that it provides an appropriate way of conceptualizing the milder aspects of emotion if not the more intense.

The other main orientation in emotion is the behavioural, research based on which has been methodologically sounder than any other in the study of emotion. Definitions have been precise and operational. There has recently been a great proliferation of research with both Hullian and Skinnerian frameworks. However, there are some rather naive, half-explanatory, half-descriptive concepts to be found in this area, 'emotionality' for example. Also, although the behavioural approach has been highly productive of data, it has led to little in the way of grand theory. Of course, it can be argued that such theorizing is unnecessary. However, those with a behavioural approach can be questioned as to whether they are dealing with emotion at all. Data are sometimes gathered in so rarified an atmosphere that they seem far removed from emotion as it is more commonly conceived.

Analysis of the course of emotional development falls into two very distinct types. There has been some research with human subjects. Methodologically it has usually been poor and theoretically it has tended to be speculative and subjective. Research using infrahuman subjects has been more in evidence, probably because of the obvious ethical objections to manipulating the emotions of infants. It has usually taken the form of giving young animals extra or restricted experience and observing the effects of this on adult emotional behaviour. These two very different approaches to emotional development point to surprisingly similar contributory factors. For example, early experience is clearly important to later emotional development, although it interacts with genetic factors. In some species, there is evidence for the importance of critical periods in emotional development. Also, the establishment, maintenance and possible breaking of (affectional) bonds to both people and places is of prime importance, indicating the possible usefulness of analysis in terms of novelty and strangeness. There is a straightforward need in this area of study for well-conceived and well-conducted investigations with children. However, the problem which it is particularly difficult to overcome is that of artificiality. With children this involves the meaningful manipulation of realistic 'emotional' situations, and with animals it is the usual question of relevance, which appears intensified from the development viewpoint.

The topic of the expression and recognition of emotion has recently inspired some interesting research, both psychologically and ethologically. Some of this is promising at the level of observation and description rather than explanation. However, much of the theoretical structure which underlies this research is concerned with possible factors and dimensions of emotional expression. The status of such analysis is awkward to place; it may be that semantic problems are simply being studied indirectly. Of course, the study of the semantics of emotion is important in its own right, but the extent to which it is implicated in problems of expression and recognition remains to be seen. Again, this area of study is plagued by the problem of devising investigations which are representative of real-life emotion. From this viewpoint, photographs, films and tape-recordings may not be providing adequate material. The expression and recognition of emotion in a social context is self-evidently a very rapid and intricate process in everyday life. At present, we do not understand its determinants.

Although covering a very broad area, the study of pathological emotion has been less productive of fundamental research than any other aspect of emotion. It is well exemplified by its most ubiquitous concept—anxiety. This has been used in both description and explanation and has been given a multitude of definitions. At the moment, however, we are little nearer saying what it is, what are its determinants or even what is the most productive way to study it. It may be that the study of abnormal emotion should not proceed in any way distinct from the study of 'normal' emotion. Presumably, they each represent an aspect of an individual's interaction with his environment and might be more parsimoniously regarded as dependent on just one set of determinants.

In drawing together these areas of study and approaches to emotion, the salient feature seems to be that each investigator has focused on one aspect of the subject and tended to go no further. This is also reflected in the many theories of emotion. They are physiological, cognitive or behavioural, or sometimes any two of these, but never all three. There appears to be no theory which successfully provides a description of experiential feelings, physiological change and emotional behaviour. This is also evident in the huge array of research which has developed from these theories. Perhaps because they are biased according to the predilections of their exponents, each of the theories of emotion is lacking in some way. Some are too narrow, others too broad; some move hardly at all from empirical data, others are too speculative.

A CONCEPTUAL FRAMEWORK

In this final section it is not intended to present a theory or model of emotion, but a framework within which it would seem possible to study emotion in a reasonably systematic way. At best, it can perhaps be regarded as notes towards a definition of emotion. Naturally enough, these ideas represent my own, behavioural, bias but the argument is made that for the moment this, in conjunction with relevant physiological study, is the most useful and productive way to extend our knowledge of emotion.

Any stimulus can have two effects on behaviour. Firstly, it can act as a reinforcing stimulus for whatever behaviour immediately precedes it in time. That is, it makes that behaviour either more or less likely to occur on similar occasions in the future. This is a straightforward instrumental effect. Secondly, the *same* stimulus may elicit some immediate response or set of responses from the organism. It is this second type of response, the simplest form of which is a Pavlovian reflex, which is of interest here and which I would like to define as emotional. Whether such a response is unconditioned or conditioned is immaterial, although perhaps of significance for the course of emotional development. Some stimuli will clearly have built-in, unconditioned effects; others, the majority, will have similar but conditioned effects. From the viewpoint of emotional reactions, it is argued that the intensity or magnitude of these effects is of more significance than whether they are conditioned or unconditioned. If *any* stimulus is regarded as having some such effect, albeit a very mild one in some instances, this may reasonably suggest that any aspect of our behaviour or life has some emotional colouring. Intuitively, this would seem plausible.

If emotion is defined in this way, there are a number of implications as to its measurement. Direct measurement might be made at any or all of the usual three levels, behavioural (for example elicited aggression), physiological (for example changes in the ANS) and subjective (for example verbal report of experience and feelings). Also, of course, indirect measures can be taken of the effects of elicited emotion on ongoing instrumental behaviour (for example work stemming from double-runway studies or conditioned emotional responding). Such effects might elevate or depress the ongoing (rate of) behaviour. Either way, this might be enhancing or disrupting performance. In some situations an increased rate or vigour of response is preferable; in others a decreased rate or vigour. In this context 'preferable' means leading to positive stimuli or away from negative stimuli more efficiently, i.e. at less cost to the organism.

The question which should be asked about this formulation is how well the existing facts of emotion can be fitted to it. The general answer, I think, is that they accord quite well. Consider, for example, the somewhat elusive concept of emotionality. In terms of the present idea, this might be defined as an inherited predisposition to respond in particular (emotional) ways to certain stimuli. It refers to what could be called response style. It is mainly a genetically determined factor which ensures that individuals respond differentially to the same stimulus. Extending the argument, emotional development becomes a matter of changing the degree to which particular stimuli have emotional effects and the association (in the Pavlovian sense) of those which have very weak effects with those which have stronger effects. When this process goes wrong, the result may be so-called pathological emotion. For example, there may be 'strong', vigorous, high-probability responses to stimuli which would only elicit 'weak' responses from normal persons. This point of view permits us to avoid the explanatory use of ill-defined concepts such as anxiety. Instead, attention is directed to the determinants of particular responses and types of response, some of which may be conveniently described by terms like anxiety. Any knowledge of pathological (or, indeed, normal) emotion would then accrue from an elucidation of the relationship between emotion-eliciting stimuli and emotional responses, a major part of which would depend on the individual's past history.

The strictly behavioural approach to emotion is clearly in accord with the present definition; it is implicit in work on frustration and elation and CERs. Normally, in this field, emotion has not been studied directly, but rather its *effects* on ongoing instrumental behaviour have been recorded. There is a need for the direct measurement of emotion (physiologically, behaviourally and, with human subjects, subjectively) in runways, Skinner boxes and their analogues. Similarly, the problem of emotional expression also falls within this proposed framework—it is but one type of emotional response to stimuli which in this case are mainly social. Of more interest, perhaps, is the question of the recognition of emotional expression. I would suggest that this is a quite distinct matter which is best pursued by the social psychologist with whatever techniques he has available. It is taking a measure of emotion as itself a determinant of social behaviour and as such has little to do with the problems of emotion itself.

A consideration of possible cognitive factors in emotion is a little more difficult to make, since it seems to imply a very different approach to the subject. The main problem is whether or not cognitive factors are assigned a causal role in emotion; do cognitive appraisals cause emotion? I would argue that this is not a useful orientation to take. It is possible, and simpler, just to study the stimuli and responses which are involved. For example, in Schachter's original studies, the stimuli provided by his euphoric and angry stooges would have certain emotional effects, and not surprisingly these could be made to depend on an artificial manipulation of the physiological state of the subjects. It is unnecessary to invoke cognitions to account for 'euphoric' and 'angry' stimuli having differential effects. Of course, this is not an attempt to say that cognitions do not exist, but rather to deny them a necessary function, and also to suggest that there are more productive, less debatable ways of studying emotion. As has already been pointed out, the present framework is a perfectly valid one within which to ask questions about subjective feelings (cognition?), but these are seen as part of emotion itself rather than as underlying conditions. Also, under some circumstances a stimulus (perhaps a mild one) might have some of its emotional effects more cognitively than in any other way. And, as the organism is dynamic rather than static, changed cognitions might affect *subsequent* emotional responses. Equally, physiological or behavioural changes could affect one another, or cognition.

Giving any stimulus the dual role of strengthening or weakening responses emitted by the organism and eliciting emotional responses has much in common with the original rationalist doctrine. However, it carries no implications about free will or choice. Man is not regarded as striving to overcome his 'baser' emotions with 'purer', rational behaviour. All of his behaviour is simply viewed as categorizable in these two ways. Such a definition allows emotions or emotional reactions to be intense or mild, long or short lived, and disruptive or enhancing in their effects on instrumental (rational?) behaviour. No claim is made for this as a grand theory of emotion. It is a somewhat self-evident way of defining emotion and hence of structuring any study which is made of it. It has two important implications. Firstly, that any theory, and hopefully whenever possible any research, should take into account *all* of the measures of emotion and also its *effects*. Secondly, it promotes a focusing of attention on the characteristics (qualities) of stimuli and on the relationship between stimulus and response. Although this sounds like a thoroughly behavioural (or even behaviouristic) way of viewing emotion, I would suggest that it is not. Certainly, more behavioural terms have been used in this account and often a behavioural technology would be appropriate for the study of emotion. But the main argument is that our knowledge of emotion should be gleaned from all sources, this bringing us back to emotion in its everyday richness.

References

Abelson, R. P., and Sermat, V. (1962). 'Multidimensional scaling of facial expressions', *J. exp. Psychol.*, **63**, 546–54.

Adelman, H. M., and Maatsch, J. L. (1956). 'Learning and extinction based upon frustration, food reward, and exploratory tendency', *J. exp. Psychol.*, **52**, 311–15.

Alexander, B. K. (1966). *The Effects of Early Peer-deprivation on Juvenile Behaviour of Rhesus Monkey*. Unpubl. doctoral dissn. University of Wisconsin. (Quoted in Harlow and Harlow 1970.)

Alexander, F. (1950). *Psychosomatic Medicine. Its Principles and Applications*. Norton, New York.

Allerand, A. M. (1967). *Remembrance of Feelings Past: A Study of Phenomenological Genetics*. Unpubl. doctoral thesis. University of Colombia. (Quoted in Davitz 1969.)

Ambrose, J. A. (1961). 'The development of the smiling response in early infancy', in B. M. Foss (Ed.) *Determinants of Infant Behaviour*, Vol. 1. Wiley, New York.

Amsel, A. (1950). 'The combination of a primary appetitional need with primary and secondary emotionally derived needs', *J. exp. Psychol.*, **40**, 1–14.

Amsel, A. (1958). 'The role of frustrative nonreward in noncontinuous reward situations', *Psychol. Bull.*, **55**, 102–19.

Amsel, A. (1962). 'Frustrative nonreward in partial reinforcement and discrimination learning: some recent history and a theoretical extension', *Psychol. Rev.*, **69**, 306–28.

Amsel, A. (1967). 'Partial reinforcement effects on vigor and persistence: Advances in frustration theory derived from a variety of within-subject experiments', in K. W. Spence, J. T. Spence and N. Anderson (Eds.) *The Psychology of Learning and Motivation: Advances in Research and Theory*. Academic Press, New York, London.

Amsel, A., and Cole, K. F. (1953). 'Generalization of fear motivated interference with water intake', *J. exp. Psychol.*, **46**, 243–7.

Amsel, A., and Maltzman, I. (1950). 'The effect upon generalized drive strength of emotionality as inferred from the level of consummatory response', *J. exp. Psychol.*, **40**, 563–9.

Amsel, A., and Prouty, D. L. (1959). 'Frustrated factors in selective learning with reward and nonreward as discriminanda', *J. exp. Psychol.*, **57**, 224–30.

Amsel, A., and Roussel, J. (1952). 'Motivational properties of frustration: I. Effect on a running response of the addition of frustration to the motivational complex', *J. exp. Psychol.*, **43**, 363–8.

Amsel, A., and Ward, J. S. (1954). 'Motivational properties of frustration: II. Frustration drive stimulus and frustration reduction in selective learning', *J. exp. Psychol.*, **48**, 37–47.

Amsel, A., and Ward, J. S. (1965). 'Frustration and persistence: Resistance to discrimination following prior experience with the discriminanda', *Psychol. Monogr.*, **79** (4, Whole No. 597.)

Anastasi, A. (1958). 'Heredity, environment and the question "how?"', *Psychol. Rev.*, **65**, 197–208.

Anderson, D. C., Cole, J., and McVaugh, W. (1968). 'Variations in unsignalled inescapable preshock as determinants of responses to punishment', *J. comp. physiol. Psychol.*, **65**, (3), Part 2.

Annau, Z., and Kamin, L. J. (1961). 'The conditioned emotional response as a function of the intensity of the US', *J. comp. physiol. Psychol.*, **54**, 428–32.

Argyle, M. (1967). *The psychology of interpersonal behaviour.* Penguin, Harmondsworth.

Argyle, M. (1969). *Social interaction.* Methuen, London.

Argyle, M., and Kendon, A. (1967). 'The experimental analysis of social performance', in L. Berkowitz (Ed.) *Adv. in Exp. Soc. Psychol*, **3**.

Arieti, S. (1970). 'Cognition and feeling', in M. B. Arnold (Ed.) *Feeling and Emotion.* Academic Press, New York, London, 135–43.

Arnold, M. B. (1945). 'Physiological differentiation of emotional states', *Psychol. Rev.*, **52**, 35–48.

Arnold, M. B. (1950). 'An excitatory theory of emotion', in M. L. Reymert (Ed.) *Feelings and Emotions.* McGraw-Hill, New York.

Arnold, M. B. (Ed.) (1960). *Emotion and personality* (2 volumes). Columbia Univ. Press, New York.

Arnold, M. B. (1968). *The nature of emotion: Selected readings.* Penguin, Baltimore, U.S.A.; Harmondsworth, England.

Arnold, M. B. (1970a). *Feelings and emotions: The Loyola Symposium.* Academic Press, New York, London.

Arnold, M. B. (1970b). 'Brain function in emotions: A phenomenological analysis', in P. Black (Ed.) *Physiological correlates of emotion.* Academic Press, New York, London.

Aronfreed, J. (1968). *Conduct and conscious: The socialization of internalized control over behaviour.* Academic Press, New York.

Ax, A. F. (1953). 'The physiological differentiation of fear and anger in humans', *Psychosom. Med.*, **15**, 433–42.

Azrin, N. (1956). 'Some effects of two intermittent schedules of immediate and nonimmediate punishment', *J. Psychol.*, **42**, 3–21.

Azrin, N. H., and Hake, D. F. (1969). 'Positive conditioned suppression: Conditioned suppression using positive reinforcers as the unconditioned stimuli', *J. exp. Anal. Beh.*, **12**, 167–73.

Azrin, N. H., and Holz, W. C. (1966). 'Punishment', in W. K. Honig (Ed.) *Operant behavior: Areas of Research and Application.* Appleton-Century Crofts, New York, 380–447.

Azrin, N. H., Hutchinson, R. R., and Hake, D. F. (1966). 'Extinction-induced aggression', *J. exp. Anal. Beh.*, **9**, 191–204.

Baccelli, G., Guazzi, M., Libretti, A., and Zanchetti, A. (1965.) 'Pressoceptive and chemoceptive aortic reflexes in decorticate and in decerebrate cats', *Amer. j. Physiol.*, **208**, 708–14.

Bard, P. (1928). 'A diencephalic mechanism for the expression of rage with special reference to the sympathetic nervous system', *Homer. J. Physiol.*, **84**, 490–515.

Bard, P. (1929). 'The central representation of the sympathetic nervous system as indicated by certain physiologic observations', *Arch. Neurol. Psychiat.*, **22**, 230–46.

Bard, P. (1934). 'Emotion 1. The neuro-humonol basis of emotional reactions', in C. Murchison (Ed.) *Handbook of general experimental psychology.* Clark University Press, Worcester.

Bard, P. (1950). 'Central nervous mechanisms for the expression of anger in animals', in M. L. Reymert (Ed.) *Feelings and Emotions: The Mooseheart Symposium.* McGraw-Hill, New York, 211–37.

198

Bard, P., and Mountcastle, V. B. (1948). 'Some forebrain mechanisms involved in expression of rage with special reference to suppression of angry behaviour', Research Publication, *Assoc. Res. nerv. ment. Dis.*, **27**, 362–404.

Barker, R., Dembo, T., and Lewin, K. (1941). 'Frustration and regression: an experiment with young children', *University of Iowa Studies in Child Welfare*, **18**, No. 1.

Baron, A. (1963). 'Differential effects of fear on anxiety in novel and familiar environments', *Psychol. Rep.*, **13**, 251–7.

Baron, A., and Antonitis, J. J. (1961). 'Punishment and shock as determinants of bar-pressing behavior', *J. comp. Physiol. Psychol.*, **54**, 716–20.

Barry, H. III, Wagner, A. R., and Miller, N. E. (1962). 'Effects of alcohol and amobarbital on performance inhibited by experimental extinction', *J. comp. physiol. Psychol.*, **55**, 464–8.

Beatty, W. W., and Schwartzbaum, J. S. (1967). 'Enhanced reactivity to quinine and saccharine solutions following septal lesions in the rat', *Psychon. Sci.*, **8**, 483–4.

Beatty, W. W., and Schwartzbaum, J. S. (1968). 'Consummatory behaviour for sucrose following septal lesions in the rat', *J. comp. physiol. Psychol.*, **65**, 93–102.

Becker, H. S. (1953). 'Becoming a marihuana user', *Amer. j. Sociol.*, **59**, 235–42.

Belanger, D., and Feldman, S. M. (1962). 'Effects of water deprivation upon heart rate and instrumental activity in the rat', *J. comp. physiol. Psychol.*, **55**, 220–5.

Beldoch, M. (1964). 'Sensitivity to expression of emotional meaning in three modes of communication', in J. L. Davitz (Ed.) *The Communication of emotional meaning*. McGraw-Hill, New York, 31–42.

Berkowitz, L. (1962). *Aggression: A social psychological analysis*. McGraw-Hill, New York.

Bevan, W., Bell, C., and Lankford, H. G. (1967). 'The residual effect of shock upon bar-pressing for water', *Psychol. Rec.*, **17**, 23–8.

Billingsea, F. Y. (1942). 'Intercorrelational analysis of certain behaviour salients in the rat', *J. comp. Psychol.*, **34**, 203–11.

Bindra, D. (1959). *Motivation: A systematic reinterpretation*. Ronald Press, New York.

Bindra, D. (1968). 'A neuropsychological interpretation of the effects of drive and incentive-motivation on general activity and instrumental behaviour', *Psychol. Rev.*, **75**, 1–22.

Bindra, D. (1969). 'A unified interpretation of emotion and motivation', *Ann. New York. Acad. Sci.*, **159**, 1071–83.

Bindra, D. (1970). 'Emotion and behavior theory: Current research in historical perspective', in P. Back (Ed.) *Physiological correlates of emotion*. Academic Press, New York, London.

Blackman, D. (1966). 'Response rate and conditioned suppression', *Psychol. Rep.*, **19**, 687–93.

Blackman, D. (1967). 'Effects of response pacing on conditioned suppression', *Quart. j. exp. Psychol.*, **19**, 170–4.

Blackman, D. (1968a). 'Conditioned suppression as a function of the behavioural baseline', *J. exp. Anal. Beh.*, **11**, 53–61.

Blackman, D. (1968b). 'Response rate, reinforcement frequency and conditioned suppression', *J. exp. Anal. Beh.*, **11**, 503–16.

Blau, S. (1964). 'An ear for an eye: Sensory compensation and judgments of affect by the blind', in J. L. Davitz (Ed.) *The communication of emotional meaning*. McGraw-Hill, New York, 113–27.

Block, J. (1957). 'Studies in the phenomenology of emotions', *J. Abnorm. Soc. Psychol.*, **54**, 358–63.

Bloemkolb, D., Defares, P., Van Enckevert, G., and Van Gelderen, M. (1971). 'Cognitive processing of information on varied physiological arousal', *Europ. j. Soc. Psychol.*, **1-1**, 31–46.

Bolles, R. C. (1967). *Theory of Motivation.* Harper & Row, New York.

Bonvallet, M., and Allen, M. B. (1963). 'Prolonged spontaneous and evoked reticular activation following discrete bulbar lesions', *Electroenceph. Clin. Neurophysiol.*, **15**, 969–88.

Bousfield, W. I., and Orbison, W. D. (1952). 'Ontogenesis of emotional behaviour', *Psychol. Rev.*, **59**, 1–7.

Bower, G. H. (1962). 'The influence of graded reductions in reward and prior frustrating events upon the magnitude of the frustration effect', *J. comp. physiol. Psychol.*, **55**, 582–7.

Bower, G., and Grusec, T. (1964). 'Effect of prior Pavlovian discrimination training upon learning an operant discrimination', *J. exp. Anal. Beh.*, **7**, 401–4.

Bowlby, J. (1951). *Maternal care and mental health.* World Health Organisation, Geneva.

Bowlby, J. (1953). 'Critical phases in the development of social responses in man', *New Biology*, Vol. 14. Penguin, London.

Bowlby, J. (1960). 'Separation anxiety', *Internat. j. psychoanal.*, **41**, 1–25.

Bowlby, J. (1961). 'Separation anxiety: a critical review of the literature', *J. child Psychol.*, **15**, 9–52.

Bowlby, J. (1969). 'Psychopathology of anxiety: The role of affectional bonds', in M. H. Lader (Ed.) *Studies of anxiety.* Headley Bros., Ashford, 80–6.

Brackbill, Y. (1958). 'Extinction of the smiling response in infants as a function of reinforcement schedule', *Child Developm.*, **29**, 115–24.

Brady, J. V. (1955). 'The extinction of a conditioned "fear" response as a function of reinforcement schedules for competing behavior', *J. Psychol.*, **40**, 25–34.

Brady, J. V. (1958a). 'The paleocortex and behavioral motivation', in H. F. Harlow and C. Woolsey (Eds.) *Biological and biochemical bases of behavior.* University of Wisconsin Press, Madison.

Brady, J. V. (1958b). 'Ulcers in "executive" monkeys', *Scient. Amer.*, **199**, 95–100.

Brady, J. V. (1960). 'Emotional behavior', in J. Field, H. W. Magoun, and V. E. Hall (Eds.) *Handbook of Physiology*, Vol. III. Williams & Wilkins, Baltimore.

Brady, J. V. (1961). 'Motivation—emotional factors and inter-cranial self-stimulation', in D. E. Steer (Ed.) *Electrical stimulation of the brain.* University of Texas Press, Austin, 413–30.

Brady, J. V. (1962). 'Psychophysiology of emotional behavior', in A. Backrach (Ed.) *Experimental foundations of clinical psychology.* Basic Books, New York.

Brady, J. V. (1963). 'Further comments on the gastro intestinal system and avoidance behaviour', *Psychol. Rep.*, **12**, 742.

Brady, J. V. (1970a). 'Emotion: Some conceptual problems and psychophysiological experiments', in M. B. Arnold (Ed.) *Feelings and emotions: The Loyola symposium.* Academic Press, New York, London.

Brady, J. V. (1970b). 'Endocrine and autonomic correlates of emotional behaviour', in P. Black (Ed.) *Physiological correlates of emotion.* Academic Press, New York, London.

Brady, J. V., and Conrad, D. G. (1960). 'Some effects of limbic system self-stimulation upon conditioned emotional behavior', *J. comp. physiol. Psychol.*, **53**, 128–37.

Brady, J. V., and Hunt, H. F. (1955). 'An experimental approach to the analysis of emotional behavior', *J. Psychol.*, **40**, 313–24.

Brady, J. V., and Nauta, W. J. H. (1953). 'Subcortical mechanisms in emotional behaviour: affective changes following septal forebrain lesions in the albino rat', *J. comp. physiol. Psychol.*, **46**, 339–46.

Brady, J. V., and Nauta, W. J. H. (1955). 'Subcortical mechanisms in emotional behavior: The duration of affective changes following septal and labenular lesions in the albino rat', *J. comp. physiol. Psychol.*, **48**, 412–20.

Brannigan, C. R., and Humphries, D. A. (1971). 'Human non-verbal behaviour. A means of communication', in N. Blurton-Jones (Ed.) *Ethological studies of infant behaviour.* Cambridge University Press, Cambridge.

Bridges, K. M. B. (1932). *The social and emotional development of the pre-school child.* Kegan Paul, London.

Brierley, M. (1937). 'Affects in theory and practice', *Internat. Psychoanal.*, **18**, 256–68. (As quoted in Rapaport 1950.)

Broadhurst, P. L. (1957a). 'Determinants of emotionality in the rat: I. Situational factors', *Brit. j. Psychol.*, **48**, 1–12.

Broadhurst, P. L. (1957b). 'Emotionality and the Yerkes–Dodson law', *J. exp. Psychol.*, **54**, 345–52.

Broadhurst, P. L. (1959). 'The interaction of task difficulty and motivation: the Yerkes–Dodson law revived', *Acta Psychol.*, **16**, 321–38.

Broadhurst, P. L. (1960). 'Studies in psychogenetics: applications of biometrical genetics to the inheritance of behavior', in H. J. Eysenck (Ed.) *Experiments in Personality*, Vol. 1. Routledge & Kegan Paul, London.

Broadhurst, P. L. (1967). 'The biometrical analysis of behavioural inheritance', *Sci. Prog. Oxf.*, **55**, 123–9.

Bronson, G. (1965). 'The hierarchical organization of the central nervous system: implication for learning processes and critical periods in early development', *Behav. Sci.*, **10**, 7–25.

Brown, J. J., and Farber, I. E. (1951). 'Emotions conceptualized as intervening variables—with suggestions toward a theory of frustration', *Psychol. Bull.*, **48**, 465–95.

Brown, J. S. (1961). *The motivation of behavior.* McGraw-Hill, New York.

Brown, R. (1965). *Social Psychology.* Free Press, New York.

Brown, R. T., and Wagner, A. R. (1964). 'Resistance to punishment and extinction following training with shock or nonreinforcement', *J. exp. Psychol.*, **68**, 503–7.

Bruell, J. H. (1965). 'Mode of inheritance of response time in mice', *J. comp. physiol. Psychol.*, **60**, 147–8.

Bruell, J. H. (1970). 'Heritability of emotional behaviour', in P. R. Black (Ed.) *Physiological correlates of emotion.* Academic Press, New York, London, 23–35.

Brunswick, D. (1924). 'The effect of emotional stimuli on the gastro-intestinal tone', *J. comp. Psychol.*, **4**, 19–79.

Bull, N. (1951). 'The attitude theory of emotion', *Nerv. Ment. Dis. Monogr.*, No. 81.

Bures, J., and Buresova, O. (1960). 'The use of Leao's spreading depression in the study of inter-hemispheric transfer of memory traces', *J. comp. physiol. Psychol.*, **53**, 558–65.

Buss, A. H. (1961). *The Psychology of aggression.* Wiley, New York.

Buss, A. H. (1966). *Psychopathology.* Wiley, New York, London.

Cannon, W. B. (1915). *Bodily changes in panic, hunger, fear and rage*, 2nd edn., 1929. Appleton-Century, New York.

Cannon, W. B. (1927). 'The James–Lange theory of emotion; a critical examination and an alternative theory', *Am. j. Psychol.*, **39**, 106–24.

Cannon, W. B. (1931). 'Again the James–Lange and the thalamic theories of emotions', *Psych. Rev.*, **38**, 281–95.

Cannon, W. B. (1932). *The Wisdom of the Body*, 2nd edn., 1939. Norton, New York.

Cannon, W. B., and Britton, S. W. (1927). 'The influence of emotion on medulliadrenal secretion', *Amer. j. Physiol.*, **79**, 433–65.

Cantril, H., ahd Hunt, W. A. (1932). 'Emotional effects produced by the injection of adrenaline', *Amer. j. Psychol.*, **44**, 300–7.

Carlton, P. L., and Didamo, P. (1960). 'Some notes on the conditioned suppression', *J. exp. Anal. Beh.*, **3**, 255–8.

Cattell, R. B. (1963). 'The nature and measurement of anxiety', *Scient. Amer.*, March. See *Contemporary Psychol.*, 1971. W. A. Freeman, New York, 358–65.

Cattell, R. B., and Scheier, I. H. (1958). 'The nature of anxiety: A review of thirteen multivariate analyses comprising 814 variables', *Psychol. Rep.*, **4**, 351–88.

Cattell, R. B., and Scheier, I. H. (1961). *The Meaning and Measurement of neuroticism and anxiety*. Ronald Press, New York.

Child, I. L., and Waterhouse, I. K. (1952). 'Frustration and the quality of performance: I. A critique of the Barker, Dembo and Lewin experiment', *Psychol. Rev.*, **59**, 351–62.

Child, I. L., and Waterhouse, I. K. (1953). 'Frustration and the quality of performance: II. A theoretical statement', *Psychol. Rev.*, **60**, 127–39.

Church, M. (1969). Unpublished study described in Wagner (1969).

Cline, M. G. (1956). 'The influence of social context on the perception of faces', *J. Pers.*, **25**, 142–58.

Cohen, M. E. (1951). 'The high familial prevalence of neurocirculatory asthenia (anxiety neurosis, effort syndrome)', *Amer. j. hum. Genet.*, **3**, 126–58.

Cohen, P. S. (1967). 'Response suppression as a function of intensity and delay of response-contingent shock'. Paper read at Eastern Psychological Association Meeting. (Described by Lyon 1968.)

Coleman, J. (1949). 'Facial expression of emotion', *Psychol. Monogr.*, **63**, 1.

Coles, M. G. H. (1970). 'Individual differences in relation to attention and arousal'. Unpubl. Ph.D. thesis: University of Exeter.

Coulson, G., and Walsh, M. (1968). 'Facilitation of avoidance responding in white rats during a stimulus preceding food', *Psychol. Rep.*, **22**, 1277–84.

Dana, C. L. (1921). 'The anatomic seat of the emotions: a discussion of the James–Lange theory', *Arch. Neurol. Psychiat.*, **6**, 634–9.

Darrow, C. W. (1947). 'Psychological and psychophysiological significance of the electroencephalogram', *Psychol. Rev.*, **54**, 157–68.

Darrow, C. W. (1950). 'Neurophysiological effect of emotion on the brain', in M. L. Reymert (Ed.) *Feelings and Emotions: The Mooseheart Symposium*. McGraw-Hill, New York.

Darrow, C. W., Pathman, J., and Kronenberg, G. (1946). 'Level of autonomic activity and electrocephalogram', *J. exp. Psychol.*, **36**, 355–65.

Darwin, C. R. (1872). *The expression of emotions in man and animals*. Murray, London.

Davis, H. (1968). 'Conditioned suppression: a survey of the literature', *Psychon. Monogr. Supp.*, **2**. (Whole No. 30.)

Davison, G. C. (1968). 'Systematic desensitization as a counter conditioning process', *J. abnorm. Psychol.*, **73**, 91–9.

Davitz, J. L. (1964). *The communication of emotional meaning*. McGraw-Hill, New York.

Davitz, J. L. (1964). 'Personality, perceptual and cognitive correlates of emotional sensitivity', in J. L. Davitz (Ed.) *The Communication of emotional meaning*. McGraw-Hill, New York, 57–68.

Davitz, J. R. (1969). *The Language of emotion*. Academic Press, New York, London.

Davitz, J. R. (1970). 'A dictionary and grammar of emotion', in M. L. Arnold (Ed.) *Feelings and emotion: The Loyola Symposium*. Academic Press, New York, London, 251–58.

Davitz, J., and Davitz, L. (1959a). 'The communication of feelings by content free speech', *J. Communication*, **9**, 6–13.

Davitz, J., and Davitz, L. (1959b). 'Correlates of accuracy in the communication of feelings', *J. Communication*, **9**, 110–17.

Deaux, E., and Kakolewski, J. W. (1970). 'Emotionally induced increases in effective osmotic pressure and subsequent thirst', *Science*, **169**, 1226–8.

Delgado, J. M. R. (1970). 'Modulation of emotions by cerebral radio stimulation', in P. Black (Ed.) *Physiological correlates of emotion*. Academic Press, New York, London.

202

Delgado, J. M. R., Roberts, W. W., and Miller, N. E. (1954). 'Learning motivated by electrical stimulation of the brain', *Amer. j. Physiol.*, **179**, 587–93.

Denenberg, V. H. (1964). 'Critical periods, stimulus input, and emotional reactivity: A theory of infantile stimulation', *Psychol. Rev.*, **71**, 335–51.

Denenberg, V. H., and Kline, N. J. (1964). 'Stimulus intensity vs. critical periods: A test of two hypotheses concerning infantile stimulation', *Canad. j. Psychol.*, **18**, 1–5.

Denenberg, V. H., and Morton, J. R. C. (1962). 'Effects of environmental complexity and social groupings upon modification of emotional behaviour', *J. comp. physiol. Psychol.*, **55**, 242–6.

Denenberg, V. H., and Smith, S. A. (1963). 'Effects of infantile stimulation and age upon behavior', *J. comp. physiol. Psychol.*, **56**, 307–12.

Dennis, W. (1935). 'Experimental test of two theories of social smiling in infants', *J. soc. Psychol.*, **6**, 214–23.

De Toledo, L., and Black, A. H. (1966). 'Heart rate: Changes during conditioned suppression in rats', *Science*, **152**, 1404–6.

Dittman, A. T. (1962). 'The relationship between body movements and mood in interviews', *J. consult. Psychol.*, **26**, 48.

Dittman, A. T., Parloff, M. B., and Boomer, D. S. (1965). 'Facial and bodily expression: A study of receptivity of emotional cues', *Psychiatry*, **28**, 239–44.

Dollard, J., Doob, L. W., Miller, N. E., Mowrer, O. H., and Sears, R. R. (1939). *Frustration and aggression.* Yale University Press, New Haven.

Douglas, K. J. (1967). 'The hippocampus and behaviour', *Psychol. Bull.*, **67**, 416–22.

Drever, J. (1952). *A Dictionary of psychology.* Penguin, Harmondsworth.

Ducharme, R., and Belanger, D. (1961). 'Influence d'une stimulation electrique sur le niveau d'activation et la performance', *Canad. j. Psychol.*, **15**, 61–8.

Duffy, E. (1934). 'Emotion: An example of the need for reorientation in psychology', *Psychol. Rev.*, **41**, 184–98.

Duffy, E. (1941). 'An explanation of "emotional" phenomena without the use of the concept "emotion" ', *J. gen. Psychol.*, **25**, 283–93.

Duffy, E. (1951). 'The concept of energy mobilization', *Psychol. Rev.* **58**, 30–40.

Duffy, E. (1962). *Activation and Behaviour.* Wiley, New York, London.

Dusser de Barenne, J. G. (1920). 'Recherches experimentales sur les fonctions du système nerveux central, failes en particulier sur deux chats donc le neopallium a été enlevé', *Arch. Neurol. Physiol.*, **4**, 31–123.

Easterbrook, J. A. (1959). 'The effect of emotion on cue utilization and the organization of behaviour', *Psychol. Rev.*, **66**, 183–201.

Eibl-Eibesfeldt, I. (1970). *Ethology—The biology of behaviour.* Holt, Rinehart & Winston, New York, London.

Ekman, P. (1965a). 'Communication through nonverbal behaviour: A source of information about interpersonal relationships', in S. S. Tomkins and C. E. Izard (Eds.) *Affect, Cognition, and Personality.* Springer, New York, 390–442.

Ekman, P. (1965b). 'Differential communications of affect by head and body cues', *J. pers. soc. Psychol.*, **2**, 726–35.

Ekman, P., and Friesen, W. V. (1967a). 'Head and body cues in the judgment of emotion: a reformulation', *Percept. Mot. Sk.*, **24**, 711–14.

Ekman, P., and Friesen, W. V. (1967b). 'Nonverbal behavior in psychotherapy research', in J. Schlein (Ed.) *Research in Psychotherapy*, Vol. 3. A.P.A., Washington.

Ekman, P., and Friesen, W. V. (1969). 'Non-verbal leakage and clues to deception', *Psychiatry*, **32**, 88–106.

Ellis, N. R. (1957). 'The immediate effect of emotionality upon behavior strength', *J. exp. Psychol.*, **54**, 339–44.

Elshout, J. J. (1967). 'Computation of factor scores by complete regression', *Technical Reports*, Psychology Laboratory, Amsterdam University. (Quoted in Frijda 1969.)

Epstein, S. (1967). 'Toward a unified theory of anxiety', *Prog. exp. res. pers.*, **4**, 1–89. Academic Press, New York.

Estes, W. K. (1948). 'Discrimination conditioning: II Effects of a Pavlovian conditioned stimulus upon a subsequently established operant response', *J. exp. Psychol.*, **38**, 173–7.

Estes, W. K. (1969). 'Outline of a theory of punishment', in B. A. Campbell and R. M. Church (Eds.) *Punishment and Aversive Behavior*. Appleton-Century-Crofts, New York, 57–82.

Estes, W. K., and Skinner, B. F. (1941). 'Some quantitative properties of anxiety', *J. exp. Psychol.*, **29**, 390–400.

Ewart, E. (1970). 'The attitudinal character of emotion', in M. L. Arnold (Ed.) *Feelings and emotion: The Loyola Symposium*. Academic Press, New York, London.

Eysenck, H. J. (Ed.) (1964). *Experiments in motivation*. Pergamon, Oxford.

Eysenck, H. J. (1965). 'The effects of psychotherapy', *Internat. j. Psychiat.*, **1**, 99–142.

Eysenck, H. J. (1967). *The biological basis of personality*. Springfield, Illinois.

Eysenck, H. J. (1969). 'Psychological aspects of anxiety', in M. H. Lader (Ed.) *Studies of Anxiety*. Headley Bros., Ashford, 7–20.

Farmer, C. (1967). *Words and feelings: A developmental study of the language of emotion in children*. Unpubl. doctoral thesis, University of Colombia. (Quoted in Davitz, 1969.)

Federn, P. (1933). 'Die Ichbesetzung bie den Fehlleistungen', *Imago*, **19**, 312–38, 433–53. (As quoted by Rapaport 1950.)

Federn, P. (1936). 'Zur Unterscheidimg des gesunden und krankhaften', *Narzimus*, **22**, 5–39. (As quoted by Rapaport 1950.)

Fehr, F. S., and Stern, J. A. (1970). 'Peripheral physiological variables and emotion: The James–Lange theory revisited', *Psychol. Bull.*, **74**, 411–24.

Felecky, A. M. (1914). 'The expression of emotion', *Psychol. Rev.*, **21**, 33–41.

Felecky, A. M. (1916). 'The influence of emotions on respiration', *J. exp. Psychol.*, **1**, 218–41.

Ferrier, D. (1875). The Gornian Lecture. 'Experiments on the brain of monkeys' (second series), *Phil. Trans.*, **165**, 433–88.

Ferster, G. B. (1958). 'Control of behavior in chimpanzees and pigeons by time out from positive reinforcement', *Psychol. Monogr.*, **72**, 8. (Whole No. 461.)

Festinger, L. (1954). 'A theory of social comparison processes', *Human Relations*, **7**, 114–40.

Festinger, L. (1957). *A theory of cognitive dissonance*. Row, Peterson, Evanston, Ill.

Fischer, W. F. (1970). *Theories of anxiety*. Harper & Row, New York.

Flores d'Arcais. (1961). 'Forming impressions of personality in situations of contrast between verbal and minoric expressions', *Acta Psychol.*, **19**, 494–5.

Folkins, C. H. (1970). 'Temporal factors and the cognitive mediators of stress reaction', *J. person. soc. Psychol.*, **14**, 172–83.

Freeman, G. L. (1948). *Physiological psychology*. Van Nostrand, New York.

Frijda, N. H. (1953). 'The understanding of facial expression of emotion', *Acta Psychol.*, **9**, 294–362.

Frijda, N. H. (1956). *Het Bergrijpen van Gelaatsexpressies*. Van Oorschot, Amsterdam.

Frijda, N. H. (1958). 'Facial expression and situational cues', *J. abnorm. soc. Psychol.*, **57**, 149–54.

Frijda, N. H. (1969). 'Recognition of emotion', in L. Berkowitz (Ed.) *Advances in experimental social psychology*, **4**, 167–223.

Frijda, N. H. (1970). 'Emotion and recognition of emotion', in M. L. Arnold (Ed.) *Feelings and emotions: The Loyola Symposium*. Academic Press, New York, London, 241–50.

Frijda, N. H., and Philipszoon, E. (1963). 'Dimensions of recognition of emotion', *J. abnorm. soc. Psychol.*, **66**, 45–51.

Frisch, K. V. (1950). *Bees—their vision, chemical senses and language.* Cornell University Press, New York.

Frisch, K. V. (1968). 'Honey bees: Do they use direction and distance information provided by their dancers?', *Science*, **158**, 1072–6.

Frois-Wittman, J. (1930). 'The judgement of facial expression', *J. exp. Psychol.* **13**, 113–51.

Fulton, J. F. (1951). *Frontal lobotomy and affective behaviour.* Norton, New York. (As quoted by Arnold 1960.)

Fulton, J. F., Pribram, K. H., Stevenson, J. A. F., and Wall, P. D. (1949). 'Interrelations between orbital gyrus, insula, temporal tip, and anterior cingulate', *Trans. Amer. neurol. Assoc.*, **74**, 175–9.

Funkenstein, D. H,, King, S. H., and Drolette, M. E. (1957). *Mastery of Stress.* Harvard University Press, Cambridge, Mass.

Gelder, M. G., and Marks, I. M. (1966). 'Severe agarophobia: a controlled prospective trial of behaviour therapy', *Brit. j. Psychiat.*, **112**, 309.

Geller, I. (1960). 'The acquisition and extinction of conditioned suppression as a function of the base-line reinforcer', *J. exp. anal. Behav.*, **3**, 235–40.

Gellhorn, E. (1964). 'Motion and emotion: The role of proprioception in the physiology and pathology of the emotions', *Psychol. Rev.*, **71**, 457–72.

Gellhorn, E. (1968). *Biological foundations of emotion.* Scott, Foresman, Glenview, Ill.

Gellhorn, E., and Loufbourrow, G. N. (1963). *Emotions and emotional disorders.* Hoeber, New York.

Gladstones, W. H. (1962). 'A multidimensional study of facial expression of emotion', *Austral. j. Psychol.*, **14**, 95–100.

Glickman, S. E., and Schiff, B. B. (1967). 'A biological theory of reinforcement', *Psychol. Rev.*, **74**, 81–109.

Goldman, R., Jaffa, M., and Schachier, S. (1968). 'Yom kippur, Air France, dormitory food and the eating behavior of obese and normal persons', *J. person. soc. Psychol.*, **10**, 117–23.

Goldstein, M. L. (1968). 'Physiological theories of emotion: A critical historical review from the standpoint of behavior theory', *Psychol. Bull.*, **69**, 23–40.

Goltz, F. (1892). 'Der Hund ohne Grosshirn', *Pflüg. Arch. ges Physiol.*, **51**, 570–614.

Goodenough, F. L. (1932). 'Expression of the emotions in a blind–deaf child', *J. abnorm. soc. Psychol.*, **27**, 328–33.

Grinker, R. R. Sr. (1953). *Psychosomatic research.* Norton, New York.

Grinker, R. R. Sr. (1966). 'The psychosomatic aspects of anxiety', in G. D. Spielberger (Ed.) *Anxiety and behavior.* Academic Press, New York, London, 129–42.

Grinker, R. R. Sr., Miller, J., Sabshin, M. A., Nunn, R., and Nunnally, J. C. (1961). *The phenomena of depressions.* Harper (Hoeber), New York.

Grinker, R. R. Sr., and Spiegel, J. P. (1945). *Men under stress.* Blakiston, Philadelphia. 1961 McGraw-Hill, New York.

Grossman, S. P. (1963). 'Chemically induced epileptiform seizures in the cat', *Science*, **142**, 409–11.

Grossman, S. P. (1964). 'Effects of chemical stimulation of the septal areas on motivation', *J. comp. physiol. Psychol.*, **58**, 194–200.

Grossman, S. P. (1967). *Physiological Psychology.* Wiley, New York, London.

Grossman, S. P. (1970). 'Modification of emotional behaviour by intercranial administration of chemicals', in P. Black (Ed.) *Physiological correlates of emotion.* Academic Press, New York, London.

Grusec, J. (1966). 'Some antecedents of self-criticism', *J. pers. soc. Psychol.*, **4**, 244–52.

Guhl, A. M., Craig, J. V., and Mueller, C. D. (1960). 'Selective breeding for aggressiveness in chickens', *Poultry Science*, **39**, 970–80. (Quoted in Bruell 1970.)

Gurney, C., and Roth, M. (1969). 'The classification and clinical differentiation of anxiety states from depressive disorders, II' (in preparation). (Quoted in Slater and Roth 1969.)

Hale, E. D., and Schein, M. W. (1962). 'The behaviour of turkeys', in E. S. E. Hafez (Ed.) *The behaviour of domestic animals*. Bailliere, Tindall & Cox, London.

Hall, C. S. (1934a). 'Emotional behavior in the rat: I. Defacation and urination as measures of individual differences in emotionality', *J. comp. Psychol.*, **18**, 385–403.

Hall, C. S. (1934b). 'Drive and emotionality: factors associated with adjustment in the rat', *J. comp. Psychol.*, **17**, 89–108.

Hall, C. S. (1941). 'Temperament: a survey of animal studies', *Psychol. Bull.*, **38**, 909–43.

Hall, C. S. (1951). 'The genetics of behavior', in S. S. Stevens (Ed.) *Handbook of experimental psychology*. Wiley, New York.

Hammond, L. J. (1966). 'Increased responding to CS in differential CER', *Psychon. Sci.*, **5**, 337–8.

Hammond, L. J. (1967). 'A traditional demonstration of the active properties of Pavlovian inhibition using differential CER', *Psychon. Sci.*, **9**, 65–6.

Hammond, L. J. (1968). 'Retardation of fear acquisition by a previously inhibitory CS', *J. comp. physiol. Psychol.*, **66**, 756–9.

Hammond, L. J. (1970). 'Conditioned emotional states', in P. Black (Ed.) *Physiological correlates of emotion*. Academic Press, New York, London, 245–59.

Harlow, H. F., and Harlow, M. K. (1962). 'Social deprivation in monkeys', *Sci. Amer.*, **207**, 136–46.

Harlow, H. F., and Harlow, M. K. (1970). 'Developmental aspects of emotional behaviour', in P. R. Black (Ed.) *Physiological correlates of emotion*. Academic Press, New York, London, 37–58.

Harlow, H. F., and Stagner, R. (1933). 'Psychology of feelings and emotions. II. Theory of emotions', *Psychol. Rev.*, **40**, 184–95.

Harlow, H. F., and Zimmerman, R. R. (1959). 'Affectional patterns in the infant monkey', *Science*, **130**, 421–32.

Harrower, M., and Grinker, R. R. Snr. (1946). 'The stress tolerance test: preliminary experiments with a new projective technique utilizing both meaningful and meaningless stimuli', *Psychosom. Med.*, **8**, 3–15.

Harvey, J. A., Jacobson, L. E., and Hunt, H. F. (1961). 'Long-term effects of lesions in the peptal forebrain on acquisition and retention of conditioned fear', *Amer. Psychol.*, **16**, 449.

Head, H. (1921). 'Release of function in the nervous system', Proc. Roy. Soc., **926**, 184. (As cited in Cannon 1927.)

Hearst, E. (1969). 'Aversive conditioning and external stimulus control', in Campbell, B. A., and Church, R. M. (Eds.) *Punishment and aversive behavior*. Appleton-Century-Crofts, New York, 235–77.

Hebb, D. O. (1949). *The organization of behaviour*. Wiley, New York.

Hebb, D. O. (1955). 'Drives and the CNS (conceptual nervous system)', *Psychol. Rev.*, **62**, 243–54.

Henton, W. W., and Brady, J. V. (1970). 'Operant acceleration during a pre-reward stimulus', *J. exp. anal. Behav.*, **13**, 205–9.

Herrnstein, R. J. (1955). 'Behavioral consequences of the removal of a discriminative stimulus associated with variable-interval reinforcement'. Unpubl. Ph.D. Thesis. Harvard University.

Herrnstein, R. J., and Morse, W. H. (1957). 'Some effects of response independent positive reinforcement on maintained operant behavior', *J. comp. physiol. Psychol.*, **50**, 461–7.

206

Hess, E. H. (1959). 'The relationship between imprinting and motivation', in M. R. Jones (Ed.) *Nebraska Symposium on Motivation*. University of Nebraska Press, Lincoln, Neb.

Hess, E. H. (1962a). 'Ethology: an approach toward the complete analysis of behavior', in *New Directions in Psychology*, Vol. 1. Holt, Rinehart & Winston, New York.

Hess, E. H. (1962b). 'Imprinting and the "critical period" concept', in E. L. Bliss (Ed.) *Roots of Behavior*. Harper & Bros., New York.

Hess, W. R. (1936). 'Hypothalamus und die Zentien des autonomen nerveu systems: Physiologie', *Arch. Physhiat. Nerveuk*, **104**, 548–57.

Hess, W. R. (1949). *Das Zeisdenhirn: Syndrome, Lokalizationen, Funktionen*. Schwabe, Basel.

Hess, W. R. (1954). *Diencephalon: autonomic and extrapyramidal functions*. Grune & Stratton, New York.

Hillman, J. (1961). *Emotion*. North Western University Press, Evanston, Ill.

Hillman, J. (1970). 'C. G. Jung's contributions to "Feelings and emotions": Synopsis and implications', in M. B. Arnold (Ed.) *Feelings and emotions*. Academic Press, New York, London, 125–34.

Hinde, R. A. (1955). 'The following response of moorhens and coots', *Brit. j. Anim. Behav.*, **3**, 121–2.

Hinde, R. A., Thorpe, W. H., and Vince, M. A. (1956). 'The following response of young coots and moorhens', *Behav.*, **11**, 214–42.

Hoch, P. H., and Zubin, J. (Eds.) (1950). *Anxiety*. Grune & Stratton, New York.

Hoffman, H. S. (1969). 'Stimulus factors in conditioned suppression', in B. A. Campbell and R. M. Church (Eds.) *Punishment and aversive behavior*. Appleton-Century-Crofts, New York, 185–234.

Hoffman, H. S., and Fleshler, M. (1961). 'Stimulus factors in aversive controls: the generalization of conditioned suppression', *J. exp. anal. Beh.*, **4**, 371–8.

Hoffman, H. S., and Fleshler, M. (1965). 'Stimulus aspects of aversive controls: the effects of response contingent shock', *J. exp. anal. Beh.*, **8**, 89–96.

Hoffman, H. S., Selekman, W. L., and Fleshler, M. (1966). 'Stimulus aspects of aversive controls: long-term effects of suppression procedures', *J. exp. anal. Beh.*, **9**, 659–62.

Hohmann, G. W. (1962). 'The effects of dysfunctions of the autonomic nervous system on experienced feelings and emotions'. Paper read at Conference on Emotions and feelings at New School for Social Research, New York. (Quoted by Schachter 1964.)

Hohmann, G. W. (1966). 'Some effects of spinal cord lesions on experienced emotional feelings', *Psychophys.*, **3**, 143–56.

Howe, E. S. (1958). 'GSR conditioning in anxiety states, normals and chronic functional schizophrenic subjects', *J. abnorm, soc. Psychol.*, **56**, 183–9.

Hull, C. L. (1943). *Principles of Behavior*. Appleton-Century-Crofts, New York.

Hunt, H. F., and Brady, J. V. (1951). 'Some effects of electro-convulsive shock on a conditioned emotional response ("anxiety")', *J. comp. physiol. Psychol.*, **44**, 88–98.

Hunt, H. F., and Otis, L. S. (1953). 'Conditioned and unconditioned emotional defecation in the rat', *J. comp. physiol. Psychol.*, **46**, 378–82.

Hunt, H. F., and Brady, J. V. (1955). 'Some effects of punishment and intercurrent anxiety on a simple operant', *J. comp. physiol. Psychol.*, **48**, 305–10.

Hyde, T. S., Trappold, M. A., and Gross, D. M. (1968). 'Facilitative effect of a CS for reinforcement upon instrumental responding as a function of reinforcement magnitude: A test of incentive–motivation theory', *J. exp. Psychol.*, **73**, 423–8.

Isaacson, R. L., Douglas, R. J., and Moore, R. Y. (1961). 'The effect of radial hippocampal ablation on acquisition of avoidance responses', *J. comp. physiol. Psychol.*, **54**, 625–8.

Isaacson, R. L., and Wickelgren, W. D. (1962). 'Hippocampal ablation and passive avoidance', *Science*, **138**, 1104–6.

Israel, N. R. (1969). 'Levelling-sharpening and anticipatory cardiac response', *Psychosomatic Medicine*, **31**, 499–509.

Izard, C. E. (1960). 'Personality similarity and friendship', *J. abnorm. soc. Psychol.*, **61**, 47–51.

Izard, C. E. (1964). 'The effects of role-played emotion on affective reactions, intellectual functioning and evaluative ratings of the actress', *J. clin. Psychol.*, **20**, 444–6.

Izard, C. E. (1965). 'Personal growth through experience', in S. S. Tomkins, and C. E. Izard (Eds.) *Affect, cognition and personality*. Springer, New York, 200–41.

Izard, C. E., Randall, D., Nagler, S., and Fox, J. (1965a). 'The effects of affective picture stimuli on learning, perception and the affective value of previously neutral symbols', in S. S. Tomkins and C. E. Izard (Eds.) *Affect, cognition and personality*. Springer, New York, 42–70.

Izard, C. E., and Tomkins, S. S. (1966). 'Affect and behavior: Anxiety as negative affect', in G. D. Spielberger (Ed.) *Anxiety and Behavior*. Academic Press, New York, London.

Izard, C. E. Wehmer, G. M., Livsey, W., and Jennings, J. R. (1965b). 'Affect, awareness and performance', in S. S. Tomkins and C. E. Izard (Eds.) *Affect, cognition and personality*. Springer, New York, 2–41.

Jaanus, H. (1966). *Het Aspect Activiteit by de Beoordeling van Gelaatexpressies*. M. A. Thesis. Amsterdam University. (Quoted in Frijda 1969.)

Jacobson, E. (1932). 'The electrophysiology of mental activities', *Amer. j. Psychol.*, **44**, 677–94.

Jacobson, E. (1938). *Progressive relaxation*. University of Chicago Press, Chicago.

Jacobson, E. (1939). 'Variation of pulse rate with skeletal muscle tension and relaxation', *Annals internat. Med.*, **12**, 1194.

Jacobson, E. (1940). 'Variations of blood pressure with skeletal muscle tension and relaxation', *Annals internat. Med.*, **13**, 1619.

Jacobson, E. (1951). 'Muscular tension and the estimation of effort', *Amer. j. Psychol.*, **64**, 112–17.

James, W. (1884). 'What is an emotion', *Mind*, **9**, 188–205.

Jeness, A. F. (1932a). 'Differences in the recognition of facial expressions', *J. genet. Psychol.*, **7**, 192–6.

Jeness, A. F. (1932b). 'The effect of coaching subjects in the recognition of facial expressions', *J. gene:. Psychol.*, **7**, 163–78.

Jeness, A. F. (1932c). 'The recognition of facial expressions of emotion', *Psychol. Bull.*, **29**, 324–50.

Johnson, D. L. (1967). 'Honeybees: Do they use the direction information contained in their dance manoeuvre?', *Science*, **155**, 844–7.

Jones, H. E. (1950). 'The study of patterns of emotional expression', in M. L. Reymert (Ed.) *Feelings and emotions*. McGraw-Hill, New York.

Kamin, L. J. (1961). 'Trace conditioning of the conditioned emotional response', *J. comp. physiol. Psychol.*, **54**, 149–53.

Kamin, L. J. (1965). 'Temporal and intensity characteristics of the condition stimulus', in W. E. Prokasy (Ed.) *Classical conditioning*. Appleton-Century-Crofts, New York, 118–47.

Kamin, L. J., Brimer, C. J., and Black, A. H. (1963). 'Conditioned suppression as a monitor of fear of the CS in the course of avoidance training', *J. comp. physiol. Psychol.*, **56**, 202–5.

Kamiya, J. (1969). 'Operant control of the EEG alpha rhythm and some of its related effects on consciousness', in C. Tait (Ed.) *Altered states of consciousness*. Wiley, New York.

Karabenick, S. A. (1969). 'Effects of reward increase and reduction in the double runway', *J. exp. Psychol.*, **82**, 79–87.

208

Karas, G. G., and Denenberg, V. H. (1961). 'The effects of duration and distribution of infantile experience on adult learning', *J. comp. physiol. Psychol.*, **54**, 170–4.

Karsten, L. (1965). 'Dimensies van de Gelaatsexpressie: Een Replicatie met de Marjorie Lightfoot photos'. M.A. Thesis. Amsterdam University. (Quoted by Frijda 1969.)

Katkin, E. S., and Murray, E. N. (1968). 'Instrumental conditioning of autonomically mediated behavior', *Psychol. Bull.*, **70**, 52–68.

Kaufman, A., Baron, A., and Kopp, R. E. (1966). 'Some effects of instructions on human operant behavior', *Psychon. monogr. supp.*, **1**, 243–50.

Kelly, A. H., Beaton, L. E., and Magoun, H. W. (1946). 'A mid-brain mechanism for facio-vocal activity', *J. Neurophysiol.*, **9**, 181–9.

Kelly, D. H. W. (1966). 'Measurement of anxiety by forearm blood flow', *Brit. j. Psychiat.*, **112**, 789–98.

Kelly, D. H. W. (1967). 'The technique of forearm plethysmography for assessing anxiety', *J. psychosom. Res.*, **10**, 373–82.

Kelly, D. H. W., and Walter, C. J. S. (1968). 'The relationship between clinical diagnosis and anxiety, assessed by forearm blood flow and other measurements', *Brit. j. Psychiat.*, **114**, 611–26.

Kelsey, J. E., and Grossman, S. P. (1969). 'Cholinergic blockade and lesions in the ventromedial septum of the rat', *Physiol. Beh.*, **4**, 837–45.

Kennard, M. A. (1955). 'Effect of bilateral ablation of cingulate area on behavior of cats', *J. Neurophysiol.*, **18**, 159–69.

Kety, S. S. (1966). 'Catecholamines in neuropsychiatric state', *Pharmacol. Rev.*, **18**, 787–98.

Kety, S. S. (1970). 'Neurochemical aspects of emotional behaviour', in P. Black (Ed.) *Physiological correlates of emotion.* Academic Press, New York, London.

Kimble, G. A. (1961). *Hilgard and Marquis' Conditioning and learning.* Methuen, London.

King, F. A. (1958). 'Effects of septal and amygdaloid lesions on emotional behavior and conditioned avoidance responses in the rat', *J. nerv. ment. Dis.*, **126**, 57–63.

Klages, L. (1950). 'The life of feeling'. Excerpts from *Grundlegung der Wissenschaft rom Ausdruck*, Bouvrer, 1950. 6th Edn. 1964. Transl. by M. B. Arnold in *The Nature of Emotion* (1968) (Ed. Arnold). Penguin, Harmondsworth.

Klüver, H., and Bucy, P. C. (1937). ' "Psychic blindness" and other symptoms following bilateral temporal lobectomy in rhesus monkeys', *Amer. j. Physiol.*, **119**, 352–3.

Klüver, H., and Bucy, P. C. (1938). 'An analysis of certain effects of bilateral temporal lobectomy in the rhesus monkey, with special reference to "psychic blindness" ', *J. Psychol.*, **5**, 33–54.

Klüver, H., and Bucy, P. C. (1939). 'Preliminary analysis of functions of the temporal lobe in monkeys', *A.M.A. Arch. Neurol. Psychiat.*, **42**, 979–1000.

Knapp, P. H. (1963) (Ed.) *Expression of the emotions in man.* International University Press, New York.

Koehler, O. (1954). 'Das Lächeln ab angerborene Ausdrucksbewegung', *Zeitschr. menscht. Vererb-u. Konstitutionslehre*, **32**, 390–8. (Quoted in Schneirla 1959.)

Krause, M. S. (1961). 'The measurement of transitory anxiety', *Psychol. Rev.*, **68**, 178–89.

Krieckhaus, E. E., Simmon, H. J., Thomas, G. J., and Kenyon, J. (1964). 'Septal lesions enhance shock avoidance behavior in the rat', *Exp. Neurol.*, **9**, 107–13.

Krueger, F. (1928). 'The essence of feeling'. Abridged from 'Das Wesen der Gerfühle', *Arch. f. d. ges Psychol.*, **65**, 91–128. Transl. by M. B. Arnold in *The nature of Emotion* (1968) (Ed. Arnold). Penguin, Harmondsworth.

Lacey, J. I. (1950). 'Individual differences in somatic response patterns', *J. comp. physiol. Psychol.*, **43**, 338–50.

Lacey, J. I. (1956). 'The evaluation of autonomic responses toward a general solution', *Annals N.Y. Acad. Sci.*, **67**, 123–63.

Lacey, J. I., and Lacey, B. C. (1958). 'Verification and extension of the principle of autonomic response stereotypy', *Amer. j. Psychol.*, **71**, 50–73.

Lacey, J. I., and Lacey, B. C. (1970). 'Some autonomic–central nervous system interrelationships', in P. Black (Ed.) *Physiological correlates of emotion.* Academic Press, New York, London.

Lacey, J. I., Kagan, J., Lacey, B. C., and Moss, H. A. (1963). 'The visceral level: Situational determinants and behavioural correlates of autonomic response patterns', in P. H. Knapp (Ed.) *Expressions of the emotions in man.* International University Press, New York.

Lader, M. H. (1967). 'Palmar skin conductance measures in anxiety and phobic states', *J. Psychosom. Res.*, **11**, 271–81.

Lader, M. H. (1969a). 'Psychophysiological aspects of anxiety', in M. H. Lader (Ed.) *Studies of Anxiety.* Headley Bros., Ashford, 53–61.

Lader, M. H. (1969b). (Ed.) *Studies of anxiety.* Headley Bros., Ashford, for the World Psychiatric Association and the Royal Medico-Psychological Association.

Lader, M. H., and Wing, L. (1964). 'Habituation of the psychogalvanic reflex in patients with anxiety states and in normal subjects', *J. neurol. neurosurg. Psychiat.*, **27**, 210–18.

Lader, M. H., and Wing, L. (1966). *Physiological measures, sedative drugs and morbid Anxiety.* Oxford University Press, London.

Landis, C. (1925). 'Studies of emotional reactions IV: Metabolic rate', *Amer. j. Physiol.*, **74**, 188–203.

Landis, C. (1929). 'The interpretation of facial expression in emotion', *J. genet. Psychol.*, **2**, 59–72.

Landis, C. (1932). 'An attempt to measure emotional traits in juvenile delinquency', in K. S. Lashley *et al.* (Eds.) *Studies in the dynamics of behavior.* University of Chicago Press, Chicago.

Landis, C., and Hunt, W. Z. (1932). 'Adrenalin and emotion', *Psychol. Rev.* **39**, 467–85.

Lange, C. G. (1885). *The emotions.* Eng. transl. publ. 1922. Williams & Wilkins, Baltimore.

Latane, B., and Schachter, S. (1962). 'Adrenaline and avoidance learning', *J. comp. physiol. Psychol.*, **65**, 369–72.

Lawson, R. (1965). *Frustration.* Macmillan, New York.

Lawson, R., and Marx, M. H. (1958). 'Frustration: Theory and experiment', *Genetic Psychol. Monogr.*, **57**, 393–464.

Lazarus, A. A. (1963). 'The results of behavior therapy in 126 cases of severe neuroses', *Behav. res. Ther.*, **1**, 69–79.

Lazarus, A. A. (1965). 'A preliminary report on the use of directed muscular activity in counter-conditioning', *Behav. res. Ther.*, **2**, 301–3.

Lazarus, A. A. (1972). *Behavior therapy and Beyond.* McGraw-Hill, New York.

Lazarus, R. S. (1966). *Psychological stress and the coping process.* McGraw-Hill, New York.

Lazarus, R. S. (1968). 'Emotions and adaptation: Conceptual and empirical relations', in W. J. Arnold (Ed.) *Nebraska Symposium on motivation.* University of Nebraska Press, Lincoln, Nebraska.

Lazarus, R. S., Averill, J. R., and Opton, E. M. Jr. (1970). 'Towards a cognitive theory of emotion', in M. B. Arnold (Ed.) *Feelings and emotions: The Loyola Symposium.* Academic Press, New York, London, 207–32.

Lazarus, R. S., Deese, J., and Osler, S. F. (1952). 'The effects of psychological stress upon performance', *Psychol. Bull.*, **49**, 293–317.

Lazarus, R. S., and Opton, E. M. Jr. (1966). 'The study of psychological stress: A summary of theoretical formulations and experimental findings', in C. D. Spielberger (Ed.) *Anxiety and Behavior*. Academic Press, New York, 225–62.

Lazarus, R. S., Opton, E. M. Jr., Nomikos, M. S., and Rankin, N. O. (1965). 'The principle of short-circuiting of threat: Further evidence', *J. Person.*, **33**, 622–35.

Lazarus, R. S., Spiesman, J. C., Mordkoff, A. M., and Davison, L. A. (1962). 'A laboratory study of psychological stress produced by a motion picture film', *Psychol. Monogr.*, **76**, No. 34. (Whole No. 553.)

Lazarus, R. S., Tomita, M., Opton, E. Jr., and Kodama, M. (1966). 'A cross-cultural study of stress-reduction patterns in Japan', *J. person. soc. Psychol.*, **4**, 622–33.

Leeper, R. W. (1948). 'A motivational theory of emotion to replace "emotion as disorganized response" ', *Psychol. Rev.*, **55**, 5–21.

Leeper, R. W. (1962a). 'The motivational theory of emotion', in C. L. Stacey and M. F. De Martino (Eds.) *Understanding Human Motivation*. Howard Allen, Cleveland, Ohio, 657–65.

Leeper, R. W. (1962b). 'Learning and the fields of perception, motivation and personality', in S. Koch (Ed.) *Psychology: a study of a science*, Vol. 5. McGraw-Hill, New York, 365–487.

Leeper, R. W. (1965). 'Some needed developments in the motivational theory of emotions', in D. Levine (Ed.) *Nebraska Symposium on motivation*. University of Nebraska Press, Lincoln, Nebraska, 25–122.

Leeper, R. W. (1970). 'Feelings and emotions', in M. D. Arnold (Ed.) *Feelings and emotions: The Loyola Symposium*. Academic Press, New York, London, 151–68.

Leitenberg, H. (1965). 'Is time-out from positive reinforcement an aversive event? A review of the experimental evidence', *Psychol. Bull.*, **64**, 428–41.

Leitenberg, H. (1966). 'Conditioned acceleration and conditioned suppression in pigeons', *J. exp. anal. Behav.*, **9**, 205–12.

Leitenberg, H., Bertsch, G., and Coughlin, R. (1968). ' "Time-out from positive reinforcement" as the UCS in a CER paradigm with rats', *Psychon. Sci.*, **13**, 3–4.

Levine, S. (1956). 'A further study of infantile handling and adult avoidance learning', *J. Pers.*, **25**, 70–80.

Levine, S. (1957). 'Infantile experience and consummatory behaviour in adulthood', *J. comp. physiol. Psychol.*, **50**, 609–12.

Levine, S. (1958). 'Noxious stimulation in infant and adult rats and consummatory behaviour', *J. comp. physiol. Psychol.*, **51**, 230–3.

Levine, S. (1959). 'Differential emotionality at weaning as a function of infantile stimulation', *Canad. j. Psychol.*, **13**, 243–7.

Levine, S. (1962). 'Psychophysiological effects of infantile stimulation', in E. L. Bliss (Ed.) *Roots of Behavior*. Harper & Bros., New York.

Levine, S. (1965). 'Water consumption: Emotionally produced facilitation or suppression?', *Psychon. Sci.*, **3**, 105–6.

Levine, S., and Lewis, G. W. (1959). 'Critical periods and the effects of infantile experience on the maturation of a stress response', *Science*, **129**, 42–3.

Levitt, E. A. (1964). 'The relationship between abilities to express emotional meanings vocally and facially', in J. L. Davitz (Ed.) *The communication of emotional meaning*. McGraw-Hill, New York.

Levy, P. K. (1964). 'The ability to express and perceive vocal communications of feeling', in J. L. Davitz (Ed.) *The communication of emotional meaning*. McGraw-Hill, New York, 43–55.

Liddell, R. D. (1944). 'Conditioned reflex method and experimental neurosis', in J. McV. Hunt (Ed.) *Personality and the behavior disorders*. Ronald Press, New York, 389–412.

Lindholm, B. W. (1962). 'Critical periods and the effects of early shock on later behaviour in the white rat', *J. comp. physiol. Psychol.*, **55**, 597–9.

Lindsley, D. B. (1950). 'Emotions and the electroencephalogram', in M. L. Reymert (Ed.) *Feelings and emotions: The Mooseheart Symposium*. McGraw-Hill, New York.

Lindsley, D. B. (1951). 'Emotion', in S. S. Stevens (Ed.) *Handbook of experimental psychology*. Wiley, New York, 473–516.

Lindsley, D. B. (1957). 'Psychophysiology and motivation', in M. R. Jones (Ed.) *Nebraska symposium on motivation*. University of Nebraska Press, Lincoln, Nebraska, 44–105.

Lindsley, D. B. (1970). 'The role of nonspecific reticulo-thalamocortical systems in emotion', in P. Black (Ed.) *Physiological correlates of emotion*. Academic Press, New York, London.

Longo, N., Klempay, S., and Bitterman, M. E. (1964). 'Classical appetitive conditioning in the pigeon', *Psychon. Sci.*, **1**, 19–20.

Lubar, J. F. (1964). 'Effects of medial cortical lesions on the avoidance behavior of a cat', *J. comp. physiol. Psychol.*, **58**, 34–6.

Luchins, A. S. (1958). 'Definitiveness of impression and primacy in communications', *J. soc. Psychol.*, **48**, 275–90.

Lykken, D. T. (1957). 'A study of anxiety in the sociopathic personality', *J. abnorm. soc. Psychol.*, **55**, 6–10.

Lyon, D. O. (1963). 'Frequency of reinforcement as a parameter of conditioned suppression', *J. exp. anal. Behav.*, **6**, 95–8.

Lyon, D. O. (1964). 'Some notes on conditioned suppression and reinforcement schedules', *J. exp. anal. Behav.*, **7**, 289–91.

Lyon, D. O. (1968). 'Conditioned suppression: Operant variables and aversive control', *Psychol. Rec.*, **18**, 317–38.

Lyon, D. O., and Felton, M. (1966a). 'Conditioned suppression and variable ratio reinforcement', *J. exp. amal. Behav.*, **9**, 245–8.

Lyon, D. O., and Felton, M. (1966b). 'Conditioned suppression and fixed ratio schedule of reinforcement', *Psychol. Rec.*, **16**, 433–40.

Mahl, G. F. (1950). 'Anxiety, HCL secretion, and peptic ulcer etiology', *Psychosom. Med.*, **12**, 158–69.

Maier, N. R. F. (1949). *Frustration*. McGraw-Hill, New York.

Maier, N. R. F. (1956). 'Frustration theory: restatement and extension', *Psychol. Rev.*, **63**, 370–88.

Malmo, R. B. (1950). 'Experimental studies of mental patients under stress', in M. Reymert (Ed.) *Feelings and emotions*. McGraw-Hill, New York, 169–80.

Malmo, R. B. (1957). 'Anxiety and behavioral arousal', *Psychol. Rev.*, **64**, 276–87.

Malmo, R. B. (1959). 'Activation: a neuropsychological dimension', *Psychol. Bull.*, **66**, 367–86.

Malmo, R. B., and Heslam, R. M. (1951). 'Blood pressure response to repeated brief stress in psychoneurosis: a study of adaptation', *Canad. j. Psychol.*, **5**, 167–79.

Malmo, R. B., and Shagass, C. (1952). 'Studies of blood pressure in psychiatric patients under stress', *Psychosom. Med.*, **14**, 82–93.

Mandler, G. (1962). 'Emotion', in *New Directions in Psychology*, **1**. Holt, Rinehart & Winston, New York, 269–353.

Maranon, G. (1924). 'Contribution a l'étude de l'action emotive de l'adrenoline', *Revue Franc d'Endocrin*, **21**, 301–25. (As quoted in Fehr and Stern 1970.)

Markes, I. M. (1967). 'Classification of phobic states'. Communication to RMPA quarterly meeting Feb. 1967. (Quoted in Slater and Roth 1969.)

Martin, B. (1961). 'The assessment of anxiety by physiological behavioral measures', *Psychol. Bull.*, **58**, 234–55.

Martin, I. (1956). 'Levels of muscle activity in psychiatric patients', *Acta Psychol.*, **12**, 326–41.

Martin, I. (1960). 'Somatic reactivity', in H. J. Eysenck (Ed.) *Handbook of abnormal psychology*. University of London Press, London.

Marx, M. H. (1956). 'Some relations between frustration and drive', in M. R. Jones (Ed.) *Nebraska Symposium on Motivation*. University of Nebraska Press, Lincoln, Nebraska.

Marzocco, F. N. (1951). *Frustration effect as a function of drive level, habit strength, and Distribution of Trials During Extinction*. Unpubl. Ph.D thesis. State University of Iowa. (Cited by Brown, J. S. 1961.) *The motivation of behavior*. McGraw-Hill, New York.

Masserman, J. H. (1943). *Behavior and neurosis*. University of Chicago Press, Chicago.

May, H. S. (1938). 'A study of emotional expression among Chinese and Americans'. Unpubl. master thesis. Colombia University. (Quoted in Davitz, 1964.)

May, R. (1950). *The meaning of anxiety*. Ronald Press, New York.

Mayer-Gross, W., Slater, E., and Roth, M. *See* Slater and Roth (1969).

Meltzer, D., and Brahlek, J. A. (1970). 'Conditioned suppression and conditioned enhancement with the same positive UCS: an effect of CS duration', *J. exp. anal. Behav.*, **13**, 67–73.

Melzack, R. (1952). 'Irrational fears in the dog', *Canad. j. Psychol.*, **6**, 141–7.

Melzack, R., and Casey, K. L. (1970). 'The affective dimension of pain', in M. B. Arnold (Ed.) *Feelings and emotions: The Loyola Symposium*. Academic Press, New York, London.

Melzack, R., Penick, E., and Beckett, A. (1959). 'The problem of "innate fear" of the hawk shape: An experimental study with mallard ducks', *J. comp. physiol. Psychol.*, **52**, 694–8.

Meyer, P. A., and McHose, J. H. (1968). 'Facilitative effects of reward increase: An apparent "elation effect" ', *Psychon. Sci.*, **13**, 165–6.

Michotte, A. E. (1950). 'The emotions as functional connections', in M. L. Reymert (Ed.) *Feelings and emotions: The Moosehart Symposium*. McGraw-Hill, New York.

Miczek, K. A., and Grossman, S. (1971). 'Positive conditioned suppression: effects of CS duration', *J. exp. anal. Behav.*, **15**, 243–7.

Millenson, J. R. (1967). *Principles of behavioural analysis*. Macmillan, New York; Collier-Macmillan, London.

Millenson, J. R., and de Villiers, P. A. (1971). 'Motivational properties of conditioned anxiety', in R. M. Gilbert and J. R. Millenson (Eds.) *Reinforcement processes: Schedule induced and schedule dependent effects*. Academic Press, New York, London.

Miller, G. A., Galanter, E. H., and Pribram, K. H. (1960). *Plans and the structure of behaviour*. Holt, New York.

Miller, N. E. (1948). 'Studies of fear as an acquirable drive: I. Fear as motivation and fear-reduction as reinforcement in the learning of new responses', *J. exp. Psychol.*, **38**, 89–101.

Miller, N. E. (1951). 'Learning drives and rewards', in S. S. Stevens (Ed.) *Handbook of experimental psychology*. Wiley, New York.

Miller, N. E. (1958). 'Central stimulation and other new approaches to motivation and reward', *Amer. Psychol.*, **13**, 100–8.

Miller, N. E. (1959). 'Liberalization of basic S-R concepts: Extensions to conflict behavior, motivation and social learning', in S. Koch (Ed.) *Psychology: A study of a science*, Vol. 2. McGraw-Hill, New York.

Miller, N. E. (1960). 'Learning resistance to pain and fear: effects of overlearning, exposure, and rewarded exposure in context', *J. exp. Psychol.*, **60**, 137–45.

Miller, N. E. (1969). 'Learning of visceral and glandular responses', *Science*, **163**, 434–45.

213

Miller, N. E., and Stevenson, S. S. (1936). 'Agitated behavior of rats during experimental extinction and a curve of spontaneous recovery', *J. comp. Psychol.*, **21**, 205–31.
Miller, R. E., Banks, J. H., and Kuwahara, H. (1966). 'The communication of affects in monkeys: cooperative reward conditioning', *J. genet. Psychol.*, **108**, 121–34.
Miller, R. E., Banks, J. H., and Ogawa, N. (1962). 'Communication of affect in "cooperative conditioning" of rhesus monkeys', *J. comp. physiol. Psychol.*, **5**, 343–8.
Miller, R. E., Banks, J. H., and Ogawa, N. (1963). 'Role of facial expression in "cooperative-avoidance conditioning" in monkeys', *J. abnorm. soc. Psychol.*, **67**, 24–30.
Miller, R. E., Murphy, J. V., and Mirsky, I. A. (1959a). 'Non-verbal communication of affect', *J. clin. Psychol.*, **15**, 155–8.
Miller, R. E., Murphy, J. V., and Mirsky, I. A. (1959b). 'The relevance of facial expression and posture as cues in the communication of affect between monkeys', *Arch. gen. Psychiat.*, **1**, 480–8.
Mirsky, A. F. (1960). 'Studies of the effects of brain lesions on social behavior in *Macaca mulatta*: methodological and theoretical consideration', *Ann. N.Y. Acad. Sci.*, **85**, 785–94.
Mirsky, I. A. (1958). 'Physiologic, psychologic and social determinants in the etiology of duodenal ulcer', *Amer. j. Digest. Diseases*, **3**, 285–314.
Mirsky, I. A., Miller, R. E., and Murphy, J. V. (1958). 'The communication of affect in rhesus monkeys: I. An experimental method', *J. Amer. Psychol. Ass.*, **6**, 433–41.
Moltz, H. (1960). 'Imprinting: empirical basis and theoretical significance', *Psychol. Bull.*, **57**, 291–314.
Moltz, H., Rosenblum, L., and Halikas, N. (1959). 'Imprinting and level of anxiety', *J. comp. physiol. Psychol.*, **52**, 240–4.
Morse, W. E., and Skinner, B. F. (1958). 'Some factors involved in the stimulus control of operant behavior', *J. exp. anal. Behav.*, **1**, 103–7.
Moruzzi, G., and Magoun, H. W. (1949). 'Brain stem reticular formation and activation of the EEG', *Electroenceph. and Clin. Neurophys.*, **1**, 455–73.
Mowrer, O. H. (1939). 'A stimulus–suspense analysis of anxiety and its role as a reinforcing agent', *Psychol. Rev.*, **46**, 553–65.
Mowrer, O. H. (1950). *Learning theory and personality dynamics.* Ronald Press, New York.
Mowrer, O. H. (1960a). *Learning theory and behavior.* Wiley, New York.
Mowrer, O. H. (1960b). *Learning theory and the symbolic processes.* Wiley, New York.
Moyer, K. E. (1965). 'Effect of experience with emotion provoking stimuli on water consumption in the rat', *Psychon. Sci.*, **2**, 251–2.
Moyer, K. E., and Benninger, R. (1963). 'Effect of environmental change and electric shock on water consumption in the rat', *Psychol. Rep.*, **13**, 179–85.
Munn, N. L. (1946). *Psychology: The fundamentals of human adjustment.* Houghton and Mifflin, Boston.
Murphy, J. V., Miller, R. E., and Mirsky, I. A. (1955). 'Interanimal conditioning in the monkey', *J. comp. physiol. Psychol.*, **48**, 211–4.
Myer, J. S. (1971). 'Some effects of noncontingent aversive stimulation', in *Aversive conditioning and learning.* Academic Press, New York, London, 469–536.
Maclean, P. D. (1949). 'Psychosomatic disease and the "visceral brain"', *Psychosom. Med.*, **III**, 338–53.
MacLean, P. D. (1954). 'The limbic system and its hippocampal formation: studies in animals and their possible application to man', *J. Neurosurg.*, **II**, 29–44.
MacLean, P. D. (1957). 'Chemical and electrical stimulation of hippocampus in unrestrained animals. II: Behavioral findings', *Arch. Neurol. Psychiat.*, **78**, 128–42.
MacLean, P. D. (1970). 'The limbic brain in relation to the psychoses', in P. D. Black (Ed.) *Physiological correlates of emotion.* Academic Press, New York, London.

McCleary, R. A. (1961). 'Response specificity in the behavioral effects of limbic system lesions in the cat', *J. comp. physiol. Psychol.*, **54**, 605–13.

McCleary, R. A. (1966). 'Response-modulating functions of the limbic system: Initiation and suppression', *Prog. physiol. Psychol.*, **1**, 209–72.

McCleary, R. A., Jones, C., and Ursin, H. (1965). 'Avoidance and retention deficits in septal cats', *Psychon. Sci.*, **2**, 85–6.

McDougall, W. (1910). *Introduction to social psychology*. Luce, Boston.

McDougall, W. (1923). *Outline of Psychology*. Scribner, New York.

McDougall, W. (1928). 'Emotion and feeling distinguished', in M. L. Reymert (Ed.) *Feelings and emotions*. Clark University Press, Worcester, Massachusetts.

McHose, J. H. (1963). 'Effect of continued nonreinforcement on the frustration effect', *J. exp. Psychol.*, **65**, 444–50.

Nash, J. (1970). *Developmental psychology: A psychobiological approach*. Prentice Hall, New Jersey.

Nisbett, R. E. (1968). 'Taste, deprivation, and weight determinants of eating behavior', *J. person. soc. Psychol.*, **16**, 107–16.

Nisbett, R. E., and Schachter, S. (1966). 'Cognitive manipulation of pain', *J. exp. soc. Psychol.*, **2**, 227–36.

Nowlis, V. (1953). 'The development and modification of motivational systems in personality', in M. R. Jones (Ed.) *Current theory and research in motivation*. University of Nebraska Press, Lincoln, Nebraska.

Nowlis, V. (1959). 'The experimental analysis of mood' (Abstract), XVth International Congress of Psychology. *Acta Psychol.*, **15**, 426.

Nowlis, V. (1963). 'The concept of mood', in S. M. Farber and R. H. L. Wilson (Eds.) *Conflict and creativity*. McGraw-Hill, New York.

Nowlis, V. (1965). 'Research with the mood adjective check list', in S. S. Tomkins and C. E. Izard (Eds.) *Affect, cognition and personality*. Springer, New York.

Nowlis, V. (1970). 'Mood: Behavior and experience', in M. B. Arnold (Ed.) *Feelings and Emotions: The Loyola Symposium*. Academic Press, New York, London, 261–72.

Nowlis, V., and Nowlis, H. H. (1956). 'The description and analysis of moods', *Ann. N.Y. Acad. Sci.*, **65**, 345–55.

Oakley, D. A., and Russell, I. S. (1968). 'Mass action and Pavlovian conditioning', *Psychon. Sci.*, **12**, 91–2.

O'Kelly, L. I. (1940). 'The validity of defecation as a measure of emotionality in the rat', *J. gen. Psychol.*, **23**, 75–87.

Olds, J. (1955). 'Physiological mechanisms of reward', in M. R. Jones (Ed.) *Nebraska symposium on motivation*. University of Nebraska Press, Lincoln, Nebraska.

Olds, J. (1958). 'Self-stimulation of the brain', *Science*, **127**, 315–24.

Olds, J., and Milner, P. (1954). 'Positive reinforcement produced by electrical stimulation of the septal area and other regions of the rat brain', *J. comp. physiol. Psychol.*, **47**, 419–27.

Orbach, J., Milner, B., and Rasmussen, T. (1960). 'Learning and retention in monkeys after amygdalahippocampal resection', *Arch. Neurol.* (Chicago), **3**, 230–51.

Osgood, C. E. (1955). 'Fidelity and reliability', in H. Quastler *Information theory in psychology*. Free Press, Glencoe, 374–84.

Osgood, C. E. (1966). 'Dimensionality of the semantic space for communication via facial expressions', *Scand. j. Psychol.*, **7**, 1–30.

Papez, J. W. (1937). 'A proposed mechanism of emotion', *Arch. neurol. Psychiat.*, **38**, 725–43.

Papez, J. W. (1939). 'Cerebral mechanisms', *Research publication, Association for Research in Nervous and Mental Disorders*, **89**, 145–59.

Pare, W. P. (1965). 'Stress and consummatory behavior in the albino rat', *Psychol. Rep.*, **16**, 399–405.

Parke, R. D., and Walters, R. H. (1967). 'Some factors influencing the efficacy of punishment training for inducing response inhibition. Experiment 2', *Monogr. Soc. Res. Child. Developm.*, 32, No. 1.

Pavlov, I. P. (1928). *Conditioned Reflexes.* Trans. and ed. G. V. Anup. Oxford University Press, London, New York.

Peckham, R. H., and Amsel, A. (1967). 'Within-subject demonstration of a relationship between frustration and magnitude of reward in a differential magnitude of reward discrimination', *J. exp. Psychol.*, **73**, 187–95.

Peiper, A. (1926). 'Untersuchungen über die Reaktionzeit ein Sanglingsalter: II. Reaktionzeit auf Schmerzreiz', *Monatschr. Kinderheilk*, **32**, 136–43. (Quoted in Schneirla 1959.)

Persky, H., Gamm, S. R., and Grinker, R. R. Sr. (1952). 'Correlation between fluctuation of free anxiety and quantity of hippuric acid secretion', *Psychosom. Med.*, **14**, 34–40.

Persky, H., Grinker, R. R. Sr., and Mirsky, J. A. (1950). 'Excretion of hippuric acid in subjects with free anxiety', *J. clin. Invest.*, **29**, 110–14.

Pichot, P. (1969). 'Discussion of "Biological aspects of anxiety" ', in M. L. Lader (Ed.) *Studies of Anxiety.* Headley Bros., Ashford, 26–7.

Pliskoff, S. (1961). 'Rate-change effects during a pre-schedule-change stimulus', *J. exp. anal. Behav.*, **4**, 383–6.

Pliskoff, S. (1963). 'Rate-change effects with equal potential reinforcements during the "warning" stimulus', *J. exp. anal. Behav.*, **6**, 557–62.

Plutchik, R. (1962). *The emotions: facts, theories and a new model.* Random House, New York.

Plutchik, R. (1965). 'What is an emotion?', *J. Psychol.*, **61**, 295–303.

Plutchik, R. (1966). 'Emotions as adaptive reactions: Implications for therapy', *Psychoanalyt. Rev.*, **53**, 105–10.

Plutchik, R. (1970). 'Emotions, evolution and adaptive processes', in M. D. Arnold (Ed.) *Feelings and emotions: The Loyola Symposium.* Academic Press, New York, London, 3–24.

Polack, I., Rubenstein, H., and Horowitz, A. (1960). 'Communication of verbal modes of expression', *Language and Speech*, **3**, 121–30.

Pradines, M. (1958). *Traite de Psychologie*, 6th Edn., Vol. 1. Presses Universitaines de France. Transl. by Y. Begin and M. B. Arnold. Excerpts reprinted in M. B. Arnold (Ed.) (1968) *The nature of emotion.* Penguin, Harmondsworth, 189–200.

Pribram, K. H. (1970). 'Feelings as monitors', in M. B. Arnold (Ed.) *Feelings and emotions: The Loyola Symposium.* Academic Press, New York, London, 41–53.

Pribram, K. H., and Fulton, J. F. (1954). 'An experimental critique of the effects of anterior cingulate ablations in monkey', *Brain*, **77**, 34–44.

Pribram, K. H., Mishkin, M., Rosvold, H. E., and Kaplan, S. J. (1952). 'Effects on delayed response performance of lesions of dorsolateral and ventromedial frontal cortex of baboons', *J. comp. physiol. Psychol.*, **45**, 565–75.

Pribram, K. H., and Weiskrantz, L. A. (1957). 'A comparison of the effects of medial and lateral cerebral resections on conditioned avoidance behavior of monkeys', *J. comp. physiol. Psychol.*, **50**, 74–80.

Prick, J. J. G. (1969). 'The role of anxiety in psychoses', in M. H. Lader (Ed.) *Studies of anxiety.* Headley Bros., Ashford, 105–8.

Prytula, R. E., and Braud, W. G. (1970). 'Sucrose pellet incentive shifts in the double alley', *Psychol. Rep.*, **27**, 391–7.

Ranson, S. W. (1939). 'Somnolence caused by hypothalamic lesions in the monkey', *Arch. Neurol. Psychiat.*, **41**, 1–23.

Ranson, S. W., and Magoun, H. W. (1939). 'The hypothalamus', *Ergebn. Physiol.*, **41**, 56–163.
Rapaport, D. (1950). *Emotions and memory*. International Universities Press, New York.
Reis, D. J., and Fuxe, K. (1969). 'Brain norepinephrine: Evidence that neuronal release is essential for sham rage behavior following brain-stem transection in the cat', *Proceedings of the National Academy of Sciences of the United States of America*, **64**, 108–12. (Quoted by Kety 1970.)
Remington, R. E., and Strongman, K. T. (1970). 'Instruction-dependent facilitation during a pretimeout stimulus in human subjects', *Psychon. Sci.*, **20**, 348–9.
Remington, R. E., and Strongman, K. T. (1972a). 'Operant facilitation during a pre-reward stimulus: differential effects in human subjects', *Brit. j. Psychol.* (In press.)
Remington, R. E., and Strongman, K. T. (1972b). 'Baseline dependent facilitation. Effects of a prereward stimulus', *Brit. j. Psychol.* (In press.)
Rescorla, R. (1967). 'Pavlovian conditioning and its proper control procedures', *Psychol. Rev.*, **74**, 71–80.
Rescorla, R. A. (1968). 'Probability of shock in the presence and absence of CS in fear conditioning', *J. comp. physiol. Psychol.*, **66**, 1–5.
Rescorla, R. A. (1969). 'Conditioned inhibition of fear resulting from negative CS–US contingencies', *J. comp. physiol. Psychol.*, **67**, 504–9.
Rescorla, R. A., and Lolordo, V. M. (1965). 'Inhibition of avoidance behavior', *J. comp. physiol. Psychol.*, **59**, 406–12.
Rescorla, R. A., and Solomon, R. L. (1967). 'Two-process learning: Relationships between Pavlovian conditioning and instrumental learning', *Psychol. Rev.*, **74**, 151–82.
Reynolds, G. S. (1961). 'Behavioral contrast', *J. exp. anal. Behav.*, **4**, 57–71.
Rodnick, E. H., and Garmezy, N. (1957). 'An experimental approach to the study of motivation in schizophrenia', in M. R. Jones (Ed.) *Nebraska symposium on motivation*. University of Nebraska Press, Lincoln, Nebraska, 109–84.
Rosenzweig, S. (1934). 'Types of reaction to frustration: an heuristic classification', *J. abnorm. soc. Psychol.*, **29**, 298–300.
Rosenzweig, S. (1938). 'A general outline of frustration', *Char. person.*, **7**, 151–60.
Rosenzweig, S. (1944). 'An outline of frustration theory', in J. McV. Hunt (Ed.) *Personality and the behavior disorders*. Ronald Press, New York.
Ross, G. S., Hodos, W., and Brady, J. V. (1962). 'Electroencephalographic correlates of temporally spaced responding and avoidance behaviour', *J. exp. anal. Behav.*, **5**, 467–72.
Ross, R. B., and Russell, I. S. (1967). 'Subcortical storage of classical conditioning', *Nature*, **214**, 5084, 210–11.
Ruckmick, C. A. (1936). *The psychology of feeling and emotion*. McGraw-Hill, New York.
Russell, I. S. 1967. 'Animal learning and memory', in D. Richter (Ed.) *Aspects of learning and memory*. Heinemann, London.
Ryan, T. J., and Watson, P. (1968). 'Frustrative nonreward theory applied to children's behavior', *Psychol. Bull.*, **69**, 111–25.
Rylander, G. (1939). *Personality changes after operations on the frontal lobes. A clinical study of 32 cases*. Munksgaard, Copenhagen.
Rylander, G. (1948). 'Personality analysis before and after frontal lobotomy', *Res. Pub.*, *Assoc. res. nerv. ment. Dis.*, **27**, 691–705.
Salzen, E. A. (1962). 'Imprinting and fear', *Symp. Zoo. Soc. London*, No. 8, 197–217.
Salzen, E. A. (1963). 'Visual stimuli eliciting the smiling response in the human infant', *J. genet. Psychol.*, **102**, 51–4.
Salzen, E. A., and Tomlin, F. J. (1963). 'The effect of cold on the following response of domestic fowl', *Anim. Behav.*, **7**, 172–9.

Sargant, W. (1957). *Battle for the Mind*. Heinemann, London.

Sartre, J. P. (1948). *The Emotions*. Philosophical Library, New York.

Sawrey, W. J., and Weisz, J. D. (1956). 'An experimental method of producing gastric ulcers', *J. comp. physiol. Psychol.*, **49**, 269–70.

Schachter, S. (1957). 'Pain, fear and anger in hypertensives and A psychophysiologic study', *Psychosom. Med.*, **19**, 17–29.

Schachter, S. (1959). *The Psychology of affiliation*. Stamford University Press, Stamford, California.

Schachter, S. (1964). 'The interaction of cognitive and physiological determinants of emotional state', in L. Berkowitz (Ed.) *Advances in experimental social psychology*, Vol. 1. Academic Press, New York, 49–8.

Schachter, S. (1965). 'A cognitive–physiological view of emotion', in Klineberg and Christie (Eds.) *Perspectives in social psychology*. Holt, Rinehart & Winston, New York, 75–105.

Schachter, S. (1967). 'Cognitive effects on bodily functioning: Studies of obesity and eating', in D. C. Glass (Ed.) *Neurophysiology and emotion*. Rockefeller University Press and Russell Sage Foundation, New York.

Schachter, S. (1970). 'The assumption of identity and peripherilist–centralist controversies in motivation and emotion', in M. B. Arnold (Ed.) *Feelings and Emotion: The Loyola Symposium*. Academic Press, New York, London.

Schachter, S., Goldman, R., and Gordon, A. (1968). 'Effects of fear, food deprivation and obesity on eating', *J. pers. soc. Psychol.*, **10**, 91–7.

Schachter, S., and Gross, L. P. (1968). 'Manipulated time and eating behavior', *J. pers. soc. Psychol.*, **10**, 98–106.

Schachter, S., and Latane, B. (1964). 'Crime, cognition and the autonomic nervous system', in D. Levine (Ed.) *Nebraska symposium on motivation*. University of Nebraska Press, Lincoln, Nebraska, 221–73.

Schachter, S., and Singer, J. (1962). 'Cognitive, social and physiological determinants of emotional state', *Psychol. Rev.*, **69**, 378–99.

Schachter, S., and Wheeler, L. (1962). 'Epinephrine, chlorpromizine and amusement', *J. abnorm. soc. Psychol.*, **65**, 121–8.

Schaffer, H. R. (1958). 'Objective observations of personality development in early infancy', *Brit. j. Med. Psychol.*, **31**, 174–83.

Schaller, G. B., and Emlen, J. T. (1962). 'The ontogeny of avoidance behaviour in some precocial birds', *Anim. Behav.*, **10**, 370–81.

Schlosberg, H. (1952). 'The description of facial expression in terms of two dimensions', *J. exp. Psychol.*, **44**, 229–37.

Schlosberg, H. (1954). 'Three dimensions of emotion', *Psychol. Rev.*, **61**, 81–8.

Schneirla, T. C. (1959). 'An evolutionary and developmental theory of biphasic processes underlying approach and withdrawal', in M. R. Jones (Ed.) *Nebraska symposium on motivation*. University of Nebraska Press, Lincoln, Nebraska, 1–42.

Schneirla, T. C. (1965). 'Aspects of stimulation and organization in approach/withdrawal processes underlying vertebrate behavioral development', in Lehrman, Hinde and Shaw (Eds.) *Advances in the study of behavior*. I. Academic Press, New York.

Schreiner, L. H., and Kling, A. (1953). 'Behavioral changes following injury in the cat', *J. Neurophys.*, **16**, 643–59.

Schwartzbaum, J. S. (1965). 'Discrimination behavior after amygdalectomy in monkeys: Visual and somesthetic learning and perceptual capacity, *J. comp. physiol. Psychol.*, **60**, 314–19.

Schwartzbaum, J. S., Green, R. H., Beatty, W. W., and Thompson, B. 'Acquisition of avoidance behavior following septal lesions in the rat', *J. comp. physiol. Psychol.*, **63**, 95–104.

218

Schwartzbaum, J. S. (1960). 'Changes in reinforcing properties of stimuli following ablation of the amygdaloid complex in monkeys', *J. comp. physiol. Psychol.*, **53**, 388–95.

Scott, J. P. (1962). 'Critical periods in behavioural development', *Science*, **138**, 949–58.

Scott, J. P. (1967). 'The process of primary socialization in the dog', in G. Newton and S. Levine (Eds.) *Early experience and behaviour*. Thomas, Springfield, U.S.A.

Scott, J. P. (1968). *Early experience and the organization of behaviour*. Wadsworth, California, U.S.A.

Scott, J. P., and Fuller, J. L. (1965). *Genetics and the social behaviour of the dog*. University of Chicago Press, Chicago.

Sears, R. R. (1950). 'Relation of fantasy aggression to interpersonal aggression', *Child Dev.*, **21**, 5–6.

Sears, R. R., Maccoby, E. E., and Levin, H. (1957). *Patterns of Child Rearing*. Row, Peterson, Evanston, Illinois.

Seward, J. P., Pereboom, A. C., Butler, B., and Jones, R. B. (1957). 'The role of prefeeding in an apparent frustration effect', *J. exp. Psychol.*, **54**, 445–50.

Shepard, R. N. (1963). 'The analysis of proximities: multidimensional scaling with an unknown distance function', *Psychometrica*, **27**, 125–40.

Sherrington, C. S. (1900). 'Experiments on the value of vascular and visceral factors for the genesis of emotion', *Proc. Roy. Soc. (London)*, **66**, 390–403.

Sidman, M. (1960). 'Normal sources of pathological behavior', *Science*, **132**, 61–8.

Siegel, P. S., and Brantley, J. J. (1951). 'The relationship of emotionality to the consummatory response of eating', *J. exp. Psychol.*, **42**, 304–6.

Siegel, P. S., and Siegel, H. S. (1949). 'The effect of emotionality on the water intake of the rat', *J. comp. physiol. Psychol.*, **42**, 12–16.

Siegel, P. S., and Sparks, D. L. (1961). 'Irrelevant aversive stimulation as an activator of an appetitional response: a replication', *Psychol. Rep.*, **9**, 700.

Siminov, P. V. (1970). 'The information theory of emotion', in M. B. Arnold (Ed.) *Feelings and emotions: The Loyola symposium*. Academic Press, New York, London, 145–9. (From an original report at the Congress of Psychology, Moscow, 1966.)

Singer, J. L. (1961). 'The effects of epinephrine, chlorpromazine and dibenzyline upon the fright responses of rats under stress and nonstress conditions'. Unpubl. doctoral diss. University of Minnesota. (Quoted by Schachter 1964; 1965.)

Singer, J. L. (Ed.) (1971). *The Control of Aggression and Violence*. Academic Press, New York, London.

Singer, R. D., and Singer, A. (1969). *Psychological development in children*. W. S. Saunders, Philadelphia, London.

Skinner, B. F. (1938). *The behavior of organisms*. Appleton-Century-Crofts, New York.

Skinner, B. F. (1953). *Science and human behavior*. Macmillan, New York.

Skinner, B. F. (1957). *Verbal behavior*. Appleton-Century-Crofts, New York.

Slater, E., and Roth, M. (1969). *Mayer-Gross, Slater and Roth; Clinical Psychiatry*, 3rd Edn. Bailliere, Tindall & Cassell, London.

Slater, E., and Shields, J. (1969). 'Genetical aspects of anxiety', in M. H. Lader (Ed.) *Studies of anxiety*. Headley Bros., Ashford, 62–71.

Sluckin, W. (1960). 'Towards a theory of filial responses', *Bull. Brit. psychol. Soc. No. 40*, 5A.

Sluckin, W. (1964). *Imprinting and early learning*. Methuen, London.

Smart, R. G. (1965). 'Conflict and conditioned aversive stimuli in the development of experimental neuroses', *Canad. j. Psychol.*, **19**, 208–3.

Smith, W. K. (1950). 'Non-olfactory functions of the pyriform-amygdaloid-hippocampal complex', *Fed. Proc.*, **9**, 118.

Solomon, P., Kubzansky, P. E., Leiderman, P. H., Mendelson, J. H., Trumbull, R., and Wexler, D. (1961). *Sensory deprivation*. Harvard University Press, Cambridge.

Soskin, W. F., and Kaufman, P. E. (1961). 'Judgment of emotion in word-free speech samples', *J. Communic.*, **11**, 73–80.

Spence, K. W. (1956). *Behavior theory and conditioning*. Yale University Press, New Haven.

Spence, K. W. (1958). 'A theory of emotionally based drive (D) and its relation to performance in simple learning situations', *Amer. Psychol.*, **13**, 131–41.

Spielberger, C. D. (1966). 'Theory and research on anxiety', in Spielberger (Ed.) *Anxiety and behavior*. Academic Press, New York, London, 3–20.

Spielberger, C. D. (Ed.) (1966). *Anxiety and behavior*. Academic Press, New York, London.

Spielberger, C. D., and Smith, L. H. (1966). 'Anxiety (drive); stress and serial-position effects in serial-verbal learning', *J. exp. Psychol.*, **72**, 589–95.

Spiesman, J. C., Lazarus, R. S., Mordkoff, A. M., and Davison, L. A. (1964). 'The experimental reduction of stress based on ego-defence theory', *J. abnorm. soc. Psychol.*, **68**, 367–80.

Spitz, R. A., and Wolf, K. (1946). 'Anaclitic depressions', *Psychoanal. Stud. of Child.*, **2**, 313–42.

Staddon, J. E. R., and Innis, N. K. (1966). 'An effect analogous to "frustration" on interval reinforcement schedules', *Psychon. Sci.*, **4**, 287–8.

Staddon, J. E. R., and Innis, N. K. (1969). 'Reinforcement omission on fixed-interval schedules', *J. exp. anal. Behav.*, **12**, 689–700.

Stanley-Jones, D. (1970). 'The biological origin of love and hate', in M. B. Arnold (Ed.) *Feelings and emotions: The Loyola symposium*. Academic Press, New York, London.

Stein, L., Sidman, M., and Brady, J. V. (1958). 'Some effects of two temporal variables on conditioned suppression', *J. exp. anal. Behav.*, **1**, 154–62.

Stern, R. M., and Kaplan, B. E. (1967). 'Galvanic skin response: Voluntary control and externalization', *J. Psychosom. Res.*, **10**, 349–53.

Sternbach, R. A. (1966). *Principles of Psychophysiology*. Academic Press, New York, London.

Sterritt, G. M. (1962). 'Inhibition and facilitation of eating by electric shock', *J. comp. physiol. Psychol.*, **55**, 226–9.

Stotland, E. (1969). 'Exploratory investigations of empathy', in L. Berkowitz (Ed.) *Advances in experimental social psychology*, **4**, 271–314.

Stoyva, J., and Kamiya, J. (1968). 'Electrophysiological studies of dreaming as the prototype of a new strategy in the study of consciousness', *Psychol. Rev.*, **75**, 192–205.

Stringer, P. (1967). 'Cluster analysis of nonverbal judgments of facial expression', *Brit. j. Math. Stat. Psychol.*, **20**, 71–9.

Strongman, K. T. (1965). 'The effect of anxiety on food intake in the rat', *Quart. j. exp. Psychol.*, **17**, 255–60.

Strongman, K. T. (1967). 'The effect of prior exposure to shock on a visual discrimination by rats', *Canad. j. Psychol.*, **21**, 57–68.

Strongman, K. T. (1969). 'Analysing emotional behavior', *New Scient.*, Aug., 242–343.

Strongman, K. T. (1970). 'Communicating with the eyes', *Science Journal*, **6**, 47–53.

Strongman, K. T., and Champness, B. G. (1968). 'Dominance hierarchies and conflict in eye contact', *Acta Psychol.*, **28**, 376–86.

Strongman, K. T., Coles, M. G. H., Remington, R. E., and Wookey, P. E. (1970). 'The effect of shock duration and intensity on the ingestion of food of varying palatibility', *Quart. j. exp. Psychol.*, **22**, 521–5.

Strongman, K. T., and Wookey, P. E. (1969). 'Frustrative reward', *J. exp. Psychol.*, **82**, 183–4.

Strongman, K. T., Wookey, P. E., and Remington, R. E. (1971). 'Elation', *Brit. j. Psychol.*, **62**, 481–92.

Sullivan, H. S. (1953). *The interpersonal theory of psychiatry*. Horton, New York.

Tart, C. (1969). *Altered states of consciousness*. Wiley, New York.

Taylor, J. A. (1956). 'Drive theory and manifest anxiety', *Psychol. Bull.*, **53**, 303–20.

Thierry, A. M., Javoy, F., Glowinski, J., and Kety, S. S. (1968). 'Effects of stress on the metabolism of noxepinephrine, dopamine and serotonin in the central nervous system of the rat. I. Modification of noxepinephrine turnover', *J. Pharmacol. exp. Therap.*, **163**, 163–71. (Quoted by Kety 1970.)

Thompson, D. F., and Meltzer, L. (1964). 'Communication of emotional intent by facial expression', *J. abnorm. soc. Psychol.*, **68**, 129–35.

Thompson, J. (1941). 'Development of facial expression of emotion in blind and seeing children', *Arch. Psychol.*, **37**, No. 264.

Thorpe, W. H. (1956). *Learning and instinct in animals*. Harvard University Press, Cambridge, Mass.

Tobach, E., and Schneirla, T. C. (1962). 'Eliminative responses in mice and rats and the problem of "emotionality"', in E. L. Bliss (Ed.) *Roots of Behavior*. Harper, New York.

Tomkins, S. S. (1962). *Affect, imagery and consciousness: Vol. 1. The positive affects*. Springer, New York.

Tomkins, S. S. (1963). *Affect, imagery and consciousness: Vol. II. The negative affects*. Springer, New York.

Tomkins, S. S., and McCarter, R. (1964). 'What and where are the primary affects? Some evidence for a theory', *Percept. Mot. Sk.*, **18**, 119–58.

Trenholme, I., Baron, A., and Kaufman, A. (1969). 'Effects of signated time-out from and loss of monetary reinforcement on human operant behavior', *Psychon. Sci.*, **15**, 295–6.

Triandis, H. G., and Lambert, W. W. (1958). 'A restatement and test of Schlesberg's theory of emotions, with two kinds of subjects from Greece', *J. abnorm. soc. Psychol.*, **56**, 321–8.

Tryon, R. C., Tryon, C. M., and Kuznets, G. (1941). 'Studies in individual differences in maze ability: IX Ratings of hiding, avoidance, escape and vocalization responses', *J. comp. Psychol.*, **32**, 407–35.

Valenstein, E. S. (1959). 'The effect of reserpine on the continued emotional response in the guinea pig', *J. exp. anal. Behav.*, **2**, 219–25.

Valins, S. (1963). *Psychopathy and physiological reactivity under stress*. Unpubl. Masters thesis: Colombia University. (Quoted in Schachter and Latane 1964.)

Valins, S. (1966). 'Cognitive effects of false heart-rate feedback', *J. person. soc. Psychol.*, **4**, 400–8.

Valins, S. (1967a). 'Emotionality and information concerning internal reactions', *J. person, soc. Psychol.*, **6**, 458–63.

Valins, S. (1967b). 'Emotionality and autonomic reactivity', *J. exp. res. Pers.*, **2**, 41–8.

Valins, S. (1968). *Persistent effects of information concerning internal reactions: ineffectiveness of debriefing*. Unpubl. manusc. (Quoted in Valins 1970.)

Valins, S. (1970). 'The perception and labeling of bodily changes as determinants of emotional behavior', in P. Black (Ed.) *Physiological correlates of emotion*. Academic Press, New York, London, 229–43.

Valins, S., and Ray, A. A. (1967). 'Effects of cognitive desensitization on avoidance behavior', *J. person. soc. Psychol.*, **7**, 345–50.

Vandenberg, S. G. (1967). 'Hereditary factors in normal personality traits (as measured by inventories)', in Wortis (Ed.) *Recent advances in Biological Psychiatry*. Vol. 9. Plenum Press, New York.

Vine, I. (1970). 'Communication by facial-visual signals', in J. H. Crook (Ed.) *Social behaviour in birds and mammals*. Academic Press, New York, London, 279–354.

Wagner, A. R. (1959). 'The role of reinforcement and nonreinforcement in an "apparent frustration effect" ', *J. exp. Psychol.*, **57**, 130–6.

Wagner, A. R. (1963). 'Conditioned frustration as a learned drive', *J. exp. Psychol.*, **66**, 142–8.

Wagner, A. R. (1966). 'Frustration and punishment', in R. N. Haber (Ed.) *Current research in motivation*. Holt, Rinehart & Winston, New York, 229–39.

Wagner, A. R. (1969). 'Frustrative nonreward: A variety of punishment', in B. A. Campbell and R. M. Church (Eds.) *Punishment and aversive behavior*. Appleton-Century-Crofts, New York, 157–81.

Walker, A. E., Thompson, A. F., and McQueen, J. D. (1953). 'Behavior and the temporal rhinecephalon in the monkey', *Bull. Johns Hopk. Hosp.*, **93**, 65–93.

Walter, W. G., Cooper, R., Aldridge, V. J., McCallum, W. C., and Winter, A. L. (1964). 'Contingent negative variation: An electric sign of sensorimotor association and expectancy in the human brain', *Nature*, **203**, 380–4.

Walther, R. (1956). *Das vegetative–affektive syndrom und seine Bedeut ung fur die Psychiatrie*. Berlin: VE3 Verlog. (Quoted in Gellhorn and Loufbourrow 1963.)

Warries, E. (1963). *Sitantie en expressie*. M. A. Thesis. Amsterdam University. (Quoted in Frijda 1969.)

Watson, J. B. (1929). *Psychology. From the Standpoint of a Behaviourist*. (3rd Ed. Rev.). J. B. Lipincott Co., Philadelphia, London.

Watson, J. B. (1930). *Behaviourism*. (Rev. ed.). University of Chicago Press, Chicago.

Watson, J. B., and Rayner, R. (1920). 'Conditioned emotional reactions', *J. exp. Psychol*, **3**, 1–14.

Webb, W. B., and Goodman, J. J. (1958). 'Activating role of an irrelevant drive in absence of the relevant drive', *Psychol. Rep.*, **4**, 235–8.

Weisberger, C. A. (1956). 'Accuracy in judging emotional expressions as related to college entrance', *J. Psychol.*, **44**, 233–9.

Weiskrantz, L. (1968). 'Emotion', in L. Weiskrantz (Ed.) *Analysis of behavioural change*. Harper & Row, New York, London, 50–90.

Weiss, K. M. (1968). 'Some effects of the conditioned suppression paradigm on operant discrimination performance', *J. exp. anal. Behav.*, **11**, 767–75.

Weiss, K. M. (1969). *Experimental analysis of emotional behavior*. Unpubl. Ph.D. Thesis. University of Exeter.

Wenger, M. A. (1950). 'Emotion as visceral action: An extension of Lange's theory', in M. L. Reymert (Ed.) *Feelings and emotions: The Mooseheart symposium*. McGraw-Hill, New York.

Wenner, A. M. (1967). 'Honeybees: Do they use the distance information contained in their dance manoeuvre ?', *Science*, **155**, 847–9.

West, L. J., and Farber, I. E. (1960). 'The role of pain in emotional development', in *Explorations in the physiology of emotions*. L. J. West and M. Greenblak (Eds.) *Psych. res. reps. of the Amer. Psychiat. Assoc.*, **12**, 119–26.

Wike, E. L. (1966). *Secondary reinforcement: Selected experiments*. Harper, New York.

Wilton, R. N., and Strongman, K. T. (1967). 'Extinction performance as a function of reinforcement magnitude and number of training trials', *Psychol. Rep.*, **20**, 235–8.

Wilton, R. N., Strongman, K. T., and Nerenberg, A. (1969). 'Some effects of frustration in a free responding operant situation', *Quart. j. exp. Psychol.*, **XXI**, 367–80.

Wolf, S., and Wolff, H. G. (1947). *Human gastric function*. Oxford University Press, New York, Oxford.

Wolpe, J. (1952). 'Experimental neurosis as learned behaviour', *Brit. j. Psychol.*, **43**, 243–68.

Wolpe, J. (1958). *Psychotherapy by reciprocal inhibition.* Stamford University Press, Stamford.

Wolpe, J. (1961). 'The systematic desensitization treatment of neuroses', *J. nerv. ment. Dis.,* **112,** 189–203.

Wolpe, J. (1966). 'The conditioning and deconditioning of neurotic anxiety', in C. D. Spielberger (Ed.) *Anxiety and behavior.* Academic Press, New York, London, 179–90.

Wolpe. J., and Lazarus, A. A. (1966). *Behavior therapy techniques.* Pergamon Press, London.

Woodworth, R. S. (1938). *Experimental Psychology.* Holt, New York.

Woodworth, R. S., and Schlosberg, H. (1955). *Experimental psychology* (Rev. ed.). Holt, New York.

Wookey, P. E., and Strongman, K. T. (1971). 'Emotional and instrumental effects of reward shift', *Psychol. Rec.,* **21,** 181–9.

Wookey, P. E., and Strongman, K. T. (1972). 'Quantitative reward shift in the double runway', *Brit. j. Psychol.* In press.

Wrightsman, L. S. (1960). 'Effects of waiting with others on changes in level of felt anxiety', *J. abnorm. soc. Psychol.,* **61,** 216–22.

Wynne, L. C., and Solomon, R. L. (1955). 'Traumatic avoidance learning: acquisition and extinction in dogs deprived of normal peripheral autonomic functioning', *Genet. Psychol. Monogr.,* **52,** 241–84.

Yarrow, L. J. (1961). 'Maternal deprivation: toward an empirical and conceptual re-evaluation', *Psychol. Bull.,* **58,** 459–90.

Yarrow, L. J. (1964). 'Separation from parents during early childhood', in M. L. Hoffman and L. W. Hoffman (Eds.) *Review of child development research.* Russel Sage Foundation, New York.

Yates, A. J. (1962). *Frustration and conflict.* Wiley, New York.

Yerkes, R. M., and Dodson, J. D. (1908). 'The relation of strength of stimulus to rapidity of habit-formation', *J. comp. neurol. Psychol.,* **18,** 459–82.

Young, P. T. (1961). *Motivation and emotion.* Wiley, New York, London.

Author Index

Abelson, R. P., 157, 158
Adelman, H. M., 104
Alexander, B. K., 143
Alexander, F., 179
Allen, M. B., 43
Allerand, A. M., 166
Ambrose, J. A., 128
Amsel, A., 96, 97, 100–7, 112
Anastasi, A., 141
Anderson, D. C., 98
Annau, Z., 112
Antonitis, J. J., 98
Argyle, M., 160
Arieti, S., 30
Arnold, M. B., 4, 5, 6, 22–5, 31, 32, 58, 59, 62–5, 66, 80, 81, 90, 91, 132, 176
Aronfreed, J., 131–3, 134
Ax, A. F., 42, 43, 66, 182
Azrin, N. H., 8, 98, 110, 112, 113, 114, 115, 116

Baccelli, G., 43
Bard, P., 14–7, 53, 55, 56, 146
Barker, R., 101
Baron, A., 98
Barry, H. III., 104
Beatty, W. W., 123
Becker, H. S., 72
Belanger, D., 47, 98
Beldoch, M., 152, 153
Benninger, R., 97
Berkowitz, L. 83, 100
Bevan, W., 98
Billingsea, F. Y., 94
Bindra, D., 3, 4, 11, 19–21, 87
Black, A. M., 47, 110, 112, 120
Blackman, D., 111, 114, 115
Blau, S., 153
Block, J., 165

Bloemkolb, D., 77
Bolles, R. C., 10, 88, 102, 122
Bonvallet, M., 43
Bousfield, W. I., 133
Bower, G. H., 107, 114, 124
Bowlby, J., 129, 130, 183–4
Brackbill, Y., 128
Brady, J. V., 36, 37, 47, 48, 53, 56, 57, 109–14, 178
Brahlek, J. A., 114
Brannigan, C. R., 168
Brantley, J. J., 97
Braud, W. G., 108
Bridges, K. M. B., 127–8, 134, 146, 147
Brierley, M., 31
Britton, S. W., 15
Broadhurst, P. L., 94, 95, 180, 184
Bronson, G., 134
Brown, J. J., 4, 102, 103
Brown, J. S., 87
Brown, R., 150
Brown, R. T., 105
Bruell, J. H., 135, 136
Brunswick, D., 41
Bucy, P. C., 55–6
Bull, N., 90
Bures, J., 51
Buresova, O., 51
Buss, A. H., 83, 177

Cannon, W. B., 4, 14–7, 30, 33, 43–7, 54, 70–1, 146
Cantril, H., 67
Carlton, P. L., 111
Casey, K. L., 59–60
Cattell, R. B., 175, 181
Child, I. L., 101
Champness, B. G., 160
Church, M., 104

Cline, M. G., 161
Cohen, M. E., 184
Cohen, P. S., 112
Cole, K. F., 96
Coleman, J., 149–52
Coles, M. G. H., 41
Conrad, D. G., 111
Coulson, G., 115

Dana, C. L., 54
Darrow, C. W., 42
Darwin, C. R., 3, 149, 166
Davis, H., 110
Davison, G. C., 77
Davitz, J. L., 6, 149–54, 156–7, 164–6
Davitz, L., 150
de Villiers, P. A., 112
Deux, J., 99
Delgado, J. M. R., 49–50, 65
Denenberg, V. H., 130, 141–3
Dennis, W., 146
Descartes, 2–3
DeToledo, L., 47, 110, 112, 120
Didamo, P., 111
Dittman, A. T., 150, 159
Dodson, J. D., 95, 180
Dollard, J., 100–1
Douglas, K. J., 123
Drever, J., 1
Ducharme, R., 98
Duffy, E., 6, 10, 16, 19, 28, 32, 33, 74, 87,
        158, 165
Dusser de Barenne, 53

Easterbrook, J. A., 180
Eibl-Eibesfeldt, I., 167–8
Ekman, P., 85, 150, 159–60
Ellis, N. R., 98
Elshout, J. J., 158
Emlen, J. T., 139
Epstein, S., 174–5
Estes, W. K., 34, 92, 109, 111, 112, 114
Eysenck, H. J., 180, 181, 186

Farber, I. E., 4, 102, 103, 128, 129
Farmer, C., 166
Federn, P., 31
Fehr, S., 45–7
Feldman, S. M., 47
Felecky, A. M., 41
Felton, M., 111
Ferrier, D., 57

Ferster, G. B., 116
Festinger, L., 72, 162
Fischer, W. F., 173
Fleshler, M., 111, 112
Flores d'Arcais, 161
Folkins, C. H., 82, 83
Freeman, G. L., 45
Freud, S., 30, 31, 100, 173, 187
Friesen, W. V., 85, 159, 160
Frijda, N. H., 148–51, 155–9, 161, 169
Frisch, K. V., 168
Frois-Wittman, J., 149
Fuller, J. L., 136
Fulton, J. F., 56, 58
Funkenstein, D. H., 134
Fuxe, K., 52

Gelder, M. G., 172
Geller, I., 111
Gellhorn, E., 61, 62, 65, 188–90
Gladstones, W. H., 158
Goldman, R., 75
Goldstein, M. L., 46
Goltz, E., 53
Goodenough, F. L., 152
Goodman, J. J., 98
Grinker, R. R., Sr., 177–81
Gross, L. P., 75
Grossman, S., 114
Grossman, S. P., 40, 50, 51, 57, 63
Grusec, J., 114, 132
Guhl, A. M., 136
Gurney, C., 172

Hake, D. F., 113–5
Hale, E. D., 136
Hall, C. S., 94, 135, 136
Hammond, L. J., 117, 121–3
Harlow, H. F., 33, 34, 143–5, 147, 165
Harlow, M. K., 143–5
Harrower, M., 178
Harvey, J. A., 57
Head, H., 15
Hearst, E., 110
Hebb, D. O., 87, 134
Henton, W. W., 114
Herrnstein, R. J., 113, 115, 116, 124
Hess, E. H., 136, 139, 140
Hess, W. R., 53
Hillman, J., 30
Hinde, R. A., 139
Hoch, P. H., 173

Hoffman, H. S., 110–2
Hohman, G. W., 46, 71
Holz, W. C., 8, 110
Howe, E. S., 182
Hull, C. L., 92, 93, 96, 100, 102, 103, 106, 192
Humphries, D. A., 168
Hunt, H. F., 56, 94, 109, 110, 112
Hunt, W. A., 67
Hyde, T. S., 114

Innes, N. K., 106
Isaacson, R. L., 56
Israel, N. R., 44
Izard, C. E., 5, 6, 88–90

Jaanus, H., 161
Jacobson, E., 41, 186
James, W., 3, 4, 13, 14, 30, 38, 43–7, 70, 71, 90, 91, 146
Jeness, A. F., 152
Johnson, D. L., 168
Jones, H. E., 73

Kakolewski, J. W., 99
Kamin, L. J., 110, 112, 116, 120
Kamiya, J., 80
Kaplan, B. E., 74
Karabenick, S. A., 106–8
Karas, G. G., 142
Karston, L., 158
Katkin, E. S., 47
Kaufman, A., 115
Kaufman, P. E., 150
Kelly, A. H., 182
Kelly, D. H. W., 53
Kelsey, J. E., 49
Kendon, A., 160
Kennard, M. A., 56. 58
Kety, S. S., 51, 52
Kimble, G. A., 184
King, F. A., 57, 123
Klages, L., 16
Kline, N. J., 142
Kling, A., 55
Klüver, H., 55, 56
Knapp, P. H., 149
Koehler, O., 146
Krause, M. S., 175–6
Krieckhouse, E. E., 57
Krueger, F., 16

Lacey, B. C., 40, 43, 44, 46, 178
Lacey, J. I., 40, 43, 44, 46, 65, 163, 178
Lader, M. H., 173, 182–4
Lambert, W. W., 152
Landis, C., 40, 67, 73, 161
Lange, C. G., 14, 38, 146
Latane, B., 70, 72–4, 76
Lawson, R., 100–2
Lazarus, A. A., 184, 186, 187
Lazarus, R. S., 28, 29, 66, 76, 80, 82–5, 88, 90, 91, 173, 182
Leeper, R. W., 2, 4–6, 21, 24, 28–30, 33, 66, 85–8, 90, 91, 145
Leitenberg, H., 104, 110, 112, 116
Levine, S., 95, 97, 112, 130, 141, 142
Levitt, E. A., 153
Levy, P. K., 152, 153
Lewis, G. W., 141
Liddell, R. D., 185
Lindholm, B. W., 142
Lindsley, D. B., 4, 5, 11, 19, 41, 42, 62
Lolordo, V. M., 122, 123
Longo, N., 113
Loufbourrow, G. N., 61, 188–90
Lubar, J. F., 57
Luchins, A. S., 161
Lykken, D. T., 73, 74
Lyon, D. O., 109–11

Maatsch, J. L., 104
Magoun, H. W., 41
Mahl, G. F., 178
Maier, N. R. F., 101
Malmo, R. B., 173, 176, 182
Maltzman, I., 96, 97, 112
Mandler, G., 44, 71
Maranon, G., 67, 70, 71
Markes, I. M., 172
Martin, B., 176, 182
Martin, I., 182
Marx, M. H., 102
Marzocco, F. N., 102
Masserman, J. H., 185, 186
May, R., 152, 173
Mayer-Gross, W., 171, 172
Meltzer, D., 149
Meltzer, L., 114
Melzack, R., 59, 60, 137
Meyer, P. A., 107, 124
Michotte, A. E., 162
Miczek, K. A., 114

Millenson, J. R., 5, 6, 28, 34, 35, 109–12, 118–9, 124, 125
Miller, G. A., 24
Miller, N. E., 49, 92, 93, 100–3, 105, 120, 180
Miller, R. E., 149, 151, 154, 155, 162
Milner, P., 49
Mirsky, I. A., 56, 154, 155, 178
Moltz, H., 140
Morse, W. H., 113–5, 124
Morton, J. R. C., 142
Moruzzi, G., 41
Mountcastle, V. B., 55, 56
Mowrer, O. H., 92, 93, 103, 117, 121–3, 140, 173
Moyer, K. E., 97, 98, 112
Munn, N. L., 86
Murphy, J. V., 154, 155
Murray, E. N., 47
Myer, J. S., 95, 98
Maclean, P. D., 54, 59, 62
McCarter, R., 156
McCleary, R. A., 57, 123
McDougall, W., 4, 16, 17
McHose, J. H., 104, 107, 124

Nash, J., 133
Nauta, W. J. H., 36, 37, 57
Nisbett, R. E., 75, 76
Nowlis, H. H., 78–80
Nowlis, V., 70, 78–80, 90, 91

Oakley, D. A., 51
O'Kelly, L. I., 94
Olds, J., 49, 64
Opton, E. M. Jr., 82, 182
Orbach, J., 56
Orbison, W. D., 133
Osgood, C. E., 149, 157
Otis, L. S., 94

Papez, J. W., 17, 18, 59
Pare, W. P., 98
Parke, R. D., 131, 132
Pavlov, I. P., 122, 123, 185
Peckham, R. H., 104
Peiper, A., 146
Persky, H., 179
Philipszoon, E., 157
Pichot, P., 181
Pliskoff, S., 113, 114
Plutchik, R., 5, 16, 21, 22, 34, 165

Polack, I., 150
Pradines, M., 31, 32
Pribram, K. H., 24, 25, 56
Prick, J. J. G., 173, 174
Prouty, D. L., 102, 103
Prytula, R. E., 108

Ranson, S. W., 41, 189
Rapaport, D., 30, 31
Ray, A. A., 77, 78
Raynor, R., 18, 107
Reis, D. J., 52
Remington, R. E., 114–7
Rescorla, R., 105, 115, 120, 122, 123
Reynolds, G. S., 124
Rosenzweig, S., 100
Ross, G. S., 48
Ross, R. B., 51
Roth, M., 172
Roussell, J., 102, 104
Ruckmick, C. H., 25
Russell, I. S., 51
Ryan, T. J., 105
Rylander, G., 58

Salzen, E. A., 128, 139, 140
Sargant, W., 189
Sartre, J-P., 165
Sawrey, W. J., 48
Schachter, S., 5, 25, 26, 43, 45, 62, 65–79, 84, 85, 90, 91, 120, 147, 154, 156–63, 182, 191, 195
Schaffer, H. R., 129
Schaller, G. P., 139
Schein, M. W., 136
Scheier, I. H., 175
Schlosberg, H., 151, 157, 158, 165
Schneirla, T. C., 94, 127, 134, 137, 145, 146, 183
Schreiner, L. H., 55
Schwatzbaum, J. S., 55, 123
Scott, J. P., 130, 136, 137, 141
Sears, R. R., 100, 130, 131
Sermatt, V., 157, 158
Seward, J. P., 103
Shagass, C., 182
Shepard, R. N., 157
Sherrington, C. S., 46
Shields, J., 184
Sidman, M., 48, 109, 111, 117
Siegel, H. S., 96
Siegel, P. S., 96–8

Siminov, P. V., 24, 26, 27
Singer, A., 127
Singer, J. E., 67–9, 70, 75, 130
Singer, R. D., 127
Skinner, B. F., 34, 72, 92, 108, 109, 111, 114, 120, 131, 192
Slater, E., 184
Sluckin, W., 139, 140
Smart, R. G., 185
Smith, L. H., 176
Smith, S. A., 141
Smith, W. K., 55
Solomon, P., 188
Solomon, R. L., 71, 105, 120, 122, 123
Soskin, W. F., 150
Sparkes, D. L., 98
Spence, K. W., 106, 173
Spiegel, J. P., 178
Spielberger, C. D., 173, 175–7, 180, 182
Spiesman, J. C., 82
Spitz, R. A., 128, 129, 146
Staddon, J. E. R., 106
Stagner, R., 33, 34, 165
Stanley-Jones, D., 60, 61
Stein, L., 111, 112
Stern, J. A., 45–7
Stern, R. M., 74
Sternback, R. A., 40, 177
Sterritt, G. M., 98
Stevenson, S. S., 102
Stotland, E., 151, 162–4
Stoyva, J., 80
Stringer, P., 158
Strongman, K. T., 97, 98, 103, 106–9, 112, 114–7, 124, 160
Sullivan, H. S., 173

Tart, C., 80
Taylor, J. A., 173
Thierry, A. M., 52
Thompson, D. F., 149
Thompson, J., 152
Thorpe, W. H., 137
Tobach, E., 94
Tomkins, S. S., 5, 6, 88–90, 156
Tomlin, F. J., 140
Trenholme, I., 116
Triandis, H. G., 152
Tryon, R. C., 94

Valenstein, E. S., 110
Valins, S., 70, 73–8, 90, 91
Vandenberg, S. G., 184
Vine, I., 149, 160

Wagner, A. R., 103–5
Walker, A. E., 55
Walsh, M., 115
Walter, C. J. S., 182
Walter, W. G., 44
Walters, R. H., 131, 132
Walther, R., 189
Ward, J. S., 102–4
Warries, E., 161
Waterhouse, I. K., 101
Watson, J. B., 18, 33–5, 92, 107, 109, 118–27
Watson, P., 105
Webb, W. B., 98
Weisberger, C. A., 152
Weiskrantz, L., 59, 94, 120, 121
Weiss, K. M., 109, 112
Weisz, J. D., 48
Wenger, M. A., 4, 45, 71
Wenner, A. M., 168
West, L. J., 128, 129
Wheeler, L., 69, 70, 75
Wickelgreen, W. D., 56
Wike, E. L., 122
Wing, L., 182, 184
Wilton, R. N., 103, 106
Wolf, K., 128, 129, 146
Wolf, S., 42, 66, 182
Wolff, H. G., 42, 66, 182
Wolpe, J., 77, 184–7
Woodworth, R. S., 151
Wookey, P. E., 106–8, 124
Wrightsman, L. S., 70
Wynne, L. C., 71

Yarrow, L. J., 129, 130, 141
Yates, A. J., 100
Yerkes, R. M., 95, 180
Young, P. T., 27, 28

Zimmerman, R. R., 144
Zubin, J., 173

Subject Index

Abreaction, 189–90
Action patterns, 63–4
Activation, *see* Arousal
Activity, 113, 156
Actors, 149–51, 157
Adaptive functions, 22, 85, 87, 135, 177
Adjective check list (ACL), 79, 149, 152, 157–8
Adolescence, 171–2
Adoption, 130
Adrenaline, *see* Epinephrine
Adrenals, 134
Adulterated food, 97–8
Adventitious reinforcement, 115–16
Affection, 136, 143–5, 192
Affective disorders, 170
Affective memory, 23–4, 63–4, 81
Affective processes, 27–8, 88–90, 156
Agarophobia, 171–2
Aggression, 55, 56, 83, 98, 109, 116–19 126, 130–1, 136, 143–5
Alertness, 179
Allocortex, 53–4
Alpha rhythm, 19, 41–2, 80
Alphabet, 150
Ambivalent stimuli, 185
Ambulation, 94
Amusement, 69–70
Amygdala, amygdaloid complex, 50, 55–6, 59
Anaclitic depression, 129
Analgesia, 129
Anger, 35, 42, 62, 63, 68, 109, 116–19 151, 154, 195
Anger-inners, anger-outers, 134
Animal phobia, 172
Animal studies, 91, 93, 126, 135–45, 192
Antidepressants, 52
Anxiety, 42, 53, 58, 70, 73–4, 75, 77–8,

88–90, 92, 96, 109, 110–13, 118–19, 126, 130–1, 140, 160, 165, 170–90, 193, 194
  affection, 183–4
  behaviour, 180–1
  causation, 183–7
  conditioned, 185
  cortical, 42
  definition, 170, 171–80
  free-floating, 172
  general, 171–2
  genetics, 184
  hierarchies, 186
  manifest, 176
  mastery, 174–5
  measurement, 180–3, 187
  moral, 174
  neurotic, 56, 173, 187
  'normal', 177
  objective, 173, 187
  phobic, 172
  psychophysiology, 172, 174–5, 176–7, 181–3
  separation, 183–4
  simple, 172
  social, 172
  state, 175–7, 181, 187
  'system', 179
  theories, 173–7
  trait, 175–7, 181, 187
Appetitive behaviour, 57
Appraisal, 22–5, 26, 28–9, 59, 62–4, 80–5, 91, 132–3, 176, 195
  benign, 83–4
  threatening, 83–4
Apprehension, 179
Approach, 122–123, 156, 162
Approach-to-food, 94
Arousal, 4, 10–11, 19, 25–8, 32–3, 38–41,

Arousal—Contd.
  59, 62, 67–84, 86–7, 91, 142, 154,
    157, 163, 165, 167, 174–5, 182–3
Artificiality, 8–9, 58, 149, 154, 168, 169,
    192
'As if' feelings, 67–72
Assertive responses, 186
Asthma, 178
Atropine, 50
Attack, 53, 143–5
Attention-rejection, 157–8
Attractiveness, 76–8
Autonomic-affective syndrome, 189
Autonomic nervous system (ANS), 36–65,
    120, 171–90, 191, 193
Autonomic reactivity, 73, 178
Autoregulation, 80
Aversive stimulation, 47, 49, 98, 100, 185
Avoidance, 48, 49, 56, 58, 64, 72–4, 92,
    104–5, 120–3, 142, 154–5
  active, 37
  cooperative, 155
  passive, 37, 50, 123
  Sidman, 48, 115, 123
Awareness, 33, 80

Balance theory, 61–2
Battle fatigue, 178, 189
Behaviour therapy, 184–7
Benzedrine, 78–80
Biology, 17, 21–2, 28, 133–5
Biphasic mechanisms, 146
Birth order, 164
Blind subjects, 152, 153
Blood-flow, 182
Body changes, perception, 66–80
Body posture and movement, 159–60
Brain stem, reticular formation (BSRF),
    41–2, 50, 53, 134

Carbachol, 50, 51
Cardiovascular system, 43–4, 182
Caudate nucleus, 61
Central motive state, 19–21
Central nervous system (CNS), 28, 36–65,
    191
  ablation, 37
  stimulation, 37
  transmitters, 52
Cheating, 72–3
Chemical stimulation, 36

Child rearing, 129–31, 134
Child studies, 126–35, 192
Chlorpromazine, 61, 69, 72–3
Cingulate gyrus, 56–7
Circulation, 40, 47
Cognition, 22–6, 28–9, 62–4, 66–91, 120,
    131–3, 154, 156, 165–6, 176, 191,
    194, 195
Cognitive style, 44
Cold, 60
Competence, 165
Complex feelings, 17
Conditioned emotional state, 121–3
Conditioned emotional responding (CER),
    37, 48, 50, 51, 56, 57, 58, 64, 92,
    108–25, 194
  methodology, 109–10
  species, 110
Conditioned stimuli, 109–17
Conditioned suppression, 110–13, 118–21
  CS duration and intensity, 111
  interference, 112
  negative drive, 112–13
  punishment, 112
Conditioning, 33–5, 92, 108–24, 175, 193–4
  classical (Pavlovian), 34–5, 51, 93, 105,
    108–24, 193–4
  instrumental, 98–9, 105, 108–24, 193–4
Conflict, 119, 139–40, 185
Consummatory behaviour, 96–8
Contempt, 151
Content-standard behaviour, 152–4
Contingent negative variation (CNV), 44
Cooperative bar-pressing, 155
Coping, 29, 82–5
Cortex, 15–16, 17, 51, 54–8, 59, 62–4,
    133–4, 188–9
Cortical levels, 62
Counterconditioning, 186
Criminal behaviour, 72–4
Critical periods, 137–8, 139, 141, 147, 192
Cross-cultural studies, 152
Crouching, 93–4
Crying, 128–9
Culture, 28–9

Danger signal, 121
Deception, 67–78, 159–60
Decerebration, 53, 60
Decortication, 51, 54
Deep relaxation, 186
Definition, 1, 2, 28, 193–5

Deliberate actions, 24
Delinquents, 73–4
Depersonalization, 171–3
Depression, 119, 171, 173, 179, 182, 187
Deprivation, 129–30, 143–5
Desensitization, 77–8, 170, 184–7
Diencephalon, 54
Differential reinforcement of low rates of responding (DRL), 113–15
Dimensions of emotion, 21–2, 34–5, 157–8, 166, 192
Disappointment, 93, 121–3
Disgust, 151
Disorganisation, 21, 29–30, 31, 33, 86–8
Dominance hierarchies, 144
Double runway, 102–3, 125
Dramamine, 78–80
Drawings, 161
Drive, 10, 20–1, 92, 95, 96, 102, 121, 133, 139, 180, 185
Drive stimuli, 87
Dynamotor theory, 45
Dysthymic personality, 181, 184

Early experience, 126–47, 192
Ecstasy, 118–19
Elation, 35, 84, 107–8, 109, 113–16, 118–19, 124, 194
  apparent, 107
  human, 115–16
  qualitative change, 108
Electrical stimulation, 36, 52–4
Electroconvulsive shock (ECS), 52
Electroencephalogram (EEG), 19, 41–2, 49, 50, 80, 120, 182
Electronic filtering, 150
Elimination, 93–5, 135–6, 141–2, 171, 185
Emergence-from-cage, 93
Emotional behaviour, 4, 8, 18, 33–5, 36, 92–125, 192, 194–5
Emotional complexes, 45
Emotional development, 126–47, 192, 194
Emotional disturbance, 130, 138
Emotional experience, 4, 148
Emotional meaning, 148, 150, 152, 158, 162, 164–6, 169, 192
Emotional sensitivity, 152, 154
Emotional situations, 148
Emotional space, 156–158
Emotional state, 152, 166
Emotional stimuli, 4, 7
Emotionality, 36–7, 56, 57, 92, 93–100, 111, 114, 123, 125, 130, 135–6, 147, 185, 192, 194
  early experience, 95, 130, 140–3
  genetics, 94–5, 135–6
Empathy, 149, 151, 155, 162–4
Endocrine system, 47–8
Energy, 33
Epinephrine, 42, 61, 67–72, 85, 134, 171
Ergotrophic activities, 61–2, 188–90
Escape, 95, 104, 183
Ethical problems, 9
Ethology, 130, 137, 166–8
Euphoria, 62, 67–70, 84, 195
Evaluative need, 72
Excitement, 127
Excitation, 64, 122–3
Executive monkeys, 178
Experimental neurosis, 119, 170, 184–7
Expression of emotion, 3, 148–69, 192–3, 195
  accuracy, 150
  categories, 155–6
  context, 160–2, 169
  dimensions, 151, 156, 157–8, 165–6, 169
  facial, 89, 149–55, 168
  hierarchies, 156
  personality, 152–4
  scales, 151
  vocal, 149–55
External cues, 66–80, 91
Extinction, 102, 103
Extraversion–introversion, 180–1
Eye gaze, 160

Facial regions, 151
Facilitation, 96–8
Factor analysis, 156, 175, 181
Fear, 18, 53, 56, 63, 70, 86, 89, 92, 93, 96, 99, 103, 104–5, 108, 121–3, 126, 137, 139–40, 143–5, 151, 174–5, 178, 180
Feelings, 16–17, 25, 30–1, 34, 47, 63–4
Feelings as monitors, 24–5
Fever, 188
Film, 82, 150–1, 153, 159
Fixed interval (FI), 106, 111
Fixed ratio (FR), 106–7, 111
Flooding, 98
Food, 74–5
Following response, 138–40
Food intake, 96
Fractional anticipatory goal response, 103

Free reward, 113–16
Frontal ablation, 58
Frontal lobes, 57–8, 63–4
Fronto-temporal cortex, 55, 56
Frowning, 148, 161, 168
Frustration, 100–8, 123, 194
  aggression, 100, 131
  anticipatory, 103–5
  aversive, 104–5
  comparative, 106–8
  choice, 102–3
  fixation, 101
  human, 105–6
  motivational block, 100
  regression, 101
  Skinner box, 106–7
  theory, 92
  tolerance, 119
Frustration effect (FE), 100, 102–3, 105–7
Frustrative nonreward, 103–5
Functional decortication, 133

Galvanic skin response (GSR), 40–1, 163
'Gap-filling' hypotheses, 161
Gastric fistula, 42, 66
Gastric lesions, 48
Gastrointestinal activity, 41
Grief, 175
Grill-box, 110, 112
Group cohesion, 168
Guilt, 35, 60, 119, 173

Habituation, 182
Handling, 99, 141–3, 147
Hate, 60
Hawk and goose, 137
Heart rate, 43–4, 76–9, 110, 120
Heat, 60
Hedonic tone, 165
Hedonism, 27–8
Heritability, 135–6
Hippocampus, 56, 59, 62–3
Hippuric acid, 179
Homeostasis, 60
Hope, 93, 103, 121–3
Hormonal mechanisms, 56, 61–2, 64, 133–4
Hydrochloric acid, 178
Hypertension, 43–4, 178, 188
Hypnosis, 90
Hypochondria, 171–2
Hypothalamus, 46, 49, 52, 53, 57, 59, 60, 61–2, 188–90

Identification of emotion, 148–69
Illness, 177–80
Images, 24–5
Imagination, 23–4, 31
Imitation, 132
Immediate reflexes, 46
Imprinting, 128, 136, 138–40, 144
Individual differences, 152
Information theory, 26–27
Inhibition, 122–3
Innate fear, 137
Insoluble problems, 101
Institutionalization, 129–30
Intelligence, 153, 154
Intercranial chemical stimulation, 50–1
Intercranial stimulation (ICS), 48–50, 111, 113
Intermediate physiological mechanisms, 47–52
Internal cues, 66–80, 91
Internalization, 131–3
Interoceptive events, 47
Interstressor stereotypy, 46
Intervening variables, 4
Intrastressor stereotypy, 46
Inverted-U, 142, 180
Isolation, 144

Jews, 75
Joy, 118–19, 154
Juxtallocortex, 54–5

Kissing, 167
Klüver–Bucy syndrome, 55–6

Labelling of emotion, 72, 74, 75, 91, 156, 157, 165–6, 191
Language of emotion, 164–6
Learning theory, 180
Lesions, 36, 52–4, 56
Levels of discourse, 7–8
Libido, 173
Limbic system, 49, 52, 54–8, 59, 62, 111, 123, 191
  lateral, 55–6
Lobotomy, 58
Localization of function, 37, 50, 51, 65
Love, 18, 60, 84, 126, 151
Love-withdrawal, 132–3
Lust, 60
Lysergic acid diethylamide (LSD), 52

Marihuana, 72
Mass action, 37, 51, 65
Maternal separation, 129–30
Maturation, 139
Measurement, 193–4
Medulla, 53
Methodology, 126, 147, 182–3
Mid-brain, 51
Migraine, 179
Monetary reward, 115
Monoamines, 51–2
Mood, 48, 52, 61, 70, 78–80, 91, 189
Motivation, 4, 10, 19–21, 29–30, 33, 57, 86–90, 109, 121, 141–2, 145, 167
Motor reactions, 162
Mourning, 183
Movement, 162, 167
Moving rectangles, 162
Muscle potential, 41

Nature–nurture, 126–47, 152
Nausea, 188
Need, 133
Negative affect, 88–90
Negative baseline, 109–10
Negative stimuli, 108–9
Neocortex, 49, 52, 57
Neurochemistry, 51–2, 65
Neurohumours, 61
Neurological activators, 89
Neuromuscular homeostasis, 45
Neurophysiology, 17–18, 19–21, 24–5
Neurosis, 101, 170, 171–2, 180–1, 184–90
Neuroticism, 180–1
Nonverbal leakage, 85
Nonveridical perceptions, 70, 76–8
Noradrenaline, see Norepinephrine
Norepinephrine, 42, 52, 134
Novelty, 97–8, 139–40
Noxious stimuli, 92, 128, 180
  perseverative effects, 95–100, 125
Nude pictures, 74, 76–8

Obesity, 74–5
Old age, 170
Olfaction, 55, 59
Open-field tests, 92, 93–5, 135–6, 14–12
Operants, 95, 120–1, 129
Organization, 29–30, 86–8

Pain, 16–17, 27–8, 59–60, 163
Panic, 179

Parachutists, 174–5
Paradoxical sleep, 52
Paraplegia, 71
Parasympathetic nervous system (PNS), 36–65, 178
Partial reinforcement, 49, 104
Pathological emotion, 119, 170–90, 193, 194
Peer groups, 143–5
Perception, 29–30, 81, 86–90, 145
Peripheral mechanisms, 38–47, 51, 65
Permissiveness, 131
Personality, 89
Phenomenology, see Cognition
Phobias, 171–3, 182, 185
Photographs, 149–51, 155, 157, 161
Physiological feedback, 74
Physiology, 22–4, 25–6, 36–65, 80, 81, 163–4, 166, 191, 194
Placidity, 55–6
Plans, 25–6
Play, 142
Pleasure (pleasantness), 16–17, 27–8, 157–8
Positionality, 156, 161
Positive affect, 88–90
Positive baseline, 109–10
Positive stimuli, 108–9
Predictive empathy, 163
Prescientific thought, 2, 3
Primary emotion, 17, 158
Primary feelings, 46
Primary localization, 138
Primary reinforcers, 109
Projection, 150
Proprioception, 45
Psychoanalysis, 30–1
Psychopathy, 73–4, 181
Psychophysiology, 36, 38–41, 65, 171, 176–7, 181–3
Psychosis, 170, 171–2, 173, 189
Psychosomatic disorder, 170, 177–80
Psychotherapy, 160, 178
Punishment, 110, 111–12, 131, 132, 173

Quinine, 97–8, 123

Rage, 18, 53, 56, 60, 63
Rapid eye movement (REM), 52
Rating scales, 149
Rationalist doctrine, 2, 3, 86, 195
Reaction time (RT), 43–4
'Real' emotion, 151, 158

Reappraisal, 29, 76
Recognition of emotion, 148–69, 192–3
Reductionism, 8, 65, 191
Regression, 177, 178
Reinforcement, 35, 49, 109–25, 138
  density, 115
  schedules, 111
Reinforcements 'lost' hypothesis, 111, 112
Relatedness, 165
Relief, 93, 109, 117, 118–19, 121–3
Representational processes, 88
Repression, 173
Rescorla control, 115–16
Reserpine, 52
Respiration, 41, 47
Respondents, 95, 120–21, 129
Response acceleration (facilitation),
  109–10, 124
Response bias, 150
Response patterning (differentiation), 42–4,
  64, 66, 70, 84–5, 90, 135, 163, 182,
  191
Response suppression, 96–8, 103, 107,
  109–10, 124
Reward change, 124
Ritualization, 167

Safety signal, 121
Schizophrenia, 170, 174, 175, 181, 182,
  189
Seconal, 78–80
Secondary reinforcement, 180
Selective breeding, 135–6, 184
Self-control, 131–3
Self-criticism, 133
Self-ratings, 164
Self-report, 79, 176
Self-stimulation, 48–9, 64
Semantic differential, 154
Sensory deprivation, 188
Sentiment, 31–2
Septum, 50, 57, 113
Serotonin, 52
Sexual behaviour, 136, 143–5, 186
Sham rage, 43, 54
Shock, 82, 96–100, 108–13, 141–3, 147,
  154–5
Situational cues, 147
Situational stereotypy, 46
Sleep-tension, 157–8
Smiling, 128, 146, 161, 168
Snakes, 77–8

Social attachment, 132, 135, 138, 143–5,
  147, 183
Social communication, 148–69
Social grooming, 167
Social reward, 105
Socialization (social development), 139,
  143–5
Sorrow, 119
Spinal cord, 53
Spinal lesions, 46, 53, 71
Spreading cortical depression, 51
Stereotyped behaviour, 167
Steroids, 48
Stimulus intensity, 141, 175, 193–4
Stress, 47–8, 82–3, 91, 95, 133–4, 171–2,
  176, 178, 182, 188, 189
Subincision, 82
Subcortex, 15–16, 17, 52–4
Sucrose, 98, 108, 115
Surprise, 151
Sympathetic activity, 66–75
Sympathetic nervous system (SNS), 26,
  36–65, 66–75, 178
Sympathectomy, 46, 71

Tachycardia, 43–4
Taste, 74–5
Telemetry, 49–50
Temporal extension, 159
Temporal lobe, 55
Terminology, 6–7, 10, 21–2
Terror, 35
Thalamic theory, 14–15
Thalamus, 44–5, 53–4, 63
Theories of emotion, 13–35
  good, 5–6
  behavioural, 5, 118–24, 193
  central, 58–64, 193
  cognitive, 5, 80–90, 193
  peripheral, 3, 14, 43–7, 70, 193
  thermostatic, 60
Therapy, 186–7
Threat, 167–8, 175, 176, 178, 184
Tickling, 59
Time-out (TO), 104, 106, 110, 114, 116–17
Time-zone changes, 75
Timidity, 136, 139–40
Timing response, 115
Trophotropic activities, 61–2, 188–90
Tuning, 62
Tunnel-emergence, 136
Twin studies, 166, 184

Ulcers, 178, 188
Unconditioned responses, 33–5, 92, 109–17
Unpleasantness, 157–8

Variable interval (VI), 109, 111, 113–15
Variable ratio (VR), 111
Vasoconstriction, 163
Verbal report, 7

Veridical perceptions, 75–6
Viscera, 14, 44–7, 65, 86

Water intake, 96, 141
Weaning, 142
Will, 60
Withdrawal, 156, 162

DATE DUE

OC 12 '80			
JA 15 '84			
NO 13 '84			
NO 7 '85			
GAYLORD			PRINTED IN U.S A.